TRIUMPH OF ORDER

COLUMBIA HISTORY OF URBAN LIFE

TRIUMPH OF ORDER

Democracy & Public Space in New York and London

LISA KELLER

COLUMBIA UNIVERSITY PRESS   NEW YORK

COLUMBIA UNIVERSITY PRESS

Publishers Since 1893

New York   Chichester, West Sussex

Copyright © 2009 Columbia University Press
Yehuda Amichai, "Some Lines Against the Light," copyright © 2006 Conde Nast
Publications. Originally published in *The New Yorker*. All rights reserved.
All rights reserved

Library of Congress Cataloging-in-Publication Data

Keller, Lisa.
Triumph of order : public space and democracy in
New York and London / Lisa Keller.
p. cm. — (The Columbia history of urban life)
Includes bibliographical references and index.
ISBN 978-0-231-14672-2 (cloth : alk. paper) — ISBN 978-0-231-51847-5 (e-book)
1. New York (N. Y.)—Politics and government. 2. London (England)—
Politics and government. 3. Civil rights—New York (State)—New York.
4. Civil rights—Great Britain—London. 5. Liberty. I. Title. II. Series.

JS1230.K45 2008
320.9747´1—DC22

2008019144

Columbia University Press books are printed on permanent and durable acid-free paper.
This book is printed on paper with recycled content.

Printed in the United States of America

c 10 9 8 7 6 5 4 3 2

References to Internet Web sites (URLs) were accurate at the time of writing.
Neither the author nor Columbia University Press is responsible for URLs that
may have expired or changed since the manuscript was prepared.

DESIGN BY VIN DANG

For my father, who taught me how to drive.

Sometimes I stumble into history
The way a small animal, a rabbit or a fox,
Stumbles into a passing car's beam of light.
Sometimes I am the driver.

—YEHUDA AMICHAI—
"Some Lines Against the Light"

CONTENTS

ILLUSTRATIONS

PREFACE

In 1850, London was the largest and most important city in the world. No city on earth had ever been so enormous. With 2.2 million inhabitants, it stretched east and west along the Thames River from Paddington to Bromley, and north and south from Islington to Camberwell. The houses of Parliament and the primary residence of the Queen sat squarely at the center. The great metropolis was home to the very rich and the very poor. Regent's Street attracted posh shoppers from fine areas such as Mayfair, while a hodgepodge of crooked streets led to slums like Seven Dials, so dangerous that police would not venture there and so unredeemable that it had to be razed.

At midcentury, New York was a third of London's size but still an extraordinary metropolis. Founded in 1624 by the Dutch as a trading post, it had grown to become the largest agglomeration in the Western Hemisphere by 1850, with about 700,000 residents (from only sixty thousand a half-century before), most of them crowded below Chambers Street.[1] The "Marble Palace," A. T. Stewart's innovative department store, exemplified the city's booming mercantile prowess; Fifth Avenue had become a status address. Already the most heterogeneous place on the planet, the city was the prime destination for an influx of immigrants, overwhelmingly poor and foreign, who crowded into tenement districts such as the notorious Five Points. Manhattan already had the largest hotel, the largest department store, and the busiest public-transit system anywhere.

In 1900, London was still the largest and most influential city in the world. The national capital, and more importantly the center of the greatest empire in human history (one-fourth of the world), it had grown to 4.7 million people (greater London had 6.5 million). Despite its noise and effluvia, people from all walks of life flocked to the booming city for the opportunity to prosper. Lush green squares hosted expensive townhouses, glittering carriages and nightly soirees, while dark gritty slums were havens for desperate piecework laborers, struggling families, and emigrants escaping even worse deprivations and discrimination. New department stores, including Harrods and Selfridges, catered to the material needs of both the wealthy and the middle class, as miles of affordable row houses sprang up in nearby suburbs accessible through the expanding underground transit system.

By 1900, New York had grown to 3.6 million people and was the second largest and most dynamic city in the world. Skyscrapers made it the first vertical city, as Manhattan developers had nowhere to go but up on the crowded island. Wall Street became the world's financial center in the twentieth century, home to robber barons and virtually limitless wealth. The Brooklyn Bridge connected the first- and third-largest cities in America in 1883 and led to the huge five-borough consolidation in 1898. The Lower East Side became the center of the world's greatest concentration of immigrants. New York's diversity was unprecedented: it was home to more Irish than Dublin, more Germans than Hamburg, more Italians than Naples, more Jews than Warsaw, and more African Americans than Atlanta.

In 2000, New York was self-described as the greatest city in the world, and no other place seriously disputed the moniker. Capital of the twentieth century and capital of capitalism, the skyscraper city was defined by glamour, sophistication, and a yearning for success, whatever that may be. The city's street names had become synonymous with the economic and cultural institutions that thrived there: Wall Street for finance, Broadway for theater, Seventh Avenue for fashion, Fifth Avenue for shopping, and Madison Avenue for advertising. And even after the devastating terrorist attack on the Twin Towers of the World Trade Center, local property values remained strong despite national trends.

London in 2000 was also a world-class city. The center of international finance, it was experiencing its greatest building boom in more than a century, and it ranked as one of the most costly cities on Earth. From the London Eye to Canary Wharf, the city was home to record-high real estate prices, a booming stock exchange, and an influx of foreign investment. Its airports were the busiest in Europe, and tourism surged. Winning the bid to host the 2012 Olympics would give London yet another reason to celebrate its modern triumph and plan its building boom.

It is remarkable that London and New York remain the two most influential cities on the planet. After all, decentralization and deindustrialization devastated their economies in the second half of the twentieth century, as did crime, pollution, faltering municipal services, and troubled public education.

Gotham's port declined, and its middle class decamped for the suburbs. World War II bombing made daily life exhausting and challenging, and it left an entire generation of Londoners tired and grim. Meanwhile, the British overseas empire declined and almost disappeared.

Paris, Tokyo, Singapore, Hong Kong, Beijing, Sao Paolo, and Mexico City are population, business, cultural, and tourist centers, and each enjoys a certain global preeminence in its own way. In the next decades, these cities may rival London and New York, but in 2008, they do not share all the characteristics of the two global leaders. The dominance of London and New York reflects their overwhelming success as global capitalism centers that offer a vast financial services sector and a remarkable infrastructure. The "success" of these urban centers reflects more than just aggregate wealth: these are places where capitalism is inspired, given incentives, and nurtured by openness, tolerance, diversity, and stability. Commerce, from large corporations to small-scale retail, flocks there, because both cities offer a large market and a supportive environment conducive for expansion and advancement.

Financial success in turn reflects a constellation of broader political, legal, and social factors, which individually are not unique but when put together become distinctive. London and New York have fortuitous geographical locations, the ability to attract and sustain a diverse ethnic, racial, and religious population with little civil conflict, and offer virtually limitless opportunities for residents to profit from work. They foster an urban culture that promotes achievements in art, theater, dance, and music, and this culture is distinguished by innovation and diversity, making these cities trendsetters and enabling the intellectual, the artistic, and the unusual to flourish.

All this nestles in two countries that are home to stable democratic and constitutional systems. The rule of law reinforces the principles of fairness, equality, and liberty that have served as a bulwark for both the United Kingdom and the United States. London and New York are dependable, organized, and ordered places where there is sustained confidence that daily life runs smoothly and without disruption. Their civil governments are led by technocrats and allow no role for the military.

This book acknowledges these two cities have achieved this world preeminence due to all these factors, but it also argues that one of the most compelling—and least credited—attributes that has made this possible is the establishment of a solid foundation of public order at the cost of fraying liberty. What has bolstered London and New York as leading world cities are two seemingly contradictory guiding principles. On the one hand, each megalopolis provides safety and security for its residents, mostly through the controls of laws, policing, and municipal government. On the other hand, each seems to tolerate an expansive level of individualism and personal rights, in which one is free to do as one pleases as long as no infringement of others' rights is committed. A city can only succeed, as Jane Jacobs suggested, when people feel safe on the sidewalks, which are, with their users, "active participants in the drama of civilization versus barbarism in cities."[2]

This book investigates these premises and asks whether the scales have been tipped in favor of order and control. While liberty still is a cornerstone in both cities, does it play the compelling role that we would like to think it does? Jacobs's civilized city is an important legacy, one in which the heart of liberty, freedom of expression in speech and assembly, exists. If criticism and dissent diminishes, can freedom of expression exist?

In the nineteenth century, these critical underpinnings were established, creating a template for urban life. City dwellers and city governments focused on making things work and on enacting policies that would facilitate large numbers of people living in a small space. London and New York served as models for their nations; after the nineteenth century, the majority of people moved to cities, where the concern for safety and security and the ideal of freedom were married and could facilitate commercial expansion and personal achievement.

As the twenty-first century starts, London and New York have achieved a precarious balance between freedom and order—open enough to allow for free speech, free assembly, and freedom of religion, and yet orderly enough to allow citizenry to sleep peacefully in their beds and for investors and real-estate moguls to invest in what is a safe bet. Many other major metropolises lack this balance. Singapore is glittering, clean, prosperous, and safe, but it has moved so far to the side of order that basic human freedoms are trampled. Hong Kong, a strong democracy, nevertheless enacted legislature empowering police with sweeping surveillance authority, including over journalists.

The opposite holds for Mexico City, Sao Paulo, and Johannesburg. Their crime rates are stratospheric and even the police are reportedly dangerous. Motorists prefer not to stop at red lights for fear of being carjacked or molested. A vast criminal network killed five hundred people in a weekend in Sao Paulo in 2006, closing down the city. Police admitted they could neither catch nor control the perpetrators. These cities, not famous for free democratic expression, have similarly failed to develop an adequate infrastructure of order.

London and New York have, thus far at least, followed a more moderate course. They have allowed enough freedom to sustain the democratic principles upon which they were founded, but at the same time they have constructed "rules" for orderly everyday life. Their citizens operate in an atmo-

sphere of stability and certainty, in which chaos is mostly banished. This was achieved through a consensus process, in which "rules" were not imposed from the outside but were the result of a negotiated process between resident and government.

This book is about that negotiation. It focuses on how two great cities have, in different degrees, limited free speech and assembly in return for order. Their intellectual and cultural traditions are similar, as are their legal, police, and government systems. Both cities lure people with the promise of opportunity and excitement, and both cope with the problems of immense size and diversity.

These cities also diverge in important ways, as is reflected in the chapter structure. Comparisons are not exact in terms of dates and specific kinds of events, but are meant to highlight the basic principles the cities share. London has for a thousand years been a national city administered by the national government. Not only do all roads, railroads, and careers lead to it, but all politics do, too. Even as a colonial Roman outpost it was a major city. Its dominance was never questioned, even with the rise of powerful and money-churning industrial centers in the nineteenth century. The British political system underscored London's importance as a center for dissent as well as for free speech and assembly. Every major political and social movement expressed itself on the streets of the great metropolis, often marching down Pall Mall or massing in Trafalgar Square. Even its police are part of a national fabric, reporting to the Home Office.

New York is not officially the capital of anything and has not housed the federal bureaucracy since 1790. It is administered by local officials elected by residents, and it answers to New York State. Its police report to local authority. But Gotham's longstanding and ongoing importance on the national and world stage has given the city a meaning that elevates it symbolically, politically, and financially to a level equal to a national capital. The September 11 terrorist attack itself underscored New York's representational place in the United States. As the media, financial, cultural, and communications center, and as the site of the headquarters for many national news organizations, it is the place where the public's vision is often focused. For the past two centuries, New York has been the original staging ground for an extraordinary array of political, social, and cultural movements that have tested the limits of free speech and assembly activities. When one wants to get the word out, one goes to New York.

Gotham's strength and influence also results from the empowerment that the American federal system gives the states, which produces a distinct political and legal authority. Cities compete for power, prestige, and influence, making for an interesting dynamic. Washington D.C., the formal seat of federal government, shares few characteristics with other big American cities or other national capitals. As one expert has said, "In no other American city were governing institutions so removed from public pressure."[3]

From its start, Washington's designers sought to exclude people from the center to protect its role as a government hub, a center of "political deliberation and national ceremonies."[4] It had few public demonstrations in the nineteenth century, a critical period in establishing the principles of order versus freedom. Moreover, public speech and assembly in Washington were always rigidly controlled, and the large-scale events that marked the 1960s and 1970s occurred only with the sanction of the federal government, making Washington D.C. the only place in America where this was the case. And the U.S. capital was, and still is, a place of last resort for protest, which is voiced there only after it has been well established elsewhere. Americans went, and still go, to Washington D.C. to protest on "special" or planned occasions, when they are bussed in at great expense and planning.

Public speech and dissent brew in the shops, streets, and open spaces that are the doorsteps of citizens' lives across the nation. This must take place locally, where citizens can turn to people and symbols they connect with their causes. Such public expression has served as a conduit for legitimate grievances for centuries. When crowds get the opportunity to vocalize their beliefs, their desires and discontents are also visualized for society to see. This has been at the heart of democracy since its inception in the Athenian city-state. Today, press reports, lithographs, photographs, television, and now Internet images of thousands of people on city streets are impressive and important expressions of popular opinion in democratic societies. And even when the process goes awry, resulting in violence, the impact of the public voice and the legitimacy of the causes remain cogent, giving agency to those who might otherwise be subsumed in the politics of the majority.

New York, when this story starts, is an island, not an open expanse like London, and it lacked a central place that symbolized a city center, such as London's Trafalgar Square, Paris's Place de la Concorde, Athens's Constitution Square, Moscow's Red Square, Amsterdam's Dam Plaza, Berlin's Brandenburg Gate, or Beijing's Tiananmen Square. At the end of the nineteenth century, London abounded in green spaces while New York struggled to create them. The very type and quality of public spaces a city offers is another critical element in the order-freedom equation.

This book is written both for the specialist and the general reader, and for all who confront on a daily basis the issues of freedom and order. It presents a nineteenth-century panorama in which these two great cities made critical decisions regarding order—decisions that have shaped our lives today. It asks the reader to consider historical tradeoffs and how this legacy has prioritized our values.

This book focuses primarily on the nineteenth-century roots of this debate, and it suggests how these negotiations spilled over into the twentieth century and will spill over into the twenty-first. It explores the nature of democracy and free speech, the way we use our streets and public spaces, how large cities develop, the creation of modern policing practices, the place of government regulation, the profile of the lives of ordinary people, and the social effects of financial and economic pressures to succeed. Evidence for the argument is drawn mostly from original sources in both cities, so that we can hear nineteenth-century voices tell us about their motivations. It asks why in one city a crowd can assemble for protest in a public square, while in the other city a speaker must get a permit to speak in public at an approved venue. This is not a celebratory story, but it is a provocative one.

MAP 1. Central London, 1890s. *Source:* By John Tauranac.

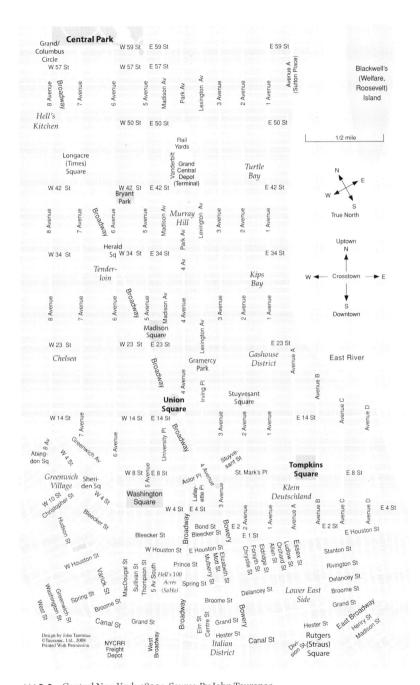

Central Park

Grand/ Columbus Circle
W 57 St
W 59 St   E 59 St

W 57 St   E 57 St

E 59 St

Blackwell's (Welfare, Roosevelt) Island

8 Avenue
Broadway
7 Avenue
6 Avenue
5 Avenue
Madison Av
Park Av
Lexington Av
3 Avenue
2 Avenue
1 Avenue
Avenue A (Sutton Place)

Hell's Kitchen

W 50 St   E 50 St

E 50 St

1/2 mile

Rail Yards

Vanderbilt
Grand Central Depot (Terminal)

Turtle Bay

N
E
W
S
True North

Longacre (Times) Square

W 42 St
W 42 St   E 42 St

E 42 St

Bryant Park

Uptown
N

8 Avenue
7 Avenue
Broadway
6 Avenue
5 Avenue
Madison Av
Murray Hill
Park Av
Lexington Av
4 Av
3 Avenue
2 Avenue
1 Avenue

W   Crosstown   E

Herald Sq
W 34 St
W 34 St   E 34 St

E 34 St

S
Downtown

Tender-loin

Broadway

Kips Bay

8 Avenue
7 Avenue
6 Avenue
5 Avenue
Madison Av
4 Avenue
Lexington Av
3 Avenue
2 Avenue
1 Avenue

Madison Square

W 23 St
W 23 St   E 23 St

E 23 St

Chelsea

Broadway
4 Avenue
Irving Pl

Gramercy Park

Gashouse District

Avenue A

East River

Union Square

Stuyvesant Square

Avenue B
Avenue C
Avenue D

W 14 St
7 Avenue
6 Avenue
W 14 St   E 14 St
University Pl
Broadway
3 Avenue
2 Avenue
1 Avenue
E 14 St

Abing-don Sq
8 Av
Greenwich Av
4 St

Greenwich Village   Sheri-den Sq

W 8 St   E 8 St
5 Avenue
Astor Pl
Lafay-ette Pl
4 Avenue
St. Mark's Pl
3 Avenue

Stuyve-sant St

Tompkins Square

E 8 St

Klein Deutschland

W 10 St
Christopher St
4 St

Washington Square

W 4 St   E 4 St

Avenue A
Avenue B
Avenue C
Avenue D
E 4 St

E 2 St

Hudson St
Bleecker St

Broadway
Bond St
Bleecker St

Bowery
E 2 St
1 Avenue
E 1 St

Avenue A
Avenue B
Avenue C
Avenue D
E 2 St
E Houston St

Bleecker St

W Houston St   E Houston St

Stanton St

W Houston St

Prince St

Mulberry St
Mott St
Elizabeth St
Chrystie St
Forsyth St
Eldridge St
Allen St
Orchard St
Ludlow St
Essex St

Rivington St

Varick St
MacDougal St
Sullivan St
Thompson St

Hell's 100 Acres (SoHo)

5 Av South
Spring St

Delancey St

Delancey St

Greenwich St
Washington St
West St

Spring St

Broome St
Canal St
Grand St

Broome St

Broadway

Broome St

Grand St

Lower East Side

Broome St

Grand St

East Broadway

Henry St
Madison St

NYCRR Freight Depot

West Broadway

Elm St
Centre St

Grand St

Hester St

Bowery

Canal St

Hester St

Italian District

Div-ision St

Rutgers (Straus) Square

Design by John Tauranac
©Tauranac, Ltd., 2008
Printed With Permission

MAP 2. Central New York, 1890s. *Source:* By John Tauranac.

TRIUMPH OF ORDER

PROLOGUE

INTRODUCTION

A Perfect Storm of People

On a bleak February day in 2003, a "perfect storm of people" made their way to the largest public rally ever held in London, to protest the war in Iraq. The sea of humans was unprecedented, a panoply of socialists and nuns, barristers and housewives, pensioners and children, some on their first-ever march.[1] From Bloomsbury and the Embankment about a million marchers wound past Trafalgar Square on their way into the vastness of Hyde Park. On a Saturday, the biggest shopping day of the week, the marchers cut off London's main thoroughfares.

Just a few weeks earlier, British Culture Secretary Tessa Jowell had supported the Royal Parks' ban on the Hyde Park meeting, which was issued to prevent damage to the grass and because the muddy turf would cause people to slip. A fortnight before the event, she changed her mind, admitting that there was no other place for such an enormous demonstration. Trafalgar Square, the usual site of such rallies, would be too small for the anticipated 100,000 to 500,000 demonstrators. "The right of protestors to organize and take part in peaceful marches and rallies has never been questioned," she asserted.[2]

London had a long history of public protest, particularly in the nineteenth century, when large-scale demonstrations were commonly held over issues as intrinsic as voting and as necessary as Sunday shopping. In the late twentieth century, nonpolitical public-street assemblages still drew huge crowds: a million for the Queen's Jubilee in 2002, hundreds of thousands for Princess Diana's funeral, and more than a million at the annual Notting Hill carnival, held every August. The February 2003 demonstration was important to show that "the scepticism of British public opinion will be made vivid in Hyde Park."[3] In 2002, British Prime Minister Tony Blair told protestors outside Downing

Street: "I may not like what they call me, but I thank God they can. That's called freedom."[4]

Across the Atlantic, in August 2004, hundreds of thousands of protestors braved sweltering heat for a "tense, shrill, largely choreographed trek from Chelsea to Midtown and back to Union Square … without a rally."[5] Their intended audience was the Republican Convention meeting in Madison Square Garden, but that Sunday the venue was empty. For four hours, protesters wended their way on a two-mile route up Seventh Avenue, across Thirty-fourth Street, south on Fifth Avenue and Broadway to Union Square, boomeranging their way back to where they started. With no central place to convene, protestors could do little but disperse after marching. Some breakout protests went to Times Square, but for the most part, the crowds simply melted away. As in London, they consisted of young and old, students, professionals, religious figures, and a myriad of groups representing all sorts of political, cultural, and social spectrums.

Gotham's authorities did everything they could to prevent this "festival of democracy," as one demonstrator called it, from happening.[6] The protest organization United for Peace and Justice, along with lawyers from the American Civil Liberties Union, had negotiated for months for a permit to hold the rally in Central Park. In May, the Parks Department, under pressure from the Central Park Conservancy, an organization of park lovers that included New York Mayor Michael Bloomberg, turned down the request. The protestors appealed to the U.S. federal court, which denied the request, citing considerations of time, place, and manner, the modern standard for granting permits for any public meeting of twenty or more persons. "We are not going to permit another en masse march to the park—you can't take over the streets without a permit," said a spokesman for the police department.[7]

Anticipating trouble, Mayor Michael Bloomberg assured Republican convention workers that protestors would be "reasonable," but "if we start to abuse our privileges, then we lose them."[8] He may have been thinking about the free-for-all that had occurred in Boston a month earlier during the Democratic convention, when an attempt to establish a "free-speech zone," a post-9/11 device, had been ignored. Previously, many huge cultural and social events had been held in Manhattan and in Central Park with little objection. On September 21, 2001, for example, a Dalai Lama gathering drew sixty-five thousand people; in 1999, one had drawn forty thousand. A Paul Simon concert in 1991 attracted at least 750,000 people to the Great Lawn. And, of course, New York regularly allowed ethnic and holiday parades. The Puerto Rican Day and Thanksgiving Day parades annually draw millions of spectators and shut down miles of streets.

Yet Gotham's officials refused a protest in Central Park out of concern for the welfare of the grass.[9]

No doubt, such easy dismissal of basic political freedoms, the right of assembly guaranteed by the Constitution of the United States, was affected by the world situation. The 2003 war in Iraq had crystallized quickly as an unpopular cause. Just two years earlier, the United States had experienced its worst terrorist attack ever, the destruction of the World Trade Towers in downtown Manhattan on September 11, which killed several thousand people. A nervous nation scurried to create new policies and agencies to protect the "homeland." The 2001 Patriot Act, renewed in 2006, allows abridgment of civil liberties to a degree unknown since the 1950s: telephone, e-mail, and other forms of electronic communication could be monitored, people who displayed behavior even mildly critical of government could be held or arrested, and the right of habeas corpus was being circumvented, leading some to conclude there was an "assault on civil liberties."[10] Public protests were monitored, videotaped, and attended by plainclothes law enforcement officials. In Iowa, anti–Iraq War protestors had been the focus of a grand jury investigation before federal prosecutors dropped the case under public pressure; in St. Louis, the Flying Rutabaga Bicycle Circus was not allowed to protest the biotech industry. Although officials denied that free speech was an issue, the public became suspicious. As a *New York Times* columnist wrote, "So it has come down to this: You are at liberty to exercise your First Amendment right to assemble and to protest, so long as you do so from behind chain-link fences and razor wire, or miles from the audience you seek to address."[11]

In Great Britain, a terrorist attack in 2005 increased unhappiness over that country's involvement in the war.[12] Public protests grew in strength and number, leading up to the 2003 monster demonstration in London. Such large-scale protests demonstrated that public opinion could be ignored only at the peril of jeopardizing constitutional legitimacy.[13] Just after the war started, Brian Haw camped down in Parliament Square, intent on staying there until Great Britain withdrew its forces from Iraq. Parliament passed the Serious Organized Crime and Police Act in 2005, with a provision aimed specifically at blocking Haw from Parliament Square and limiting public assembly and speech.[14]

Free speech took different turns during the 2003 London and 2004 New York marches. If Tony Blair asserted it was the backbone of freedom, he did so not in a theoretical sense but in a pragmatic one. If Mayor Bloomberg asserted free speech was a privilege, he transformed freedom into a relative and theoretical concept that eludes pragmatic application. Freedom was public ground under the feet of these millions of protestors, and these two massive demonstrations brought to the forefront the tension between government authorities and private citizens over the right to use public spaces, a defining aspect of democracy.

Over the course of several centuries, Great Britain and the United States had established constitutional and democratic systems in which freedom was the conceptual underpinning. These two demonstrations in London and New York could not have been more different—or predictable. They reflect an historical dynamic dating back 150 years, a dynamic that laid the foundation for establishing the way such events would be handled for generations and that provided a new layer of complexity for the idea of freedom. Where there is democracy, there is dissent and disorder, necessary byproducts of this extraordinary system of government. Only democracies tolerate criticism of its processes.

Freedom is difficult to define. Eric Foner asserts it "lies at the heart of our sense of ourselves as individuals and as a nation."[15] Sir Isaiah Berlin said "liberty is liberty, not equality or fairness or justice or culture, or human happiness or a quiet conscience."[16] Musician and pop icon Janis Joplin told a cynical generation that "Freedom is just another word for nothing left to lose."[17] Freedom can be defined in political, economic, social, racial, legal, religious, linguistic, artistic, civil, cultural, sexual, and personal contexts, and its meaning changes depending upon the circumstances.[18]

The words "freedom" and "liberty" in the early twenty-first century tend to be used interchangeably, although "liberty" has a longer historical pedigree, as it was in broad use in English since Roman times. While the Latin word *libertas* and the ancient Greek word *eleutheria* are closest to the modern ones, in both cultures there were numerous words used that varied according to the specific concept being applied, a mirror of our own many applications. In particular, both words carried a particular meaning of individual independence. Because slavery was such a defining institution for thousands of years, and only ceased to be one in the West in the past two centuries, freedom/liberty has been understood as much in relation to the individual as to society in general.

For most people today, freedom/liberty tends to be personal. Americans regard themselves as the freest people in the world because they can carry concealed weapons, travel without official identification cards, live where they please, select from hundreds of television channels, and eat and sleep at any hour of the day or night. Despite the word's political connotations, it is now linked strongly to economic issues. The freedom to emigrate has deep political and religious roots, but its economic causation is preeminent. The husband of a murdered Chinese woman in New York in 2006 was asked why his family had come to America, where they worked grueling hours to make a living. Mired in grief over his wife's violent death, he "looked surprised" at the question and answered, "Freedom."[19]

This is not a word that would have resonated across the ages. In most Western societies, people's lives were defined not so much by what they could do as by what they couldn't. For example, in most of Europe since the Middle Ages, only the privileged could carry weapons. Passage in and out of villages and cities was limited and taxed (and even today most Europeans must carry identification cards). Sumptuary laws limited to certain social and economic classes the right to eat or dress as one desired. There were strict and codified rules, religious and civil, regulating gender and who and when one could marry. From fifth-century Athenian law to the eighteenth-century Frederician Code, even marital relations could be mandated.

While freedom remains a broad and multifaceted concept, its abridgement is acknowledged within the Western tradition. We may have a hard time defining it, but we know that its absence can have disastrous results, such as slavery, poverty, or muted speech. As Foner has warned, "Efforts to delimit freedom along one or another axis of social existence have been a persistent feature of our history,"[20] and John Tchen has added that capitalism and equality don't always go hand in hand, creating a "precarious balance."[21]

Notwithstanding the philosophical debate over whether liberty is a natural state, ensuring or restoring it has produced tensions. Freedom is in constant conflict with authority. It is the foundational Western societal conflict, as John Stuart Mill asserted in the nineteenth century: "The struggle between Liberty and Authority is the most conspicuous feature in the portions of history with which we are earliest familiar, particularly in that of Greece, Rome, and England."[22]

Regulating the balance between authority and liberty then becomes society's clockwork. Mill called it "the practical question, where to place the limit—how to make the fitting adjustments between individual independence and social control."[23] Well schooled in utilitarian principles, Mill realized that liberty could only triumph if its principles were applied in a workable way. U.S. Supreme Court Justice Stephen Breyer echoed this a century and a half later: "in the real world, institutions and methods of interpretation must be designed in a way such that this form of liberty is both sustainable over time and capable of translating the people's will into sound policies."[24] How we live out our freedom depends upon how we construct our order.

This book addresses the dynamic between freedom and order in New York and London, the world's two dominant cities since about 1850. It examines how they defined modes of public behavior, created public policies regarding order, and established the machinery for enforcing it. It looks at how democratic processes emerged in the form of public expression and popular protest, barometers of freedom's health. It investigates disorder, including violence, challenges to state authority, and the polarization of urban communities. It explores how urban authorities both accepted and limited dissent and the right to use public spaces for the free expression of popular will. And it measures the degree to which nascent police forces succeeded, government sensitivity emerged, and the public demanded accountability from both.

The advent of coherent and organized urban public order arose in the nineteenth century in response to increased population density, newly energized democratic political systems, class and race friction, administrative bureaucratic growth, and physical stress on the city. As these dynamics produced an increase in demonstrations and parades as well as in violence and crime, challenges to civil liberties grew. If modern democracy requires the cultivation of an ear sensitive to the noises of the streets, the nineteenth century became the time of testing for democratic institutions.[25]

The Victorian era was marked by a sense of optimism, progress, and anxiety. In Great Britain, the "long" nineteenth century began with the defeat of Napoleon in 1815 and ended with the bloodletting of World War I; in that same time period, the population grew from nine million to more than thirty-two million. In America, the century began with a republic of four million and ended with seventy-six million in the Gilded Age, over which time phenomenal industrial and technological development made the United States the world's richest and most powerful nation by 1920. Politically, both countries shifted between 1815 and 1920 away from their conservative roots to a wide democratic base.

Economic expansion brought pressure: nothing typified the century better than mid-Victorian Samuel Smiles's notion of self-help: "Heaven helps those who help themselves." The changing social structure was confusing, as money became more important than class. Utilitarianism, socialism, Marxism, anarchism, and evolution coincided with individualism, rising literacy, women's rights, and a dazzling array of technological advances ranging from the railroad to the icebox. Even time and space became transformed as the steam engine shrank distances and turned night into day. Anxiety brought fear, which in turn brought a desire for solace, solidity, stability, and order.

This book considers five topics: the cities, the police and the militia, the public, free speech and assembly, and the law. As crucibles of democracy, London and New York represented the field for the battle between personal needs and societal demands. This civic discourse, which could be constructive or contentious, took place in the streets, squares, and parks, much as it had in the original, classical democracies. Cities provided "a variety of sites [that] could function as new areas of public discourse"[26] in an era that demanded visible and accessible popular expression.

Places such as Hyde Park and Trafalgar Square in London and Tompkins Square and Central Park in New York became the settings for how public spaces would or would not be used for civic purposes. Such defined areas had not existed since ancient times. For the first time in the modern era, citizenry and government tested legal boundaries regarding personal liberties and public space. In London, Hyde Park emerged as the paradigm of a people's park, Trafalgar Square as that of the public square. In New York, the city administration refused to accept Tompkins Square and Central Park as permissible places for civic engagement. Instead, its "concern for maintaining social order" made them officially off limits.[27] While Union Square was used for many demonstrations, it never became the city's central meeting place, for many reasons. But the issue was always in dispute, and these places were frequently the scene of popular protest and unrest.

The establishment and utilization of police forces in both cities represented one of the most radical shifts in the modern era. This new force, first in London and soon after in New York, was fluid in the empirical application of its duties. The nineteenth century was critical in establishing police identity and clarifying responsibilities, laying the foundation for future actions. The idea of a civil force to control public order was novel and met with resistance. Indeed, policing remains contentious in our time. And lurking in the background in both cultures was the military, which acted as an auxiliary or backup force during times of civil disorder. In both cases, the mandate to maintain civil order generally trumped the right of assembly.

Civil disorder was hardly new. But the modern city's great size and pluralism made for a potent brew of problems. The legitimacy of broad public participation in society has undergone revision over the centuries. In ancient Athens, such participation was unquestioned; in ancient Rome, the "mob" was acknowledged as a negative force; in the post-1500 era, crowds played key roles in symbolic and economic popular protest within autocratic societies; in the nineteenth century, such groups took on new political meaning as Western governments became democracies; and the contemporary interpretation of "associational life" defines the modern polity and civic engagement of the public. Over time, class and violence became defining characteristics of whether any particular group coming together in public was "legitimate" or not.

The notion of the legitimacy of public expression was born in the nineteenth century. Only then did democracy take center stage, coming to full realization as it was tested, in Britain by its initial modern emergence and in the United States by its application to all groups within society. Free speech and assembly were the conduits for public expression, but not everyone liked the idea that one could say anything one wanted. Free speech and assembly were messy, difficult to apply, and subject to interpretation. In Britain, free speech and assembly were latent concepts within the common law, while in the United States they were ensconced in the Constitution. In both countries, the nineteenth century brought a new consciousness of the role of such rights and a new conviction that "when we are wronged there must be remedies, that patterns of illegitimate authority can be challenged, that public power must contain institutional mechanisms capable of undoing injustice."[28] Free speech and assembly emerged as foundational elements of freedom. As it turned out, they were on the one hand sacred and on the other hand expendable.

The law is traditionally held to be the guarantor of these rights, but for most of the nineteenth century, the law was either secondary or a passive participant in terms of rights. The application of law was an interpretative process, so one must turn to the agencies that enforced them in order to see how law was interpreted and how policies that helped shape laws were created. Civil liberty, a concept that contemporary Britons and Americans hold dear, has been legally endorsed for less than a century. Not surprisingly, form followed function: codification and enforcement of laws regarding free speech and assembly in the twentieth century occurred after testing these rights in the nineteenth century. The nineteenth century was also the time in which the framework for public-order law was constructed, with virtually every aspect of daily life subject to state regulation. By 1900, public order existed not as a concept but as a mandated way of life.

The evolution of public order in London can be illustrated by four major studies: the Chartist disturbances of the 1830s and 1840s, the 1855 Sunday Trading Bill riots, and the Black Monday and Bloody Sunday riots and their aftermath. Each provides singular insight into the "order versus freedom" debate. The Chartist disturbances, almost fifteen years of political protests throughout London, underscored how persistent public protest could be, how policing expanded, and how spying and surveillance emerged as tools of public order. The Sunday Trading Bill riots illustrated how freedom of speech and assembly were shaped by social and economic class, whether public parks would be places of leisure or protest, and how economic issues could produce public dissent. Black Monday and Bloody Sunday were lessons of how police authority could be abused, how principles of free speech and assembly ultimately triumphed, and how public space became the centerpiece for fierce debate. All these events show the degree to which usage of streets was endorsed by public demand and sustained by government.

New York similarly fits into the public-order model through four major studies: the period leading up to the Draft Riots of 1863, the crisis over Tompkins Square in the 1870s, the controversy over armories and the National Guard in the 1870s and 1880s, and the challenges of creating ordered public streets in the last quarter of the century. The disorder leading up to the Draft Riots of 1863 produced a rethinking of what public order was, why it was needed, and what rules were necessary to enforce it. What emerged was zero tolerance for disorder. The Tompkins Square case underscores the difficulty public authorities had in formulating policies regarding public space and the triumph of leisure over free speech and assembly. The debate over building armories amid labor strife in the 1870s demonstrates that while order was an accepted priority, the city was confident in local policing ability and loathe to spend money unwisely. At the same time, the 1877 national railroad strikes cast a long shadow over the city, and anxieties over organized labor, pluralism, and class stratification issues crystallized fears of disorder and heightened xenophobia and intolerance. Finally, street regulations made possible the development of intricate controls on daily life.

These case studies underscore several important points. In both London and New York, authorities would not tolerate disorder. They would infringe on freedom in exchange for security. Yet there was also a fervid public challenge to the more draconian measures, showing the tensile strength of public beliefs. To stem disorder, these cities tried to take measures to prevent it and to deploy the police when it was anticipated. Public order entailed implementing mechanisms to ensure the security of the personal, everyday world and vanquish disorder, in a city landscaped by new extremes of poverty, striations of class, and racial, ethnic, and gender prejudices.

By the time the nineteenth century ended, the dance between freedom and order was well choreographed: a public-order mentality had been constructed that remains with us today. The framework for how, where, and when we express our liberty was in place by 1900. Mill's warning about the tyranny of the majority came true, as order exacted a heavy price. His mandate that society must allow absolute freedom of opinion, absolute freedom of choice by the individual, and freedom to unite (subject to public-safety concerns) proved to be difficult to fulfill. In the strictest interpretation, that would have meant the failure of liberty to Mill: "No society in which these liberties are not, on the whole, respected, is free."[29] Yet Mill tempered his argument with the consideration that individual rights are always subject to the idea of doing no harm to the community.

Three main arguments emerge from this discussion. First, London and New York were able to strike a balance between freedom and order that helped them in their rise to world leadership. In their quest for commercial success, these cities experimented to see how much order was needed and how much freedom could be relinquished. This balance was achieved with the full cognizance of both government and public, which created what could be called a de facto public-order contract much in the mode of John Locke's social contract. Each side tolerated certain types of public behavior and official limitations that were respected by the other side. But when these boundaries were overstepped, the agreement was broken. The result was either civil disturbance or overbearing civil authority. Both cities were beset by tensions and conflicts, in the context of an increasingly fractious public discourse. While the need for free speech and assembly was acknowledged, both cities enacted curbs on them. They created police forces to ensure order and prevent disorder. That meant not just intervening when a problem arose but preventing the problem from arising in the first place.

Second, despite strong ideological similarities, London preserved the substance of freedom better than New York, endorsing wholly the notion of "inalienable rights." London was more dominated by "moral conscience." By the end of the nineteenth century, its policies were more tolerant concerning free speech and assembly, and despite challenges, the city allowed almost unlimited meeting rights. There was more official toleration of street activities in London, with regulation coming later. In the "Empire City," by contrast, liberty took a back seat to the pragmatic concerns of daily life. Quietly, New York regulated the use of public places, deciding when and how they could be used; there, streets met with extensive if unevenly applied regulation. In Britain, early recognition of the juncture of public space and civil liberties led to greater sensitivity and the formation of prototype organizations specifically aimed at addressing these concerns. Britain's liberal position was aided by its common-law traditions, which endorsed free speech and assembly. American statute law provided less protection and more confusion; combined with the new regulatory local governance, New York lost spaces devoted to public speech. The British also developed a better process for accountability of the actions of both police and public, along with a greater abhorrence of violence and death as consequences of public action.

Third, the nineteenth century yielded an important long-term legacy. By the start of the twenty-first century, freedom declined and civil order prevailed in both cities. This was not linear—there were several points in the twentieth century in which freedom was clearly triumphant. But what was eroded was the belief that these two things could coexist. As material and consumer demands increased along with national pressure for economic expansion, the two world cities became pragmatic in their actions, adjusting any intellectual and moral precepts. The twentieth century brought new threats of destruction and tore at the fragile fabric of democracy, with free speech an early victim.[30] In the twenty-first century, the ascendancy of terrorism further bifurcated the worlds of order and freedom. The de facto public-order contract has been challenged increasingly, despite its workability and usefulness as a foundation in cities. Pragmatic concerns now challenge freedom more than ever and underscore its fragility as a concept. To this observer, the current trajectory is not promising.

A century ago, both London and New York had acknowledged through laws, policies, and public dialogue that order was necessary for the city to exist. But the degree to which order would trump freedom was unexpected. The nineteenth century's democratizing energies and pluralistic tone resulted in the broadest inclusion ever in the public dialogue. That public discussion evolved from the classical idea that the public could speak its mind; in almost every city, the town center functioned as a public forum where people went en masse to speak their minds, in protest or in support of those who governed. The idea of the public forum has dramatically faded in the twenty-first century, and non-celebratory public gatherings have declined. Public space has been replaced by cyberspace, where anonymity and disjointed communication rule. To offset this, it has even been suggested we return to our roots and reinstate old-style national political meetings, called "Deliberation Day," so that voters, subsidized by the government, can gather in groups of up to several hundred to discuss issues.[31] Numerous initiatives have been proposed to decrease voter apathy and return to practices that favor direct citizen participation.[32]

Recent changes that are part of the nineteenth-century legacy underscore the fragility of freedom and are examined in the last chapter of this book. In the United Kingdom, the Serious Organized Crime and Police Act of 2005 (SOCPA) promises to limit public assembly and speech. The Data Protection Act of 1998 presents potential barriers to access information that could affect freedom. In the United States, the Patriot Act may have the same chilling effect on civil liberties. Attempts to limit public demonstrations in both cities have started as public spaces are declared not suitable for demonstrations. And London has become the most watched city in the world, with the largest number of closed-circuit cameras in public places anywhere; in New York, authorities are increasing the use of public surveillance methods with all possible speed.

The anti–Iraq War protests of the twenty-first century are a foreboding example of the erosion of access to public space and the clash between the state and the public regarding free expression. This reflects the view that the city's triumph is pegged to economic success, that policing forces have new mandates to control order, that popular protest is a nuisance to be limited, and that free speech and assembly are relative, not absolute, rights. This book is about how we got to this point.

1

THE ELEMENTS OF DEMOCRACY

Free Speech, Free Assembly, and the Law

THE WEAPON THAT'S BEST

Democracy was a novel idea in the nineteenth century. The United States was first to implement its modern manifestation, although imperfectly; Great Britain passed major franchise expansions in 1832 and 1867 that helped close its gaps. In the shifting Victorian landscape of new ideas, citizens learned that they could influence national policy. Cities, "always ... the cradles of liberty,"[1] became the staging ground for the rebirth of the classical Greek idea that all citizens should participate in state governance and that open debate in a popular forum was the best way to anchor a democratic state.

From the nineteenth century onward, democracy became linked with liberty, the ability of the individual to act as a sovereign agent and express all sorts of personal convictions. In the linkage between democracy and liberty, free speech combined the rights of the individual with the ability of society to respond organically to changes within it. Free speech and assembly served as an outlet for popular discontent.

In England, this was considered a "birthright" in that it was an implicit part of the national heritage to vocalize opinions when unpopular issues or crises occurred. The right of crowds to collect to protest, the right of nobility to present petitions to the king, and the right of merchants to present remonstrances to parliaments are examples of such birthright free speech and assembly notions. Sometimes this expression was positive and supportive, such as celebratory parades and royal marriages. In general, though, there was little that could be clearly identified with the modern democratic form, as historically such expression had not been without restriction, or, even worse, had failed to exist in many societies and across the eras.

In the nineteenth century, the rights of free speech and assembly became transformative in Europe. A century earlier, free speech and assembly had become a volatile force in the French and American revolutions. In the maelstrom of change in the Victorian era, popular protests catapulted European and American cities into centers for vocalizing discontent. Throughout European cities, nationalist and liberal movements propelled people onto the streets; "death or liberty" became a constant cry as Berlin, Milan, Amsterdam, Budapest, Florence, Venice, Vienna, Paris, and Frankfurt were roiled in revolt.[2]

As later chapters will show, London was a sophisticated free-speech center from the 1830s onward. In New York, such expression took on a more raucous and violent nature. By the second half of the century, public-protest aspects of free speech and assembly became driving forces in the clash to create an ordered city. In London, such expression was by then a fact of life. There, the Socialist newspaper *Justice* spread its message of dissent by brandishing the weapon of words: "From the East to the West / When our enemies reach / The weapon that's best / Is the right of free speech."[3] In New York, a citizens' group petitioned the common council for a free hall in a central location "of the largest capacity for indoor meetings . . . at the command of the people." The request was based on a clear principle: "The discussion of political questions is necessary for the existence of the Republic."[4]

That two different voices on either side of the Atlantic had such similar expression is not surprising. They are both born from enduring "birthright" beliefs. Such beliefs cross centuries and emerge in different ways, but they essentially support the idea that people have the right to voice their opinion in a manner that can be heard by others. This voice can manifest itself in different ways, but it is almost always a civic one: assembling and speaking in a public place is most forceful. So entrenched was this idea of civic speech that it became a joke in the nineteenth century: "The Anglo-Saxon who does not call a meeting and make speeches has forfeited his birthright," said a New York editorial.[5]

Equally old and compelling is the idea that such expression must be controlled so that the community is not thrown into disorder by such openness. The desire of authorities to provide a framework for order into which that expression can fit is present whatever the form of government. This creates the potential for abuse in conflicts between public and private needs, government and private citizen, and private and public government.[6]

Urban public order sits in the Western European landscape the same way a willow tree is rooted in the pastoral one. Its graceful, solid presence belies its shallow roots; the first storm can end its tenuous existence. For the twenty-first century, our willow tree is the functioning police, legal, constitutional, and political system that we expect to govern our cities. In 1800, the police did not exist, the legal system was untested, the constitutional framework was fragile, the bureaucracy was just created, and the political party system in both the United States and Great Britain was burgeoning. As even a mild storm can uproot the willow, even partial failure could result in the breakdown of public order. What can be uprooted in this case are human lives. When public order failed, loss of life and the destruction of property ensued, and public confidence in government failed.

Facilitating access across the city for people to work, shop, and engage in recreation was of paramount importance for the success of London and New York. Cities created infrastructure to deal with the physical exigencies of daily existence such as food and water supplies, waste disposal, transportation, and communication. These new urban agencies reported to a central administrative structure that we still use: in London, the Home Office, and in New York, the mayor and the City Council. They determined policies, did long-term planning, and facilitated relations with the various political, economic, legal, and social interests in the city. All this gave rise to new laws governing every aspect of daily life, from the placement of streetlamps to the right to sell apples.

Popular response to the new regulated city was mixed and reflected class, race, ethnic, religious, and political differences. The degree to which control was embraced usually mirrored economic interests: the working class tended to support less regulation, while the prosperous favored more. As the nineteenth century became the breeding ground for new beliefs such as socialism and communism, the ability to maintain order while upholding democratic standards was tested.

AN EVOLVING INSTITUTION

An unimpressive scraggly hill in contemporary Athens belies the monumental significance of the events its earth once witnessed. Across the way is the Acropolis, the ruins of an ancient civilization, where religion, culture, and governance triumphed. Visitors admire the symmetry of the Doric columns on the Parthenon, gawk at the Karyatids, and marvel at the breathtaking view of this modern city of four million. Few visit that other stark hill, known as the Pnyx, where ancient Athenians met to practice their original and innovative political system known as democracy. From the sixth to the fourth centuries BC, the *demos*, the people, came together with the *kratos*, the state, to create the world's first system of popular representation of citizens in the governing process.

As imperfect as Greek democracy was, its advent was a great innovation. Popular participation in government was hardly practiced up to this time, with autocratic and monarchical systems dominant. On the side of the Pnyx, citizens gathered to listen to orators, and sometimes demagogues, to debate issues and controversies. These assemblies averaged six thousand citizens in the fifth century, and it may have reached double that number later, when stipends were given for attendance. So important were the assemblies that city officials would dip a rope in red dye and drag reluctant participants over to the hill. The community was the source of all authority, and "a full share in the decision-making process meant the full right to influence decisions by speaking in the sovereign body as well as voting." The onus was on the citizen to participate when the herald called the assembly and asked who had advice for the polis: "every citizen present had the right in principle to make or amend proposals, to speak for or against the motions presented by others."[7]

In addition to political gatherings, cultural or religious large-scale events were common. Comedies and tragedies packed open-air amphitheaters; religious festivals filled the streets with processions of thousands. Parades and processions, such as those of the ancient spring Thesmophoria and Dionysios festivals, were public statements in which societies validated religious, cultural, or social beliefs. Unfettered speech and popular assembly in these venues revealed much about the Athenian state: the political savagery of the playwright Aristophanes, for example, marked both literary sophistication and the tolerance of his society for self-criticism, highlighting the "effectiveness of Athenian *eleutheria* and *parrhesia*, liberty and freedom of speech."[8]

The lynchpin of the Athenian system was participation. The participatory process in which laws were made demanded public attendance as well as voting.[9] The notion that public assembly and speech were intrinsic to the success of democratic processes is foundational. Such processes inevitably produced dissent and disorder. But only democracies could tolerate criticism of its processes through the channels of public debate.

Yet this was the Achilles' heel of the innovative system. Open discussion was not always a reality, and the participatory base was limited. Many dissenting voices were purposefully silenced. The early democracy depended on a limited membership. Only about a fifth of the estimated 250,000 population qualified for citizenship, and the most disenchanted were automatically disenfranchised: foreigners, chattel-like women, and oppressed slaves. For these groups, only the public festivals and processions afforded the opportunity to make public statements.

While civil strife (*stasis*) was common among Hellenic city-states (*poleis*), it was less a factor in Athens than other places. Conformity dominated politics because Athenians feared a lack of cohesion. Athens needed "a broad consensus," "a sense of community and a genuine willingness on the part of its members to live according to certain traditional rules, to accept the decisions of legitimate authorities, to make changes only by open debate and further consensus."[10]

While the public arena was the legitimate place for civic discussion, violent or antistate public expression would have shattered any notion of consensus. Instead, war shifted attention away from such discussion, limiting criticism. The biting political satire of Aristophanes came to a chilling halt as Socrates faced execution for perceived criticism of the state. Popular political dissent was channeled into the notorious *ostraka*, the pottery shard on which citizens would write the name of a politician who had fallen into disfavor. Such a vote would send the man into exile and bring down the most popular of politicians.[11]

As the Greek city states disintegrated into kingdoms and Roman fiefs, the transfer of democratic ideals to Rome produced changes in the place and role of free speech and assembly. Rome's constitutional republican phase was more fractious than any Greek precedent, and as a city it was more cosmopolitan, tolerant, heterogeneous, and accessible than Athens. Its sophisticated legal code, extensive bureaucracy, and large army could better deal with unrest in the packed city, which was estimated to include from a half million to a million by the end of the first century BC. Political turmoil peaked as the Roman mob became a tool for political manipulation. Public disorder changed with the death of the republic in the first century BC and the shift to autocratic government and truncated legal modes. In the Roman Empire, unruly masses could be appeased and riots averted by "bread-and-circuses" social and economic policies, and public energies could be diverted by imperial expansionist efforts.[12]

But Rome provides clues about constructing public order, even when it was unraveling. Roman society was middle class and materialistic; its political system, whose machinations Cicero detailed so carefully, depended on a governing elite. With a quarter-million citizens enfranchised, Rome featured a "full-scale 'politicization' of elective office, and with it a vastly increased level of violence as deployed in the competition for office" in the first-century BC republic.[13] The whole system hinged on open-air meetings in the Forum, a capacious area, as the assemblies were still responsible for legislating.

Nothing replaced Rome in the West for many centuries. Later, in Constantinople, the Byzantine Empire did not tolerate public dissent. Not until cities recovered from the population decimation of the mid-fourteenth-century Black Death did order once again become an issue. Well into the Renaissance and Reformation era, most European cities had such draconian ordinances that there was never any question of disorder; there were some exceptions, such as sixteenth-century Nuremberg, a free imperial city of the Holy Roman Empire and one of the best run in Western Europe.[14]

European society did not consider urban order a major issue. Popular unrest tended to manifest itself in rural areas and was associated with food shortages, poor harvests, bread riots, wage and price protests, protests against sumptuary laws, demonstrations for "King and Country," and, in the post-Industrial era, machine breaking. In Britain, the Rebecca, Captain Swing, Gordon, and Luddite riots typified popular discontent, while in France crowds attacked the Bastille, the Tuilleries, and the Hotel de Ville, symbols of autocratic and class rule.[15]

Only in two cases was urban disorder a major focus in the eighteenth century—the French Revolution, in which public protest dominated Paris, and the American Revolution.[16] In both cases, the abrupt shift in political system, class tensions, economic struggles, legal and constitutional crises, and populist politics produced a breakdown of order that affected cities. Not surprisingly, Napoleon restored order in France with a vengeance, and subsequently Metternichian Europe became obsessed with imposing law and order in the *ancien régime* mode, one doomed for failure.

By the eighteenth century, Enlightenment thinkers had cracked open the doors of democratic reform, providing a new platform for developing the individual's relationship with the state. In Great Britain, this coincided with the world's first industrialized economy, which was accomplished "without abandoning its traditional reliance on a 'constitution' composed of statue, precedent, and custom." This was the new marriage of urban society with the evolving notion of individual rights, replete with "problems emerging from the material and social transformation engendered by industrialism."[17] Rising consciousness of constitutional rights was the inevitable consequence of the heady brew of nineteenth-century ideas; this produced a potent dialectic that carried the conviction that "when we are wronged there must be remedies, that patterns of illegitimate authority can be challenged, that public power must contain institutional mechanisms capable of undoing injustice."[18]

The most significant modern manifestation of individual rights occurred in London and New York. One might have expected America, with free speech guaranteed in the Constitution and the country's national origin cemented in dissent, to be a better guardian of its freedoms. But a broader free-speech framework emerged in British law, which reached its apogee of liberalism midcentury. Its Magna Carta inheritance, buried for centuries and resurrected in the turbulence of the civil unrest of the seventeenth century, came into full fruition in the nineteenth, as universal male suffrage triumphed. John Stuart Mill's *On Liberty*, published in 1859, crystallized Victorian British attitudes. We don't, said Mill, need to define what we are allowed to do, as that is unrestricted, but rather only what we are *not* allowed to do, which is a narrow area: "the only purpose for which power can be rightfully exercised over any member of a civilized community, against his will, is to prevent harm to others." Mill's classic definition asserted that "there is a considerable amount of feeling ready to be called forth against any attempt of the law to control individuals in things in which they have not hitherto been accustomed to be controlled by it," indicating there is little in their history of such control. We are defined, he said, by liberty of conscience, liberty of thought and feeling, and even liberty of expression, which could possibly affect other people and hence be subject to some limits, but "being almost of as much importance as the liberty of thought itself and resting in great part on the same reasons, is practically inseparable from it."[19]

In the first half of the nineteenth century, Britons reacted strongly against attempts to repress basic rights. The infamous "Peterloo" massacre in 1819 became a rallying point for the preservation of rights and initiated opposition to any crackdown on liberty. When government officials panicked at a mass rally in St. Peter's Fields, Manchester, troops were called out, an unusual act in the nineteenth century, and soldiers fired at the crowd, killing eleven people, including two women. That was followed by government attempts to limit public meetings and newspaper criticism through the notorious Six Acts. Public outcry at this proved formidable, and for the next several decades significant reform enlarged public participation in government. At the same time, authorities rethought how to deal with disorder and replaced the military with police in the expanding cities.

London was more tolerant than New York in allowing unfettered access to public spaces. Its plentiful and well-formed squares and parks, particularly the two most prominent and central, Hyde Park and Trafalgar Square, became the megalopolis's most popular gathering places for demonstrations, still the case in the twenty-first century. Hyde Park's unique Speaker's Corner reflects the city's tradition of allowing citizens to use public space for free speech, and by the end of the nineteenth century no guidebook failed to mention it as a tourist destination.

In virtually every nineteenth-century public demonstration in London, the issue of rights was a focus and caused police to think twice before acting. During the 1887 labor demonstrations, for example, press suggestions that the right of free speech was endangered resulted in even larger crowds assembling, often fifty thousand strong. The "Dod Street trick," as George Bernard Shaw called it, would be familiar to political activists today: it involved repeated and flagrant violation of the law in order to be arrested, to test the validity of the law, garner publicity, and gain public sympathy.[20]

New York authorities, on the other hand, paid lip service to free speech and assembly but were more likely to curtail rights in the face of expediency. During the nineteenth century, they systematically limited citizen use of public spaces for political dissent, as the city strove to appear orderly, well run, and mannered, despite its proclivity to be just the opposite. A premium was placed on street paving, lighting, sewers, water supply, fountains, street signs, animal control, and open roadways.

Unlike the London force, Gotham's police were not guided by adherence to common-law principles or by governmental infrastructure. Instead, the New York force reveled in its broad discretionary powers, particularly after the deadly Draft Riots. The post–Civil War period marks a dramatic increase in repressive tactics by police and politicians; this was partially made possible in 1870 after the restoration of authority over the police to the city following a thirteen-year transfer to the state of New York.

New York was the first major American city in which public meetings were sanctioned and allowed by permit only; London had only some temporary restrictions in the late nineteenth century. Up to the 1860s in New York and the 1880s in London, crowds took to the streets as a natural outlet for protest or public political statement without legal regulation. It would never have occurred to anyone at that time, as it would never have occurred to an ancient Athenian or Roman citizen, that permission was needed to do so. Yet both London and New York enacted legislation that effectively required permission to speak in public. Authorities used their Parks and Public Works departments to create ordinances that appeared nonpolitical and nonpartisan. In New York's highly charged political bureaucracy, however, the fight for the Parks Board presidency earned the comment "A more undignified squabble for the spoils of office has rarely been seen."[21] By the 1870s, as later chapters will show, New York's regulations were more draconian than London's, it becoming almost impossible for a person to take up a soapbox on a corner and make a speech without prior permission.[22]

That freedom came at the price of order was realized early on both sides of the Atlantic. New York, the setting for much popular violence in the first half of the century, lusted after order and looked askew at British insistence on rights:

> The London police dare not touch a man unless he has committed some offence, or the officers have a warrant. Well-known thieves and burglars walk defiantly by the guardians of the law. . . . A mob of ten thousand may gather in St. James's Park [to sack] Buckingham Palace, yet, until they begin to tear down the fence . . . the police or troops have no power. . . . But our police can arrest on suspicion or at pleasure.[23]

At the same time, the increasingly heavy-handed techniques of maintaining order in New York led some to question whether rights were being trampled. After a brief visit to Manhattan, popular author Lydia Maria Child perceived the effects of placing expediency before principle. "The ungenerous strife, which has of late been going on between natives and foreigners, has been painful to me," she wrote of the Astor Place riots. "It is not American freedom for which our fathers struggled; but the principle of freedom."[24] During the aftermath of the 1874 Tompkins Square riots, there was serious questioning of the authorities' position even by those who squarely condemned the demonstrators, whose "oracular utterances . . . are bladders of wind." No act of violence had been committed and yet the demonstrators were attacked: "American citizens have the right to hold meetings and parade so long as they keep the peace. There is no law that forbids people making foolish speeches. . . . The police went one step too far, and by their excessive zeal for order made an attack which looks despotic and has turned the current of sympathy against them. They overstepped a principle which Americans regard as sacred."[25] Sacred went out the window when disorder occurred.

THE LAW

"The beginning of tumult," said English Lord Chief Justice Tindal in 1832, "is like the letting out of water; if not stopped at first, it becomes difficult to do so afterwards; it rises and increases, until it overwhelms the fairest and most valuable works of man."[26] In warning that no one could foresee what might happen at a public assembly, Tindal hit at a vexing legal problem surrounding public assemblies: once a meeting had started, no one could really stop it. One might try to ban a meeting beforehand or stop it after mischief began; both presented significant legal problems. Interfering once a meeting had started but before disorder had occurred was legally difficult and logistically a nightmare.

The right to meet is a basic tenet of free speech in contemporary England and America, and it is commonly assumed to be a protected right. Historically, this is not the case. In the nineteenth century, there was little public debate over legal rights or the concept of civil liberties and few court cases dealing with legal challenges. Yet it was that century which witnessed the critical role of public meetings in pressing for major societal political and social changes. This underscores an important point: people assumed they had a right to free expression, and governments understood that blocking this brought problems. Decisions about this were made not so much in the courts as in the streets, police departments, and city halls. There was danger in preventing meetings but also folly in allowing them.

Public assemblies caused constant problems in both cities, and involved law and law-enforcement officials in opposite ways. In London, government and police felt the burden was on them to justify their actions when it came to interfering with public assembly. Their view was that meetings were a matter of public right, and interference had to be based on clear legal ground, even though there was not a large body of law upon which to make decisions. Officials constantly discussed the legality of meetings and interference and solicited opinions by government lawyers before determining what course of action to take. A narrow body of laws, such as the Riot Act, proscribed meetings under special circumstances, but they required that specific conditions be met in order to be used. In general, public meetings were viewed as a right under common law, only deniable when a violation of the handful of laws or a significant breach of the peace occurred.

The case was different in New York. In America, statute law replaced common law; while a strong tradition of public meeting existed since the Revolutionary era, there was an amorphous legal framework supporting it, and as an issue it was not asserted as strongly as in England.[27] One reason for this was that public meetings in America tended to be accompanied by more disorder and violence and were considered threats to the well-being of the city, particularly after the Civil War. Even the existence of a federal constitutional amendment guaranteeing rights of speech and assembly had limited power in the nineteenth century, as it did not apply to state law. The First Amendment only applied to states starting in 1925, with the *Gitlow* decision, when the courts determined that the Fourteenth Amendment could be applied to state action.[28] Prior to that, speech and assembly decisions were issued on a local basis, and for the most part, courts ruled against free-speech principles in the few cases that came up.[29]

When it came to the issue of the right of access to public spaces, the laws were not clear on either side of the Atlantic. The bias was in favor of the public in London and against it in New York. In this area, the two cities exerted their will most forcefully, defining public usage relative to their needs. In the nineteenth century, the demands of work, commerce, transportation, and leisure influenced how the city would allow its residents to use these public spaces. Authorities in the form of citizens, government agencies, representative bodies, and individuals established new legal codes to govern them; these codes spelled out how the spaces were to be used and who would regulate them. The codes could be ignored, modified, or enforced, and they sometimes needed clarification or interpretation.

In Great Britain, common-law tradition stood behind all codified law. There was no general right of public meeting, but there was a right for individuals to assert their civil rights to express themselves, according to common law.[30] This is sometimes referred to as "residual in nature," meaning that it is allowed because nowhere is it specifically not allowed. In the nineteenth century, there were three general guiding principles regarding assembly. Unlawful assemblies were not necessarily those that were purposefully unlawful. That is, what starts out as a legal meeting can turn into an illegal one. Second, the Crown and its servants, particularly the Metropolitan Police, had the right to control the use of parks and highways for the purposes for which they were intended to be used. The notion that parks were for recreation and highways for passage was crucial in understanding the legal restrictions governing them. Third, the rights of assemblers were not always clear in any meeting situation, because of the difficulty in ascertaining the legal status of a meeting. That information was necessary to state positively whether a meeting or a procession went beyond the rights of the individual.

No nineteenth-century statutes were aimed specifically at public meetings, as legal expert A. V. Dicey pointed out, nor was there any clarity in the common law to help guide courts.[31] When Dicey wrote in 1889, it was at the height of the controversy over holding meetings in Trafalgar Square, when few jurisprudential experts were writing about it. Despite the general principle that no right of legal meeting existed, the government, as well as Dicey, asserted that interference with meetings was itself illegal. For much of the century, discretionary judgment on the part of police, magistrates, and judges was used in dealing with assemblies. One result of this discretion, as a modern critic has said, was "a lack of clear-cut legal process for preventing political discrimination on the part of a local authority in controlling public meetings."[32]

Legal scholars said the right of people to gather together is a compounding of the rights of individuals to be at liberty and to speak at liberty. A public assembly is the statement by any number of persons of their natural, individual rights. On the other hand, this competes with the duty of all subjects to keep the peace, and when this comes into conflict with the rights of the individual, the outcome is negative, and a breach of the peace occurs.

Early in the nineteenth century, as concern over popular disturbances grew, the prevalent view was that the instant that public peace was breached, suitable controlling action had to be mounted. As the House of Commons was told in 1819: "Every subject of this realm had an undoubted right to the protection of the laws . . . any assembly of the people held under such circumstances as to excite in the minds of the King's peaceable and loyal subjects reasonable grounds of alarm in this respect, were illegal assemblies, and liable to be dispersed as such."[33] When three or more people assembled "to do an unlawful act, in such a manner as cannot but endanger the peace" or "raise Terror" in Her Majesty's subjects, a gathering became an unlawful assembly.[34]

This was a precursor to a riot: unlawful assembly was created "by persons barely assembling together, with the intention to do a thing, which if it were executed would make them rioters."[35] If people have made motions toward an unlawful end, it is a rout; when action actually begins, it is a riot. All these offences are misdemeanors, unless the Riot Act is read, in which case they are a felony. Under common law, there is no right to stay and remain (*jus spatiandi vel manendi*) on any land unless the law specifically allows such a right (see the discussion about public squares, below), as land is considered to be private. In most cases, the intent and the act (*actus reus*) must both be criminal for a meeting to be illegal, as bad intention alone (*mens rea*) is not sufficient for the assembly to become unlawful.

Separate from all this were meetings that clearly breached specific sedition or treason laws, a tiny proportion of cases, for which there were a number of laws.[36] These include riot statues, treason statutes, sedition statutes, and those that covered other areas, such as special constables, London, and damages from riots.[37] The most famous was the Riot Act, a 1714 statute that sought to prevent riot by increasing its severity as a crime; it was rarely used. If twelve or more people gathered in order to commit an unlawful act, authorities could read the Riot Act and compel them to disperse within an hour, or else their acts would be felonious and punishable by life imprisonment (originally, this was a capital offense). The purpose behind all these laws was to preserve the peace, but their use was limited.

Dicey, a great nineteenth-century jurisprudential mind, pointed out several vexing issues regarding public meetings, issues that remain problematic today. The first is that even if a meeting starts out as lawful, individuals can provoke a breach of the peace that can transform it into an unlawful assembly. Second, meetings can be limited if peace can only be maintained by dispersing it. Third, issuing a notice forbidding a meeting has little actual preventative power. Unless absolute proof can be produced that a meeting would become violent and illegal, which is difficult, then the meeting cannot be prevented. Fourth, the Crown and its servants, including the police, have the right to control the use of parks and highways for the purposes for which they were intended, traffic and leisure.

In England, the Home Office was the arbiter of public meetings, setting national and London policies. Courts were seldom used in the nineteenth century for policy assistance in this area, only for prosecuting after arrests had been made. By the second half of the century, the Home Office increasingly relied on its own law officers for guidance, but it remained sensitive to the political context of the issues at hand; with rare exception, meetings were allowed to occur. An 1831 Special Commission had determined that when terror and alarm are unquestionably aroused, even if no destruction or injury followed, suppression was justified. But Home Secretary Lord John Russell warned that "the presence of *some persons* armed might not be of itself . . . enough to make the general meeting unlawful . . . for it is possible the attendance of such persons might be entirely unconnected with the general purposes and objects of the meeting."[38] In 1842, a police magistrate had disallowed meetings because their hours were unreasonable and they were violent and seditious, but he actually never declared the meetings illegal.[39]

When an 1848 Chartist demonstration was declared illegal because it inspired terror and alarm, Commissioner Rowan admitted that he was not sure what to do about it: he considered the dispersion to be possibly illegal. This is an example of what the later chapters of this book show: the intersection of law and politics proved tricky. Government and police maintained they would only stop a meeting because of potential disorder, but there were times when there was clearly a latent desire to stop assemblies with unpopular causes. It is important to note that there is little evidence that assemblies were stopped just because of government disapproval; in the limited cases of meetings that were stopped, there was credible evidence that public order was the cause.

Not until 1868 did government legal opinion assert that "meetings and precessions . . . cannot legally be prevented simply because they may tend to breach of the peace," a position that became an important legal principle on both sides of the Atlantic.[40] This occurred as a variety of contentious issues in the late nineteenth and early twentieth centuries arose, including politics, temperance, religion, and Irish nationalism, all of which tested government tolerance of dissent. An 1873 legal opinion said only sworn testimony that unquestionably would support a definite disruption could be used to block a meeting—a thing not easily obtained.[41] So by the 1890s, the 1868 principle remained firm: "meetings should not be interfered with or suppressed when there is no actual breach of peace, merely because there *may* be."[42] The government essentially denied the right of interference with peaceable meetings while never actually admitting the positive right of meeting.

Police were instructed never to interfere with a public meeting unless specifically ordered to. They had been empowered to deal with these issues when the forces were created, but indirectly. They gained the right to control traffic and prevent obstruction of thoroughfares for the preservation of peace under the Metropolitan Police Acts of 1829 and 1839, which included all meetings and processions on streets, street corners, and in public places.[43] Gradually, police were empowered to do the same for commons, local parks, royal parks, and Trafalgar Square, although technically they were never given jurisdictional control of these spaces, only the power to enforce codes set by other authorities.[44]

One of London's great meeting places, Hyde Park, was only placed under police jurisdiction in 1867.[45] The other major site, Trafalgar Square, technically was not a legal meeting place: under the Seditious Meetings Act of 1817 (57 Geo III c. 19), it was illegal to hold assemblies within one mile of a sitting Parliament (chapter 12 discusses the twenty-first-century manifestation of this). The law was either ignored or challenged, and most politicians came down in favor of using Trafalgar Square for purposes of assembly. When the Home Office tried to stop a March 1848 Chartist meeting, the attempt failed when Home Secretary Sir George Grey told the House of Commons that such meetings were legal as long as they were orderly.[46] Trafalgar Square saw sporadic usage from 1860 to 1886, with only twenty-one meetings there, including four in 1867 and five in 1872.[47] Severe traffic problems brought Trafalgar Square back into the spotlight as a meeting place in the 1880s, as will be discussed later.

Many spaces fell under the jurisdiction of other agencies, such as the Metropolitan Board of Works or H.M. Board of Works. Controlling order on them, however, always stayed with the police. This was the source of contention in the 1870s and 1880s; ironically, in the twenty-first century, similar jurisdictional issues have arisen. In the last quarter of the nineteenth century, argument over the legality of assemblies in squares and commons increased, as these popular venues were "sites steeped in the collective traditions of metropolitan radicalism."[48]

Meanwhile, America's broad-based and exalted principle of freedom has been compromised. The First Amendment of the Constitution states that "Congress shall make no law . . . abridging the freedom of speech, or of the press." Such a provision is powerful but vague, and "most Americans would be surprised to learn that their cherished 'constitutional liberties' have no specific content."[49] The agent, Congress, has been expanded to apply broadly to all public government and officials—but not to the private sector. Over the past two centuries, the meaning and application of this law has gone through testing and refinement. It remains a cornerstone of liberty but comes with restrictions and cautions.

English law served as the basis for most American law, so most of Blackstone's principles applied. As in England, no special set of laws existed to deal with speech and assembly. Divergence from the English law (aside from the written constitutional platform) emerged in two ways: special legislation enacted during unusual circumstances (such as war) and the creation and administration of laws by states, for local application, which was critical up to 1925. As many scholars have pointed out, the young republic's policies were shaped by prosperous federalists who were inclined to distrust the masses. The early democracy excluded many groups, including slaves, women, and the poor. Concerned with the stability of the new nation, the founders did not view popular protest as constructive, and they wanted to block anything that could destabilize the country.[50] The contraction of liberties resulted from fear of both internal and external threats to stability.

Many repressive measures have occurred during wartime.[51] The short-lived Sedition Act marked the first contraction of the notion of liberty. Passed in 1798, with a set expiry of 1801 to coincide with the start of the next presidency, the Sedition Act was a free-speech encroachment aimed at quelling political opposition against Republicans by Federalists. That same year, three Alien Acts were passed, aimed at limiting or blocking the influence of foreigners, an odd tactic for a country in which every citizen started out as a foreigner. The significance of the Sedition Act, under which twenty-five people were arrested and fifteen prosecuted, went beyond political machinations: it was the first nick in the skin of First Amendment rights. The resultant backlash among Americans who felt the new laws betrayed the ideal of freedom helped Thomas Jefferson win the presidential election of 1800.

Special legislation abridging rights during war was considered necessary for national security. Abraham Lincoln abrogated civil liberties during the Civil War and suspended habeas corpus, the legal mandate that requires charges before arrest. Thousands of people, including newspaper editors and civilians, were arrested for speech that was perceived to threaten or question the Union war effort, and hundreds of Democratic newspapers were forced to suspend publication temporarily.[52] Once again, the net effect of this was to make the press fight back, and there was little permanent legal aftermath from this. The positive effect was definite: it opened up a new legal path for free speech, one that rejected English common-law limitations and linked freedom with an open political discourse.[53]

For most of the nineteenth century, there were few cases in which constitutional cases of free speech and assembly issues arose.[54] Most cases fell into state courts; these were not numerous and occurred mostly in the last quarter of the century, when unionization and obscenity laws were challenged. Thus legal guidance for civil liberties was nonexistent. Instead, policy direction came from local agencies in cities, who created and administered the rules for how speech and assembly would be tolerated. In New York City, this gave power to the police, parks department, and the mayor's office. The 1870s was the single most critical decade for this divesting, with cities across America enacting municipal ordinances empowering them to govern legally and totally.[55]

The enforcer of these ordinances was usually the police, a novel concept in the nineteenth century. Some of the resulting problems, which are discussed in the next chapter, reflect the fact that vesting such power in ordinary, nonmilitary personnel was jarring to contemporaries. One of the early debates about the police in both England and America concerned suitability and compensation for service. Factors such as age, ethnicity, religion, domicile, sobriety, and physical stature were important, but education was not. When it came to applying and interpreting the law, the police played a decisive role in two ways: they were either primary in determining suitable actions of enforcement or they were bound to follow administrative orders.

Police in the nineteenth century were molders of the law in the way they chose (or not) to carry it out. While critics tend to identify police with the most severe enforcement and abuse of authority, the record of the formative first fifty years shows that this was not always the case. Modern scholars point out that "police are naturally biased in favor of preserving order, and are unlikely to give proper regard to demonstrators' constitutional rights." This is combined with the "necessity for some police discretion," which in the twentieth century has been looked upon with suspicion by the courts.[56]

In 1892, prominent journalist and muckraker Lincoln Steffens saw the police relationship with the law in a more pragmatic if clearly cynical way: "The law is just a club, then, the police are a weapon to be used or denounced."[57] When police failed to maintain order, they suffered severe criticism; when they maintained order with too much force, they suffered another kind of criticism. The early use of public inquiry into disorder was critical in trying to ensure that abuse by police be prevented, that public misbehavior be monitored, that accountability be assigned, and that basic rights be protected. Interestingly, these inquiries were more numerous, earlier, more thorough, and of more consequence in London than in New York.

Some scholars argue that "free speech ideals were first systematically repressed by arbitrary enforcement of municipal ordinances."[58] In New York City, ordinances were focused on regulating daily life in order to make it manageable. The prevention of crime, the need to control traffic, and the importance of responding to the demands of residents and visitors were legitimate demands. But infringement of basic rights did occur, sometimes purposefully and often accidentally. New York City required a permit for anyone who wanted to use the public streets and squares in any manner—be it selling, transporting, or assembling, and this created many limitations curtailing unrestricted rights. In 1871, open-air preaching in the city's streets and parks was banned. By 1872, anyone who wanted to hold a meeting on the street or have a procession had to request a permit from the police, making New York among the first cities in the nation to sanction free speech.

As the case studies in this book show, the degree to which infringement occurred depended on who was in charge, what the political context was, what the economic situation was like, and who was challenging authority. There was a growing awareness that liberty and democracy did mean the right to speak out loud and move about at will. At the same time, authorities and the public made a clear distinction between popular speech and unpopular speech in terms of content, and there was no clear, consistent policy linking all this. The first generation of civil-liberty scholars saw this early period, from the Civil War to World War I, as formative in developing a "new concept of freedom of speech . . . which freed it from the mainstream of democratic privileges. From that period forward, the principle would remain intimately connected with the protection of minority rights."[59]

In New York City, the last quarter of the nineteenth century was foundational in this formative change, as the clash between the needs of the regulated city and the right to free speech intensified. The first two national organizations ever to deal with the legal aspects of civil liberties had significant ties to New York. The National Defense Association, started in 1878 to oppose the censorship that the Comstock Act had created, was formed by Edward Bond Foote and his father Edward Bliss Foote, who had been a sole opponent of an 1872 New York law that was the model for the Comstock Act. The Free Speech League, founded in 1902 and housed in the city, extended its reach beyond Comstock to include all issues, such as radical political speech and antiwar speech; New York City activists Emma Goldman and Margaret Sanger were aided by this organization. Theodore Schroeder, one of the forces behind the League, cut his teeth on radical speech in a formative period spent in New York in 1901.[60]

As the center for the labor movement in America, New York was a natural home for new defensive legal organizations. Crackdowns on labor had increased after Chicago's 1886 Haymarket riot, during which a bomb killed a policeman and fatally wounded six others during a labor protest; four men were executed the following year, sparking even more protest. New York anarchist Johann Most spent years engaged in free-speech battles following his arrests. In 1902, following President William McKinley's assassination, New York State passed a law against advocating overthrow of government by force and violence. The Free Speech League fought a ten-year battle over infringement of free speech and assembly rights of the Industrial Workers of the World, or Wobblies, as they were known.[61]

The Wobblies were particularly adept at using city streets as forums for their ideas, and they were as provocative as the English socialists of three decades earlier. Until World War I, they were the most visible group in the battle for civil liberties across America. As was the case with the "Dod Street trick," the Wobblies wanted both confrontation and arrest to test laws. They usually failed, in the sense that they received no endorsement or major court victories of their right to speak, but they succeeded in that they persevered in getting their message across and in focusing on the concept of free speech. Their success depended upon the politics of local government. In New York, an unusual tolerance emerged for Wobblies, one based less on publicly held libertarian views than on pragmatic ones. Allowing and controlling public demonstrations of any sort proved less cumbersome and disruptive than banning them. Police Commissioner Arthur Woods followed this policy and allowed meetings under controlled circumstances, changing the profile of Union Square from a gathering place for celebration into a venue for dissent—at least for a while (see chapter 12).

Outside of New York City, the situation was less than rosy. During World War I, there were 1,956 prosecutions and 877 convictions for free speech and assembly issues, and the Espionage Act of 1917 drew a tight line against speech perceived to be advocating forcible action against law or government. [62] The federal Sabotage Act and Sedition Act also contributed to the demise of the Wobblies, and prominent socialist Eugene Debs faced a ten-year imprisonment for antiwar rhetoric.

The year 1920 was marked by the Palmer raids, when thousands of aliens were seized for deportation; the fight over seating socialists in the New York Assembly; the Lusk commission and its legislation aimed at ferreting out possible revolutionaries and protecting schoolchildren; the prosecution of Benjamin Gitlow under the Anti-Anarchy Act in New York for printing the *Communist Manifesto*; and, not coincidentally, the founding of the American Civil Liberties Union, also in New York, under the leadership of Roger Baldwin.[63] Gitlow's case led to the federal case that established application of First Amendment principles to the states. Gitlow was convicted under the revived Anti-Anarchy Act, and the New York Appeals Court sustained the conviction. Few thought this case would be able to qualify as a constitutional one, including Zechariah Chaffee Jr. Gitlow lost the battle but won the war: three years into his five-to-ten-year sentence, he was pardoned by Governor Alfred E. Smith, who had the Lusk legislation repealed when he regained the governorship in 1923.

It took another decade after *Gitlow* for civil liberties to establish terra firma in the Supreme Court. The court moved away from the "clear and present danger" test, which judged meetings from the immediate results, and toward a broadening of interpretation of rights. Judges on federal courts, appointed for life and theoretically less likely to be influenced by current politics when making decisions, increasingly acknowledged that unpopular speech was unfairly treated judicially. While agreeing that limitations on free speech and assembly existed, in the 1930s the Supreme Court moved to apply these equally—to regulate but not discriminate—so that content was less significant. The Salvation Army, which used streets and squares in ways similar to that of leftist political groups, for example, was rarely prosecuted, and this had not escaped notice.

The 1939 *Hague v. Committee for Industrial Organization* decision established the still used principle that while meeting conditions could be set to ensure that access to public spaces be protected, the rules had to apply equally and be made regardless of content of event or speech.[64] *Hague* also gave the Supreme Court and its friends the opportunity to affirm the importance of public assembly in American life and democracy, as well as the place of dissent. The court had reaffirmed what most Americans had believed by custom for the previous century, and it had denied the acceptability of subverting these principles. For, as the next chapters show, taking one's voice to the streets was a natural course of action.

THE WORLD OF THE GREAT CITY

THE CITIES

"Roaming far and wide over the island of Manhattan" in 1844, Edgar Allen Poe commingled his awe and enthusiasm over the "Doings of Gotham" with cynicism over its chaos. The Irish shanties, the "decrepitude" of the old mansions, the "absurd" fountain at Bowling Green, the "insufferably dirty" streets, "entire districts . . . left for weeks in outer darkness," and newspaper hoaxes that produced instant mobs had Poe wondering how the city could function and who was in charge. But he also acknowledged the endemic excitement of Manhattan, the "legitimate liveliness—the life of money-making, and the life of pleasure"—that encompassed its 400,000 souls.[1]

That same year, Charles Dickens's *Martin Chuzzlewit* portrayed London as a "singular sort of a place." In describing the neighborhood of Todger's, a boarding house, he presented a microcosm of vagaries, the "throats and maws of dark no-thoroughfares" and "devious mazes" in which brokers hawked damaged fruit, "paralysed old watchmen" guarded churches overgrown with "straggling vegetation," and public-house devotees "piled from morning until night" under archways, sleeping off their excesses. Yet London was a magnet for all: in novel after novel the compelling passions for the great city were integrated into the tapestry of human misery and urban decay.[2]

Poe's idea of "legitimate liveliness" and Dickens's sobriquet of a "singular sort of a place" provide important clues in understanding the fast-paced, exciting, provocative, dangerous, and exhilarating life of a large economic hub. New populations forged distinctive cultural and social patterns that produced a frenetic pace that worked as long as civic order was maintained.

London and New York were booming nineteenth-century cities, one the world capital, the other on its way to becoming one. London dwarfed all other major European cities: in 1800, it had 1.1 million people; by 1850, it rose to 2.6 million, and by 1900, greater London had 6.5 million.[3] By 1900, there were nineteen cities with population of more than a half million, including New York at 3.4 million, Paris at 2.7 million, Berlin at 1.8 million, Vienna at 1.6 million, St. Petersburg at 1.2 million, and Moscow at one million.[4]

Nineteenth-century cities were meccas, attracting people as places of economic possibility and individual fulfillment. Their growth was accomplished through two means: migration from other places and an excess of births over deaths.[5] In New York, the foreign born outstripped natives by 1900; in London, the permanent foreign born were a smaller and more insular group, but as the imperial capital, there were many transients from the British Empire.[6] The population influx was accompanied by problems—insufficient housing, inadequate sewage systems, clogged thoroughfares, poor schools, and periodic public-health crises.[7]

In 1850, London was the world's financial and cultural capital. No other city in history had ever reached such a size, producing what one historian has called "urban elephantiasis."[8] Its administration was a nightmare, and as it grew so did a myriad of vestigial bodies controlling services, none of them coordinated or accountable to the general public. Some functions, such as police, remained under central government, with the Home Office serving as the decision-making body. Other functions, such as streets, markets, and water, were either in the hands of the parishes or vestries, which were small or large local areas or independent companies with municipal monopolies. It made for a chaotic and uncoordinated life.

Greater London, as it was known, had spread out like an ink stain, with people settling in new "suburbs" that were not, like American ones, distinct from the city but rather extensions of it, with a total of thirty-two boroughs. This expansion was facilitated by new rail lines serving the greater London area. The London and Greenwich Railway Company was the first steam line to open in 1836, and it kicked off the first stage of pre-1840 rail development.[9] It was an expensive mode of transport for city workers, and many resorted to walking (about 200,000 people walked every day into London's business center, the City) or to the seven thousand omnibuses that went there daily. A second wave of railway development, from 1850 to 1875, established a cobweb of routes that made for speedy commuting and established rail as the preferred mode of transport. By 1900, more than 55,000 arrived daily at Liverpool Street station.[10] The first subway, the Metropolitan Railway Company, opened a line from Paddington to Farringdon Street in 1863. In the 1870s, there were an estimated 150 to 170 million rail journeys a year within London, and forty-nine million omnibus passengers. Horse-drawn street railways were the dominant mode of transportation and between 1890 and 1914 the most frequently used form of transport.[11]

Demographic expansion brought an environmental and physical debacle. The Great Stink of 1858 confirmed Victorian suspicions that "miasma," the malevolent stench from effluvia, was indeed the cause of disease and death. In midcentury, only 10 percent of London was connected to sewers; cattle were still slaughtered downtown; black clouds of pollution hung over dimly lit streets; the erratic water supply contributed to frequent outbreaks of cholera, infant diarrhea, and typhus; and housing was substandard beyond imagination. Traffic was abysmal, made worse by peddlers and markets, and to cross the street one needed to pay a street urchin to clean the manure and night soil in order to pass. This was the world of Jo the crossing sweeper:

> a black, dilapidated street, avoided by all the decent people; where the crazy houses were seized upon, when their decay was far advanced, by some bold vagrants . . . these tumbling tenements contain, by night, a swarm of misery . . . vermin parasites appear, so these ruined shelters have bred a crowd of foul existence that crawls in and out of gaps in wall and boards; and coils itself to sleep, in maggot numbers, where the rain drips in.[12]

Still, the availability of jobs, from the most menial to the most lucrative, drew an unending stream of emigrants to the capital. The Great Exhibition of 1851 showcased Great Britain's material and cultural hegemony, and 6.6 million visitors marveled at Joseph Paxton's Crystal Palace, a symbol of empire and technology's triumph and home to 13,000 exhibitors. Red pillar boxes dotted London's streets as the penny post enabled millions to use this 1840 innovation. Gaslights lit the streets, public drinking fountains were established in 1859, and parks and squares relieved the density.

The realization that urban chaos could erode prosperity led to a wave of reform and regulation in the second half of the century. It is hard to believe that in midcentury there was no central authority or municipal agencies governing the entirety of London; there were about ten thousand "commissioners" overseeing hundreds of local acts.[13] Only in 1855, with the creation of the Metropolitan Board of Works, did the first superstructure emerge to govern everyday life. It turned out to be an imperfect one, but nevertheless it was revolutionary, as it provided for general oversight of sewage and streets. In the subsequent three decades, new laws and new agencies created the structure for a city reeling from its own success. The creation of the London County Council in 1888 extended the mantle of local control, replacing hundreds of ad hoc boards empowered by about two hundred and fifty local acts to pave, light, or maintain specific areas.[14]

New York's growth was more spectacular than London's. Almost exclusively populated by foreign emigrants, its heterogeneity proved particularly daunting. For most of the century, New York consisted only of Manhattan, and its people were concentrated on the lower half of the island, creating, by 1900, the world's highest population density. With twenty-nine miles of waterfront, its location at the entrance to the Hudson River, and great ports, the city quickly flourished as a mercantile center. After the completion of the Erie Canal in 1825, its harbor soon became the busiest on the planet.

In midcentury, transportation infrastructure was well established: one thousand horse-drawn railway cars, 267 omnibuses, twelve thousand licensed vehicles, and forty thousand horses plied the 490 miles of streets, of which 291 were paved. Commuter rail lines had been well established to the north, fifteen ferries connected Manhattan with Brooklyn, Staten Island, and New Jersey, and four bridges connected the island. The subway was not constructed until 1904.

As in London, cleanliness fell victim to the city's success. A British visitor on Broadway described a scene of "confused debris . . . ashes, vegetable refuse, old hats without crowns, worn-out shoes" waiting for the pigs to poke about.[15] As the older, substandard housing stock was inadequate for the surging immigrant newcomers, dumbbell tenements were erected until the end of the century, notorious for cutting off light and air. The vast majority of buildings had little indoor plumbing or bathing facilities. This was ironic given that New York had what was probably the best water supply system in the world: 340 miles of Croton Aqueduct water pipes had been bringing clean water to all parts of the city since 1842.[16]

Unlike London, New York had an extensive local government system, with a mayor and common council. Partisan politics leached into every aspect of municipal government, including police, streets, public works, fire, and public parks. Corruption was widely acknowledged and numerous attempts at reform were launched. Like London, New York was tied financially and governmentally to a central governmental structure, in this case, the state of New York, which needed to approve legislation and expenditure.

People came to London and New York for success, not for a life of ease or the vain pursuit of "sweetness and light."[17] Access to wealth by even the poorest became a reality in the nineteenth century, and the new sizeable and influential middle class was less concerned with how it made its money than with what kind of carriage would convey it in public. In a world striated by social class, this sudden shift was jarring. "The surface smelt a little too much of the workshop and was a trifle sticky," said Charles Dickens of the fictional Veneerings, icons of the nouveau riche.[18] In Central Park, "splendid coaches may be seen, in which sit large, fat, coarse women, who carry with them the marks of the washtub," noted a cynical New Yorker unhappy over the invasion of the city's new park.[19]

Money, said a sharp-eyed New York observer, "makes up for every deficiency in morals, intellect, or demeanor."[20] The new middle class had enough money and education to make them players in the civic drama, and the wealthy became centrally involved in trying to reshape the city. Interest in the physical state of the city became paramount—navigable streets, pleasant parks, and personal safety became the hallmark of the consumer society. For those striving to achieve success, especially the vast numbers of immigrants, the novel prospect of participatory democracy contributed to the importance of public spaces.

In nineteenth-century London and New York, residents demanded order in their cities and the government was the agency to deliver it. Taxes were to be used to maintain the mechanisms of civic order, not build a king's palace or pay for his soldiers. Urban authorities had to facilitate the achievement of what a popular Victorian writer termed "National Progress" by removing anything that might hinder it.[21] People had to get to stores and businesses, transportation had to facilitate this, and no one had to feel at risk in going out. Streets weren't paved of gold, but they were the pathways to it—shops projected "tributaries of silks and velvets, flowers and feathers . . . you gaze on the universal prodigality of the exterior, and wonder what fills the multitude of pockets that pay for it!"[22] The lurking thieves and dangerous streets portrayed in picaresque eighteenth-century novels such as *Tom Jones*, *Barry Lyndon*, and *Tristram Shandy* were to be banished from the modern city.

PUBLIC SPACES: STREETS, PARKS, SQUARES

Theoretically, the streets, squares, parks, and commons of London and New York were places of passage or recreation. In reality, these public spaces were opportunities for challenge, where new behavior conflicted with old and where legitimate activity crossed with transgression. There the rich could interact with the poor, the cultured with the uncultured, the populace with government, new tropes with old customs. They also served an important economic role, as streets could be places of trade and business could be conducted on a park bench. Public spaces could also be the setting for social tableaux, where prostitutes enticed customers on streets, children were paraded for public display, and seductions were carried out. They also served as the backdrop for political dramas, scenes of public speech, and protest.

In the past two decades, scholars have examined class, gender, spatial relations, economics, politics, and religion in relation to open spaces to understand how urban dynamics were affected by them.[23] What emerges is that these spaces were places of risk, anonymity, and modernity. Their openness and greenness contrasted with the colorless built environment around them. They broke up the density by facilitating access to light in dark cities, which only saw the widespread use of gas light toward the end of the century. And rivers, canals, and aquifers became public spaces for commercial, leisure, and utility purposes. Increasingly, privately owned land was used routinely for activities of a public nature: leisure or tea gardens, theaters, halls, department stores, government buildings, workhouses, prisons, asylums, and hotels. Public spaces helped relieve city dwellers of noxious air by dispersing it over green spaces; they became literal conveyors of life and death.

Public spaces retained an air of romanticism. Nothing better typifies this than the two hundred acres of London's Greenwich Park, the oldest royal park, dating from the fifteenth century. A favorite Victorian destination for a picnic, it was a haven on the Thames waterway otherwise bustling with commercial ships, a place where the world of business met the world of emotion. It was, and still is, one of the city's most beautiful parks, a destination where one could have a "delightful" time "looking at the ships and steamboats making their way to the sea with the tide that was running down."[24] But Greenwich was also the place where time was kept for the world in the Royal Observatory, a seat of pragmatic action in a sentimental setting, a blending of a place of leisure with the seat of progress.

If parks were the lungs for a densely packed populace, then London's were capacious. With forty-two thousand acres of open space, London was and still is one of the greenest cities in the world. In the era before the discovery of microbes, Victorians believed that fresh air mitigated disease. Open space was seen as a public-health facilitator and an outlet for recreation for the population. The parks, squares, and commons owed their existence to historical tradition: land sold or ceded for public use by the elite, and the existence of common land. In the English legal tradition, some land was open to all by custom, meaning that by dint of time and usage, land that was used by the public, whether it be for grazing animals or passageway, remained forever in the public domain. Private land, which accounted for the bulk of real estate, was restricted. Indeed, poaching and hunting on land that wasn't yours was a capital offense until the nineteenth century.

The belief that the public had a right to access certain lands was deep seated. The story goes that when Queen Caroline, wife of George II, asked how much it would cost to enclose royal land to keep out the public, she was told by Prime Minister Walpole "three crowns"—meaning the royal heads, not the old coins with that name. By the eighteenth century, private grounds began to be turned into fee-paying pleasure gardens, where tea, music, and entertainment were available in exotic settings. Many were lost to development. What took their place were public parks, small and large, resplendent in their verdure, with fountains, elegant walks, and benches. In the nineteenth century, responsibility for all these open spaces shifted from local to central authority. Dozens of laws were created to administer and control these spaces, and new agencies, such as the Metropolitan Board of Works (1855) and the London County Council (1889), were granted jurisdiction over them; these two agencies also greatly increased the number of London's open spaces. London's Metropolitan Police were empowered to keep order in them.[25]

Some parks had been royal lands, which had been opened to public use since the seventeenth century. While technically owned by the Crown, their management and financing shifted in stages to the state. This includes St. James Park, Green Park, Hyde Park, Kensington Gardens, Regent's Park, Greenwich, Richmond, Nonsuch, and Hampton Court, making up about 13 percent of open lands. Another large group of parks are municipal, land acquired by government to provide relief for nearby residents. They are usually located in working-class areas and include Victoria Park (one of the largest), Meath Gardens, Battersea Park, Kennington Park, Finsbury Park, Southwark Park, Dulwich Park, West Ham Park, Queens Park, and Embankment Gardens, which runs along the Thames.[26]

Commons are the open spaces all over London that are vestiges of older times. Like the forests, heaths, and greens that are now used by the public, these lands are from time immemorial and in the public domain. Commons include Clapham, Wandworth, Streatham, Mitcham, Wimbledom, Barnes, Woolwich, Eltham, Plymstead, Chiselhurst, Shepherd's Bush, Ealing, Clapton, Chiswick, Stoke Newington, Well Street, Wormwood Scrubs, Totting Bec, and Tooting Graveney. Greens include Islington, Clerkenwell, Camberwell, Bethnal, Woodford, Havering, Hadley, Turnham, Kew, and Richmond. The other major category of open spaces are the squares; while many are now public, a number have remained private, open only to keyholders, usually local residents. As London grew in the century, so did the number of squares.

Even less than Philadelphia, Boston, or Savannah, New York had little historic tradition of public open space. Land was divested and developed on a first-come, first-served basis, with the highest bidder winning. A master plan, the 1811 grid, mapped out Manhattan above Houston Street, and provided for no public parks; the grid was a "monument to the primacy of commercial and speculative values."[27] The disappearance of rural and mostly unoccupied areas north of Forty-second Street in midcentury and the rapid rate of population growth coincided with a new aesthetic wave that shifted values back to a pastoral level. Nature, the archenemy of development, experienced a city revival as proselytizers of the parks movement proliferated.

Travelers to Europe, particularly England, were overwhelmed by the stunning park landscapes of cities there: "Every intelligent New Yorker that went abroad must have made the same comparison," wrote a contemporary.[28] Seduced by lingering romantic preoccupations with nature, Americans also saw parks pragmatically as a way to deal with sanitary reform and overcrowding. Open spaces would tame nature, civilize the working classes, and energize the population. Leaders in the mid-nineteenth century parks movement, such as Frederick Law Olmstead, Andrew Jackson Downing, and Calvert Vaux, set out to change "mere grassplats of verdure" into green vistas of democracy. It was an expensive challenge, and one that met with limited success.

The most significant open-space transformation was Central Park, in which 843 acres of shanties and countryside were converted into a manicured and carefully planned pleasure space, with fountains, lakes, walks, refreshments, and sports areas.[29] A very expensive project, it was correctly anticipated that increased real-estate tax revenues would more than make up for the costs, an argument that would later be brandished by advocates of municipal purchasing of land for conversion into parks.[30] Perhaps, said an *Atlantic Monthly* article, the park would teach good habits to the masses.[31] But it was more likely that "the order which prevailed in the park represented the victory of its fundamental premise: that the disorder, rudeness and criminality which prevailed elsewhere in the city were not necessary aspects of city life."[32] The "People's Park" was, from its outset, an elite leisure ground, shunning "undesirables" and demanding that patrons adhere to its codes of acceptable behavior and regulations for licit activities. There was also a virtual ban on any use of the park for political purposes.[33]

By the time Central Park opened in 1859, there were eleven public squares and parks below Forty-second street, serving the bulk of Manhattan's population: Tompkins Square, which served a working-class neighborhood and was an important meeting place for decades; Union Place, which was formed in 1831 from the intersection of local streets and became the sole sanctioned place for demonstrations and civic events; Washington Square, which had been a potter's field with more than twenty thousand buried there and then made into a parade ground in 1826; Madison Square; Abingdon Square; The Battery; Bowling Green; Gramercy Park; Hamilton Square; The Park (City Hall Park), the meeting place in the first half of the century; and St. John's Park. "Almost every stranger who visits us, whether from our sister States or from Europe, speaks of the paucity of our Public Squares," said the city fathers in 1831, in endorsing the extension of Union Square.[34]

Private supporters of the parks movement in New York fought to increase public spaces, but land was simply too valuable to convert to parks. The New York Parks Association pointed out the salubrious effects of parks on health but argued most forcefully that "but for the existence of Central Park a very considerable part of the tax paid by the enhanced real estate in the Twelfth, Nineteenth and Twenty-Second Wards would be imposed upon the rest of the city." Tax revenues from higher assessments would more than make up for the absence of businesses, buildings, and any tax revenue from them.[35]

They pointed to Europe for inspiration. The main parks of London consisted of more than eleven thousand acres, while New York (still Manhattan) had a total of a bit more than one thousand, including all the squares and the newly added Riverside Park; if kept in proportion to London, New York should have had five thousand acres, a highly unrealistic figure even for the time. During the battle for more parks, advocates reminded politicians that New York's population was increasing at so rapid a rate that it would overwhelm the existing parks by 1900. In the 1880s, the ratio of parks to population in major cities in the United States and Europe was startling: in New York, there was one acre of publicly owned open space for every 1,363 persons; London, for every 205; Berlin, for every 235; Vienna, for every hundred; Paris, for every thirteen; Chicago, for every two hundred; Boston, for every 190; and Philadelphia, for every three hundred.[36] By the end of the century, a concerted effort was made to create small, local parks to act as safety valves in the most congested neighborhoods, mostly to serve as children's playgrounds. "The children seem to have been forgotten," said Mayor William Strong.[37]

Open, public spaces in these two cities may have served recreational, sanitary, and social purposes in the nineteenth century, but they also aided in the formation of civic identity. They were places for expressing a wide array of political, social, and economic messages, a public conduit for private opinion.[38] Parks, streets, squares, and other open spaces became sites to be used "as new arenas of public discourse" (with the significant exception of Central Park).[39] Together with the new vision of urban space, there were competing views of how urban social order would be manifested, how desired commercial and civil relationships would be designed,[40] and how "public life transpired in streets, squares and parks, places of informal, casual, largely unplanned social interaction."[41] Some scholars have argued that the very survival of capitalism is vitally connected to the way urban spaces are used, and that this reshapes societal structures, which in turn reshape the urban spaces.[42]

London had an advantage over New York in its tradition of open land accessible to all, the commons, and this influenced the use of much of its public land. The ability of vast new populations to interact in public was formative in forging this civic identity. New York, with its limited open spaces and unhappy history in the first half of the nineteenth century of public disorder, decidedly turned its back on using its open spaces for political speech.

THE CROWD

Big cities gave rise to big crowds. The modern city surpassed all others in size—big, powerful, unfriendly, and unyielding. This was where population congregated, where thousands came to work, shop, and play. The unprecedented numbers of humans living in one place redefined the nature of city life. This was also Bartleby's world, filled with people hurrying along the streets, paths of awe and fear, isolation and alienation, wealth and poverty; this was the world of Dicky Perrott, the doomed *Child of the Jago*, filled with "contorted forms of those who made for sleep on the pavement" and rolled through the gutters of the impassible rookeries.[43] Literature about the city teems with explosive images and a mixture of admiration and apprehension when discussing crowds.[44]

The crowd is benign; the mob is violent. In the public arena, they are urban actors, contributing vitally to the city's drama, to the new discourse on the public sphere, and to the new tensions of a pluralistic society.[45] Every public place, event, or gathering has a crowd; when the crowd becomes disorderly or commits acts of aggression, it turns into a mob. The classic study by Gustave Le Bon in 1896, the first major one of the modern era, saw this mass only in a negative light, imbued with a primitive anthropomorphic character. It was savage, on the lowest order of mankind (after animals, children, and women), irrational, and implicitly devoid of good people. The state of collective mentality that existed precluded morality because of the impulsiveness and mobility of the group. "Popular" became "vulgar," in placement before the word "protest." From "vulgar" it is a short distance to "criminal," and this short span was traversed easily in the nineteenth century.

Le Bon's work reflects a dominant attitude in the century: there existed a bottom-feeding, permanent underbelly class, bordering on animal. For Clarendon they were "dirty people without name," for Hippolyte Taine they were *la canaille*, and for Jules Michelet they were *le peuple, gens sans feu et sans aveu*; even Karl Marx saw a permanent underbelly of public participants, the *lumpenproletariat*, in France the *canaille* or *menu people*, in Italy the *lazzaroni*.[46]

Both in England and America the idea of the mob was connected to the poor. In the mid-nineteenth century people believed that while some poor might turn out to be honest, all the crooks started out poor. Henry Mayhew's pioneering *London Labour and London Poor* substantiated the theory with massive testimony. Mayhew could clearly point to a class of poor "who will not work," indicative of their moral failure. And those who were in contact with criminals painted a frightening picture of a class seeped in vice and ignorance, genetically self-perpetuating.[47] By the end of the century, the British attitude had begun to change, as Charles Booth identified the poor as the "submerged third," victims of the imbalances of society rather than morally deficient.[48] As the Royal Statistical Society correlated death rates with income (concluding that the poor tend to die younger and the rich older), the poor began to be disassociated with criminal tendencies. This was the era of labor politics, modern psychology, criminology, sociology, statistics, and socioeconomic mobility.[49]

Historians in the twentieth century rejected the automatic branding of the mob as criminal, instead identifying those who challenged the status quo as people who rightfully questioned authority, were denied rights, or had legitimate complaints because of a grievous issue. They examined specific events, time periods, or themes: for New York, these include the Revolutionary period and its politics;[50] antebellum political, racial, and artisanal Republicanism;[51] and individual riots.[52] For London, they include eighteenth-century mob violence,[53] early nineteenth-century political dissent,[54] and specific riots. For both cities, they include the formation and role of police and public order in British and American societies in general.[55]

As they became identified with the public disposition of grievances, urban crowds gained legitimacy in nineteenth-century Great Britain and America. The negative "mob" label was considered inappropriate in most situations because it reflected class or social biases, and the urban crowd was usually poor but certainly not criminal. The crowd could be a barometer of society's political and social health, a marker for economic change;[56] it could be imbued with a political psychology that compelled it to grow, absorb, seek density, and lose the individual in an attempt to achieve a perfect and impossible egalitarianism.[57]

Increasingly, the legitimization of the crowd occurred when beneficial change resulted from their actions. For the past fifty years, scholars from many disciplines have reexamined history from the "bottom" up, with a view to both disassociating violence as a hallmark of crowd behavior and to analyzing police and government contributions to disorder.[58] Experts examined court, arrest, and bail records[59] and questioned police operations and stereotyping. Police would, and could, identify people from their past actions and establish a negative record of behavior that could be used against a person if he or she acted in any antiauthoritarian fashion.

For the most part, crowds in nineteenth-century London and New York were as diverse as the society around them: working class, middle class, upper class, immigrant, native, young, old, white, African American, male, and female. Contemporaries were consumed with who was in the crowd in an effort to establish how legitimate a public assembly was. Police might allow or disallow an event based on their view of the crowd; the press would approve or disapprove of an event on the same basis. Sometimes the police or press could say the crowd was criminal in order to delegitimize the validity of the complaint, which usually reflected class, race, or ethnic bias; examples of this were the London Chartist disturbances and New York's Tompkins Square riot. On the other hand, there were numerous examples of contemporaries legitimizing crowds by showing sympathy for causes even during violent protests, such as was the case with the 1887 Trafalgar Square protests and the 1837 New York Flour Riots.

The redefinition of mobs reflects a new perspective on the way people were integrated into public life. Democratic societies became more inclusive, and new groups emerged to vocalize publicly their interests and perspectives. This accelerated in the nineteenth century, leading to the late-century Progressive movement in America and a host of reformist movements in England, which brought dissenting or alternative views to the public forum. As the common good became a driving ideal, it became clear that "people with different values, backgrounds and desires could define the public and its interests in different, often contradictory ways," making for a noisy outcome but not necessarily a bad one.[60] By the end of the century, the crowd was considered a legitimate conduit for public opinion and a symbol of fulfilled democratic ideals; the expression of mass opinion in open forums was seen as a critical societal right.[61]

The degree to which violence was present on public streets or at events was a vexing one. The new police served a prophylactic function: for the first time, a body existed to thwart disorder or keep it in check. Uniformed authorities learned to control public spaces, and the citizenry acknowledged that control. Violence did recede in both cities, more so in London than New York. Perhaps, as Arthur M. Schlesinger Jr. has said, violence is an American tradition.[62]

Throughout the nineteenth century, public order in New York was not achieved without bloodshed and death, which was greeted by the public and authorities as unfortunate but not disastrous. The middle and well-off classes paid little attention to the loss of poor or ethnic protestors. After the 1863 Draft Riots, the worst case of civil violence in American history, New York moved to ensure such an event would never happen again, by passing new laws and reorganizing the police.

Up until the mid-eighteenth century, London had been marked by casual violence. The tradition of violent popular protest usually had been aimed at property rather than at people. By the eighteenth century, crimes against property had risen dramatically; to curb this, drastic punishments were enacted to dissuade perpetrators, resulting in the existence of more than two hundred capital offences.[63] By the nineteenth century, and particularly after the Metropolitan Police was formed in 1829, violence declined, and legal reforms reduced the number of capital offences. Public toleration for violence fell in London, and its occurrence usually resulted in demands for accountability and reform, as evidenced by lengthy Parliamentary investigations mounted following riots in 1833, 1856, 1864, 1886, and 1887. The death of even one protestor or policeman was considered horrifying. Questions were often raised in Parliament concerning any sort of public demonstration, and the public eye was keenly on the subject. In both cities, there was outrage at property destruction, although in England there was more of an effort to address the financial and restitutional aspects of this.

The two cultures differed drastically concerning the use of firearms. New York police in the nineteenth century tended to be armed, as were civilians in many cases. By contrast, after the Coldbath Fields debacle in 1833, British forces went out of their way to avoid firing on crowds, and London police in general did not carry firearms. Historically, firearms in Britain were accessible only to the nobility or the wealthy, whereas Revolutionary Americans reacted against this notion of privilege and asserted their right to firearms, creating a sacrosanct right to bear them unknown in any other culture.

Much of America's civil violence has emanated from conservative roots, from those who tried to maintain the status quo and prevent newcomers from accessing basic institutions.[64] The 1863 Draft Riots were indicative of this conservatism. Its chief victims were African Americans. Such violence had not been seen during the Revolutionary era, which was marked by a singular absence of summary executions, decapitations, or bloodthirsty mobs.

And while violence—"a common agent of historical change everywhere"[65]— is endemic to all human societies, America tolerated a more careless use of it. A century after the Draft Riots, in the 1960s, a new pattern of violence erupted in America's cities. Books, magazine articles, television, and Congressional and state committees asked why Americans were so careless with human life and so destructive of cities.[66] Some felt the explanation was rooted in history: we "have imprinted upon our citizenry a propensity to violence."[67] If anyone had reflected on urban life a hundred years before, they would have found the pattern disturbingly portentous. In almost every riot and civil disturbance in New York, with the exception of the Draft Riots, there was little cause for weapons of any kind to be used nor were there any clear or pressing threats to respond to. But weapons were everywhere: guns, truncheons, staves, rocks, brickbats, and whatever implement came to hand. Perhaps, as psychologists are prone to say, aggression is embedded in the human fabric and loosened by the irrational hatreds and jealousies we nurture.

Race and class loosened those hatreds. New York was more heterogeneous and fragmented by race and ethnicity than London, whose external emigration was limited.[68] In the antebellum period, virtually every civil disturbance in New York was connected to race or ethnicity, even when other issues, such as employment, were involved (see chapter 5). Many of these incidents so seethed with hatred that twentieth-century disturbances such as Newark or Watts, which became the banner for race and class fractionalization, pale beside them. Even orphaned African American children were targets in the Draft Riots.[69]

If London was less affected by race and ethnicity than New York, the two forces were equally vexed by issues of class. England, typical of European societies, was mired in class rigidity and traditions, which only started to erode with the advent of new mercantile wealth in the eighteenth century and new industrial wealth in the nineteenth century. Speech, dress, deportment, and schooling remained markers for status long after income had leveled the playing field. The new police, who were working-class salarywise, were representatives of government and should have been as immune to class prejudice as a blindfolded Lady Justice. They were forced, from the beginning, to make judgments based on class in order to carry out their responsibilities: they were required to determine whether people looked "respectable" or were known to be of "bad character." The 1855 Sunday Trading Bill riots are a good example of a civil disturbance based on class, as there was a universal perception that Sabbatarian legislation was anti–working class. If the wealthy could spend Sundays as they pleased, riding through the park and going to their clubs, then the working people should "throw off the shackles of oligarchal oppression and misrule," as a speaker in Hyde Park put it.[70]

British novelist and prime minister Benjamin Disraeli drew a vivid picture of his nation's bifurcated world of the "haves" and "have-nots" in his 1845 novel *Sybil*, engaging the public's attention on the need to reform vast economic inequities. As cognizance of problems increased, nineteenth-century reforms tackled some of the worst abuses the new industrialism had produced and established the basis for a regulatory and welfare-minded government. [71] In tandem with voting reform, which made working men part of the electoral process, the perception of class began to change, and poverty was reconsidered not as a character defect but a societal one.

In New York, the general attitude toward the poor grew increasingly venomous as the century wore on. "The government is not expected to do social and moral reform," piously preached the New York Association for Improving the Condition of the Poor.[72] The Association praised the police for ridding the "wharves and streets of beggars in forty-eight hours, thus at once proving the power and the responsibility of the government for the removal and continuance of this disgraceful evil."[73] That civil disorder and riot were associated with "homeless loafers on the Battery," "human swine sleeping on benches," and "bloated night walkers" was clear to many middle- and upper-class New Yorkers, who thought that those in the penitentiary "had it easy."[74] Newspapers and contemporaries commentators tended to take the position that nobody reputable would have been caught in this sort of fracas.

Even when the disturbances were condemned and rioters blamed, there was often much support for the cause behind the actions. Despite class arrogance, a singular sense of egalitarianism prompted many to question the fairness of a situation, particularly when disturbances were linked to economic recessions or political infighting. In 1837, prior to the formation of the New York police, the gathering that led to the Flour Riot was endorsed by the *New York Herald*. It was a meeting about "exorbitant prices" and not a political meeting—the "usurers, speculators and extortioners went on in their career" and "have increased the absolute necessaries of life—flour, fuel, food, rent, until hunger, cold, thirst and starvation compel men to throw off their lethargy—to come forth, *en masse*, to take into deep consideration the condition of the times."[75] Distaste for Tammany Hall politics surfaced many times, such as in the 1857 riots, when the gangs were considered to be political pawns. Sympathies tended to erode in the lean and conservative decades of the 1880s and 1890s.

THE POLICE

No one in the twenty-first century could envision a city without a police force, but less than two centuries ago, no city had one. Of course there was crime. The literature of the mid-Victorian era abounds with stories of the criminal classes establishing an underworld composed of lairs, gangs, initiation rites, methods for disposal of goods, and even its own language. Nor was there any coherent set of regulations about daily life: in both England and the United States, commercial travel was common and dangerous, and roads and streets were perilous frontiers to be crossed. Even harsh punishments failed to deter criminals.

The modern police are distinguished by four characteristics differentiating them from the constabulary prior to the nineteenth century. First, they were a paid, professional force that was trained and disciplined. Initially, appointments were made on connections as well as merit, but over time the police became part of a civil service system. They also replaced the military, which had been called upon to deal with civil unrest.[76] Second, police served the public and were accountable to the public, not to any private or political interests. Previously, policing forces had served special interests, individuals, groups, leaders, and royalty. However, now their pay was delivered through new taxes meant to create an equalized burden of costs.

Third, the mandate given to police was broad and unprecedented: to keep order, whatever that entailed. Among the array of activities were new ones such as morals laws and municipal-code enforcements. Earlier forces tended to have specific goals, such as catching crooks or keeping crowds in control. The new police created a safe environment and they dealt with a distinct criminal class they sought to deter and arrest. While robbery, murder, and assault were always unacceptable in Western societies, there had not been a consistent and dedicated group of people concerned only with controlling them.

Fourth, they became the first official and secular organization to oversee the city entirely; they became integrated into the entire urban community, forming (for better and for worse) a consistent local authority. In London, this meant equalizing the roles of the parishes; in a growing New York, it meant equalizing all new neighborhoods in the city, leading to the establishment of a functional municipal corporation. In this capacity, the police became direct interpreters of the law and symbols of justice. This was not always done perfectly, but it was a new delivery system.

Numerous factors prompted the formation of police. Foremost was the need to ensure the city was livable, unfettered by hindrances that would block growth, and free from anxiety and fear. Who would get coshed in the streets of London? Whose silver plate would be stolen from the mansions of New York? How would people get to work and shops if the streets were blocked by refuse or rioters? There was potential insurrection, spreading political dissidence, and simmering civil unrest. In England, even the monarchy contributed to national disorder.[77] Modern historians have examined the origins of the police extensively. Some argue the police were formed to prevent crime and disorder, while others maintain their mission was to retain class structure and elitist control. There is evidence to support both contentions, but this book argues another perspective.[78] The mandate for the city to grow and prosper propelled the formation of policing. The new attitude was one of zero tolerance for anything that promoted disorder. The nineteenth century marks the first time that it was widely believed that police could accomplish such a goal. If hegemonic forces made the city prosperous, then their interests would be served. The early establishment of police in these two world cities (New York predated Boston and Philadelphia, older cities)[79] helped pave the way for their economic success by providing stability.

Police were the first modern mechanism for regulating the rhythms of city life and creating a language of authority within the new urban discourse. Guided (and to a large extent bounded) by laws, ordinances, and administrative directives, they were required to make daily decisions and create informal policies that gave form to city functions. From creating a category of criminals "known to the police" in London, to determining peddlers' rights on New York's Lower East Side, to deciding who would remove snow from fire hydrants, to determining who would use public squares, the police cut a broad swath of discretionary power. And the nineteenth century marked the first time that citizens were routinely punished for unacceptable waste-disposal methods, unsightly appearances of homes and businesses, and annoyances to and interference with the lives of other citizens. In both London and New York, police decided how to patrol streets, enforce regulations, and guard the city.[80]

Neither the British nor the American national governments wanted to use the army to quell disturbances after 1829. One of the last major military deployments in London was during the 1780 Gordon riots, when seven hundred were killed. As England was embroiled with the American Revolution, internal political and religious rifts precipitated the London rampage. Thousands of soldiers took over the streets of the capital. Once peace was restored, the reaction was as fierce as the violence: such arbitrary authority was unacceptable. After the formation of police in both cities, the military was rarely used; up through the twenty-first century, the idea of using armed forces to maintain urban order was universally repugnant and during its rare usage the source of even more problems.[81]

Policing changed perceptions. In May 1844, Edgar Allen Poe indicated with relief that order in New York had been restored "by the firmness and prudence of the new authorities."[82] Dickens had made it clear in *Oliver Twist* that there would always be a Bumble to apprehend a young boy nicking a handkerchief.[83] On the simplest level, the police stemmed violence and reduced property crime;

as it turned out, they also reshaped the way the city functioned. Uniformed authority was in itself a symbol of the city—structured, accountable, and service oriented. The formation of police forces started a tidal wave of municipal legislation and reform that reshaped the metropolis by providing a new infrastructure and operating system.[84]

Before the existence of the police, there were private watches, household associations, constables, local patrols, and harsh punishments, all aimed at reducing crime and chaos.[85] A few laws, such as England's Michael Angelo Taylor's Act (1817) and New York's limitations on animals on streets, aimed at making streets cleaner and safer and provided penalties for abuse.[86] Ordinary citizens served as lookouts and had to protect their own property and lives.

The London police became a model for the world.[87] It was not technically the first—Vienna, Berlin, St. Petersburg, and Paris all had forces in the eighteenth century, but those gendarmes were militaristic. In Britain, Sir Robert Peel saw his proposal for police blocked for years on the grounds that it would be too expensive and would signal the beginning of authoritarianism on the much detested Continental model. This reflected the English emphasis on personal liberty.

Even if Peel had not faced opposition on principle, he had problems. In an official sense, there was no such place as "London." The City of London was a distinct, small, and self-governed area in the center of the conurbation.[88] The metropolis itself consisted of two hundred vestries and parishes, which were self-governed, took care of the streets, and handled peacekeeping. And many urban responsibilities were in the hands of private entities. So an area had to be defined that was to constitute the "beat" of this new force, and that was drawn as a twelve-mile radius from Charing Cross, in central London, with nineteen police divisions within it and 3,444 men. By 1839, this jurisdiction was increased to a fifteen-mile radius and covered 688 square miles, an area only partially populated at the time. The districts established for the first time a universal urban administrative structure. Along with this came a universal rate (tax) to pay for the force, one of the first of its kind anywhere.

Given the lack of a realistic "city" administrative reality, the new police had to be administered by central government, the Home Office. This was suspiciously reminiscent of a military structure. Ensuring that the police be a civil force rather than a military one led to decisions that were defining, including the sensitive one of uniforms. The blue swallow-tailed coat was different from a military uniform, as was the leather top hat, and men were to carry no weapons. The uniform was intended to make the policeman visible, a prophylaxis against those who would break the peace. In the United States, cops were initially loathe to be identified as such, and rejected uniforms initially as too servile. They wore only badges until the 1850s, the same period in which weapons were authorized.

Perhaps the most astonishing aspect of the new police force was its first two commissioners, who brought stability and leadership to the office. Richard Mayne was a lawyer, Charles Rowan a military officer, and both stayed in office until death, Rowan in 1850 (mortally ill for two years) and Mayne in 1868. Their leadership was intelligent, constant, firm, and prescient. Their odd personality combination worked well. Rowan, brigade major of the Light Brigade, was "imbued with the spirit of Sir John Moore's Moral Training"[89] and he dealt with daily administration, discipline, and training. Evidence of his strict standards was the fact that of the first 2,800 recruits, 2,238 were dismissed.

Mayne, only thirty-three years old at the time of his appointment, had learned his criminal law at Lincoln's Inn and became an innovator who questioned everything, handled complaints, and founded the detective force. In particular, he was responsible for solidifying the preventive nature of the force: "the principal object is 'the Prevention of Crime.' . . . The security of person and property, the preservation of the public tranquility . . . will thus be better effected than by the detection and punishment after he has succeeded in committing the crime."[90] He saw the men as disciplined—no drinking or sitting was an early order—officers of the law who could make their own daily decisions with no political bias.

Who was qualified to be on the force, how big the force would be, and how much its members would be paid were perplexing questions whose answers established critical precedents. While the Metropolitan Police started at just under three thousand men, by 1848, it approached five thousand, by 1880, almost eleven thousand, and by 1900, more than fifteen thousand. Mayne realized quickly that he had underestimated how large the force should be: in 1830, he wrote to Home Secretary Peel, pointing out that London's physical expansion with inclusive city suburbs drained resources. Mayne told Peel, "it is found that from the exposure of the back parts of many houses in the suburbs it becomes more difficult effectually to protect them than those in the streets of the Town."[91] Peel had made sure recruits would not be political appointments by establishing tough standards; police were to be apolitical, not even voting—in contrast to New York's patronage system of police appointments. Good physical health, literacy, citizenship, and good character were the basic requirements. The minimum age was twenty-two, the maximum, thirty (lowered after the initial decade from thirty-five), height a minimum five feet, seven inches, which was on the tall side for the time.[92]

Residency requirements shifted in both cities. At one point, police in both cities were required to live in the area in which they worked, to improve their knowledge of and relations with locals. To ensure professionalism and emotional distance from subjects, London's bobbies were mostly drawn from the country—it was important that they came into their neighborhoods fresh, with no previous connections with the locals, but then they had to live within the districts they patrolled, to gain familiarity with the residents. In New York, the familiarity of the cops on the beat with the neighborhood was considered a way to thwart crime, so recruitment for neighborhoods was encouraged. But that was a double-edged sword, as it added a temptation to corruption. After joining the force local residence was strongly emphasized, although legally it changed over the century. Originally a requirement, it was eliminated with the 1857 Metropolitan Police Act, but by the 1870s new rules of local residence brought police back into their counties.

The New York Police Department was founded in 1845 with 1,132 policemen, in a system modeled on London's. Younger men were also preferred, but the maximum age was higher, thirty-five. With the same English five feet, seven inches height requirement and a minimum weight of 138 pounds,[93] good character and references were just as important, but until civil-service reform, politics was just as important for getting an appointment. The force developed an early reputation for being heavily Irish, but in 1888, a police census claimed that two-thirds were classified as American or native, 28 percent Irish, 4 percent German, and the rest a mix.[94] It is likely the number of Irish was undercounted, as had been the case in 1855, when an official report showed only a quarter of the force to be Irish, but another one by the city's aldermen estimated that figure to be double.[95]

By the end of the century, there were just over five thousand police, with a starting salary of $1,200 for a patrolman.[96] In New York, as in London, calls to increase the size of the force cited better European ratios and the dearth of police in expanding neighborhoods: in 1896, New York had one patrolman for every 540 people, London one for every 330, Paris one for 306, and Berlin one for 447.[97] Both cities continued to grow, and the number of police increased in both places, but much more so in London, prompting comments about the visibility of police on the streets there. By 1901, there were almost 16,000 police for about 4.5 million Londoners, one bobby for every 408 citizens; in Gotham (with 308 square miles, half that of London), there were about 7,500 cops for 3.4 million, one for every 458 citizens.[98]

Unlike London, New York's police suffered from unreliable leadership that changed with the political administration. From the start, the force was subject to the patronage system of Tammany Hall, the Democratic political system that dominated much of New York's politics for more than a century. Tammany's "Boss" Tweed and his ring reshaped the police force by giving out appointments to Irish immigrants—by one account more than three hundred in the mid-1850s.[99] In American cities, machine rule "has been made possible only through control of the police"; New York was no exception.[100] Investigations during the Progressive era pointed to the almost impossible task of extricating the police from this arrangement but, not surprisingly, intense partisanship was a hallmark of American urban life.[101]

When it came to determining salaries, it was not clear where on the socioeconomic pecking order a policeman would be. For the most part, salaries placed police in the ranks of the lower middle class, and they failed to rise substantially in either city as citizens grumbled about taxes. On the eve of the Civil War, a New York policeman earned three times that of his London counterpart. In 1890, a London constable earned the equivalent of a manual laborer, starting at twenty-four shillings a week and rising to a maximum of thirty-four.[102] By the early twentieth century, New York cops had longer hours but better pay—London spent $8.5 million on its force, New York $11.2 million.[103] In both places a policeman could augment his salary in several ways: in London there were supplements for clothing and fuel, and single men could live in barracks; in both places there were periods in which men could receive "rewards" from the public with department approval, a practice which eventually was eliminated.[104]

In New York, two rival forces existed for a while in 1857, as the state wrested control of the force away from the city, producing confusion and conflicting authority. Between 1857 and 1870, New York State's Metropolitan police force was in charge of the city. When the conflict arose, it was called a "Civil War in Metropolis," according to the *New York Herald*. [105] This was a brutal era, and conflicting authorities did not help (see chapter 8).

For both forces, defining what they did was critical and problematic. Beyond the broad instruction that they were to keep the peace and prevent crime and disorder, judgment and discretion played a major role in formulating police behavior. Few wanted to offend the public with a heavy-handed approach or increase fears that the new police were like Continental gendarmes, out to squelch liberty and terrorize the public. Early resistance to the London force quickly dissipated, despite a rocky start with the 1832 Coldbath Fields incident, in which a policeman was killed during a riot. In New York, the creation of the police coincided with 1840s street disorder. Police critics were strange bedfellows, ranging from right-wing moral reformers such as Charles Parkhurst to left-wing agitators such as anarchist Johann Most.

The London police force professionalized quickly, creating an efficient body, while New York dealt with an ongoing slew of personnel problems. By the end of the century, one of the many New York committees looking into the "police problem" reported admiringly on the efficient way London police handled a crowd, the "orderly and obedient" way the crowd responded to police instructions, and the "considerate and polite" responses the "bobbies" gave to public. The London police were younger, more fit, and more civil—and less likely to fall prey to the temptations of graft that had plagued the New York police.[106] Yet policing was difficult, demanding, underpaid, dangerous, and subject to criticism from every quarter. The cop or bobbie was in the public eye all the time, and expectations were high. Even a severe police critic in 1887 still believed "a policeman should be brave, fearless and discriminating. His judgment should be constantly, actively, exercised."[107]

At the same time, the middle class on both sides of the Atlantic, concerned with property protection, grudgingly accepted the police as a service organization out to assist them, thus affording them a new legitimacy. Accountability was important, more so in London than in New York. There had always been concern about the cost of police, but expense was accepted as long as there appeared to be adequate return for the investment. Disgruntled taxpayers in New York, for example, who had formed one of the new citizen lobbying organizations in the mid-1870s, complained to the mayor of New York that "a demoralized and inefficient Police ... has proved itself utterly unable (or unwilling) to check the increase of crime in this city which has been going on for years past" and demanded "judicious retrenchment and *real* reform" in the name of efficiency and economy.[108]

The press in both cities delighted in pointing out any police transgressions. Government investigations of events in which police were involved were constant in England, with Parliamentary inquiries producing substantive results. In New York, official investigations of the police themselves, such as the Mazet and Lexow commissions, produced mostly noise and smoke.[109] More potent was the effect of political fallout on a politician, which produced anything from a shakeup to a resignation. The New York force was strongly tied to the local political machine, unlike London, where local politics were removed from policing. Constant battles were waged between the mayor and the force. A grand jury's finding that "the alarming increase of crime in this community, especially murder, robbery" along with the "steady growth of public indignation" convinced Mayor William Wickham in 1875 that the three police commissioners could no longer garner public confidence and should resign.[110] Two decades later, an equally blunt and excoriating letter was sent from the mayor to the police commissioner asking for the resignation of the commissioner himself. "You have lost your influence with the public and the board," wrote Mayor Strong to Police Commissioner Andrew D. Parker in May 1896. "Consequently I feel that your resignation would be for the best interest of the Police Department."[111]

By the end of the nineteenth century, New York and London were safer places than they had been eighty years earlier. The original charge to the police had been to keep the order, not reduce crime, and only after several decades was crime reduction an acknowledged focus of their mission. In London, the mid-century formation of the Criminal Investigation Division (CID) facilitated this, by allowing a group of police to work only on crime. In general, crimes against property and murder declined in both cities, although sensational crimes, such as the Whitechapel (Jack the Ripper) murders, brought the public to a fevered pitch. In London, a series of laws provided police with the ability to track the newly identified criminal class. According to police statistics, as London's population grew, the gross number of felonies declined somewhat, but the rate—the proportion per thousand felonies to the estimated populations—fell dramatically, from 6.17 in 1867, the year of the Reform Bill riots in Hyde Park, to 3.3 in 1892.[112] Also impressive was the very low rate of homicide in London throughout the nineteenth century. New York had from five to ten times as many murders, indicative of the America's higher tolerance for violence, greater presence of firearms, and what some say is its greater emphasis on the individual.[113]

New York had no structure similar for tracking criminals—the "known to the police" category—to that of the London force. Many in Gotham had reservations about vesting too much power in the police. There is ample evidence in both cities that the police dealt with anything that was considered a problem, either because there was no other agency available or empowered to do so or because they were increasingly burdened with regulation enforcement; crime, though, was not the original focus.

That meant that in London police had to control traffic, assist in fires, find missing people, return lost children, take care of foundlings, muzzle and capture stray dogs, deal with licensing (hackneys, stages, and horses), move on vagrants, charge people with wanton or furious driving, issue summonses for various reasons (pubs, beer and refreshment houses, and carriages, carts, and wagons), transport people to the hospital, operate a lost-property bureau, and enforce pollution, adulterated food and drink, housing, and disease laws. Then they dealt with crime. Commissioner Mayne was concerned with the amount of time devoted to traffic control, which took away from broader control of streets.

With a few variations, the New York cop did the same. Police stations were used as flophouses, and snow removal had to be enforced. A New York sergeant in the 1880s was responsible for keeping twenty-three books: in addition to the ones pertaining to crime, he had to deal with the telegraph messages, corporation ordinances, permits, street lamps, and night medical services.[114] In one week, December 12–19, 1897, the New York police arrested 1,807 people, of which more than five hundred were either drunk or drunk and disorderly; at the same time, the police dealt with 648 noncriminal issues, including aiding 333 people, reporting eighty-three open buildings, taking care of twenty-seven lost children and six foundlings, dealing with forty-five stray animals, disposing of thirteen dead bodies, reporting 216 corporation ordinance violations, and issuing twelve masked-ball permits and thirteen pistol permits. That week they recovered more than $24,000 worth of property.[115]

In both cities, drinking, prostitution, and gambling fell under a new kind of regulation unprecedented in history: police were to regulate public behavior, including determining how citizens could congregate, drink, or fornicate. The regulation of benign street activities, whether peddling, processions, or dissident speech on sidewalks, also fell under the police aegis.

Much of what police did was not specified in code but interpreted over time as falling under supervision. In both cities, every new municipal regulation meant new police enforcement. Responsibility for parks, for example, was moved into a new department in both cities, but criminal activities in parks still fell under police jurisdiction. Police became the "managers" of the city, carrying out, interpreting, reformulating or contradicting governmental policies and legal constructs.

These new managers sometimes stumbled: "when constabulary duty is to be done, a policeman's lot is not a happy one." When *The Pirates of Penzance* premiered in New York on New Year's Eve, 1879 (months before its official London opening), one of Gilbert and Sullivan's most enduring images in this well-received operetta was the parodied police sergeant. The uniformed authorities had become the target of both humor and criticism, showing how firmly they were integrated into urban society by this time. The policeman on the street, in his neighborhood or local beat, displayed the best and the worst of the force: he could be viewed as the kind and protective local or hated as a brutal bully looking for payoffs. Throughout the century, New York and London police received monetary rewards and honors for meritorious service but they also received criticism, disciplining, and opprobrium following publicized incidents and investigations.

As purveyors of municipal authority, police were watched carefully for abuses and irregularities. In London and New York, constant disciplining was the main way top brass ensured their men would avoid temptations. Both forces liberally punished men for transgressions, resulting in reprimands, fines (docking salary anywhere from a half day to twenty days), lost privileges, or dismissal. Causes for punishment depended on the era, but could include sitting, neglect of duty, violations of rules, conduct unbecoming an officer, off post, loitering, conversation, absenteeism, intoxication, improper conduct, losing one's shield, and smoking.[116] The number of men dismissed for cause declined steadily in London: in 1882, 706 men, or 6 percent, were removed. In New York, from July 1878 until March 1879, fewer than two dozen men out of about 2,200 were dismissed, while more than 1,300 were disciplined.[117] The police were, by the last quarter of the nineteenth century, regularly accused of brutality and graft, the latter most pronouncedly in New York, where crooks' "capacity for innocent enjoyment" could be facilitated all too often with a monetary incentive, as investigative committees revealed.

Decisions about the use of public space fell into a grey area as far as law and order were concerned. London and New York police had to follow orders from the authorities but also decide on their own how to proceed in any given incident. They had little in the way of precedent or legal guidance to assist them and much in the way of political, economic, and social biases to influence them. For the most part, police acted prudently to allow or disallow public gatherings and acted as impartially as possible, but the authorities controlling them showed much bias in giving orders to police.

There was no clear legal construct in either country to guide police in any decisions relating to free speech and assembly. Aside from a general understanding that people had "rights," no one was sure what they were in this context, as law served as a port of last resort, one rarely visited. Both forces consisted of men from working-class backgrounds who reported to elitist authorities, and loyalties came into conflict. England's common-law system reassured the public that that which they did in the past they could continue doing; America's revolutionary ideals of freedom and equality persisted in the opportunities afforded for advancement for all citizens.

Police tolerance for freedom in public spaces was tested as these activities became more controversial. As "unpopular" speech that challenged authority increased on both sides of the Atlantic, freedom frayed at the edges. Police may have had no desire to impede freedom, but when it clashed with order, freedom lost, as the public mandate became well established by the second half of the nineteenth century. In the end, it was difficult to "distinguish between 'legitimate' and 'illegitimate' forms of violence against the established order."[118]

During the nineteenth century, the police became the sole arbiters of law and order, a process that by 1900 was clearly in place in both cities. This was accompanied by a dramatic decline in the use of the military to deal with law and order. While the militia was used as backup in both places, it served as a metaphorical sword of Damocles rather than a literal one. "There is not a rogue in the Union that does not know that should he overpower the civil authorities, a few sharp taps on the City Hall bell would bring ten thousand bayonets to the support of the law," noted Matthew Smith Hale, who held the New York police in high esteem but noted that "a worse population than can be found in New York does not inhabit the globe."[119] In London, where street crowds were bigger than New York's, the military similarly never played any significant part in stabilizing the city. Had civil authorities failed to keep the peace (which was the case during New York's Draft Riots in 1863, an important failure that changed police behavior), their cities would have been destabilized. Modern cities in which the military play significant roles in keeping order fail at democracy and their most basic mandate: to be livable places for their inhabitants.

THE HUMAN TIDES

"What hurrying human tides, or day or night!" exclaimed Walt Whitman in his poem "Broadway," "What passions, winnings, losses, ardors, swim thy waters! ... Could but thy flagstones, curbs, facades, tell their inimitable tales ... vast unspeakable show and lesson!"[120] In the same year that Darwin published *On the Evolution of the Species* and John Stuart Mill *On Liberty*, Charles Dickens wrote of the scary days a century before when life in London was unregulated: "there was scarcely an amount of order and protection to justify much national boasting," as burglaries and robberies were nightly affairs, people were afraid to leave their furniture alone at home, tradesmen became highwaymen, and mobs fired on musketeers.[121]

But some saw a future in which the external splendors masked morbid illnesses within. The popular and futuristic 1890 novel *Caesar's Column*, by Ignatius Donnelly, projected New York a century later as a "wonderful" city of ten million inhabitants and filled with "the radiance of its millions of magnetic lights," making it possible for people to work day and night. Glass-covered streets became pedestrian malls in business areas. Subways, electric elevators, and subterranean streets would move commuters swiftly, and all sorts of air traffic abounded. Food became "our physic," a religion and a drug, and apparently Donnelly foresaw the epidemic of plastic surgery, as his narrator noticed women and men displaying "the same soulless likeness."[122]

But the imaginary commercial capital hid the "joyless, sullen crowd," the undersized men and women with haggard faces, and children "prematurely aged and hardened." These fruits of the "iron law of wages" were "condemned, marching noiselessly as shades to unavoidable and everlasting misery," their future "the same shameful, pitiable, contemptible sordid struggle for a mere existence," their inevitable end only to wind up "consumed with disease, mere rotten masses of painful wretchedness" with corpses fit only for cremation.[123]

The corruption of wealth, said Donnelly, produced political corruption, class rule, and the death of liberty. He outlined a totalitarian society in which the masses had lost any access to free public expression or protest. "As the domination and arrogance of the ruling class increased, the capacity of the lower classes to resist, within the limits of law and constitution, decreased."[124] And, written in an era in which New York grappled with building new armories, the novel posited that the futuristic government repressed workingmen's rebellions with armed militias.

A year earlier, George Gissing's *The Netherworld* portrayed a similar sense of bleakness, but with a view toward London's seamier side: "the carts, waggons, vans, cabs, omnibuses, crossed and intermingled in a steaming splash-bath of mud; human beings, reduced to their due paltriness, seemed to toil in exasperation along the strips of pavements, bound on errands, which were a mockery, driven automaton-like by forces they neither understood nor could resist."[125] In both cities, endemic problems could eventually cobble a city's vitality, preventing it from reaching the success that was a driving force to strive for. The very notion of a "successful" city, which today is defined almost solely in economic terms, is rooted in Victorian notions that encompass broad personal moral and ethical parameters, making "success" all the more difficult to achieve. In a century of profound intellectual and technological innovations, the safety and security of the personal, everyday world gained even greater meaning, and most believed that disarray and disorder could somehow be vanquished. That a structure of public order be established in New York and London by the end of the nineteenth century became paramount, a way of offsetting anxieties about urban life.

Well into the twentieth century these cities remained magnets for those looking for opportunity. Newcomers and long-term residents had to cope with increasingly complex urban dynamics in their commercial endeavors. They had to consider how they would maintain the ideals that propelled them into the city while adjusting to the requisites of life. And they had to reconcile the city's excitement and lucrative possibilities with the dangers and temptations that ensnared many. Residents looked to urban authorities for assurances that life would not get out of hand. Whatever liveliness the city might offer, in the end it was cloaked with a sense of legitimacy.

PT
2

PUBLIC ORDER IN
VICTORIAN LONDON

Nº 3

LONDON BEFORE 1850

"The dispersion of a mob," stated an 1833 London *Times* editorial, "is something like the application of consolation in affliction. . . . If the consolation come before the calamity be digested, it is too early and is disregarded; if after it be digested, it is too late and superfluous. There is, therefore, but one crisis, as fine and sharp as a razor, to which the consolation will apply usefully, and few ever hit the mark."[1]

This comment was elicited in response to the 1833 Coldbath Fields incident, in which a policeman was killed during a political protest rally. Coldbath Fields foreshadows every major issue relating to public order in London and New York: the right of the public to protest, the authority of police and government to maintain public order, the role of law in defining how both sides can act, the degree to which disorder and violence is tolerated, the accountability of authorities, and the suitability of public places for group protests.

A year after the Great Reform Bill of 1832 had extended the right to vote in British society, still 80 percent were left out. The May 14 rally called by the National Union of Working Classes to protest this disenfranchisement ended with stones, obscenities, and truncheons flying amid the four thousand demonstrators. Three policemen were stabbed, one of them, Constable Culley, fatally.[2]

Authorities had anticipated a possible "calamity," as a similar meeting a year earlier in Finsbury Square had drawn twenty-five thousand and had resulted in tumult. A huge police presence of 1,500 men—almost half the force—meant the 1833 rally would be a challenge to the new police authority. The protest rally elicited sharp press reaction, a Parliamentary investigation with surprising results, and produced a reformulation of policies regarding public meetings.

Neither London's Metropolitan Police nor the Home Office had much experience in coping with a mass meeting. The basic rules about procedure and behavior were untested in real situations. Police had been told that "a Constable who allows himself to be irritated by any language whatsoever shows that he has not that command of his temper which is absolutely necessary in an officer vested with such extensive powers by the law."[3] How police react when taunted remains problematic even today. Coldbath Fields forced the Home Office to develop and closely monitor orders that its new policing force would follow. To further complicate matters, policies emanated from two internal sources, the permanent civil service, which oversaw administration, and political appointments, which could change at any moment. Neither the police nor the Home Office was clear about the legal ramifications of their actions, an uncertainty that would plague them for the rest of the century.

The testimony at the Parliamentary investigation following the Coldbath Fields incident provides insight into the difficulty in formulating public policy. Each side blamed the other for the melee: the Home Office blamed the ineptitude and poor hearing of the police. Home Secretary Lord Melbourne had told Police Commissioners Mayne and Rowan "that the meeting being illegal, and public notice given to that effect, was not to be allowed to take place; that the meeting, if attempted, was to be dispersed, and the leaders seized on the spot."[4] This would have meant stopping it as it began, not before. But Melbourne's public notice that the meeting was illegal had not been signed, rendering it useless as a legal document, and he claimed at the hearings that he only wanted leaders arrested when they began to speak, and not the participants dispersed. Commissioner Mayne, a Cambridge graduate and lawyer, had kept notes during their meeting that contradicted this.

Public meetings, it appeared, could not be prevented simply because tumult *might* result, an important principle in free speech. The police could not stop people from gathering in a public space, and if they did, violence could have resulted from such a process; they had little power to prevent people from moving to another location. Under the Riot Act, only extreme events with a clear aim of major disturbance could be legally prevented. The police could move people on to prevent them from loitering, under a recent statute, 57 Geo. III, c. 29, which had been passed as a result of late eighteenth-century mob violence. But in a circumstance such as Coldbath Fields, Commissioner Mayne voiced doubt about its application: the police had used this statute "occasionally; but we do not conceive they have authority to do so generally."[5] Commissioner Rowan added they had thought of using the statute to disperse people loitering in front of shop windows displaying obscene prints but "have felt great difficulty in giving any such direction."[6]

Implicit is the idea of personal or civil rights. In this formative era of policing, British authorities exercised caution. The police commissioners admitted they had rebuked constables for their overzealousness in "telling people to 'move along'" and their jostling them in the streets.[7] Public sympathy was so weighted on the side of the crowd and against the police that the coroner's jury returned a verdict of justifiable homicide against the murderer of Culley. The jury had felt the meeting was legal and therefore illegally dispersed. They said that "no Riot Act was read, nor any proclamation advising the people to disperse; that the Government did not take the proper precautions to prevent the meeting from assembling; and that the conduct of the police was ferocious, brutal and unprovoked by the people."[8] While the decision was later quashed, the message was clear: the police had better watch their step with the public.[9]

For decades, the Coldbath Fields cases were the only legal precedents for dealing with public meetings. From the 1830s to the 1870s, police and government dealt with an increasing number of public meetings. Commissioners Mayne and Rowan oversaw the Metropolitan Police together for the first two decades, and when Rowan retired in 1850, Mayne continued for another two decades, providing the stability, expertise, and intelligence that provided a foundation for operations for decades to come. This was particularly important given that there were a myriad of agencies in the second half of the century that dealt with public-order issues, including the Metropolitan Board of Works, the Board of Health, H.M. Works Office, the London County Council, the Metropolitan Boroughs, the City of London, the Metropolitan Commission of Sewers, and of course the vestries and parishes.[10]

From the 1830s on, police were often caught in the middle of administrative arguments. When it came to the ability of the public to use public spaces for assemblies of any kind, there was confusion. Conservative local agencies wanted more restrictions, and central government, more sensitive to public opinion, wanted fewer. The courts tended to side with the conservative position, though it never advocated eliminating the right of meeting. The expanding demand for parks increased pressure to limit their use to recreation, but that competed with the very strong claims of the public to use spaces for whatever they wanted.

As pressure for more park access mounted in the next few decades, public-order issues increasingly became crises. Advocates demanded green space be increased as an antidote to bad air and public-health epidemics in the overcrowded metropolis, and in response government agencies clamped down on public meetings in commons and local parks. This became the mandate of the Metropolitan Board of Works in 1877, which gained the new power to control, manage, and protect lands for the "prevention and restraint of acts or things tending to the injury and disfigurement of 'the parks' or to interference with the use thereof by the public for purposes of exercise and recreation."[11] The act specifically stated the board could make bylaws concerning public assemblies, which is just what it did.[12] That same year, the Metropolitan Open Spaces Act had empowered the Board of Works to purchase land for more parks. With its new powers, the works commissioners immediately set about to limit the right of meeting to disallow assemblies, meetings, and addresses, except with written permission of the Board.

CHARTISTS

Great Britain was undergoing a difficult transformation of its representational system in the first half of the nineteenth century. Universal manhood suffrage remained only an ideal on both sides of the Atlantic. These ideals had found new vigor in Enlightenment writings and in the resurgence of the philhellenism that accompanied them. British travelers to Greece and Rome brought back home a heady fervor for the artistic, intellectual, and political accomplishment of the past and argued for their incorporation into modern society.

The move toward democratization came with fierce public battles for change. The Great Reform Bill of 1832 had introduced the most sweeping changes ever for the British electorate, resulting in expanding it to include 20 percent of the male population. This was not impressive by the standard of the United States, where Andrew Jackson was elected president in 1828 with 56 percent of the white male population able to vote, double that of the 1824 election. By 1840, that electorate had risen to 78 percent.

Popular pressure mounted in England for genuine democratic government. The Chartists became the leading movement for such reform in the 1830s and 1840s. Their name came from their advocacy of a six-point charter, which included demands for universal male suffrage, secret elections, and proportional representation. Forming local organizations in every major English city, they published newspapers and broadsides, gathered in pubs and coffee shops, and marched in London to publicize their demands. While the charter was never formally adopted by Parliament, the reforms demanded were incorporated for the most part during the next half century. One of the most significant results of the movement was to strengthen the legitimacy of working-class politics.

As Jacksonian America experienced raucous and often violent public demonstrations in cities, Britain witnessed the noisy and energetic Chartist protests for almost two decades. The stronger the movement became, the more anxious was government. In the post-Metternichean world, conservatives feared that instability and revolution lurked around every corner. Thus order had to be preserved even if the *ancien régime* was dying.

As Chartist activism reached its first peak in 1839, the decade-young police found themselves in an impossible position. They were criticized for doing either too much or too little. The personnel attrition rate was high, costs soared, taxpayers complained, and relations with the public were unstable. In addition, for ten years they had to compete with the Bow Street Runners, the last vestige of the old system that had served as a de facto police force, which remained a separate and rival force until their incorporation with the police in 1839. Crime prevention was important, but Chartism forced the police to embrace the broader role of public-order arbiters. At the same time, they tried to differentiate themselves from the army. Coldbath Fields had served as a foundational lesson that violence on the part of the police would not be tolerated. And while the police were doing all this, they had to navigate whatever rough currents political waters offered.

The Metropolitan Police developed coherent tactics to deal with dissent and public protest. Under pressure from the Home Office, they were compelled to monitor political activities. This marked the birth of police surveillance, which became an accepted means of keeping order, even if unpopular. Usually in plain clothes, the police went to meetings to record proceedings[13] and note the age, dress, class, and number of participants. These tended to be unsystematic fishing expeditions rather than a sensitive spy network. The police made it clear they did not feel very threatened by the Chartist movement: "they have not funds, nor are they organized so as to act together," noted Mayne.[14] But under order from the Home Office, police had to fulfill their duty.[15]

The sour reception that greeted surveillance reflected fears that police would emulate continental practices and use it even more. The 1833 Popay incident had heightened concerns that in addition to surveillance, police were acting as *agents provocateur*. Popay, an overzealous constable, had been censured by a Select Committee for his "highly reprehensible" conduct in joining the National Political Union of Working Classes under disguise and inciting members to take violent actions.[16] Like Coldbath Fields, the Popay incident was less a matter of police misconduct and more a matter of the conjunction of government politics and questionable public policy and its enforcement.[17] Its significance was that it placed surveillance into the public-order system, an important tool to be used judiciously by authorities.

The military had long used intelligence, and the same principle was applied all over England during the age of the Chartists: "The spy, therefore, was still the natural source of secret information."[18] A spy could be a paid informant, a postmaster, a loyal nationalist, or a magistrate watching a public meeting. The police commissioners were not fans of surveillance, but they assiduously followed orders. Such evidence could be used in prosecutions, although it rarely was. Popay may have exacerbated public distrust of police, but the case did not turn the government away from using surveillance.[19] Some saw the "Bloody Peelers" as spies out "to worm themselves into the Chartist movement, to incite to outbreaks or at least to intemperate language."[20] In one case, constables dressed "as a Bird Catcher and equipped with Bird traps, cages" and a "journeyman" went on a fruitless search for a Chartist paramilitary drill.

Yet the police rarely used information from surveillance operations to press charges, and distrusted informants so much that they investigated each offer and rejected many of them.[21] The police were forced to follow up on the letters forwarded to them by the Home Office, which conveniently exculpated itself from blame about surveillance.[22] Rowan told superintendents that "there are gentlemen in London who are convinced that the Police follow them about the Streets as spies to catch them intriguing." Rowan warned that any man doing so would be dismissed, and he advised his police officers to avoid giving such an impression.[23]

Fears of "infiltration" also blocked for many years the formation of a separate detective force. Rowan and Mayne believed such a detail would address London's growing crime problem. Resistance to its formation was based on fear that personal freedom would be threatened. The force was finally established in 1842, with only eight men. Home Secretary Sir James Graham relented following a brutal murder case that went unsolved; he was careful to separate this from politics.[24]

In general, the Home Office distanced itself from policing political events, preferring to remain either neutral or as defenders of free speech. Embarrassed by an 1845 news report about a policeman disguised as a cobbler who arrested two counterfeiters, Home Secretary Grey responded that "I object to disguises; and the Police Constable must on no account be allowed to use artifices of this description."[25] Mayne and Rowan censured the offending officer, and clarified that "there shall be no particular men in the Division called plain clothes men and that no man shall disguise himself without particular orders from the Superintendent and that this should not be done even by them without some very strong case of necessity being made out."[26] The disagreement over plainclothes police was indicative of longstanding British fears of spying and contributed to sustaining tension between police and public. A byproduct of this was bad police-public relations, whose legacy has continued to current times; police misconduct reinforced the hostility, which in turn fed public distrust.

Sensitive to criticism, the commissioners made concerted efforts to improve relations, establishing the principle of police accountability. Commissioner Mayne kept up a constant letter-writing campaign with the London newspapers in an attempt to assuage ruffled tempers. The *Times*, *Morning Chronicle*, *Morning Herald*, and *Morning Post* received dozens of letters from Mayne, in which he not only patiently explained the nature and workings of the police but also attempted to "give the Public a more correct view than they now entertain of the comparative expense of the new police with the old nightly watch."[27]

The police commissioners constantly sent out memos warning police against exceeding their authority and improperly taking subjects into custody, following a spate of arrests where no legal charges could be found to substantiate them. Mayne defined the chain of command by telling superintendents that they would be responsible for their subordinates' misconduct. Any negative press report would open the valve of torrential memo writing. In 1842, he sent the force a memo about "several articles in the Newspaper . . . in which unnecessary violence on the part of the Police is insisted upon; also the statements privately made of a Newspaper Editor who is favourable to the Police that the general impressions appears to be that the Police are unnecessarily violent particularly towards women."[28]

When Home Secretary Sir George Grey complained about press reports of police misconduct in 1847, Mayne shot back with his own investigation of the twenty-seven cases of misconduct covering July through mid-October, along with the 835 cases of assaults on police, 122 cases of attempting to rescue from custody, and forty-eight cases of obstructing police in the same period.[29] He noted that from January to October 1847, 143 men had been wounded or hurt on duty, losing a total of 1,475 working days, and that twelve men had been forced to retire or take a leave of absence because of injuries sustained while on duty. The police, he wrote, "are often met with open resistance in enforcing the law, and have to contend with brutal violence of the most lawless characters, from which the lives of the constables are endangered."[30] The force was reminded once again to keep within the legal bounds of behavior and remain cool and temperate in manner.

Colonel Rowan handled the "gentlemen's complaints," the off-the-record, awkward situations best dealt with by tact and courtesy. Mayne developed an efficient system for the more common and widespread complaints, in which the accused constable "is immediately sent before the Police Magistrates in the usual manner," or if the complainant declined appearing before magistrates, "the Commissioners deal with the constable . . . according to the best of their judgment."[31] Mayne personally reviewed every case of complaint brought against his men.[32] In the five years from 1844 through 1848, coinciding with the peak of the Chartist movement, there were 454 cases against police constables, of whom 119 were convicted, resulting in fines and dismissal from the force; in 1844, there had been 120 cases, in 1848, 71.[33]

On the other hand, letters also poured in supporting police or asking for more police presence, particularly from high-crime areas. In Tulse Hill, one such area, residents were more than grateful for the presence of a controlling force, and even petitioned the commissioners to allow the police to carry cutlasses at night to scare off the ruffians in their isolated district. The request was quickly sanctioned by Whitehall.[34] The Lord Mayor of London grumbled that the police were shirking in their duties in not adequately protecting his procession, to which a hurt and indignant Mayne responded by reminding him of the "onerous duties" of the police.[35]

Meanwhile thousands of small and large political meetings prompted strong government and police response.[36] In Chartism's three peak periods of activity, 1839, 1842, and 1848, police policy was to leave well enough alone, despite mounting anxieties. In 1839, when Home Secretary Lord Normanby forwarded a local petition from Clerkenwell residents asking police to suppress meetings, the police responded by producing their own report of the gathering in detail, denying that any "depredations" had occurred and arguing that action was unwarranted. Anyway, they added, "should police interfere to prevent these meetings at this place, they would no doubt be adjourned to some other spot within the Metropolitan Police district, where their presence would be an equal nuisance and annoyance."[37]

The commissioners also knew that they "are not aware that they have any legal authority to prevent [meetings]," to which the Home Secretary demurred.[38] Police reluctance to stop meetings was tested by political pressures: a panic produced by unfounded rumors of a Chartist attack on the city produced a "cock and a bull" story that made the government a laughingstock.[39] Chartists watched the "Blue Devils" watching them and were wary of flying truncheons at meetings; excessive police force was a valid complaint that the commissioners tried to address. Yet demonstrators had little fear of being stopped once meetings were started, as long as things were orderly.

London emerged as peaceful in comparison with other British cities. In Lancashire, there were the Plug Plot riots; in a riot in Manchester, more than two thousand soldiers and artillery were mobilized and two policemen were killed; in Staffordshire, fifty-four men were sentenced to transportation for Chartist activity; and a general strike paralyzed much of the north, with the military patrolling.

The spring of 1842 marked a flurry of activity, as Chartists presented their 3.3 million-signature petition for change to Parliament on May 2. The police took no extraordinary precaution as a six-mile-long charter, rolled up on a frame, "took a devious route," with one end at the House of Commons and the other at Oxford Circus. By the summer, the sanguine atmosphere had disappeared. Meetings at Islington Green and Lincoln's Inn Fields brought out more than a thousand policemen.[40] At Clerkenwell Green on August 19, police taunted Chartists; at Bow Street an enraged crowed hurled brickbats, injuring an officer. On August 22, demonstrations occurred all over London. At Kennington Common, 1,400 police dispersed the crowd, and at Paddington Station ten thousand protestors threw insults, stones, and brickbats at the police, and one constable was stabbed. Police arrested seventeen people.

Yet the next day the police allowed a meeting (although not a procession) in Finsbury, with Mayne telling his men to be civil.[41] All this illustrates the degree to which politics and policing clashed. While Home Secretary Graham forbade processions, saying they were "dangerous to the public peace" and asking police to intercept them, the police declared "it is not intended to prevent the meeting and it is not desirable the Police should stop Vans or carriages." The men were also reminded "of the great importance of not using any irritating language or expressions even towards those who may be offending against the laws," advice easier to give than to follow amid such tension.[42] No meetings were stopped from happening, but some were dispersed when they appeared to be getting out of hand. Police policy had been "to take immediate steps to preserve Public Peace if any appearance of disturbance from the Meeting to be held should arise."[43] Like application of consolation in affliction, this left a vast grey area in which interference could easily miss the mark.

Chartism remained a political movement for most of the decade, and its last great public stand came in 1848, when supporters attempted to present the petition to Parliament on April 10. In 1843, London had become their national headquarters and in 1844, home to its newspaper, the *Northern Star*. In 1847, star orator Feargus O'Connor also moved to London, after his election as a member of Parliament for Nottingham.

Chartist meetings in 1848 established a benchmark for how authorities would handle such events for the rest of the century, by establishing police and government credibility in controlling order in the city. With one eye on uprisings across the Continent, police assured the public that security would be preserved while protecting basic rights. Violence and arrests were kept to a minimum; truncheons and cutlasses were scarcely used. Relations between the crowd and the police were neutral, particularly when there were not large numbers of police out.

The Chartist attempt to present the petition to Parliament on April 10 of that year is significant for several reasons. For the first time in the nineteenth century, people believed the security of London was at serious risk. Second, new tactics for controlling urban order were introduced, such as special constables and the creation of strategic sealed-off zones. Third, it was the first time that large numbers of demonstrators were arrested. Fourth, it was the first time that massive numbers of security personnel were used in such a situation. Fifth, it was the first time that interests of the business and commercial community were prioritized so that daily life could go on without interruption.

The event also highlights an enduring facet of democratic societies: whatever the issue, whatever the era, some people want to voice their opinions publicly and loudly. This enforces participatory government and defuses tension and violence, which often results when the public is denied the right to voice its opinions. The London police showed antipathy toward banning demonstrations and understood that to do so would interfere with basic rights and set the city up for disaster.

The police were previously humiliated at a March 6 demonstration in Trafalgar Square, which authorities had attempted to prevent through the use of an obscure statute. As food riots in Glasgow and a workhouse riot in Manchester were occurring, up to fifteen thousand gathered in Trafalgar, and near chaos ensued for twelve hours. Young boys pushed people into the fountains, stole handkerchiefs, and crowds of men "bonneted" police, pulling hats over the constables' eyes. Insufficient planning and numbers of police contributed to the melee, where truncheons were used but personal injury kept to a minimum. When lingering crowd members tore down the palisades around Nelson's Column and destroyed lamps, the police chased them down Pall Mall, the street of government offices and clubs, to St. James Park and then to Buckingham Palace, where they were stopped by the army. A thousand police had been deployed; 103 people arrested (of whom seventy-three were convicted). The police learned that demonstrations in Trafalgar Square needed particular attention.[44]

They were more prepared for a demonstration a week later, where they applied their new techniques of how to handle public assemblies. This event was held not in the city center but on Kennington Common, on the south bank, far from the critical economic hub. Special measures were taken to preserve safety: loose pavement bits that could become projectiles were removed, gunsmiths unscrewed barrels of firearms, special constables were appointed, and the military was put on alert. The deployment of the police force was well thought out: with small groups on constant patrol, a mass of four thousand officers were placed strategically around the common and all the bridges to prevent people from crossing the Thames into central London, where a quarter of the force was stationed. The crowd on that rainy March 13 was smaller than expected, and disorder kept to a minimum, with twenty-five people arrested.

Given the political atmosphere of the time, it is impressive that the government reacted as calmly as it did. Throughout Europe in 1848, every major city experienced popular uprising and revolt in a push for liberal and nationalist reform, and the British across the English Channel watched nervously. The April 10 presentation of the charter to Parliament marked the greatest turnout of civil and military forces London had ever witnessed. Home Secretary Sir George Grey, known for his calmness and moderation,[45] Commissioners Rowan and Mayne, and Lord Wellington, the esteemed but elderly hero of Waterloo, were in charge.[46] Grey was under pressure from Prime Minister John Russell to maintain order, as "any loss of life will cause a deep and rankling resentment."[47] This was the first time that loss of life was seriously considered, and the deep concern that it be avoided reflected the longstanding British intolerance for public violence.

London was tense, with six thousand police, more than eight thousand military (including pensioners), and tens of thousands of special volunteer constables patrolling the city. The show of force assured people that the authorities were in control, that threats to internal security would be prevented, and that interruptions of daily routine would be minimal. People hung out of their windows with avid interest instead of boarding them up with fear, and merchants who closed their shops at all did so while protestors passed in front of their stores.

The most important decision was to allow the mass meeting but to disallow any procession into the city center. Chartist leaders, although disappointed, were surprisingly cooperative and conceded the issue quickly:

> Feargus O'Connor ... was ordered by Mr. Mayne to come and speak to him. ... Upon being told that the meeting would not be prevented, but that no procession would be allowed to pass [back along] the bridges he expressed his utmost thanks and begged to shake Mr. Mayne by the hand. He then addressed the crowds, advising them to disperse, and ... he went off in a cab to the Home Office, where he repeated to Sir George Grey his thanks, his fears and his assurances that the crowd should disperse quietly.[48]

The dispersion proved more difficult. As police broke up blocks of people, they were hooted at. More invective was directed at the special constables, as civilians were viewed as traitors. Newspaper reports celebrated the "normalcy" of the day, how the "utmost order and decorum" prevailed, and how destruction was not on the charts.

These were the days of denouement for Chartism. Failure to present the petition to Parliament signaled the end of the noble movement. Even the press voiced sympathy for the working classes: "Poor fellows! By far the greater part of them, with their pale faces, and puny and ill-clad frames, were calculated to inspire much less of terror than of sympathy and pity."[49] From the Chartists' point of view, the spectacle of force was overwhelming: "As I crossed Waterloo Bridge," reported Chartist leader Thomas Frost, "I saw two lines of police drawn up; and happening to look over the parapet near Somerset House, I caught a glance of a dismounted trooper of the household cavalry. . . . I saw a line of mounted constables, expending form Ludgate Hill to the foot of Blackfriars Bridge." It was Frost who had predicted that the Kennington Common location doomed the event.[50]

In this city of millions, a mass protest occurred with little negative consequence. Order was maintained, stockbrokers were happy enough to sing "God Bless the Queen" at 2 p.m. that day, and the right to assemble was preserved. Chartist leader Thomas Slingsby Duncombe concluded that their leaders "could not stand up against the ridicule directed against them, for having permitted themselves to be outgeneraled. The most influential organs of public opinion . . . laughed them into private life."[51] It was as good a lesson in governing a city as history can provide.

N⁰ 4

THE SUNDAY TRADING BILL RIOTS

The Earl of Dartmouth complained to Home Secretary Sir George Grey in 1855 about the windows of his sister's house at Curzon Street being broken during disturbances of that year. The Home Office's reply was succinct: "He [Dartmouth] says the practice [of window breaking] is *un English*. I should have said just the reverse."[1] This jaded outlook was an outcome of the 1855 Sunday Trading Bill riots. Window breaking, along with lamppost smashing, stone throwing, and barricade bashing, had become the hallmarks of London's public protests. Grey had become accustomed to this and his comfort with street battles may have been honed by his surviving numerous political battles, serving as Home Office Secretary from 1846 to 1853, 1855 to 1858 (during which the cabinet underwent massive changes), and 1861 to 1866.

Grey had learned much from the Chartist protests, including the inadvisability of trying to ban public meetings. For months after April 10, modest demonstrations had occurred in London's open spaces as Chartists vented their final grievances. The police increased surveillance, displayed drawn truncheons, and brandished cutlasses, which they were authorized to carry on night patrol starting August 30, 1848. To ensure accountability, the commissioners demanded that a report be filed each time swords were drawn. The police took "the greatest pains to learn where indoor meetings are held, to have the parties carefully observed whilst assembling, to mark whether they appear to be in any manner armed.... To have a sufficient body of men at hand when the meeting breaks up to deal with it summarily if there be any signs of violence or riot."[2]

As the Chartist protests proved to be more smoke than fire, police gained confidence and pressed for order. Their relations with Chartists deteriorated, and Chartists complained about the "blue monster" and police brutality.

Civilians did file complaints, and they were always investigated.[3] But there is no evidence of serious injuries in these years. The public, for its part, made clear its distaste for police presence. When the police asked to stand on the platform with speakers at a July 1848 meeting, speaker Samuel Kydd gave them permission on the condition that they tell him who were the plainclothes men in the audience, and when the police refused, they were forcibly ejected from the theater by an angry audience. The next day a similar event resulted in two plainclothes constables being thrown out—one tossed down a steep flight of stairs—and both had to take refuge from the mob in a nearby house. The cry to "turn out the Bloodhounds from Scotland Yard" echoed throughout London's meeting halls.[4]

Despite the decline of London Chartism, it clearly laid the foundation for working-class participation in politics. In the cycles of debate about its success or failure, Chartism is rarely given credit for helping to establish the firm footing of public assembly as a political tool. Grey's comment on window breaking underscored the degree to which public protest had been accepted during this century of revolutionary ideas and economic transformation.

Chartism laid the groundwork for other groups, which incorporated its ideas, energy, and spirit into new political and social movements. The ideas of an obscure duo—an unemployed and exiled intellectual and the son of a wealthy German industrialist—began to catch fire in Europe at about the same time and helped propel just the sort of end the Chartists had hoped for. Karl Marx and Friedrich Engels built on the ideas of others at a time when challenges to capitalist society found fertile soil for growth. It was Marx who pronounced the 1855 riots as the beginning of the revolution.[5]

The Chartist legacy of activism and public assembly was borne out during the 1855 Sunday Trading Bill disturbance. This event demonstrated the legitimacy of expressing discontent with government action in a society not yet fully participatory. It served as a bridge between the old form of popular protest— food riots, King and country riots—and the new political and ideological protests typical of modern ones. Midcentury Victorianism presented a responsive model of government, which served citizens' needs and projected optimistically a progressive notion of societal improvement. If citizens wished to voice their opinion, there was an ever-widening forum for them to do so. From 1850 to 1900, Parliament was transformed into a body popularly elected by most males, with working class and labor members, and reform created more equal districts and fairer representation. Meanwhile, a burgeoning press served every possible constituency in the nation. And at a time when Britain was the wealthiest nation in the world, recognition of poverty produced reforms that were to ameliorate endemic problems.

The Sunday Trading Bill riots also focused attention on the role of public space in a major world city. For the next half century, the rights of the public to use parks, commons, streets, and squares were mired in a complex and confusing legal framework that reflected the vagaries of English common law. Unlike New York, there was no clear resolution to these issues, but a set of guidelines and principles did develop. While some parks were to be used primarily for leisure, there were exceptions. Significantly, the need to use some public spaces for nonleisure activities was widely acknowledged. Authorities realized that to abridge such usage would be to abridge basic rights.

The 1855 riots crystallized the changing dynamic between police and the public in an age of anxiety. That old antagonism between them remained, particularly among the "have-nots," as Benjamin Disraeli characterized the poor. But it was clear that an important shift had occurred as police had created stability that had in turn fostered economic growth. London was on its way to becoming a regulated city, in which the police acted as agents of the upper and middle classes to enforce rules of a livable city. The very idea of the police was legitimized and their responsibilities increasingly broadened. Government differentiated between the commitment of some egregious acts of violence by police and wholesale abuse of power: the latter was intolerable but the former unavoidable. In order to empower the police, government had to maintain unwavering support for the force. If we expect police to control the metropolis in the twenty-first century, it is because a century and a half ago, they assumed these roles to make the ordered city possible.

The exhaustive Parliamentary investigation into the riot exemplified new government accountability. After two weeks of hearings and 179 witnesses, the panel concluded that fault lay on both sides, that physical force had been excessive, that popular violence had been in need of control, that venues did exist for complaints against authority, and that justice could be served. The hearings served as a fascinating *vox populi*, with every social and economic class represented. In the end, three policemen were indicted for excessive force in violence that produced no major injuries.

The investigation's findings also provide broader warnings that remain unheeded today: banning a demonstration ensures it will happen; with disorder, small missteps can create large mistakes; communications among police are critical; crowds are laced with opportunistic elements; testimony is often contradictory and confusing; there must be adequate jails if arrests are made; central command must take responsibility for the actions of its representatives; and politicians are evergreen in their attempt to slither out of responsibility.

The 1855 riots were the closest thing to class warfare London had yet seen. Sabbatarian legislation had started decades earlier with efforts to control open markets in working-class districts on Sunday.[6] As Parliament considered the effect on cities of surging urban populations, a Select Committee on a Sunday Trading Bill reported in 1831 and 1832 on the "systematic and widespread violation of the Lord's day."[7] The report painted Sunday activities negatively: alcohol easily available, inferior-quality goods sold, eating houses and coffee shops havens for the derelict and disorderly, and bakers bleary from seven-day work weeks. "Respectable" people on their way to church were accosted by late-night drinkers. The committee was not concerned that Sunday was the only day the working class could shop.

By the next hearing, in 1847, the argument veered away from the traditional Sabbatarian argument of respecting the Sabbath and moved into the realm of workers' rights, arguing Sunday trade denied a tired population the rest it deserved and that bad merchandise was foisted on those who had no choice. At this hearing and at others, police reports formed the backbone of information. An 1844 example provided a comprehensive and colorful picture of street scenes in the metropolis.[8] Petticoat Lane, Spitalfields Market, Brick Lane, Church Street, Bethnal Green, White Street, Club Row, High Street, Shoreditch, Cable Street, Rosemary Lane, and East Smithfield were typical areas for this, many dominated by Jewish residents, and full of poor people. All sorts of goods were sold, and the report noted that trading had gone on long before the police were ever there. The police were sympathetic: Sunday trading was a necessity, the report concluded, and if eliminated small peddlers would be forced to go to the workhouse and thus create even more problems.

Police Commissioner Mayne realized such a law banning Sunday trading would place the onus of enforcement on the police, and with it blame for an unpopular law that he feared would "excit[e] public feeling against the object of the bill."[9] Years earlier he said that enforcing such laws would bring "odium to Police, which injures their general usefulness to the public."[10] He was not eager for his men to become embroiled in the issue, and even worse, the proposed 1850 law stipulated that the police officer, not a magistrate, would be authorized to impose a penalty, giving a legal discretion to the police, which Mayne felt was improper. With his usual tact, Mayne tried to insulate his men against an unpopular political decision with unacceptable legal implications: "I have always found it necessary to restrict the use of the police to instances in which I thought it desirable that they should interfere, as the Commissioners are responsible for their conduct; I felt it necessary to sanction their interference only in cases that I thought came within the law."[11]

The debate continued for years, highlighting class division. An 1851 report reaffirmed the patterns of selling, mostly in the poorest areas of London, which were beset by health and sanitary problems.[12] The bill's sponsor, Lord Robert Grosvenor, claimed it gave the working man and woman a rest, while others saw it as a way of strangling them by preventing them from using their Saturday night wages to purchase food and goods on their only day off. Was it "directed against a particular class," the lower classes, as Sir Joshua Walmsley stated, or was the bill introduced "in compliance with the wishes of a number of inhabitants of this metropolis, principally of the trading and lower classes," as Lord Grosvenor said? Or, as MP Massey said, might it be better for all if "tradesmen ought to be left entirely to their own individual guidance in such matters"?[13]

Mayne pressed for the matter to be left alone. In his best lawyer's manner, he reminded members of Parliament that it was not expedient "to make it the duty of the police to interfere directly in the present state of the law against Sunday Trading."[14] Regarding the crying of apples and oranges on Sundays, Mayne said "it has not been considered advisable for the police to interfere. . . . The Police must in matters of this description be guided mainly by the public feeling."[15] Only if a street were obstructed or the crying of goods was extreme would he countenance interference. His pragmatism was paramount: "the industrious classes who gain their livelihood at a distance from their homes and who generally received their wages too late on Saturday evening to enable them to spend their hard earnings" was a key factor.[16]

The 1855 bill to restrict Sunday selling and shopping was the proverbial straw that broke the camel's back.[17] When 150,000 people assembled in Hyde Park that hot July 1 Sunday, they expressed both outrage at the bill and the desire to claim the park as their own.[18] They decided to "go to Church" with Lord Grosvenor and watch the wealthy at Sunday play in the park, as a publicity campaign about the meeting pointed out the hypocrisy of the politicians. A phlegmatic Parliament dithered; Prime Minister Palmerston first said he would remove the bill, then backpedaled, saying it was a matter for the metropolitan members, whom he thought supported it (that remark was met in Parliament with cries of "no, no").[19] But when a large group assembled on the north bank of the Serpentine on June 24, annoying carriages, Mayne made a rare but colossal mistake: banning the meeting. On June 29, the commissioner posted a notice forbidding any meetings in Hyde Park because it would "endanger the Public Peace, and particularly by making loud noises and obstructing the Carriage road."[20] It was like waving a red flag in front of a bull.

Hyde Park was in its Sunday mode in pleasant weather that July 1, with people strolling, riding, and driving their carriages through the capacious green spaces. Things were quiet at 2 p.m. at the Serpentine, but that disintegrated quickly as protestors pelted strollers and carriages with stones. "Go to church" was a favorite cry. No one could pinpoint when things went wrong, but whatever the trigger, a melee ensued for hours, with the brandishing of truncheons and staves by the police. In the course of the afternoon, seventy-one people were arrested in Hyde Park and forty-nine police injured; at the investigation, many of the eighty-six complainants said they were hurt.[21] The more vociferous the crowd became, the more police swung truncheons, as they lost control for hours.

Parliament was outraged at both the protest and the assault on the park. Grosvenor refused to pull the bill, saying, "Nobody likes to be mobbed and bullied," but other MPs called it "mischievous and pernicious."[22] The metropolitan members corroborated stories of violence by the police by presenting testimonials from their constituents; others defended the police by pointing out "the rascally boys deserved much greater punishment than any one that was inflicted upon them." One law-and-order MP went so far as to suggest that for future incidents "nothing will frighten a mob more than the crash upon the pavement of the trail of a 6-pounder."[23]

The event opened an important debate on what was an acceptable activity for the parks. Were they for leisure only, or were they for the populace to use as they wanted? Would demonstrations, always held on public spaces, be banned from parks? Such a discussion had never been entertained before, and politicians were wary of entering the fray. Grey maintained that it was the privilege of Londoners to have use of the enjoyment of the parks, but he qualified this grand statement of freedom by saying that "nothing could be a greater dereliction from duty on the part of any person holding the office that I do than to allow a monster meeting . . . to take place in one of the public parks on Sunday, thus interfering with the rights of enjoyment by all persons in those parks."[24] He obfuscated further by adding that people in the park on July 1 "had a perfect right to do so. . . . They had a right to be there and to enjoy themselves quietly."[25]

With that question lurking in the background, the Home Secretary reluctantly agreed to an investigation of the melee. Police credibility was on the line, *he* was responsible for the police (who reported to him), and he had ordered the meeting banned. Members of Parliament had pressed for an inquiry, citing petitions of grievance from constituents and stories of "horror and disgust at the brutal and violent conduct of police in truncheoning the peaceably disposed people."[26] Sniffing the scent of police misconduct, the press demanded inquiry, too: "There are occasions—and this is one of them—in which injudicious orders given by [police] superiors lead to popular indignation on one hand, and to the abuse of authority on the other."[27] For some, it was yet another piece of evidence showing infringement of liberty and police violence.[28]

The bill was finally withdrawn, but another demonstration on July 8 to protest police misconduct brought more protestors in Hyde Park and mayhem to London. The park crowd was quiet and dispersed without incident into the streets, but around 5 p.m. a group of "boys," as press and witnesses described them, rushed out Apsley House gate and startled carriages, then down Grosvenor Street to Belgrave Square, where they set fire to a heap of straw. They smashed windows there and down Grosvenor Place to Eaton Square, until stopped by the police, which had been kept under low profile by Mayne.

The resulting hooliganism infuriated the residents of the well-off neighborhood in which it took place. In Hampstead, twenty-three streetlamps and 343 squares of glass in eighty-four houses were broken by a mob of five hundred. In Marylebone, two mobs of five hundred each blocked the roads while a band of fifty boys shattered the windows of the Austrian ambassador's house. In Hanover Square, the Oriental Club was attacked, while in Eaton Square 150 boys, surrounded by three hundred "well-dressed and respectable" persons, scampered off to join a larger mob in Pimlico. In the toniest areas, including Belgravia Square, Upper Belgravia Street, Grosvenor Place, Eaton Place, Upper Eaton Street, Wilton Street, Eaton Square, and Grosvenor Street, 749 panes of glass in seventy-nine houses were broken.[29]

The police were praised by both the left and the right for their performance that day. Critic MP Duncombe called their behavior "conciliatory and judicious," while the *People's Paper* said the police conducted themselves with "exemplary character."[30] As for the police, they were confused and overwhelmed. When Inspector Webb of the C division tried to arrest a stone thrower, he was assured by a "respectable" person that it was the wrong person and had to let him go. A lone hand throwing a stone just can't be identified, he said.[31] The relatively minor disruptions had become a *cause celebre* in London, a sign that the means of control had gone astray—either too much or too little—and was serious enough to warrant official investigation.

THE INQUIRY

Three men served on the commission that heard the exhaustive testimony. They had extensive experience in public life but were selected because they were considered temperate in character and political views. Robert Baynes Armstrong, seventy years old, had been Recorder at Hull, Leeds, Manchester, and Bolton, and an MP from Lancaster. Gilbert Henderson, a fifty-eight-year-old barrister, had been Recorder at Liverpool. James Stuart Wortley, a fifty-year-old barrister, had been an MP from Halifax and Bateshire and Recorder of London.[32] The 588-

page report had detailed testimony from eighty-six complainants against the police and ninety-three supporters for the police, all of whom testified between July 17 and August 2, 1855.

One of the problems facing the commission was that the complainants were strangers, most could not afford lawyers, and most were loathe to make official statements. To help them, the commission appointed an attorney who had represented a client taken into custody on July 1 at police courts to be the legal representative of those complaining against the police. The police had their own legal representation.[33]

The report's details and impartiality became a model for future ones. The commission established as clear a timeline and analysis as was possible, to demystify what had been a confusing day. Piecing together the narrative of civil disorder is difficult but critical: if done incorrectly, it can result in accusing or arresting the wrong person, or failure to vindicate. The report noted that the park was a gathering place for Londoners from all walks of life, and that class bias was present when judgments were made. It also underscored how popular dissent could be voiced in public places, that delinquent juveniles were a new urban problem, and that violence was directed at objects instead of people. The police did not fare well: the report noted latent antagonism to police and that police misconduct was unacceptable and would be punished. It also stressed how critical parks were to the city.

The heterogeneity of the crowd was considered impressive. In an era in which public meetings were gaining legitimacy, the constituency of the crowd was considered an important issue. Witnesses stressed that it was not "riff-raff" or "canaille" that met that day, but "respectable" people. "I saw 10 or 15 members of Parliament and 8 or 10 peers," reported a wine merchant. A justice of the Peace and former Commissioner of Glasgow's police said that "it was not what I should call a mob on that day ... it was a respectable body of people gathered together."[34] Clothes, an important nineteenth-century indicator of social and economic class, were constantly referred to: "There are always a great many well-dressed people in the Park, but there were ten times as many as I ever saw there before and I have known the park for 25 years," said a veteran police superintendent. The placards and bills advertising the protest had advised people to put on their Sunday best.

Prosecution witnesses were classified as 45 percent tradesmen "of a superior sort," 35 percent working men and women, and 20 percent were gentlemen, army, barristers, and professionals. Police witnesses were three-quarters police, with 8 percent working men and 4 percent professional, military, and law. Such a sampling as represented by the complainants was typical of the city mob, according to historians, which would "involve small tradesmen, craftsmen and factory workers."[35] These people lost a day's wages by testifying and had little to gain except to correct the public record.

Occupationally, they were a fascinating cross-section of London's economy: upholsterer, engineer, mining agent, building society representative, barrister, carver and gilder, newsagent, cap maker, porter, plasterer, publican, tailor, ecclesiastical estate agent, draper, solicitor's clerk, waiter, wastepaper dealer, trunkmaker, compositor, schoolmaster, servant, ship's carpenter, fruiter, grocer, carpenter, law stationer, hairdresser, boot closer, carpenter's apprentice, undertaker, glover, currier, clergyman, bookbinder, beer retailer, woolen draper, merchant, straw-hat maker, messenger, cab proprietor, writer, and assorted military men. Hyde Park had been a destination, not the park across the street: fifteen were from West London, six from Marylebone, eleven from Pimlico, eight from North London, ten from Central London, six from Westchester, fifteen from east London, three from Kensington, and six from the Temples and Inns of Court.

The report identified troublemakers in two areas, petty thieves and juveniles. The latter group was considered a major instigator on July 1. "I saw all boys," testified a master currier. An old elm was sprouting boys, said a writer from Bristol. A half-dozen boys were reported carrying pieces of broken hurdles, playing "soldiers," and throwing the sticks helter-skelter. One lad of ten "invited Lord Robert Grosvenor to hang himself with the parchment that they wrote the Bill on," eliciting laughter from the crowd in Grosvenor Street.[36]

Juvenile delinquency in the streets of London was a subject on the minds of many contemporaries. A couple of years earlier, a Select Committee on Criminal and Destitute Children had voiced severe alarm at the growing number of juvenile offenders and the lack of proper channels through which they could be controlled and mended. One of the results of this was the 1854 Reformatory School Act.[37] Recent works such as Mary Carpenter's *Juvenile Delinquents* (1853) and Alexander Thomason's *Social Evils* (1852) had drawn attention to the strange phenomenon of child "criminals" in a morbidly upright Victorian society. Moral insufficiency was still the verdict, but amelioration through corrective measures was a step in the right direction. It would be decades before poverty's role in this was fully acknowledged.

But it was freedom of speech and movement that motivated the majority of the crowd, the report concluded. Notwithstanding unruly boys and lowlife elements, most people were venting their anger at the Sunday Trading Bill and asserting their belief that they could come and go as they pleased in the city and speak and act freely. "I saw not the least disposition to riot, but more to enjoy themselves by way of a lark," said an ecclesiastical estate agent who became entangled with a policeman and whose case was a major one before the commission. When a constable tried to move people from the rails, they refused, responding that "they had as much right being in the park as we had."[38]

Who had a right to be in the park was a curious question. Sunday excursions had become defining experiences for the working class, for whom the Sabbath was generally the only non-workday. Since the eighteenth century, tea gardens had proliferated, where spring waters, coffee, tea, or wine was consumed and where music could be heard, skittles or cricket or fives played. In London, more than two hundred of these pleasure gardens existed; most charged admission, sometimes as much as a shilling, and catered to different constituencies. A few, such as the Ranelagh, catered to the upper classes, but the rest, including the famous Vauxhall Gardens, were patronized by everyone from the Prince of Wales to the bootmaker. The well-known Cremorne featured exotic entertainments including circuses and stuntmen and attracted students, clerks, and shop assistants.[39]

As these private gardens began to close in the second half of the nineteenth century, usually to make way for new buildings, there were fewer recreational outlets for the working and lower middle classes, who could not afford to go into the country for day trips. A dearth of open spaces and parks had added to the pressures of increased usage of the Royal Parks, of which Hyde Park was the most famous. Like the tea gardens, some commons had also been gradually lost; an 1866 law finally afforded them protection.[40]

The Royal Park favored by the upper classes was Hyde Park. Given to the public in the seventeenth century by Charles I, it was fashionable, and the Sunday stroll was the setting for the best of society. While the middle orders may have gone to Regent's Park, "For the Higher Orders there are Hyde Park and Kensington Gardens, where your 'people of condition' conglomerate every Sunday afternoon, 'as thick as idle moths in sunny ray,' exhibiting their taste in turnouts."[41] Four-in-hands displayed occupants in all their finery, and well-dressed women and top-hatted men strolled with children; Rotten Row was a who's who of riders between 5 and 7 p.m.[42]

By the mid-nineteenth century, that had begun to change. As one writer complained, "Nowadays the idlers in the park remind us little of the personages" who used to go there.[43] One could only witness now the "lower or middle classes of London intruding themselves in regions which … were then [in the past] given up exclusively to persons of rank and fashion."[44] The 1883 *Baedeker* summed up its new personality. It was full of "elegant equipages, and high bred horses in handsome trappings" and "some of the most beautiful and exquisitely dressed women in the world," but of late "peaceful enjoyment of the breezy walks and shady groves . . . has been frequently interrupted, even on Sundays, by the invasion of noisy organized crowds, holding demonstrations."[45]

If the parks were the "lungs" of London, they were also becoming its vocal chords. The practice of making speeches in the open had attracted people to the Reformer's tree, which burned down in 1875. That spot, at the Marble Arch end of the park, eventually became Speaker's Corner, formally acknowledged in the twentieth century. The park had been used for a grand fair replete with gambling and drinking booths in 1814 to celebrate the centenary of the Hanoverian accession to the throne; in 1837, a four-day fair celebrated Queen Victoria's coronation. Popular use of the space had increased with the Great Exhibition of 1851, during which 6.6 million visitors flocked to Hyde Park over several months to view Paxton's astonishing Crystal Palace. Two-thirds of these visitors bought middle- and lower-class tickets, and they were considered a model of the "character of the industrial classes of England and London," especially as they were "well-dressed, orderly and sedate."[46]

That Hyde Park was the people's park was the overriding theme in testimony. Both pleasure seekers and protesters demanded this access. "The pathway before me was clear, the people was perfectly quiet, there was no reason why I, a lady, with my child, should not walk on the banks of the Serpentine without interruption from the disorderly and riotous Police," testified one woman.[47] On the other hand, police notices forbidding the meeting provoked many to come to the park to assert the right to protest. As a Belgravia architect testified, "They [they crowd] were brought there . . . by the proclamation of the police. I think half of them. And it was very natural." People, he stressed, were asking, "Why should I be commanded to keep away?"[48] A cap maker admitted curiosity along with the assertion of his rights: "I went there on purpose to be satisfied what cause there could be for the caution."[49]

The commission revealed how any interference with rights or assertion of authority that was perceived to be unfounded would be resisted. Mayne's order to forbid the meeting was done under Home Office pressure and was not unusual. Many such orders had been issued, and all had been ignored. Long after the event, Mayne received law officers' opinions asserting the government's right to close the gates and exclude the public and specific individuals, though the latter was to be done only in cases of misconduct. The opinion treated the Crown as a landowner who had the right to refuse access to people,[50] stating that "the public have not acquired any legal right to use the parks by reason of the continued user under the license and by favour of the Crown."[51]

The fact that Mayne called out such large numbers of police indicated he knew the warning would be ignored. Protesters had mounted a spirited campaign to get people to come to the park. The popular bills the protest organizers had posted called for a "peaceful monster meeting," warned of the "tyrannical attack on the liberty of the people," exhorted Londoners to "come, therefore in your best clothes … and look and behave like your betters." Protestors could watch the West End clubs serve dinner, pale ale, wine, and spirits when licensed victuallers were closed by law.[52]

Other criticism was milder but hit at the heart of policing procedures. The police exercised poor judgment at several junctures, one of which was to allow tensions to increase by trying to control the crowd. "Prudence required that the experiment of removing and keeping back the crowd from the rail should have been abandoned immediately the collisions attending it were perceived," the inquiry noted. Nor should there be interference with a crowd unless something clearly illegal is going on, said the report.[53]

Even though the destruction was relatively light and no death ensued, police violence was judged excessive beyond any doubt. This was a uniquely British level of tolerance—in the United States, only deaths would have produced a similar verdict. How a simple meeting turned into chaos was traced to three factors that have remained a constant in police-public dynamics: provocation, escalation, and visibility. Short of bodily harm, police were not to respond in kind to any sort of taunting or provocation. The force was sorely tested that day, as forty-nine police were hurt, twenty-seven struck with stones, thirteen with sticks or pieces of hurdles, seven kicked and knocked down, and one thrown.[54] An officer who was censured by the commission was struck between the shoulders by a man who said "Give it to the blues."[55] Widespread taunting—"Bobby goose" was a mild one—was par for the course, but officers had been repeatedly told to act with good temper and patience and to ignore taunts.

Escalation of tension was (and is) an inevitable consequence of provocation. Police buckled under the sudden tension of the afternoon. As one witness, a hairdresser, testified, he asked a constable, "What are you going to do?" and was told, "This is what I'm going to do," and hit him on the face.[56] Police denied their use of truncheons was unprovoked, which would have led to mandatory disciplinary action with a fine. Most of the violence resulted in attempting to keep people off the roads or away from certain areas; had all vehicular traffic into the park been blocked that day, the riot probably would not have occurred.[57] Police claimed their violence was defensive. When a child in its mother's arms was struck by a stone, the mother pointed out a boy whom the constable then struck. When a fourteen-year veteran detective in plain clothes attempted to arrest a pickpocket, he lost hold of his charge three times and was assaulted by the man, who bit him and tore his coat off.[58] Truncheons were drawn over the silliest of incidents: a constable grabbed a dead eel from the Serpentine that a boy had been playing with; the boy threw a clod of earth which hit the officer in the face, and he and other officers drew their truncheons.

Visibility was the last issue. Because the origin of the provocation was not clear, the commission had difficulty in assigning responsibility. People could not positively identify officers, because the number on the collar was not visible or not correctly remembered. Uniforms were changed after this to make the officer's number more readable. The commission even tried modified lineups to identify the police, but they did not help.

Despite the finding of police brutality, the punishments were relatively light. Of the forty-eight accusations of police misbehavior, only thirteen were found to be substantiated and punishment allotted. Of the seventy-two people arrested, nine contested their case, and the commissions affirmed the arrest of six. When testimony between the police and the civilians complaining against them was contradictory, the police were favored two-thirds of the time.[59]

Overall, the commission's tone was conciliatory. While it was "our duty to report misconduct on the part of various members of the police," there was also "ample testimony . . . borne to the moderation and forbearance of other members of the same body on the same occasion; and whatever blame may attach itself to individuals, it was through the exertions of the police that accidents were prevented in the Park, and property in that vicinity protected from damage."[60] In short, the police had maintained public order, and their lapses were unfortunate and punishable but not such as to negate their positive work in controlling the park.

The commission also established the important principle of internal blame, in which someone with responsibility, but not on the highest level, would take much of the heat. In this case, culpability fell on a superintendent who was a twenty-five-year veteran of crowd control. Despite the excitement of the crowd and their irritation at the police, there was a lack of "judicious management" by officers and no justification for the violence used in crowd dispersion. Superintendent Hughes was censured by the panel and charged that "in endeavouring to discharge a difficult and embarrassing duty, gave too much sanction to the use of the staves and exercised less control over his men than a due regard for the safety of unoffending individuals required."[61] Mayne wrote Hughes of Home Secretary Grey's disapproval of "of his want of forbearance and judgment."[62] Grey decided that dismissal would be too harsh.

The censure of a top policeman was considered severe, significant, and a signal to others. It also underscored the degree to which government felt it accountable for its actions. Officers had to think clearly and use critical judgment to avoid orders that would have negative consequences for the police. Sound direction was even more important, given the fact that in general the force was young and still learning. Half the Metropolitan Police, which totaled 5,707 in 1855, had been on the force less than five years; all these men were in their twenties, and many had received small disciplinary fines for gossiping or being late.

Yet the officers present during the Sunday Trading Bill riots were an older and more experienced lot, with two-thirds having six or more years and half of those with over ten years of service, and all were over the age of thirty. The judgment was that seasoned men should have been more able to have prevented the disturbance. It was also noted that the regular Hyde Park police were from the A division, but that day, forces unused to patrolling the park had been placed there.[63]

Other punishments set precedent. While three policemen were prosecuted, most issues were dealt with internally. Public officials on all levels felt that police misconduct had to be dealt with firmly but with great discretion in order to protect reputations and avoid inflaming public opinion against them. The three constables prosecuted were suspended from the force—their actions deemed "gross and unprovoked" by the government.[64] One was found guilty at trial and sentenced to nine months' imprisonment, one of the harshest punishments ever for a policeman; the other two were acquitted due to weak prosecutorial witnesses and strong defense witnesses.[65] In deciding the punishment for the next three severest cases, length of service and performance were taken into consideration, and they received a week's suspension without pay.[66]

Home Secretary Grey emphasized the necessity of keeping police disciplining as internal as possible. He balanced his "great regret" of police violence with a statement asserting "there can be no doubt that the interference of the Police was indispensably necessary."[67] Despite the public nature of all of this testimony, Grey converted this from a public to a private issue, in the interest of protecting "this high character which the Force has acquired and which is highly creditable to it as a body and to those under whose immediate directions it has been placed."[68]

The government was also forced to question its methods of arrest and imprisonment during public protest and to consider the resultant effect on public opinion, important precedents. They learned that the public eye was focused on events such as this and that the press was particularly interested in the abrogation of rights. In addition, the 1855 events highlighted weaknesses of the criminal justice systems. Slow courts and overfilled prisons were pressing issues. Jamming too many people into inadequate jails was unacceptable, a mid-century standard that was surprising for its progressive nature. The police lockups of Vine and Marlborough Streets were equated to the "Black Hole of Calcutta," a recent sensational account of the horrible conditions in Indian jails; more than forty people at one point were in a cell eight by twenty-four feet.[69] Home Secretary Grey could not understand why all the prisoners were sent to Vine Street when there were so many other places to send them to. He would not accept the explanation that the number of arrests was much higher than had been anticipated, and he stressed that the arrangement was "defective" and resulted from "mismanagement."

Grey's annoyance at the police was bolstered by his conviction that the entire melee could have been avoided, along with a battered public and a bruised police. No one was killed, no one seriously injured, and violence had been directed more at property than at people. That the crowd had taunted the police who in turn were antagonized by the crowd was a problem the force had dealt with for years. No provocation, whatever the cause, could be accepted as a basis for police violence against the public, as the Sunday Trading Bill Riots showed.

Yet more fundamental issues remained unresolved concerning parks, the public, and meetings. Prosecuting attorney Mitchell asked, "Is it not a serious thing for a policeman to be rushing with truncheons upon a crowd of people in England?" Superintendent Nassau O'Brien answered with equanimity, "It is a very serious thing to see a disorderly mob of persons in England taking possession of the west end of London in the way that mob did in Park Street."[70] It was yet another chapter in the battle between civil liberties and civil protection.

PRELUDE TO BLACK AND BLOODY

George Bernard Shaw called it the "Dod Street trick":

> Find a dozen or more persons who are willing to get arrested at the rate of one per week by speaking in defiance of the police. In a month or two, the repeated arrests, the crowds which they attract, the scenes which they provoke, the sentences passed by the magistrates and at the sessions, and the consequent newspaper descriptions, rouse sufficient public feeling to force the Home Secretary to give way whenever the police are clearly in the wrong.[1]

The Irish playwright, known for his sharp social and political insights, embraced socialism as a young man and took his passion to the streets. Shaw joined the Fabian League, which embraced reform rather than revolution. The small but feisty group of one hundred exercised disproportionate influence on the political scene, with high-profile members such as Shaw, Annie Besant, and the intellectuals Sidney and Beatrice Webb.[2] As British authorities attempted to curtail rights in the name of public order, Shaw's use of the "Dod Street trick" in 1885 signaled a dramatic shift in the battle to retain free speech and assembly. The fight reflected the desire of authorities to ensure a safe city during a period of economic depression, in conflict with the efforts of those seeking redress from a system they felt had harmed them.

Black Monday in 1886 and Bloody Sunday in 1887, days of turmoil and violence in London, illustrate how government easily could change the balance of power to favor order over liberty and use police as tools for change. An interest in preserving economic prosperity drove one sector of the public to back curtailment of liberty, while another sector made it clear that they would not tolerate a significant infringement of basic rights. The fight that ensued was ugly, violent, and punitive. The streets and squares of London were the battleground, public oratory grew more strident, and the law became even more confusing in mediating battles. New policies emerged and quickly changed as these factors fused and conflict resulted. While all of London was at issue, two places in particular received the brunt of attention: Trafalgar Square and Hyde Park, both of which carried symbolic and strategic significance.

By Bloody Sunday, it had become clear that free speech had changed from a means to achieve political ends to an issue in and of itself. Leftist and labor politics, as well as Irish nationalism, had helped catapult the idea of liberty into the spotlight. Civil violence was on the minds of many in these decades. "Remember Mitchelstown," where police fired on a crowd of eight thousand and killed one man, became a favorite cry in the Irish campaign. One noteworthy product of all this conflict was the emergence of the first organization in Britain to ensure civil liberties.

The London that celebrated the Queen's Jubilee in 1887 was a very different place from the city that had hosted the Great Exhibition in 1851. The triumphant imperial exhibition had been replaced by draining imperial responsibilities. Still the world's largest city, greater London had grown to more than five million, spreading out physically. Its infrastructure was impressive: the transport system carried millions of passengers per day on rail, tube, bus, and water transport; improved sewer and water systems addressed daily needs and helped rid the city of epidemic disease; and new administrative agencies were set up to regulate daily life. A century of capitalist triumph produced elegant mansions, sumptuous banquets, and posh shopping arcades in the capital city, but it also produced labyrinthine and inaccessible alleys reeking of death and disease for the millions who could not gain access to prosperity. Economic weaknesses had started to surface as continuous growth during the past century faltered. Cyclical depressions left deep scars on the city, with destitution rampant and discontent simmering. Poverty, which had long been credited as the result of personal or moral failure, was in the process of being reassessed as the result of societal and economic flaws. Organizations sprang up throughout London aimed at remedying it.

Perceptions of societal inequities fueled alternative political views, and on the streets of London voices of discontent sounded. Both Conservative and Liberal politicians pressed for reforms to include more middle-class and working-class constituents. The idea of the expanded electorate faced contentious debate, as only about 20 percent of the male population voted in 1866, the year before the second Reform Bill. In 1867, that bill nearly doubled the size of the electorate in England and Wales, enfranchising about one in three males, and most importantly adding a huge swath of working-class voters in the towns. Over the next twenty years, that number quadrupled.

Civil disorder was becoming a political tool. The 1867 Hyde Park protests may or may not have convinced Parliamentarians to pass the Second Reform Bill. Yet the presence of thousands of people in the park on a hot July day, during a cholera epidemic, affected reform in a profound way. The riot resulted from perceptions that voices were not being heard and that the government was silencing participation in the public sphere. The torn railings in the park symbolized the tumbling down of other barriers, and open access to the park symbolized the widening of British democracy. When the government decided to close the park and prevent the meeting, the crowd pushed into it and tore down the railings. The ensuing melee spilled over into the adjacent wealthy local neighborhoods.

While the 1867 riot demonstrated a popular support for franchise reform, it was without question an assertion of the right of free speech and assembly by a public faced with a curtailment of liberties.[3] In the decade after the 1855 Sunday Trading Bill riots, Hyde Park had been a favored meeting ground. Regulations concerning the royal parks were numerous but confusing. Police orders in 1838, 1850, and 1859 had stipulated that open-air preaching was only to be interfered with if it caused obstruction. In 1860, a new order said police were not to interfere with anyone publicly speaking in the park.[4] With no legal clarification regarding this from the 1855 events, Mayne clearly sided with free speech. The Works Office tried to block a preacher from Hyde Park on the grounds that the parks would "become the scene of polemical strike, if not of attack upon religion, as heretofore, instead of the peaceful resort of the different classes of the community."[5]

Despite growing antiritual disturbances against the Church of England, Mayne issued orders in 1859 and 1860 reaffirming that preaching was not to be interfered with, nullifying the Works Office decision, but he did so as the increased political nature of meetings began a shift of responsibility to the Home Office. An 1859 protest meeting by the Conference of the United Building Trades forced Mayne to reiterate the Home Secretary's warning that the park was for recreational purposes. When the union refused to cancel the meeting, Mayne told him "distinctly to understand that no sanction whatsoever could be given by the authorities charged with preserving the Public Peace."[6] The August 3 demonstration of five thousand was quiet, and police kept at a distance.

This prompted the Home Office to give police complete discretion in handling meetings. When a series of meetings was announced to support Italian nationalist Giuseppe Garibaldi, Home Secretary Walpole predicted "There will be some disturbance … but Mayne will have a good strong force in the neighbourhood to prevent the combatants from coming to extremities." That the government anticipated possible violence was clear, but also clear was the fact that it did not consider such a threat sufficient to block the meetings. After all, Walpole conceded, "it would not do to prohibit the meeting altogether after the entire freedom of assembly in the park for discussion which has been allowed of late years."[7]

As the battle for the streets and squares began, convenience for the public was pitted against custom, and authorities argued and vacillated. Works Office First Commissioner Alfred Austin wanted meetings banned from Hyde Park, insisting that it be used only for recreational purposes. Mayne responded, "it appears to me that such a course could not properly be taken on this occasion, as numerous meetings with a great variety of objects have been permitted by the authorities having control in the Parks to be held there for some years past."[8] As meetings became more disruptive, Mayne admitted that they had to be limited. Although the law opinion had provided only for banning a specific meeting, in late 1862, Mayne issued an order disallowing meeting for speeches in the Royal Parks on Sundays.[9]

It went unchallenged, even when the same group that had demonstrated with Mayne and the government's approval a few years earlier, the Garibaldi supporters, was banned from meeting on Primrose Hill on July 23, 1864. The same day, fifty thousand people assembled there to watch the planting of an oak tree in commemoration of the Shakespeare Tercentenary. A simultaneous political meeting sponsored by the Working Men's Committee attracted another fifty thousand people. With the government's ear tuned to possible disruption, police had stationed more than two hundred men on the procession route from Russell Square to the site in Regent's Park. Mayne issued a notice forbidding the meeting on July 17, saying it was "inconsistent with the purposes for which the Park is thrown open to and used by the public." Yet he gave strict orders that the police were not to interfere with anyone speaking nor take anyone into custody without "special directions" from either the commissioner or assistant commissioner, an unusual step. The force was also warned not to take notice of offensive or angry language.[10]

The Primrose Hill incident led to the founding of the Reform League, a working-class group with a trades union and leftist base supporting Italian unification and the expanded ballot. They joined with the National Reform Union, manufacturers and merchants from the Midlands, to press for reform and demonstrate in public in 1866 and 1867. With 1855 lurking in the background, the government made it clear that a peaceful and well-ordered city was primary and that the use of public spaces would be limited. Home Secretary Sir George Grey told the Commons that "the Royal parks are intended for the recreation and enjoyment of the people."[11]

The law officers were not so sure. They said there was no legal authority to disperse a large meeting in Hyde Park, unless individuals broke specific laws or the license under which they originally entered.[12] They were particularly worried about what would happen if a meeting was held and then dispersed: this could not be done safely in large gatherings, and "there is no right to disperse or coerce them [the meeters] as a body of rioters or disorderly persons."[13] When Mayne issued an order on July 23, 1866, forbidding the assembly on the grounds it was "inconsistent with the purposes for which the Park is thrown open to," it had the effect of inspiring a "determined spirit of resistance" in the public.[14] The rails came down.

A year later, Walpole wept at the melee that ensued on April 19, 1867. After three days of skirmishing between outraged citizens and police, he issued a bill ordering people not to attend a proposed May 6 meeting, though he never declared it illegal.[15] Whitehall shuddered and ordered fifteen thousand special constables to prevent the demise of orderly London. When the demonstrations turned out to be peaceful and well run, the anticlimax shook the Home Office, and Walpole resigned "in humiliation."[16]

A Pandora's box had been opened regarding public meetings, and the debate grew fiercer. The government was unsure its meeting ban was legal. In 1868, Home Secretary Gathorne Hardy solicited another legal opinion, which equivocated so much it was hardly worth the paper it was on. Meetings or processions can't be prevented "because they *may* tend to breach of the peace." But if the object of the meeting or procession, or the conduct of the people participating, "inspire terror . . . the meeting might be dispersed and persons prevented from joining it."[17] The gauging of terror was not like the gauging of rainfall, and no one had any idea what instrument would help determine an acceptable threshold. Again, in 1870, another LOO advised that Mayne's 1862 order disallowing meeting for Sunday speeches "cannot be enforced and . . . it would be better to rescind it."[18]

For the first time, a British government attempted to stop summarily outdoor public meetings, and it was met with fervent opposition. Gathorne Hardy's abortive attempt to get Parliament to pass a bill eliminating all meetings in royal parks died in the face of staunch Liberal opposition.[19] The debate on the issue was impressive. Even though the Crown was the owner of the parks, the public paid for their upkeep, and many, including John Stuart Mill, considered that to mean that the parks were public property. In 1866, Lord Shaftesbury had struck a familiar historical note, citing the "great free States of antiquity in providing open spaces where the people may have the undisputed right of considering all the affairs relating to their own condition, and the state of the commonwealth at large."[20] The public's right to the streets and squares was a defining English characteristic, said Mill: meetings had to be allowed "because it has been for centuries the pride of this country and one of its most valued distinctions from the despotically-governed countries of the Continent, that a man has a right to speak his mind, on politics, or on any other subject, to those who would listen to him, when and where he will."[21]

The two great lions who dominated British politics for decades came down on the side of allowing public assemblies. Conservative Benjamin Disraeli said they were the "safety-valves of a free country," although he preferred indoor ones to outdoors. Liberal William Gladstone admitted they were not convenient, but said, "I am apprehensive of a measure the effect of which will be to limit the power of holding open-air meetings."[22] Other MPs suggested that a bill such as the one proposed would equate unlawful assembly with political offences. Liberals saw the issue of Crown rights over the park a narrow one and an excuse for the real agenda of closing the parks to the masses. "Large public meetings are the best modes of expressing public indignation and thus preventing arbitrary and oppressive legislation," said MP Denman.[23]

The fight over royal parks for the next twenty years hinged on a narrowing legal interpretation of park use and a denial of the notion of birthright access to open space. The Board of Works had no intention of letting parks become public meeting grounds, claiming ecological and environmental reasons for the refusal (reasons similar to those mounted today in New York and London). Parks were to be segregated as leisure zones of green space to offset pollution and overcrowding. This argument contradicted the position held by liberal politicians that public spaces were for the people for any purpose.

The 1872 Royal Parks and Gardens Act empowered the park ranger to set discretionary rules. No public addresses could be delivered that were not in conformity with his decision. Addresses could only be given within forty yards of the notice board on which rules were posted, effectively eliminating large gatherings.[24] Challenged in court almost immediately, the conviction of a violator was upheld by the Queen's Bench judges, who denied the concept that past usage for public speech would constitute a preexisting right or justify current usage. "The habit of using the metropolitan Parks for other purposes than those of recreation and exercise is of modern growth, and it had produced certain inconveniences which required to be modified." The offender had held his meeting 106 yards from the notice board, and park laws were broken. The courts emphasized the conservative nature of the usage: "Whatever enjoyment the public have been allowed to have of these parks," Mr. Justice Cockburn said, "has been an enjoyment which the public have had by the gracious concession of the Crown." In essence, the court tried to establish the parks as privileged havens.[25]

By the time George Bernard Shaw started his street escapades, the debate over royal parks had escalated. The public right to use the park at will remained contracted in the 1880s, but mounting challenges eventually broke down the metaphorical barriers. The rise of Labour politics, the increase in organizations seeking public forums, the diversifying social structure, and the angry confrontations of the decade contributed to the return of public addresses by the mid-1890s in most of Hyde Park.[26] Only Hyde Park and Regents Park regulations specifically allowed public addresses in certain areas; in other parks, specific authorization was needed before giving an address. Despite attempts at limitation and the absence of written statements guaranteeing meeting rights, there were twenty-eight major meetings in Hyde Park from 1877 to 1885.[27] The public clearly considered Hyde Park a meeting ground. As one woman said in 1892, her reason for attending a meeting there was that "they had been in the same place by permission in former years."[28] By the early twentieth century, the area near Marble Arch had become identified as the chosen meeting place in the park and earned the moniker Speaker's Corner.

Socialists, short on cash and long on soliloquy, knew that the best way to get their message to the public was to deliver it where people lived and worked. The British version of socialism was "reformist, permeative, and evolutionary."[29] The movement was blessed with exemplary public speakers who were focused on convincing the public that it was "absurd" and "unjust" to link socialism with physical force.[30] The Fabians were one of three Socialist groups utilizing street campaigns. The Social Democratic Federation, the largest, was headed by Cambridge-educated H. M. Hyndman, a well-to-do businessman. The circulation of their newspaper, *Justice*, and their monthly magazine, *To-day*, was far greater than their membership, which was about two thousand by the late 1880s. The Socialist League, a breakoff group from the SDF, was spearheaded by Arts and Crafts movement founder William Morris, who threw his energies into *Commonweal*, the SL's weekly newspaper. All educated and of economic means, these men chose the streets as the platform for *vox populi*. Such street usage had also been popularized by the Salvation Army, which employed proselytizing tactics at corners.

Socialist street lecturers were undaunted by hecklers, foul weather, and traffic noise. Hyndman wore his silk hat and frock coat on purpose: "I do more for the movement by wearing my Stock Exchange clothes," he told Shaw, "than you with your Norfolk suit. I do not want the movement to be a depository of odd cranks, humanitarians, vegetarians, anti-vivisectionists, anti-vaccinationists, arti-crafters and all the rest of them."[31] Edward Aveling, companion of Karl Marx's daughter Eleanor, was known for his euphoniumlike voice. Belfort Bax dealt with paid Tory agents trying to disrupt his meetings.[32] Lord Snell was giving a lecture on the Greek city beautiful as compared with Lambeth when two men with terriers and a cage full of live rats appeared, causing a quick dispersion of the crowd.[33] Shaw took to the streets thrice-fortnightly in his efforts to convince crowds "against all their prejudice that they ought to change their minds and become Socialists."[34] Unflappable, he once attempted to convert six policemen, his only audience during a rainy hour and a half in Hyde Park.

Other voices were more strident. Labor leader John Burns's "bread or lead" speeches pulled no punches, and George Lansbury admitted that while law and order should not be disregarded, "there are times though when . . . it is imperative that self-respecting men and women should revolt."[35] Audiences, which ranged in size from a handful to thousands, ran the gamut from aristocrats, to government officials, to unemployed, to loiterers. The police rarely interfered, even with large meetings such as the 1882 Coercion Bill, which brought thirty thousand to Hyde Park. Meetings could become unruly, as was the case with one in February 1885, when a gathering of unemployed at Cleopatra's Needle, addressed by John Burns, marched in heavy rain to the local Government Board offices where a deputation of men entered; some boys and roughs broke loose and wandered off to attack railings. Yet relations with the police remained amicable, with even *Justice* describing the bobbies as behaving "admirably."[36]

Women, such as Annie Hicks and Annie Besant, drew big crowds, and ironically the police clampdown started with two women speakers. Decades earlier, it would have been unthinkable to have had women addressing the public on the streets. In 1884, Jessie Craigen received a police summons for speaking on Primrose Hill. A startled and annoyed SDF could see no reason "why public meetings should not be held on Primrose Hill just as well as in Hyde Park or Regent's Park. . . . Besides at present democrats are practically shut out from public halls so the open air is their only gathering place."[37] Then in September 1885, Annie Hicks, a Dod Street regular, was arrested for obstructing the street. Suspicions arose immediately that the arrest was politically motivated, as the East End spot was popular for religious and political groups and it was in a section of warehouses with little traffic. SDF leader Hyndman flatly stated, "We are stopped from speaking because of our opinion."[38] Fabian Annie Besant noted that "Christians, Freethinkers, Salvationists, agitators of all kinds were, for the most part, left alone, but there was a regular crusade against the Socialists."[39] Police action had served to unite temporarily warring socialist factions.

Antagonism to police rose as Socialists were harassed. An indignant Hyndman said it "were as if the police, instead of being our servants, kept, and clothed, and fed with our money to do our duty . . . were petty tyrants appointed by some disreputable gang of labour-robbers to bully honest folk."[40] Open-air meetings around London gathered momentum: at Battersea Park, Hampstead Heath, the Bricklayers Arms, Burdett Road, Regent's Park, Stamford Hill, Islington Green, and Victorian Park, crowds gathered around the socialist platform.

The Dod Street trick worked beautifully. Never popular among East Enders, the Metropolitan Police became even more contemptible, and they were accused of emulating the Continental police.[41] Popular opinion churned over the endangerment of free-speech rights by police, and the public bristled as "something deepseated and hereditary in them smouldered at that news."[42] As news of the arrest got around, more people than ever came to Dod Street meetings, and by the end of September 1885, there were over fifty thousand in attendance.[43] Money poured in toward a Defence Fund, whose popularity among the working classes was evidenced by one collection plate of twenty-three shillings consisting of pennies (276 of them).

There was no such thing as bad publicity for the socialists, so when William Morris was arrested on September 20, 1885, the press had a field day. A Police Court magistrate created a travesty during Morris's obstruction trial. "What are you?" Justice Saunders asked Morris, who was famous. "I am an artist, and a literary man, pretty well known, I think, throughout Europe," replied Morris.[44] It was a publicist's dream for the free-speech cause.

By October 1885, the police had no choice but to capitulate, given public indignation. Home Secretary Cross "instantly crumpled" and called off police "with assurance that devotion to Free Speech was the first principle of its being."[45] A month before, sixty thousand people had turned out in Dod Street in an orderly fashion, affirming that "the authorities had given in,"[46] and the press approved.[47] A meeting in Victoria Park on October 11 hailed John Williams, who had been imprisoned, as the "Sufferer for Free Speech."

The socialists had become heroes for both an oppressed minority and a wronged majority. They gained legitimacy through the free-speech platform. The police mistakenly attempted to stop Dod Street meetings on the weak cry of obstruction. It is difficult to tell if the government had any coherent policy regarding all of this, as there was little in the way of public pronouncements until 1886.[48] Dod Street had given the socialists confidence. But it would prove to be a false sense of security and a premature notion of victory.

COMMONS, OPEN SPACES, AND THE LAW

Dod Street brought to the public eye a legal question that previously had not been asked. Were there limits to speech and assembly in public places? The right to use public space for a variety of purposes was widely assumed, and for centuries interference had been minimal. Historically chaotic cities had few regulations about public places. For Victorian London, an avalanche of law changed that. From midcentury on, regulation was enacted to control the way thoroughfares were used, goods and services were sold, basic urban services delivered, and public space used, to create new standards of a livable city. "Crying," for example, the age-old public announcing of goods for sale, became disruptive in a city where crowded living conditions meant noise could be a constant irritation. "Selling" political, religious, or other ideas on the streets became a possible disruption, too, and prompted authorities to consider regulation and people to think about what they were free to do.

The popular assumption that meetings could be held on any public land without permission or restriction met its first major legal challenges in this period. This was prompted by increasing amounts of speech challenging all aspects of conventional society and by the existence of new municipal agencies that sought to restrict access to their properties with a view to protect them from physical damage. The Home Office and its servants, the Metropolitan Police, continued to be caught in the confusion of the vagaries of the laws, as few dealt specifically with public meetings.

London had many kinds of spaces that were completely in the public domain, and they followed different legal guidelines.[49] Small parks, large parks, squares, and commons could be owned by the Crown, the state, or the municipality, and rules varied accordingly; Hyde Park was Crown land. Statutes for commons and open spaces provided little help where meetings were concerned. According to the oldest legal principles, while the public technically had no right to any space unless specifically allowed (*jus spatiendi vel manendi*), it had right of access for air and exercise (Halsbury's Laws). The Highway Act prevented obstruction of passage, and two other laws dealt with language or behavior that could provoke a breach of peace. Another law gave police the ability to arrest people who prevented them from doing their duty, which could be applied to public-space control.[50]

Formally, the Home Office oversaw order on commons and open spaces in its capacity as overseer of the Metropolitan Police, and it often had to seek law-officer opinions about application of the laws. At the same time, the new Metropolitan Board of Works created its own extensive collection of bylaws for its properties. It was always possible to use the Riot Act to disperse a meeting, but as the Coldbath Fields riot had shown, that was rarely used. During the Chartist era, the government rarely tried to prevent meetings, and the police commissioners had learned there were no legal grounds for banning meetings.

Parliament was drawn into an investigation of the public-space issue as confusion and confrontation heightened. The 1865 Select Committee on Open Spaces concluded that legal precedents were based upon "no very intelligent principle." While a "'*servus spatiandi*' over open ground which has in some measure been devoted to public use, is also intelligible and known to the law, yet the legal authorities appear most unwilling to admit any general public right to exercise and recreation upon the spaces, although such a right may from time immemorial have been enjoyed."[51] The next year, a new law placed all commons in the hands of government agencies, dedicated to the public forever as open and unenclosed space. Three years later, another amendment clarified that a space frequented for twenty years by the public had passed into the realm of public use and was a common.[52]

Between 1878 and 1888, significant changes in local laws prompted legal action challenging the right of the Board of Works to determine the permissibility of public meetings. The first-ever attempt to limit legally public meetings came in the late 1870s, with a Works bylaw addressing assemblages. Amid jockeying for power by new government agencies, the Board of Works felt empowered to clamp down on public meetings in commons and local parks in order to preserve existing green spaces, considered an antidote to the miasma thought to cause disease. The Works office had gained increased authority following an 1877 act, which authorized it to control, manage, and protect lands for the "prevention and restraint of acts or things tending to the injury and disfigurement of 'the parks' or to interference with the use thereof by the public for purposes of exercise and recreation."[53] The act specifically stated the board could make bylaws concerning public assemblies, which is just what it did.[54] That same year, the Metropolitan Open Spaces Act established the need to provide more open spaces for London's inhabitants to enjoy, and it empowered the Board of Works to purchase land for that purpose.

With its new powers, the Board of Works commissioners immediately set about to limit assemblies, meetings, and addresses on any subject unless it gave written permission. One of the bylaws implied there was no right of public meeting by stipulating that all assemblies and addresses were automatically disallowed and illegal without written permission. The regulations met with an immediate legal challenge in *DeMorgan v. Metropolitan Board of Works*.[55] The case addressed the notion of the privilege as opposed to the right to use public places (as had been the issue in *Bailey v. Williamson* in 1873, discussed above).

The case was decided in favor of the Board of Works, but not without a confusing argument that left many questions unanswered. The increase in public meetings, heightened political tensions, and demands of the city were factors in the decision. *DeMorgan* challenged the bylaw that permission for meetings had to be obtained, as the purpose of the land was recreational. The plaintiffs argued that the public had acquired the right to hold meetings prior to the bylaw's existence; the bylaw itself, said the brief, was *ultra vires* (beyond the powers or authority) and void. An open and unenclosed space, it said, meant there was an inherent right of assemblage, which was placed under the broad rubric of recreation.

The opinion denied any rights of the public to the land in the strongest possible way. The evidence of public meeting did not constitute a right nor prove anything more than an excused trespass. Public meetings were not recreation and did not contribute positively to the urban experience, the opinion said: "If this argument were sound it would follow that any number of public meetings might be held . . . to the disturbance of the neighbourhood and the exclusion of the portion of the public who desired to use it for the purpose of recreation." Regulation in and of itself was acceptable in order to satisfy the needs of the community, and the Works bylaw reasonable.[56]

Reaction to *DeMorgan* was fierce, loud, and negative from press and government. This became evident in the first test of the bylaw after *DeMorgan*, on Peckham Rye Common, at a meeting to protest the illegality of meetings there. As far as the Works Board was concerned, no public assemblies were to be held. After all, explained First Commissioner Sir James McGarel-Hogg, "the nuisance was found to be so great from meetings, one person lecturing on atheism, another on religion, another on politics, and a fourth on temperance, that the Board . . . amended bye-laws . . . to prevent meetings." An exception could be made for a "great public object, such as [Prime Minister] Mr. Gladstone's meeting on Blackheath," but such assemblies tended to contain "a large number of roughs . . . to the very great annoyance of respectable persons."[57]

Home Secretary Sir William Harcourt protested that "meetings of this character are found by experience to be productive of no evil, and their prohibition tend to provoke irritation and disturbance." The board claimed the bylaw was not intended to prevent peaceful and orderly meetings and that they would review it, but it was left dormant for five years.[58]

Harcourt lost his temper when the Works Office refused to allow a group of Rotherhithe taxpayers to hold a meeting in Southwark Park. They held the meeting anyway, and the board took legal action against them. The incident occasioned one of the strongest statements ever made in England about the place of free speech and assembly and the right to use public space. The Liberal Harcourt saw such space as a place for the London populace to let off steam. "It is hard to expect," he angrily wrote McGarel-Hogg,

> that working men who desire to meet for the discussion of their own affairs should be put to the cost of hiring rooms for the purpose. . . . There is not a village or a town in England which has not some open space where gatherings of this kind can take place, and it would be intolerable if the population of London, amounting to four millions of people, were destitute of such opportunities, which are naturally and legitimately desired.

He also reiterated a classic rule of public meetings: attempted repression of them "creates discontent and disturbance" and provokes "irritation and tumult."[59]

The volley between the two men continued for some time, with the Works Board maintaining a conservative stance and the Home Office defending the common man. The board made a concession in allowing a portion of Southwark Park to be used for meetings. Such events disturbed residents in houses of a "superior character," McGarel-Hogg said, to which Harcourt retorted, "the enjoyment of the public of open spaces maintained at the public expense ought not . . . to be wholly governed by the interests of the owners of adjoining houses."[60]

For Harcourt, the last straw was the arrest of a man at Shepherd's Bush Common for reading the Bible. "The knowledge that a man has been sent to prison for reading the Bible to a few people on a suburban common on Sunday is not likely to strengthen the administration of the law," he told the Works Board, whose actions he characterized as illegal, oppressive, irritating, and provocative. The Bible reader got fourteen days, although the magistrates discharged the members of the assembly who had been reading and singing.[61]

The Works Board by and large stood their ground in upholding their policy against public meetings in open spaces. *DeMorgan* had proven inadequate as a legal framework, and government policy remained the prime determinant of police action. Meanwhile, the more socialists and labor took to the streets, the greater the tensions and the attempts to stop them. As the Liberal Gladstone cabinet disintegrated in 1885, the battle cry grew louder.

TRAFALGAR SQUARE AND PROCESSIONS

The public meeting armageddon of 1886–1887 took place in Trafalgar Square, which had not been a preferred meeting ground for major political meetings for most of the century. From 1860 to 1886, only twenty-one meetings were held there, including four in 1867 and five in 1872.[62] In 1866, Home Secretary Sir George Grey asserted that "Trafalgar Square was the lawful and proper place for holding such meetings," since it was rarely used as a thoroughfare.[63] When the issue rose again, in 1881, much had changed to alter this view. In addition to the new political scene, the metropolis had grown considerably in population, and traffic had become congested in the city center. Traffic flow had been prioritized by police, and the cry of obstruction became the government hallmark for stopping demonstrators.

The emergence of Trafalgar Square as the heart of London's public meeting ground is ironic. The majestic square had served for two centuries as a symbol of empire. Now a prominent tourist destination and traffic nightmare dotted with heroic monuments, it started off not as an open square leading to the seat of government power but as a crowded Charing Cross downtown neighborhood with a mixed population of poor and gentry, who lived down the curling roads surrounding it. A hundred years earlier, the Charing Cross area had been prominent not only for the coffeehouses and taverns filling it but also for the innumerable hangings, heads on pikes, and punitive mutilations, including the excision of ears and splitting of noses, that had taken place there.

In 1812, during a decade of ambitious Regency urban planning, architect John Nash envisioned "a magnificent and beautiful termination of the street from Westminster," surrounded by government offices and royal societies and academies, a place where "the greatest part of the population of the Metropolis [would] meet and diverge."[64] Laws in 1813 and 1826 established the desirability of an open square opposite Charing Cross, monies for acquisition of the land, and the opening of streets.[65] After thirty years of complicated real-estate transactions, including a novel combination of land purchase and lease exchange estimated at more than £700,000, Sir Charles Barry completed the design of the square. In 1844, a statute was passed "to provide for the Care and Preservation of Trafalgar Square," in which the square was vested in the Queen and her successors as part of the hereditary possession of the Crown, while the care and management of the square fell to the H. M. Commissioners of Woods (later Works).[66] By the Crown Lands Act (1851), the power of the Board of Works was expanded to include Trafalgar.[67]

The post-Waterloo generation celebrated Nelson and his naval victory by creating central London's defining presence. The name was given in 1832, and in 1840 it was cleared of rubble from the construction of the National Gallery. The column was put up in 1842, and Nelson's statue, funded by public subscription, was placed atop it in 1843. The unveiling of the lions, the famous "guardians" of the square, took place in 1867.[68]

Nash also saw the square as a means of social engineering at a time when London's poor were spreading into every corner of the crowded metropolis. The new streets were engineered to create a "line of separation" between the areas occupied by nobility and gentry and those occupied by mechanics, traders, and the so-called inferior classes. Nelson's column and the fountains were placed to discourage the collection of crowds. The working-class nature of the area was killed off by regulations disallowing wagons, carts, drays, and animals from using the new area, including the park, which forced cheap food vendors out of the area. Complaints by shopkeepers, local traders, and local residents were heard formally at the time of renovation but had no effect.[69] As plans for the square were being formalized two decades later, worries still abounded in the age of the Chartists that the new square might be subverted by "other evils of a generally objectionable character," that is, urban mobs.[70]

Like the royal parks, the square also fell under the ambiguous appellation of Crown land; there were no regulatory statutes, since it was neither a park nor a local common. This was contested by Attorney General Sir Charles Russell and Home Secretary Henry Matthews during debates in Commons over the Black Monday and Bloody Sunday events. Russell argued that using public monies along with accommodating the public made this public land: "while the freehold or legal estate remains in the Queen, the beneficial use and accommodation of it lie in the public," negating the powers of the crown agency, the Commissioners of Woods and Forests, to control it. Matthews presented a novel argument that the square was not a thoroughfare because of the sculpture there, thus making it even more unsuitable as a meeting place. Russell took the opposite interpretation: since statues were placed in a public place, that place "is defined to be the one to which the public had the right of ingress, egress, regress or thoroughfare."[71] An obscure law barring meetings from the square within one mile from a sitting Parliament, the Seditious Meetings Act of 1817, was little known and hardly used.[72]

The colorful Charles Bradlaugh—freethinker, birth-control advocate, and MP—forced the government to seek legal opinion. Denied his seat in Parliament because of his insistence that he affirm rather than take an oath, Bradlaugh had attracted twenty thousand people in August 1881 to a peaceful meeting. When a group of five thousand marched to Palace Yard, the police dispersed them. Bradlaugh was long experienced in holding meetings in Trafalgar Square and had never had any problems there. The law officers' opinion advised a worried government against interference with the procession, although it did say there were two narrow grounds that could be used to stop it: one statute prevented people from collecting within Palace Yard, and the 1817 Seditious Meeting Act was still on the books. The police were told to use their discretion regarding the first and latitude toward the second.[73] Matthews later admitted the meeting was not stopped because of fear that Bradlaugh would become even more sympathetic in the public's eyes, and that it was better to avoid a collision.[74]

The dramatic shift in government policy came after Black Monday in February 8, 1886. Preventing that meeting had never been considered, because no one anticipated a large turnout, let alone a riot. The day after the riots, Queen Victoria wrote Childers: "Her Majesty believes that … a public meeting in Trafalgar Square is illegal; and, if so, asks whether after the recent riot you would not be justified in forbidding tumultuous assemblages in that place." Childers was worried and wrote Ponsonby the next day that "to withdraw a permission, granted or recognized by successive governments, would be a very grave step."[75]

In November 1887, new police commissioner Sir Charles Warren did what no one did before or after him: he banned all public meetings. Brought in after the fallout of Black Monday and the subsequent Parliamentary investigation, Warren was the law-and-order chief. But the radical action caught everyone by surprise. Bit by bit, he began in the fall of 1886 to stop meetings, in different places and for different reasons, arresting open-air speakers. In November 1886, he banned a Trafalgar Square counterdemonstration by socialists on Lord Mayor's Day, a ceremonial event, but did not enforce it. By totally banning meetings, Warren had taken the law into his own hands, and brought on Bloody Sunday.

Nº
6

BLACK MONDAY, BLOODY SUNDAY

William Booth, founder of the Salvation Army, gave a chilling description of London in the late 1880s:

> Just as Big Ben strikes two, the moon, flashing across the Thames and lighting up the stone work of the embankment, brings into relief a pitiable spectacle. Here on the stone abutments, which afford a slight protection from the biting wind, are scores of men lying side by side, huddled together for warmth, and of course, without any other covering than their ordinary clothing, which is scanty enough at the best.

The "Sunken Millions" had no "vile dens, fever-haunted and stenchful crowded courts" to go to, but slept out in the open only hundreds of yards from where British politicians decided their nation's future.[1]

A few years earlier, Andrew Mearns had published a penny pamphlet describing London's starving children, covered in vermin, living in vile conditions with hopeless parents.[2] The swelling philanthropic institutions of the country were churning out aid as a horrified public tried to process the sensational reportage. Booth and Mearns joined contemporaries Henry Mayhew, Charles Booth, George Sims, and W. T. Stead in firsthand investigation of misery. Their reportage provides unprecedented insight into the lives of the "submerged third," those with little hope of ever escaping hunger and poverty.

Booth founded the Salvation Army not to ameliorate poverty but to eliminate it in an era of prosperity. Many had benefited from a century of industrialization and imperial expansion. New millionaires had sprouted like tulips in spring, and an expanded middle class exerted its influence on the manners and mores of the nation. Yet it also produced a new layer of poor and unemployed, especially egregious in the cities. In response, government established reforms and regulations that would be the foundation for the welfare state.[3] The century marked a shift toward recognizing societal responsibility for assisting the poor, but poverty remained distasteful in the eyes of the powerful middle classes.

How to reduce the extremes of wealth and poverty and cope with the excesses of a materialistic culture became a major preoccupation. By the 1880s, the imperative for drastic change had filtered into a large sector of the public. New political organizations promised to eliminate poverty and equalize wealth. Panaceas offered by evangelical organizations such as the Oxford Movement, Toynbee Hall, and the People's Palace, along with the millions of pounds endowed in philanthropic trusts—the sharp eyes of the Charity Organization Society were always on the lookout for fraud—had not succeeded in changing the imbalance of society. Amid this landscape of distress and excess, the politics of dissent found a firm footing in the late Victorian era.

Booth was among the first social reformers to use the public spaces of London to get his message across. His fervent sermonizing became common on streets and squares, and his army of proselytizers fanned out over the metropolis. Not surprisingly, the Salvation Army became embroiled in many legal disputes over public meetings, along with socialists and labor groups,[4] and London proved to be a fertile base. Socialist organizations mostly emanated from the capital,[5] and trade unionism used London to increase its political centrality and national publicity. London was confronted by a level of political activism it had not witnessed since 1866–1867, and the Reform Bill agitation of that period was not of the scale or nature that the new political activism entailed. Street-corner oratory was popularized to a degree never before known in the metropolis; from 1882 through 1888, one could hear several street lectures a day, often as many as a dozen, in various parts of London.[6]

The combination of long-simmering political discontent, new ideologies, labor activism, high unemployment, and a terrible winter precipitated the crisis that became known as Black Monday. As cold weather and seasonal unemployment increased misery, the Lord Mayor of London started the Mansion House Fund, the first by a public official in response to destitution in "Outcast London."[7] The Charity Organization Society, the nation's leading private charity, continued to distinguish between deserving and undeserving poor, unwittingly contributing to the dissident and radical ideologies.[8] The middle and upper classes offered sympathy but seldom empathy for the poor. While "slumming," the practice of well-off women in visiting the poor and offering token gestures, may have assuaged their troubled consciences, it did nothing to lessen their fear that one day they might be the visited instead of the visitor.

Unemployment, in particular, helped unite disparate political groups to act in concert. As socialists unfolded their "popular melodrama, [its] Pilgrim's Progress through suffering, trial and combat against the powers of evil," the government and the police tried to regroup as the protectors of middle-class respectability and hegemony.[9] But it was no longer clear whose interests police were protecting, as suffrage extension for forty years had expanded the electoral base to nearly democratic proportions. The 1880s crisis in the streets of London tested the essential formulation of constitutional liberty: unpropertied classes now joined the electorate, testing and changing democratic processes. This contradicted long-held English beliefs cemented by Hobbes and Locke that only property ownership could ensure licit participation in government. As historians have pointed out, "property as the first prerequisite of civic virtue lay at the heart of the ancient political system that was under siege . . . new forms of property right . . . were subtly transforming the character of British society and the balance of power between different social groups."[10] Work was part of the process to property access and was as sacred as a right.

As demonstrations asserting the right to work and to receive proper compensation increased in the 1880s, propertied and prosperous Londoners reacted as though streets and open spaces were invaded by the discontented. Civil authorities responded as if London were at risk and its institutions in danger of collapse. City streets and spaces had to be cleared, police said, regardless of the rights of the individual. Laws were challenged, questioned, interpreted, supported, and knocked down, often without much pattern or sense. From Ireland to India, from London to the Midlands, free speech and meeting rights were challenged by diverse groups ranging from the Salvation Army to home-rule advocates.

Nowhere in the nineteenth century was the battle as fierce or focused as on the streets of London, where centuries of custom and law were challenged. Black Monday plunged London into its worst fears ever of civil chaos, bringing with it doubts about police capability, questions over government competency, and loud outcries from the commercial sector. The resultant Parliamentary investigation produced a scathing assessment of police and a major reorganization of the force. More sinister, Black Monday produced a curtailment of free speech in the public spaces of London.

BLACK MONDAY

As the unemployed slept on the Thames Embankment in the especially bitter winter of 1886,[11] socialist leader H. M. Hyndman grew fiercer in his resolution to find a remedy for unemployment. "We appeal to all who have sympathy with misery and distress to do their best to work up really threatening meetings and demonstrations," he wrote in January.[12] Large meetings were held outdoors at favorite venues such as Clerkenwell Green, despite the police crackdown. The Social Democratic Federation was no longer the main player: quickly rising in prominence was the new working-class political lobby, which in only a few decades would elect a Labour Prime Minister. Despite sharing many common interests, these groups had little unity in action or thought, and they often attacked each other. The General Labourers' Amalgamated Union and the Fair Trade League, for example, disliked the radicalism of the SDF and organized their own meetings.

The main players on February 8, 1886, then, consisted of a collection of disparate groups with different platforms but a common interest in assuaging unemployment. The meeting was called by the Labourers' League and cosponsored by the Fair Trade League, who were viewed by the socialists as nothing more than a "capitalistic working-men's" group who were "lackeys of the sugar refineries."[13] A large crowd was not expected, and the police were oblivious to the hostility between the groups, which Hyndman had noted was "likely to degenerate into a free fight."[14] The only other recent large demonstration in Trafalgar Square, against "Increased Duties on Beer" in May 1885, had been orderly. The police had only five hundred men stationed around the square; Police Commissioner Henderson anticipated that no "outrages on property were in contemplation or that the meeting would differ in any material respect from previous similar gatherings," although "a collision was feared between the 'unemployed' and the 'Social Democrats', which it was our duty to prevent or suppress."[15] In the end, the West End was left unprotected and subject to poor police communication and lack of intelligence regarding activities.[16]

The spark that turned a rally into a riot could not be traced. The twenty thousand demonstrators spilled out of the square, down the roadways leading to the square, onto the steps of St. Martin's Church, and down Pall Mall. Police tried in vain to keep people off the base of Nelson's Column, and suggested Hyndman move his supporters to Hyde Park to avoid a breach of the peace. John Burns waved the red flag, denounced the Commons, spoke of heads adorning lampposts in France, and intimated that if the government remained passive concerning unemployment their next action would be to sack bakers' shops in West London. Burns led demonstrators out of the square, down Pall Mall, up St. James Street, and along Piccadilly in mid-afternoon, with few police in sight. As fate would have it, the streets were being macadamized, and heaps of metal and stone were everywhere. That proved too much.

Fueled by the jeers hurled from the exclusive private clubs that overlooked these streets, the crowd reacted by smashing windows, targeting the clubs, including Arthur's, Brook's, Devonshire, University, and Boodles. The mayhem continued along Piccadilly and Half-Moon Street, until the crowd reached Hyde Park at about 4 p.m., where Hyndman, Burns, and others led a meeting. A thousand marchers proceeded to the high-rent districts and commercial centers of South and North Audley Street and Oxford Street, where they attacked and looted jewelers, grocers, bakers, china shops, wine merchants, perfumers, hosiers, tailors, art shops, poulterers, a portmanteau shop, the Bath Hotel, and the homes of Baroness Burdett-Coutts and the Duke of Cambridge.

The police finally stopped protestors at the end of Marylebone Lane, and by 7 p.m. the streets were finally cleared.[17] Those arrested were young, almost all under the age of thirty, and represented a wide swath of the working class, ranging from the most unskilled, such as laborers, hawkers, woodchoppers, and barmen, to the more skilled, such as carpenters, painters, printers, and tailors. They were charged in Bow Street police court with stealing, willful damages, and riotous conduct.

London was in a state of alert for the next few days. As dense fog and frost settled, rumors of marauding crowds increased. On Monday evening, gangs of men were reported to be wandering down Cheapside and St. Martin's Lane. On Tuesday, an attempt to hold a meeting in Trafalgar Square fizzled out for lack of leadership, though not before shopkeepers panicked and closed their doors, unprecedented steps. Home Office Undersecretary Godfrey Lushington said that to deal with the "possibility of fresh attempts being made to disturb the public peace," troops were being kept at hand to augment the civil forces if necessary.[18]

By Wednesday, February 10, things had reached their worst point. An unfounded rumor swept through the city that ten thousand men were marching from Deptford to London, ransacking property as they proceeded; other groups were said to be starting down from the poor areas of Whitechapel, Bethnel Green, and Camden Town, all in a pea-soup fog. "All the shops closed," the *Times* reported, "and the people stood at their doors straining their eyes through the fog for the sounds of the 10,000 men."[19] A chance visitor would have been astonished to see the unlikely sight of an empty London, a ghost town in the middle of the day, windows boarded up. Troops were ready at Chelsea Barracks, a magistrate was at hand to read the Riot Act, and the entire London police force was on alert. But there were no major crowds, just spectators waiting around to catch some action.

London reacted as if Napoleon himself had marched in. Citizens, press, police, and government were thrown into a state of anxiety, though many pointed out things were not all that bad. The tearing down of the Hyde Park rails in 1855, considered fearsome at the time, said the *Times*, seemed minor in comparison with "the wholesale destruction of property and the looting of shops" that had just occurred. [20] The English had viewed socialism with "dry grins" in 1884, but "in 1885 they seemed suddenly to realize these Socialists were in earnest . . . and after THEIR PROPERTY"—and by 1886, the dry grin was gone.[21] When Hyndman told Sir William Harcourt that troubled times were ahead, Harcourt had shrugged off the warning. "Well, it may be so," said Sir William, "but for my part I don't believe in any great popular discontent until I hear of ricks on fire and factories in flames." Apparently Harcourt had forgotten that London had few ricks and industrial factories.

At the heart of it all lay a concern for order. Nothing, said the papers grandly, could justify disruption. "Free speech and liberty of action are precious things; but order is sacred and it may become necessary to forbid pre-emptorily great gatherings of people in places or under circumstances where disturbances are certain to ensue," the *Standard* said.[22] The *Spectator* concurred: "discussion should not be limited but it ought not to be legal in London to use menaces against order, or to intimate that force would ultimately be found the remedy for social disorders. . . . Order is the very breath of life."[23]

That might be what drove Lord Walter Campbell to write to the *Gazette* that he was stocking up on Remington rifles: "It is but the beginning of the 'Divine mission from on high'—revolution . . . [that] must be taken hold of by ourselves."[24] He may well have read Matthew Arnold's gloomy 1875 warning that the Englishman's "right to do what he like . . . tends to anarchy."[25] His father Thomas had told him the only sensible course was to follow the Romans, flog the protestors, and "fling the ringleaders from the Tarpeian Rock!" Even legitimate protest should be to avoided, said Arnold, because it could end in riot: "monster processions in the streets and forcible irruptions into the parks . . . ought to be unflinchingly forbidden and repressed. . . . Because a State in which law is authoritative and sovereign, a firm and settled course of public order, is requisite if man is to bring to maturity anything precious and lasting now."[26]

Apparently the Philistines were listening. The *Times* considered Black Monday "a work of disaster and shame such as London has not known within living memory."[27] As in the case of the 1855 riots, the attack on middle- and upper-class property alarmed a metropolis unused to such attacks. Even the SDF felt the situation had gotten out of hand: "Social Democrats and English workers generally are not given to rapine and plunder, nor is it by such means that an organized Revolution can be brought about," was the SDF policy line.[28] The Fabians and Socialist League voiced disapproval of the tactics, though they were pleased with the attention socialism and the issues had been afforded.

The Continent, beset by its own nationalist and liberal uprisings, enjoyed the denouement of the smug English. In Paris, Black Monday was seen as a bread riot, and—*mon dieu*—surprise was voiced that such a thing could occur in England.[29] In Berlin, the capital of *Kulturekampf* and order, a sudden sympathy developed for starving rioters. Queen Victoria feared for national respectability and wrote Gladstone of her indignation at the disgrace to London: "If steps and very strong ones are not speedily taken to put these proceeding down, with a high hand ... the Government will suffer severely. The effect abroad is already humiliating to this country and that this should take place *just* when a Liberal Radical Government comes in ...."[30]

The psychological effect of the riot was out of proportion to the destruction it produced. About a third of the damage claims were for under £30, and the total amount claimed was only £11,000.[31] One newspaper summed up the effect succinctly: "The damage done to property by the mob this week can hardly exceed the loss by an average night's fires in London; but the commotion caused among the well-to-do resulting from the escape of Socialist steam far exceeds that caused by the more destructive element."[32] The right-wing press condemned the troublemakers en masse, whereas the left wing was careful to distinguish the respectable demonstrators from the looters.[33] All took pains to try to identify the source of the trouble, curious to discover if the revolution was really on the way, noting that working men, employed and unemployed, were central to the drama.

The *Times*, always quick to paint crowds as rabble, reported construction workers, artisans, and unemployed dock laborers coming in from the suburbs.[34] The *Pall Mall Gazette* sketches of demonstrators showed "legitimate" working-class types,[35] perhaps mindful of the SDF and Labour and Socialist League members, a mixture of "roughs and respectably-dressed people."[36] Supt. Dunlap, "A" Division, felt the meeting "was composed of as rough a class as I have seen together of late years."[37] Police assumed by people's dress that the crowd represented the "submerged third" of London.[38] One Londoner at Monday's events, connected with a charitable institution in Seven Dials, characterized protestors as 30 percent working men, 10 percent socialists, 10 percent curiosity, and 30 percent thieves and rogues.[39] When John Burns asked the crowd haw many were unemployed, nearly all the crowd held their hands up.[40] The SDF newspaper, *Justice*, was careful to point out that the mischief was done by "hangers on," not the regular Social Democrats.[41]

In the shifting late Victorian political sands, those on either side saw the event as evidence of a bifurcated city, a reminder of Disraeli's "haves" and "have-nots" four decades earlier and the proof of a breakdown of law and order. Along Pall Mall, St. James Street, and Piccadilly, "the rich men crowded to the windows to see the poor men pass along; and Dives, not noticing the absence of the police, mocked Lazarus," George Bernard Shaw acidly noted. He felt Londoners had overreacted: "Lazarus thereupon broke Dives's windows, and even looted a shop or two, besides harmlessly storming the carriage of a tactless lady near the Achilles statue."[42]

In interpreting Black Monday as the prelude to class warfare, some pointed out the insult of the crowd being attacked by missiles thrown by servants at the Reform Club. Breaking windows may have been accepted as a hallmark of English crowds, but looting was unacceptable, as socialist Belfort Bax reminded them, even if it was a protest against the social organization rooted in capitalism.[43] Violence was directed at property, no one was killed, and injuries were minor. What was shocking was the inability of police to cope, the absence of government leadership, and the idea that the city could be attacked from within. The Black Monday riot brought home the possibility that Marx and Engels might be on to something, that revolution might be possible, that society and government had failed. Victorian society "worked well so long as the sky was the limit,"[44] but once conditions were not so favorable, the cracks in the foundation appeared. The familiar and domestic was changing: wealth, as Disraeli's 1872 Crystal Palace speech suggested, was to be found not at home but abroad; humans, Darwin had suggested in 1859, were only a few steps away from the apes; and the genteel, separate sphere of the middle-class woman coexisted with revelations that the white slave trade existed in the heart of the capital of Empire.

Fear and anger from Black Monday also produced a boost for funds for the needy. At a time when charity was to be given only to the deserving, the riot drove home the reality of poverty in a tangible way. The Mansion House Fund suddenly received thousands of pounds in contributions. On Monday, February 15, the Lord Mayor announced that of the £132,000 in the Fund, £29,000 had been received in the previous five days. Both business and individual donors were eager to have their names appear on the daily lists printed in the *Times*.[45] Socialists pointed out that cowardice rather than compassion motivated the contributions, but they produced some hyperbolic numbers to prove this with a great deal of self-righteousness.[46] The avalanche of money met with criticism from another corner, the established philanthropies, who disapproved of the unfettered funds, with the powerful Charity Organization Society calling the fund positively harmful.

THE DODO OF SCOTLAND YARD

The police and government took the blame for failing to prevent the riots, and accusations of incompetence masked the unwillingness of many to believe that social distress was severe enough to precipitate a riot. F. M. Stuart-Wortley's letter was typical:

> Surely, sir, the responsibility which justly rests immediately on Hyndman and his fellows for these scandalous proceedings should be shared to some extent by those more highly placed, who have for many years now supported the system of advancing popular demands by monster meetings in thoroughfares which are quite as much an opportunity for the criminal classes for plunder as they are for the deserving for the ventilation of their just grievances.[47]

Meanwhile, Londoners turned on the police and began an attack that resulted in two Parliamentary investigations as well as the appointment of a new commissioner. The force was charged with incompetence, the commissioner called irresponsible, and the Home Office accused of negligence. It was the most devastating criticism the police had borne in decades.

The most satisfactory scapegoat, though, was the longstanding commissioner, Sir Edmund Henderson, former officer in the Royal Engineers, who was appointed to office in 1869. The *Pall Mall Gazette* started a campaign on the "Dodo of Scotland Yard"—the fat and useless bird a metaphor for the police, whom they charged with ineptitude,[48] impotence, and inability in coping with mobs.[49] After the panic on Wednesday, the dodo transformed into a "bubbly-jack which strutted and rattled and stamped and made its guttural gobble all over the metropolis yesterday, with the most alarming result." Mr. Hyndman was "a mere infant as a panic produced compared with Sir Edmund Henderson."[50]

Nor were these charges unfounded. "For heaven's sake, Burns, keep control of this meeting, for we can't," was what one inspector was reported to have said to John Burns.[51] Across the board, the London press, including the *Times*, *Gazette*, *Daily News*, *Morning Advertiser*, *Daily Telegraph*, and *Morning Post*, agreed that the police had failed and their leaders were directly responsible for the damage. The *Saturday Review* credited the origin of the "No-Police Riots" to the "scandalous mismanagement of the chiefs of police."

The man who had to answer publicly to these chargers was Home Secretary H. C. E. Childers, who had taken office the very day of the riots. Excuses for his lack of action were judged lame.[52] "After rioting actually began," said the *Times*, after a week of mulling it over, "there was ample opportunity for an energetic Home Secretary to rouse up the fossils of Scotland Yard and put down the disturbance."[53] Ever since the founding of the Metropolitan Police, the question of who was responsible for determining policies had been unclear. Black Monday was a mistake the Home Office did not want credit for, as it was at best a source of great embarrassment. The solution was typical—shift blame and find a scapegoat. Home Secretary Childers found his in Police Commissioner Sir Edmund Henderson.

Childers sleekly extricated himself from blame during debate in the Commons on February 18. Eleven notices of questions were put to him, concerning absence of police preparations, failure of police to stop the riot, police misbehavior, precautions for future meetings, faulty communications between the Home Office and the police, and culpability of the Home Office itself. Sir Robert Peel spoke for majority sentiment in the Commons and Lords when he said the riots were a "disgrace to the Metropolis and a discredit to the Police Force."[54] Childers's response was to reiterate that he had been assured by his predecessor that all necessary arrangements had been made.

But it was just that predecessor, Sir Richard Ashton Cross, who pointedly challenged Childers's remarks. Childers stated there was a misconception about the Home Office–police relationship, as the February 8 events were "purely under the responsibility of the Chief Commissioner" and had little to do with the Home Office.[55] The Home Office, he said, dealt with the police as the Secretary of State for War dealt with the army, offering only financial and administrative oversight. That statement proved to be a bombshell, striking at the heart of the nation's view of how the police were run. Sir Richard's astonishment at Childers's statement revealed the deep-seated belief that the police never were, and never would be, an independent force operating without political and directive input from the government. Most believed the government would always be accountable for police actions, whether successes or failures.

Cross said he had "constant communications with the police" during his tenure as Home Secretary. Childers remained unmoved: "I have asked the officials at the Home Office and Scotland Yard, and they both tell me that during the progress of a meeting it is not customary that communications should pass between Scotland Yard and the Home Office."[56] No one asked him about communications during a riot. He did admit that during the 1884 Reform Bill demonstrations, information was sent at regular intervals, and during the Parliamentary hearings it came out that Cross had asked for telegrams to be sent to him at his club every half hour during other disturbances.[57]

The redoubtable permanent undersecretary, Godfrey Lushington, whose hand could often be seen behind every decision, affirmed Childers's position. Lushington's comments were usually heeded and his advice to Secretaries of State usually adopted, and much of the police correspondence was handled solely by Lushington. He wrote Childers on February 21 advising him to take an early opportunity of "disabusing the public mind of the error ... that the Secretary of State is personally responsible for the Police Orders" at public meet-ings.[58] The confusion and conflicts over accountability became even worse. The police were subject to the will of the Secretary of State but "the Commissioner fully admits the responsibility is with him" and "issues the orders on his sole authority," with orders sent to the Home Office for record-keeping purposes only.[59] While conferences between the Home Secretary and the commissioner may on occasion take place as an assurance and messages sent for that purpose, Lushington added, that was the limit of their scope. Only the commissioner knew how to deal with crowds, though Lushington did say in very rare cases a military-minded secretary might interfere. "Any division of responsibility . . . is incompatible with the public safety."[60]

Given the blame game, the obvious response was to investigate. The Select Committee on the "Origin and Character of the Disturbances . . . " consisted of Childers, a Liberal MP and former First Lord of the Admiralty (1864–1865) and Secretary of State for War (1880–1882); Viscount Wolseley, Conservative MP, lieutenant general in the army, and former governor of Cyprus; Edward Cav-endish, Liberal MP, magistrate and deputy-lieutenant, from Derbyshire; H. T. Holland, Conservative MP, barrister, vice president of the committee on edu-cation, and a former charity commissioner (1866); C. T. Ritchie, Conservative MP, secretary of the Admiralty in 1885, and president of the Local Government Board in 1886; and prison expert E. Ruggles-Brise, who served as secretary of the committee. Tories were gleeful at the chance to attack Liberals. Earl For-tescue called Childers "unmoved and indifferent, like the gods described by Lucretius."[61]

After hearing only twenty-eight witnesses, the February 22 report evisce-rated the police, singling out specific officers and recommending an investiga-tion into the entire force.[62] The central criticism was blunt: "had the police authorities shown greater resource, acting upon a good and well-understood system," the "inconceivable events would have been avoided."[63] Much of the criticism focused on the absence of clear rules for crowd control and the ne-cessity for clear and permanent policies to be formulated. Police had made no dispersion arrangements, had not sent out warnings by telegraph to West End police (because no one at Scotland Yard knew what was happening), had not used mounted patrols, and had displayed poor judgment. The assistant com-missioner should have sent out reserves at once instead of trying to seek out the commanding officer in the square, who wasn't found. The district superin-tendent was useless because he was in plain clothes. An inspector Knight had failed to stop the mob in Arlington Street after it had wrecked St. James Street. An officer was wasted at Buckingham Palace once it was obvious the mob was not headed there. And the misheard order to send men from the Barracks to Pall Mall wouldn't have worked anyway.

This report was the most devastating the London Metropolitan Police had ever received, and Commissioner Henderson's demise was assured. The Tories saw Black Monday as a law-and-order watershed; for them, it was a matter of establishing the dominance of national government in such circumstances. A noteworthy criticism was Henderson's failure to notify the Home Secretary, who could have called up the military. Tory hearts were calmed by the idea the army would intervene, but such intervention is likely to have escalated tension rather than calmed it. The criticism also revealed a "damned if you, damned if you don't" attitude that has plagued police up to the present. The commissioner was criticized for not being independent and using poor judgment; at the same time, he was criticized for not sufficiently relying on the Home Office for help.

For the first time in half a century, changes were suggested in the administration, structure, and personnel of the force, and it was the first time the controversial and sensitive issue of using troops for controlling riots was made the subject for public debate. The mere suggestion of troops highlights both Tory and Liberal preoccupation with the need to maintain order at whatever cost. The report reflected the new political dynamics between the old establishment and the new working-class politics. As long as socialists, communists, and trade unionists had not posed a serious threat, they had been tolerated. But when their message became popular, public order seemed threatened, and measures had to be taken to limit their roles.

The second Parliamentary Committee suggested that an underpaid, undereducated, and understaffed force was a problem in itself. As Robert Peel had warned in 1829, good men were hard to come by at 19s a week.[64] Of the seven points of criticism, the first was an insufficient number of officers of superior rank and education, the source of the poor judgment displayed at Black Monday. District superintendents should be replaced with "chief constables" who were "gentlemen of good social standing" and former officers of the army or navy.[65] The report noted the absence of effectual inspection of stations by superior officers and a defect in the chain of responsibility. There were insufficient mounted officers and an inefficient telegraph system. It also said regulations for public meetings had to be clarified and disseminated.

Meanwhile, the confused relationship between the Home Office and the police was not clarified. While the "primary responsibility of dealing with all states of disturbance" should rest with the police commissioners, "in all cases of grave or abnormal character the Home Office should be promptly informed of circumstances as they occur." Memoranda were sent by Childers to the Police

Commissioner on July 30, 1886, and again on December 24, 1887, reaffirming the police commissioner's authority. Interference from the Home Secretary would only be in "abnormal or grave" occurrences, since it would be "undesirable to derogate from the plenary responsibilities of the Commissioner."[66]

After seventeen years as commissioner, Henderson resigned when the first Select Report was issued.[67] Because the position of commissioner was an almost sacrosanct lifetime post, this was not the kind of shakeup anyone would have anticipated. Childers emphasized that he had "always endeavoured to exclude party politics from administration" and picked as possible successors four men whose appointments would not be considered political.[68] After his first choice, Sir Revers Buller, declined, he chose the law-and-order candidate, Sir Charles Warren. It proved a regrettable choice.

Reorganization of the force was the least of the government's worries. West End merchants were incensed over the failure to control order and pressed the Home Office for compensation and Scotland Yard with complaints about the failure of police to protect property.[69] Their ire only increased when it turned out that they were not eligible for compensation. Earlier in the century, local authorities, the "hundred," had been made liable for damages to buildings, furniture, and goods,[70] but only if a felony were committed. For that to happen, the Riot Act would have had to be read, which was not the case on February 8.

Black Monday produced the first major legal reform regarding compensation for damages during riots and cemented the notion of governmental responsibility. This reform took into account both the loss of potential revenue because of suspension of shopping hours and direct monetary loss. For a commercial center, this was critical. London on the eve of the Queen's Jubilee was a consumer's paradise, where "on every available yard of wall, advertisements clamoured to the eye: theaters, journals, soaps, medicines, concerts, furniture, wines, prayer-meetings."[71] More than two hundred merchants, tradesmen, and residents vented their "indignation" on February 9 under the leadership of W. H. Smith, scion of the book and stationery world. Smith declared that a truly unemployed and hungry crowd could not have committed such damage, and Lord Dorchester nostalgically looked back at the law-and-order days of Wellington in 1848.[72]

Shopkeepers stressed their loss of confidence in authorities and demanded government compensation for losses. The speed with which Parliament passed an innovative law providing compensation for damages during civil disturbance highlights the new primacy of order. It was a de facto statement of the "contract": authorities would keep the peace or pay up. The February Compensation Act was followed by the broadly constructed Riot Damages Act of 1886, which provided that damages be paid out of the police rate, a sure sign of police responsibility for order.[73]

The merchants were mollified by money, but their desire to punish leaders of the disorder led to disastrous results. Home Secretary Childers took the unusual and ill-advised step of prosecuting the protest leaders for sedition, which was a fiasco for the government.[74] Sedition is difficult to prove under English law; the government might as well prosecute Randolph Churchill for stirring up civil war in Ireland, Annie Besant sourly noted.[75] The socialists were delighted with their martyr role, Hyndman gloated. "I cannot but know that the effect of the prosecution would be to greatly strengthen our cause. . . . It always has been so and always will be," he said, adding, "*Sub pondere crescit.*"[76]

At face value, the trial was a victory for free speech, proof that Dod Street was worth the trouble. Hyndman and Champion defended themselves, William Thompson (later editor of *Reynold's*) defended Burns and Williams, and Attorney General Sir Charles Russell prosecuted at the April 8 Old Bailey trial before Justice Cave. Burns dramatically said, "I am a Rebel, because Society has outlawed me," an arrow aimed straight at the heart of every liberal-minded Englishman.[77] To the dismay of the daily press (with the exception of the *Gazette*), the verdict on April 10 was not guilty, which socialists ascribed to the presence of "one or two good men on the jury," notably a Christian Socialist.[78] Hyndman thanked the government for elaborate propaganda "we could not have purchased for fifty thousand pounds."[79]

The verdict was a victory for civil liberties and a reaffirmation of the rights of free speech and assembly. Such a victory, however, also frightened a large sector of the city, which feared that unleashing the rhetoric of change could produce violent results. London was now not only a center of commerce and culture but also a center for change—and a potentially radical one at that. The socialist press warned that "undoubtedly during the last forty years society has learned that when the many headed mob means to have anything it will get it if the heads be only sufficiently numerous. . . . Society can see as well as we do that all the combustible elements are grouped together so closely that even spontaneous ignition is not impossible."[80]

The immediate effect was a backlash—a move to reaffirm law and order at its strictest. As the Fabian E. R. Pease said, "public opinion was justified in regarding Socialism as destructive and disorderly than as constructive."[81] Engels thought that the unemployed who followed Hyndman were "the masses of the Lumpenproletariat, whom Hyndman had taken for the unemployed." Engels chided Hyndman: "Shouting about revolution . . . is utter nonsense here among the totally unprepared masses. . . . It absolutely cannot be understood here an anything but a summons to looting."[82] Even worse, it produced one of the most repressive campaigns against free speech and assembly ever in Great Britain.

The political transformations in this quarter century cemented the use of London's parks as public free-speech forums and established some inviolable tenets. By 1886, Marble Arch had become the world-famous Speaker's Corner, "a favourite rendezvous of organised crowds, holding 'demonstrations' in favour or disfavour of some political idea or measure."[83] Fueled by midcentury liberalism, public meetings had become the means to establish the "validity of the argument for free discussion," an antidote to the "mischief of denying a hearing to opinions."[84] Between 1866 and 1886, meetings were hardly considered objectionable, even when the subject was unpleasant: "So quiet, indeed, are our daily London meetings, even when attended by roughs, that a 'policy of non-intervention' has been formulated, and it is held as a theory indisputable by sensible men that no meeting is dangerous until it is interfered with."[85]

SABER RATTLING

For the next eighteen months, the perceived threat to law and order produced abrupt changes. They encompassed all aspects of urban life: a new militaristic police commissioner, a crackdown on public meetings, the emergence of a free-speech lobby, new sensitivities to the business community, reorganization of the police, judicial remedies for disorder, a reinterpretation of the role of public spaces, and a public backlash in favor of civil liberties.

The appointment of Charles Warren as Metropolitan Police Commissioner on April 3 confirmed the fears that had blocked Peel's formation of the police force for years—the creation of a quasi-military force. Warren was a former general who had served in Egypt, Bechuanaland, and at Suakin, and his strong-arm techniques in handling public protest became apparent within a month. Home Secretary Childers was disingenuous when he said he was apolitical in his selection of a new police chief; he had obviously chosen the most conservative of candidates, one with military training, to use specifically for the control of public order. "I think that we have seen the worst of the Socialist meetings," the Home Secretary prophesized.[86]

Warren immediately directed his men to arrest speakers at meetings that were interpreted to be obstructive. He did so with the sanction of the government, which later acknowledged such a policy was not legal.[87] The Queen applied pressure on both Childers, whom she felt was "frightened at his shadow," and Warren to watch out for socialists, especially after April riots by Belgian socialists.[88] Oxford Street shops, Strand taxpayers, the Royal College of Physicians, bankers, and hoteliers kept up pressure on the police to stop West End meetings. A memorial from them on October 22, 1887, called "attention to the great danger and loss caused to our business" by the meetings, and asked that they be prevented,"[89] and the large business losses of upholsterers, traders, silversmiths, picture galleries, and opticians were cited as proof of the need to ban public meetings.[90] One high-ranking officer concurred: "I do not think meetings of this kind should be permitted in . . . such localities, for however strong and efficient the Police may be it is practically impossible to prevent some slight damage to property."[91]

For socialists, radicals, and even liberals, the result was a new burst of activism. Annie Besant, who cofounded the Law and Liberty League in reaction to Warren's policies, commented that Warren "thought it his duty to dragoon London meetings after the fashion of Continental prefects, with the inevitable result that an ill-feeling grew up between the people and the police."[92] William Morris angrily suggested that Warren "was put into Col. Henderson's place after the Trafalgar Square riots that he might make a stroke on us by driving our propaganda out of the streets."[93]

During this sudden struggle over the right of free speech and assembly, antagonism to police grew, and along with it support for socialists. The more the police tried to repress meetings, the larger they grew. When the socialists informed the police on February 17, 1887, that they would be holding a large meeting in Hyde Park on February 21, Scotland Yard panicked.[94] About seventy-five thousand people showed up on a very cold Sunday, with plenty of police and MPs to monitor the orderly meeting.[95] The only disruption occurred when mounted police tried to discharge the crowd from the park. "The policemen charged furiously among the quiet and peaceful assembly. The man standing next to me was felled like a log," reported one bystander.[96]

Open-air meetings increased in size and number in 1886. By the week of June 26, eighteen meetings had been held by the SDF alone, while the National Secular Society held gatherings in Hyde Park, Camberwell Green, Paddington, and Waltham Green Railway Station in a single week. The streets, said William Morris, were the people's drawing room, and the people had to decide whether the police would be their servants or masters.[97] Only the leftists encountered problems, and their arrests often resulted in dismissal in court.

That was not the fate of socialist H. H. Champion on July 4. While speaking at Kilburn Road, police told him he was obstructing the thoroughfare. He moved the platform so that the footway was clear and cabs could pass, but Champion was arrested anyway, along with three others, including John Williams.[98] Found guilty at Middlesex Sessions, Williams was made into a martyr, with a sentence of two months' imprisonment. Sir Charles Warren had testified that police were ordered to stop meetings at their discretion only after complaints of inconvenience, not as a general policy. Socialists called the trial a sham and used it for propaganda.[99] "It can never be too strongly insisted that through the maintenance of absolute freedom of speech and press lies the only hope that our country may escape the horrors of a revolution of violence," predicted *Justice*.[100] The instinctive public reaction was to rally around the cause. Attendance increased at socialist meetings at Bell Street and Harrow Road, and confrontations continued between the police and public.

Trafalgar Square remained the *bete noir*, however. Police bristled at an attempt to organize a mock procession during the Lord Mayor's Day parade in November 1886, and Warren prohibited the event. Shopkeepers boarded up their windows. The counterdemonstration fizzled in the rain, but police arrested labor activist Tom Mann and two SDFers. A follow-up demonstration on November 21 garnered fifty thousand but was quiet.[101]

Things heated up with the advent of the Jubilee Year, the celebration of the Queen's fiftieth anniversary on the throne. With the economy still in trouble, socialists denounced the "Jingo Jubilee" and called it circuses without bread. Ill-fed and badly clothed people marched to St. Paul's every Sunday that winter, tolerated by police until March, when their numbers swelled to ten thousand with the warmer weather. This was a labor crowd, with contingents from Limehouse, Canning Town, Hackney, Battersea, Paddington, Kensal Green, Chelsea, Fulham, and Bermondsey. Skirmishes between police and marchers occurred constantly, and at the *sanctum sanctorum*, Marble Arch, crowds were hustled by police for blocking the paths.

The crisis increased with the arrest of John Williams during an April melee. Physical violence had been on the rise between socialists and Tories.[102] Following a fight between police and a crowd in Hyde Park, Williams and five others were sentenced to six months' hard labor. The press erupted into a fusillade of charges against the police and government for abrogation of free speech. Socialists complained that "we are being exposed to bad treatment at the hands of constables and magistrates all over London, and we are informed by policemen ... who sympathized with us ... that this is only the beginning of an organized campaign against us, with the view to the suppression of our meeting altogether."[103]

The Commons debated the conflict between civil liberties and public order. Metropolitan MPs Stuart (Shoreditch), Pickersgill (Bethnal Green), Rowlands (Finsbury), and Cremer (Shoreditch) felt the sacred right of public meeting had been violated. They were joined by MPs Bradlaugh and Cunninghame Graham in placing the chief blame for the "coercion policy" upon the Home Secretary.[104] London MPs found the increased suppression issue full of potential conflict, since they also commonly used local open spaces as forums for discussion with their constituency and as safety valves for discontent.

MPs pointed to an arrest for unlawful assembly on Sancroft Street in May 1887 as evidence that civil liberties could too easily be breached. The arrest should not have occurred: it violated an 1882 court decision that a meeting did not become unlawful simply because those calling the meeting knew it might cause a breach of the peace.[105] Home Secretary Matthews's defense of police action as necessary to clear the streets appeared weak next to the seriousness of some of the charges. Socialists were stopped because their doctrines were unpopular, said an angry Cunninghame Graham: "England is a free country . . . but it appears in the future it is not going to be a free country to hold public meetings in. What with the closure in the House of Commons, Coercion in Ireland, and the suppression of meetings in London we are getting to an almost Russian pitch of freedom."[106] Bradlaugh told Matthews he'd show him two hundred to three hundred meetings on any Sunday morning, on busy streets, by street preachers who were not bothered with.[107]

BLOODY SUNDAY, 1887

Queen Victoria's year of the Jubilee was not just a celebration of fifty years on the throne but of "fifty years of Progress. National Progress, without precedent in the history of mankind! One may say, indeed, Progress of the Human Race. Only think what has been done in this half-century: only think of it! Compare England now, compare the world, with what it was in 1837. It takes away one's breath!"[108] But the celebration came with its ironies—the unemployed camped in Trafalgar Square and washed in its fountains. And the London of 1887 was the place of conflict between police and crowd, where "the burly guardians of order dealt thwacking blows, right and left, sound fisticuffs, backed with hearty oaths."[109]

Bloody Sunday marked a low point in English history, a retreat from ideals and an abandonment of principles in the face of threats to law and order, and a breach of basic legal precepts. Occurring the same week as the execution of the Chicago Haymarket anarchists, its significance was due not only to its casualties—three dead and scores injured—than the manner in which the courts, government, and press handled the case. As William Morris said, "it will be a disgrace to the British workmen . . . if they do not express themselves clearly and emphatically on this attack on the liberties which the U.S. have been supposed to guard so jealously."[110] In London, Bloody Sunday kindled a furious debate over who had "rights" to the city, who could use its spaces, and who could say what in public. It also sparked a new cognizance of civil liberties as an issue in and of itself.

By the autumn of 1887, Warren's heavy-handed tactics had brought a call for his resignation from a wide sector of the public. Called by one MP a "psalm-singing, sanctimonious swashbuckler,"[111] he ordered arrest at the least provocation; even a reporter and a Tory MP did not escape.[112] "It is quite clear," said a Bow Street magistrate, in heavily sentencing protestors from an October meeting, "that when crowds assemble in Trafalgar Square with flags and shouts such as were used they must alarm and terrify people."[113] The apology and rationale for irregularities in police conduct, explained a *Spectator* article, was that caution must be thrown to the winds for maintenance of order in the metropolis.[114] The leftist press could express only exasperation: the police were caricatured "as the foreigner in Leech's woodcut, who shoots the foxes and the owls instead of the pheasants."[115]

In the month before Bloody Sunday, Trafalgar became the central battleground. The beautiful square, London's great meeting hall, was also the center of business and government, a symbol of empire and conquest, and a psychological threat when filled with large crowds. Warren's policy was to lump all the protestors together, whatever the issue, including socialists, radicals, freethinkers, Irish nationalists, and Liberals. The initial support of Liberals was the most important in that it won over some middle-class support for public speech.[116] But when socialists attempted to proselytize to the "sleepers" in Trafalgar with midnight speeches, police decided to evict the homeless, who had been left alone up to this point.

So severe was police harassment that it fueled the creation of an organization to deal with free speech. Police began not only to block meetings and disperse crowds but actually to charge them. In October, a furious crowd in Hyde Park turned on police when told to disperse; the arrest of Alfred Oldland, an unemployed painter, caught the attention of Annie Besant, political activist.[117] She and Stewart Headlam (of the Socialist Guild of St. Matthew) started a formal defense fund, with the initial purpose of providing bail money, called the Law and Liberty League (see chapter 7).

The lack of a clear policy on the permissibility of holding Trafalgar Square meetings contributed to the imbroglio. The multiplicity of orders emanating from Commissioner Warren's office during November shows that even he was unsure of the legal boundaries. On November 2, a proclamation stated that processions would be allowed as long as they were peaceful and unobstructive. To confuse matters further, they also said there was no right to meet but "no instructions can be given to prevent the assembly of such a meeting," even for illegal purposes, "except upon sworn information showing it to be an illegal meeting."[118] The inconsistency in Trafalgar Square policy was apparent, as meetings on October 11, 15, 16, 23–31, and November 1–3 were allowed, those of October 14, 17, 18, November 4 dispersed, and on November 6 the morning meeting dispersed and the afternoon meeting allowed.[119]

By November 8, the government had had enough. A police order, approved by the Home Secretary and the Board of Works commissioner, forbade all meetings and processions in Trafalgar Square. Repeated on November 12 with an injunction against a proposed meeting the next day, it noted that "whereas the holding of meetings and the passage of processions have caused and are liable to cause public tumult and disorder in Trafalgar Square, and have created, are liable to create, obstruction in the streets," no procession and "no meetings shall be allowed to assemble, nor shall any person be allowed to deliver a public speech in Trafalgar Square or in the Streets, or Thoroughfares adjoining or leading thereto."[120] There was no legal basis for any of these orders, but Matthews suffered, as the *National Reformer* had pointed out a month earlier, from the delusion that government had unlimited rights.[121]

Much of the daily press, fed up with the crowds in Trafalgar Square, approved of the order and interpreted it as the end of vacillation by government. Others, such as the *Pall Mall Gazette* and *Reynold's*, saw the step as ominous and as a threat to democracy, warning that if the railing had not gone down in 1866, the right to meet would have.[122] The *Gazette* paid a price for its principled stance. W. T. Stead, the crusading *Gazette* editor who "exposed" the white slave trade in London, said that "our stand regarding Trafalgar Square hit us in advertisements and also in circulation."[123] The *Daily Chronicle*, which had a larger and less upper-class circulation and which had backed Coercionist policies in Ireland, also chided Warren for interfering with public rights.[124]

Home Secretary Matthews tried to reduce the ominous quality of the proscription. In statements issued on November 11 to the *Standard* and the *Daily News*, he said he had no objection to bona fide meetings, since liberty of speech and public meeting were rights and privileges. But the meetings in question, he flatly stated, were not bona fide. Matthews even introduced the long-ignored fact that technically the Queen's permission was needed for meetings on Crown property such as Trafalgar. Matthews could not have chosen a less suitable remark for the occasion. The *Pall Mall Gazette* reminded its readers of the story of the king who wanted to close the parks: the cost, he asked? "Only three Crowns," was the reply.[125]

Bloody Sunday was a fiasco for the demonstrators, who had about as much chance of getting into Trafalgar Square as of laying hands on the Crown Jewels. A third of the Metropolitan Police Force was there, fifteen hundred in the square and twenty-five hundred in the immediate vicinity, along with three hundred mounted men. And by 4 p.m., three hundred Life Guards and three hundred Grenadier Guards carrying bayoneted rifles and twenty rounds of ball cartridges had joined them. As Shaw later said about Warren: "It was, as one of Bunyan's pilgrims put it, but a word and a blow with him; for the formal summons to disperse was accompanied by a vigorous baton charge, before which the processionists, outnumbering their assailants by a hundred to one, fled in the utmost confusion and terror."[126] Most of the crowd never made it to Trafalgar, but even so, there were about twenty thousand immediately around it, "respectable persons attracted to the spot out of curiosity" and "loafers and roughs, drawn chiefly from the lowest classes, youths of 17 or 18 predominating."[127] As fights broke out in Piccadilly, Convent Garden, the bottom of Wellington Street, Bloomsbury at Broad Street, and other places, the police availed themselves of refreshments offered by the Pall Mall clubs. The square was cleared by 7 p.m., with little in the way of physical damage.

By London standards it was bloody: seventy-five injuries were treated in Charing Cross Hospital, and an equal number went untreated. Three people were killed, and fifty arrests made.[128] The predominantly working-class crowd also represented a wide spectrum of social, age, and geographical backgrounds.[129] The most tense moment came when the two meeting leaders, John Burns and MP Cuninghame Graham, attempted to break through the police cordon and get into the square. The band turned back as staves were drawn and the two men arrested.[130] Warren's military triumph meant the whole thing ended in a matter of minutes: "our comrades fought valiantly, but they had not learned how to stand and turn their column into a line, or to march on to the front. . . . I confess I was astounded at the rapidity of the thing."[131] Warren's message had been that "the Radical workers of London as a whole are still little better than an unorganized mob."[132]

Women were not spared rough treatment. Eleanor Marx Aveling, who with her partner Edward had been active for years in the socialist battle, was struck by a truncheon, and Mrs. Taylor of the Socialist League was knocked down. Annie Besant related her experience: "As we were moving slowly and quietly along one of the narrow streets debouching on Trafalgar Square, wondering whether we should be challenged, there was a sudden charge, and without a word the police were upon us with uplifted truncheons; the banner was struck down and men and women were falling under a hail of blows."[133]

The effect of all this on protestors was disillusionment. "In our innocence," Lord Snell said of Black Monday in 1886, "we believed that these futile and angry demonstrations were the birth pangs of a new order, that England was indeed rising, and that 'the day was here.'"[134] By Bloody Sunday, that sentiment was gone, as long-cherished ideals were subjugated to the principle of public order. Rather than thousands transforming public squares into the Forums and Pnyxes of ancient democracies, "lean, hungry, hopeless men" led to a day of police triumph. As one bystander watched the "army of the unemployed passing on its way from the square to the City, their only standard a red handkerchief roughly tied upon a boom stick," he asked himself, "why does authority fear them? Are these the terrible unemployed at the mention of whom the West End shopkeeper shivers with fright behind his counter?"[135] The debacle at Trafalgar Square made George Bernard Shaw into a realist, and Edward Morris dropped his "Shelleyan" notions about the invincibility of undefended millions.[136]

Warren, captivated by his military triumph, swore in thousands of special constables in anticipation of a meeting the week after Bloody Sunday and advertised in the press that Trafalgar Square meetings were forbidden.[137] The Hyde Park protest rally the following Sunday attracted forty thousand people but was dismissed by much of the press: The *Illustrated London News* shows a straggly group, "an orator," "an old broom to sweep away coercion," "plenty of pluck but not much physique."[138]

Even Liberal leaders recanted free-speech issues in support of law and order. *Commonweal* presciently pointed out they were "Digging Their Own Grave," or at least the party's, by antagonizing the working-class constituency that should be following them but would instead go down other paths.[139] Most galling was Gladstone's blatant inconsistency regarding Coercion in Ireland and London, cartooned by *Punch* in the "The Grand Old Janus," which depicted a two-faced statue of Gladstone smiling upon a London bobby knocking down a man and frowning at an Irish officer doing the same thing.[140] On November 13, when Gladstone received a note from the Bermondsey Gladstone Club condemning police violence, he replied by stating the need for the complete disassociation of London from Irish affairs and for the respect due to law, police, and the decisions of the Executive government.[141]

The grim postscript to all this was the funeral procession of Alfred Linnell, a law writer who had received fatal injuries on November 20.[142] William Morris composed "A Death Song" for Linnell:

What cometh here from west to east awending?
And who are these, the marchers stern and slow?
We bear the message that the rich are sending

Aback to those who bade them wake and know.
Not one, not one, nor thousands must they slay,
But one and all if they would dusk the day.

The Law and Liberty League organized a monster procession to Bow Cemetery on December 18, with an estimated two hundred thousand following it. "From Wellington Street to Bow cemetery the road was one mass of human being, who uncovered reverently as the slain man went by," said Annie Besant, an organizer of the procession. "At Aldgate the procession took three-quarters of an hour to pass one spot, and thus we bore Linnell to his grave, symbol of a cruel wrong, the vast, orderly, silent crowd, bareheaded, making mute protest against the outrage wrought."[143] The coffin bore not only the dead man but also symbolized the mordant aspirations of the year's struggles. Free speech and assembly had taken a body blow. Linnell's funeral marked a somber ending for the Jubilee Year. To many, Bloody Sunday seemed the Thermopylae of English liberty, the triumph of class, crass, and lucre.

7

TAKING BACK TRAFALGAR

What a vision William Morris had in 1890 when he drew a picture of England in the year 2000: "We come presently into a large open space ... the sunny site of which had been taken advantage of for planting an orchard ... of apricot trees, in the midst of which was a pretty gay little structure of wood, painted and gilded, that looked like a refreshment stall.... A long road, chequered over with the shadow of tall old pear trees," completed the scene.[1] The bucolic if somewhat banal scene Morris was describing was Trafalgar Square.

Such a utopian vision was built not on a desire for a garden of Eden but upon the bitter realization that the square had little beneficial use as anything else. By 1890, when Morris's *News From Nowhere* was published, Trafalgar Square had been officially removed as a meeting place, and the right of public meeting was roiled in controversy. Aesthetically, Morris considered the square a monstrosity, but what drove him to plow it over in his novel was the disillusionment that emanated from the Black Monday–Bloody Sunday fiasco.

On the surface, 1886 and 1887 had been a triumph of order, an assertion of police hegemony, the mortification of popular protest, and the denial of civil liberties. On closer inspection, it was a turning point with far more positive results. Black Monday and Bloody Sunday created a self-conscious movement for civil liberties and a compelling debate about public space, which asserted freedom as inviolable within the city. The Law and Liberty League was the first association in England to be concerned solely with civil rights. During its short-lived existence, it became a paradigm for many groups that came into existence in the twentieth century to defend unpopular causes and protect free speech.

It also became clear that policy making was hobbled by political rivalries and factionalism, making it impossible for any consistent policies to emerge from either the Home Office, the police, or the Works Office. Tories and Liberals were so polarized that no compromise was possible. In addition, the Metropolitan Police had become embroiled in politics, their mission distorted and their credibility tarnished, by the Home Office. As government attempted to keep order in an increasingly contentious London, conflicts became harder to resolve.

Most perplexing was the legal framework surrounding public meetings. A host of regulations and legal decisions emanated from Black Monday and Bloody Sunday, but by the beginning of the twentieth century, there was no resolution of the issue. One pivotal issue was that of street obstruction: most parties agreed it could not be tolerated, but they could not agree at what point it occurred. Newspapers, parliamentarians, people on the streets, bureaucrats, and the police were all participants in the debate. At the end of the day, no matter how unruly the streets of London became, few people were willing to suspend the freedoms of speech and assembly. London ended the century with most rights restored and a vindication of the principles behind them.

The temporary crackdown on public meetings occurred as political dissent, imperial tensions, and labor politics peaked. In its last quarter century, Victorian England was one large soapbox upon which Everyman—and now Everywoman—held sway. Every issue was contested in the public sphere, whether it be vaccinations, vivisection, Ireland, imperial ambitions, women's rights, prostitution, or exploited labor. Deeply involved in this mix was Annie Besant, whose advocacy of birth control, match-girl strikes, and mystical religion equaled that which she gave to conventional politics. Eventually Besant, always phlegmatic, was consumed in 1887 with defending Bloody Sunday arrestees and joined with journalist W. T. Stead to take the helm of the Law and Liberty League.

"We seek the Temporal Salvation of the world," she announced dramatically in November 1887.[2] As regular meetings began in January 1888, its mission became clear: to defend free speech and meeting victims, to provide bail and prosecute appeals for victims, to pursue questions of popular rights and privileges on a legal plan, and to secure the continued and uninterrupted use of places currently used for public meeting. It published its own newspaper, the *Link*, for most of 1888.[3] She started "conversazione," informal conversations in Trafalgar Square, which were aimed at thwarting police intervention by their unconventional nature.[4]

The LLL's membership was a who's who of political activism. Forty-six associations sent representatives to the first meeting on January 25, 1888, including the SDF, the Socialist League, the Fabians, the Irish National League, and local Radical and Liberal clubs. At a preliminary meeting in November, the attendees came from journalistic, religious, and political roots: W. T. Stead, William

Saunders, Rev. S. Headlam, Rev. B. Waugh, Dr. Pankhurst, G. W. Foote, Jacob Bright, Annie Besant, Josephine Butler, William Morris, and Dr. Hunter, MP. G. O. Trevalyan and nineteen other MPs sent letters expressing their sympathy with the cause.

The LLL created what it had hoped would be a major celebration, when labor leader John Burns and MP Cunninghame Graham were released from their six-week jail sentences for unlawful assembly (they had been cleared of riot and assault charges). The defendants thought the verdict too harsh, the government thought it too lenient, and public opinion was mixed but mostly favored the verdict: it was viewed as either the end of mob law in the metropolis,[5] too mild a sentence,[6] somewhat harsh,[7] or a gag on free speech.[8]

The LLL saw the February 18, 1888, "coming-out" event as the start of the martyrdom of Burns and Graham, but the tea reception at Allen's Riding School the next day was a disaster. More than five thousand people tried to get into the reception, and deep ideological divisions among the celebrants emerged during the speechmaking. Pandemonium and fistfights broke out when SDF leader H. M. Hyndman started speaking.[9] "From one end of the Hall to the other turmoil and disturbance reigned supreme. I have been in a good many rough and tumble affrays in the course of my life, but never did I see anything much more dangerous than this."[10] Instead of cementing alliances, the Riding School tea marked the shattering of the tenuous allegiance formed among political groups over Trafalgar Square.[11] By the summer of 1888, the LLL began to falter from fractured support. Despite declaring that "the pot must be kept boiling in the Square," the LLL said no formal meeting or speeches should be held in the square.[12] For all practical purposes, Trafalgar Square dropped to the bottom of the LLL's agenda.

That was not the case in Parliament, which took on the issue of civil liberties, a phrase not popularly used in the nineteenth century nor commonly recognized as an issue by itself. Thus the two-day Commons debate in 1888 is particularly noteworthy for its focus on it.[13] The debate was kicked off by Sir Charles Russell's demand for an inquiry into the conditions of holding meetings and the limits and rights of intervention by the government. The inquiry request was defeated by a Tory majority of 316 to 224 Liberals, which also killed a request for an inquiry into the November 1887 events. The debate involved a large number of MPs and government officials but only eight of the sixty-one London MPs, and it shows how deeply imbedded notions of free speech and liberty were.[14]

The debate was driven by the question of how to resolve the clash between order and freedom. Russell's message was clear: the result of the unfettered use of public meeting in British society, he said, meant that revolution was effected without violence or crime, as was the case in other countries, "because this country has lived and thriven upon the breath of free public discussion."[15] The role of order was paramount in the mind of the Attorney General, who answered Russell's broad legal, historical, and constitutional approach coldly, concerned not with historical rights but with the chaotic effects of gross license. The reality, said Home Secretary Matthews, was that "the interests of public order required that that chronic malady of disorder near Trafalgar Square should be checked."[16]

Still, free speech and assembly remained the thread of the debate, as MPs insisted this superseded any legal interpretation. The right to assemble was termed "time-honored" by one MP; the newly released Cunninghame Graham called the right "inherent": "Would they [the demonstrators] have been worthy to be called Englishmen if they had failed to remonstrate?"[17] Tories pointed out that another tradition was threatened—the sanctity of London's monuments. Burdett-Coutts envisioned a rape of London's inner core by straggly and vicious mobs. Many argued that public meetings were safety valves for the masses, and some said that the government had panicked unnecessarily.

The debate also revealed conflicts over the increasingly militaristic nature of the Metropolitan Police, especially in the area of public order. Recent policies had "divorced [men] from sympathy with authority" and had caused ill will toward police.[18] Although no one wanted to see London in a state of chaos, the least hint that police were overstepping their authority produced a fear that the Continental gendarmerie were invading. "Matters had now reached the stage that the Chief Commissioner of Police mistook himself for a sort of *prefet*," said Bradlaugh."[19] Former Home Secretary William Harcourt warned that "you ought to teach the people to regard the police as their friends, but if you employ them to restrict what people regard as a just public right, then you turn the police from what they have been and from what they have always won respect as being, a civil force, into a body of gendarmes."[20]

The debate did little to settle the question of whether public meetings could be held as a right. Russell had admitted there was a right to prohibit meetings in general, leading some to puzzle over his advocacy of them and ensuring that meeting rights remained arbitrary.[21] The LLL concluded that the salient "question remains and presses for an answer: what are we to do?"[22] In 1888 and 1889, an abortive attempt was made by a Liberal-Radical coalition to answer that question by passing a Bill for the Regulation of Meetings in Trafalgar Square (1888).[23] The act would have set up guidelines for meetings, including no unlawful address, a notice of intent for allowed meetings signed by two householders two days prior, and addresses only in daylight and only in paved portions of the square, where no obstruction would be caused. The bill was dropped on the second reading in 1888 and withdrawn in 1889.

A second bill, the Public Meetings in Open Spaces Act, which would have established similar rules for all open spaces, also failed to pass. This bill sought to positively assert the "absolute and unassailable" right to meet in any open space that had been commonly in use for such a purpose for twenty years.[24] It would have set up the novel principle that the abuser of the law was not the person who held a meeting but the person who disrupted one.

Between 1888 and 1890, the political maelstrom over public meetings hit its apex, with Tories intransigent, Liberals incensed, and no clear policy visible. The government established the principle that it would not tolerate certain activities, but it never defined what those activities were. The public asserted that the expression of opinions—of any sort—was an inalienable right. Caught in the middle were the police, who were the ones who had to act when public order and personal rights collided. The debates were spirited: if the government could "give an assurance that the police should act within the law, and not like Bashi-Bazouks, there would be scenes of disorder and bloodshed in Trafalgar Square," said a Liberal MP.[25] The Home Secretary was steely in his contempt for those who would create disorder: "Saturday after Saturday Gentlemen who ought to know better went to Trafalgar Square, where they were surrounded of course by a mob consisting partly of idle persons and partly of sightseers drawn there by curiosity," he contemptuously said.[26]

Police said they would interfere in disorderly meetings, not orderly ones, but government never clarified the difference.[27] When asked why religious meetings were not disturbed, only political ones, Matthews answered that religious ones were small and neighborhood residents did not complain about them.[28] In June 1889, he refused to consider mitigation of a particularly severe sentence of five years for a stonemason involved in Bloody Sunday, a refusal made even in the light of questionable testimony from prosecutorial witnesses.[29] From 1889 through 1891, there were no permitted meetings in Trafalgar Square, although there were hundreds of meetings in the rest of London.

THE LEGAL RESPONSE

With the possibility for legislative action on public meetings dead and with gridlock over the right to hold meetings, the law became the last bulwark to ensure rights, and it proved to be unsatisfactory. In the few cases that dealt with free speech and assembly, the decisions were contradictory. While the century ended with a decision backing the right of public meeting, it did not resolve all the remaining questions and problems.

The hypocrisy of the government toward issues involving public meetings was infuriating. Obstruction could not be tolerated in the streets of London, said Home Secretary Matthews, but no one in government would clearly ban demonstrations. When the Home Secretary was accused in June 1890 of supporting "a policy that aims at destroying piecemeal all the great rights of public meeting in the metropolis," he replied by assuring the Commons of the right of usage of London's open spaces.[30] The accusation arose after the police commissioner had restricted a proposed procession of temperance associations from Thames Embankment to Hyde Park and police had refused to protect the procession. It was the closest thing to a general prohibition of processions the authorities had ever come to. The Radical-Liberal vanguard harped on the government's "terrible fear of the democracy" and its increasing similarity to Continental authoritarianism.[31] What incensed them most was not the idea that some regulation might be necessary for processions but that Police Commissioner Monro's "ukase" seemed based on doctrines "far too high."[32]

The legal battle shows how political these decisions could be. The Home Office used law officer's opinions and a couple of legal cases to justify their decisions, but these decisions were by no means defining; the more Trafalgar Square was used, the more polarized matters became. When the police commissioner banned the November 1887 meetings, the Home Office had cited the little-used legal standing of the square as Crown land. The law officers repeatedly said that assemblies not sworn by oath to be illegal could not be stopped.

In *R. v Graham*, the unlawful assembly case that put Burns and Cunninghame Graham in jail, the judge contradicted legal precedent by saying potential danger was a legitimate reason for prohibiting a meeting. This was the first time that a curb was suggested for the broadly interpreted right of public meetings. The judge said that Trafalgar Square was a place of public resort, used "from time to time" for public meetings without objection, but that there was "no right" to do so.[33]

The law-and-order atmosphere was obvious in the judge's assertion that the preservation of lives was at stake and any possible riot had to be prevented. This seems to be the rationale behind his blanket statement that any meeting was unlawful if any violence resulted, no matter what the intent of the meeting or who committed the violence. If demonstrators wanted to defy a police ban on meetings, he told the jury, then they were heading for unlawful assembly. This was alarming: "It may well be that an assembly which is perfectly innocent at one time may be riotous and unlawful at another, and although you may have gathered together with a most innocent intention, still, if while you are so gathered together you determine to do an act of violence, then you become a member of an unlawful assembly."[34]

Had this legal precedent stood, it would have effectively cut off most public meetings permanently, by giving the government unlimited discretionary powers. The other case that arose out of Bloody Sunday, *Ex parte Lewis*, enforced these principles but addressed more technical legal points. The case argued that the Home Secretary and the police commissioner had illegally banned the meeting, conspired to prevent Her Majesty's subjects from exercising their rights, endangered public peace, prevented the lawful use of a thoroughfare, and conspired to inflict bodily harm by excessive evidence.[35]

Ex parte Lewis also endorsed the idea of limited access to public space, asserting there is only a right of passage, and any assembly that is "to the detriment of others having equal rights, is in its nature unreconcilable with the right of free passage and there is . . . no authority whatever in favour of it."[36] In a shift, the court said that the H. M. Works Board, which had authority to maintain the square, also had the right to determine its usage, instead of the Home Office. Both of these decisions were reversed, along with the ban on meetings in the square, in 1892, and later clarified as policy. In 1904, correspondence between the Works Office and the Home Office acknowledged that the Works Office had "delegated their powers to the Commissioner of Police" in 1892.[37]

During the 1888 Commons debate, the suggestion that Trafalgar was Crown property and thus private had enraged several MPs, including Russell and Cunninghame Graham, who asked what "did the proletariat of London know of the legal aspect of the question." What was manmade law in the face of birthright, forcefully asserted the liberal Harcourt: the right of meeting was "a political right which has belonged for generations to the people of this country, not asserted in the Courts of law," a sentiment echoed by numerous MPs who said forty years of rights ought not to be nullified because of a few disorderly occasions. Harcourt called on his experience as Home Secretary to declare that "the conduct of the Government is in contradiction of every tradition that existed in the Home Office when I was there."[38]

Yet the standing Tory Home Secretary Matthews denied any right of meeting *de jure*: "I say that such a right does not exist in law or in fact." One MP said the events of 1886 had "materially altered" the character of Trafalgar Square meetings, necessitating the need for control. Another said public spaces such as these were for passage only: there is no legal support for "the proposition that in a public place set aside for the people to pass and repass and to enjoy it . . . there is a right of meeting or public speaking at all."[39]

The legal precedent did not support these two cases or the Tory stance. In *R. v. Inhabitant of East Mark*, it was decided that public dedication may be presumed against the Crown following long acquiescence in the public use.[40] Another case said the right of assembly on a village green was a recognized right that could be rescinded.[41] Trafalgar Square was an unusual case, however, complicated by the proliferating number of public processions. Many groups felt that marching through London's streets was the most effective way to voice their complaints. The 1868 Law Officers Opinion (see chapter 5) had included processions in its finding that a meeting's outcome did not determine its lawfulness. The first opinion solely about processions was in 1877, which took the opposite view: processions should be prevented to prevent the commission of an offense.[42] The dusting off of obscure or little-used statutes showed how political these decisions had become.

The other precedent dealing with illegal assembly concerned a religious issue rather than a political one. *Beatty v. Gilbanks* arose out of a Salvation Army procession at Weston-super-Mare. The anti–Salvation Army group, the Skeleton Army, ran a counterdemonstration, and a riot ensued. Booth's use of processions had effectively popularized his evangelical cause in the early 1880s. The liberal Harcourt said that processions, "not being illegal in themselves cannot in the absence of other circumstances be legally prevented," but he also said local magistrates had to keep the peace and could have discretion in disallowing processions if sworn testimony showed there would be disturbance.[43] In 1882, four Salvation Army men were convicted of assaulting constables who were trying to prevent them from holding a procession because the police feared a breach of peace would result, but the conviction was overturned on the grounds that the procession was legal and could not be stopped just because it might lead others to commit unlawful deeds.[44] In another case, the Salvation Army was acquitted of disturbing the peace after a crowd following its procession made a great deal of noise and caused a disturbance of the peace.[45]

The 1882 *Beatty* case established a core principle of public meeting, debated in both British and American law. The Salvation Army argued that their meeting was legal because their purpose was legal. The government, however, said any meeting likely to produce danger to the tranquility of a neighborhood is unlawful, regardless of purpose. The court's decision was that the object of the meeting is the critical point, not the outcome. A meeting for an illegal purpose, or one that endangers public peace and raises fear among people, is an unlawful assembly. Terror must subsist in the assembly itself, its object, or the methods of carrying it out. In this case, the disturbance was "caused by other people antagonistic to [the Salvation Army]" and "no acts of violence were committed by [the Salvation Army]." In *Beatty*, "an unlawful organization" (the Skeleton Army) tried to prevent lawful demonstrators from assembling, and the court cannot convict someone "for doing a lawful act if he knows that his doing it may cause another to do an unlawful act."[46]

By the late 1880s, a decade of processions by the Salvation Army and others had occurred with no interruption by police. There was no precedent for Home

Secretary Matthews's new policy of stopping them on the grounds they caused street obstruction. The majority of Londoners disapproved of processions, he said, because they "do not afford to the eyes and ears of the public any gratification to compensate for the interference with the free passage along the streets which is the common right."[47] His hard-line position caught the public eye when he prosecuted the "Captain Amy" case, in which a Salvation Army woman was imprisoned for pulling aside a vehicle that was on the wrong side of the road in order to avoid causing injuries from a procession.

An 1888 case chipped away at the right of procession. In *Homer v. Cadman*, the court ruled that a man addressing a crowd from a chair on a highway caused obstruction even though traffic could still get by. It made the road "less convenient and commodious to the public."[48] While maintaining the prima facie lawfulness of procession, the justice took the position that "the reasonableness of a procession must be judged primarily from the standpoint of the interest of the public and not from that of the members of the procession."[49] The Home Office stopped short at requiring permission be given in advance for processions, as was the case in New York (see chapter 9), but by 1890 it did require that the police be told in advance of these events in order to regulate them by prescribing routes.

The reopening of Trafalgar Square for meetings started in 1890, when police, under Home Office pressure, relaxed the ban. "Trafalgar Square (the flagged part) is not a public thoroughfare.... Meetings are, strictly speaking, on sufferance; but as long as they are permitted, no Police intervention can take place on the ground of obstruction within the Square."[50] As relations between the Home Secretary and the police commissioner deteriorated, the Home Secretary told the commissioner he was uneasy regarding police interference with Friendly Society parades: I hope "you will not commit yourself today to a policy of prohibition," as the law regarding Trafalgar Square "was strained to the utmost." Police could keep order in the streets, and the Works Office could keep them clean, but any policies regarding the assembly of people in the square was to be set by the national government. The Home Office had gained control of the streets, for better or worse.[51]

TAKING BACK THE STREETS

The floodgates of meetings reopened after 1890. Between 1886 and 1895 there were more than 150 major demonstrations for various political causes.[52] Members of the Social Democrats, Friendly Societies, free education, Anti-Coercion, unemployed, dock laborers, temperance, anti-sweating, anti–Local Government Bill, anti–Wheel Tax, Sunday Closing Bill, Gas Workers, Postmen, Tailors, Railway Workers, printers, Eight-Hours Movement, Foresters, League of the Cross, and Radicals met in parks and paraded through London streets.

Given the dreadful climate of London—and the pervasive pollution that poisoned the air in the nineteenth century—it is astonishing how many outdoor public forums there were. In 1866, when a Commons Bill set up rules and administrative structures for governing open spaces, there were over two hundred commons and spaces within a fifteen-mile radius of London popularly used for informal speaking.[53] By 1892, after legal and jurisdictional tangles, London's forty-six major commons and parks were officially sanctioned for open-air meetings, the sanction given by either the Works Office, the London County Council, or local boards.[54] This included Hyde Park, Regents Park, and Battersea Park.

The actual number of places in which open-air meetings were daily held without police interference was greater than that. There were almost five hundred spaces, including street corners, greens, and open spaces, that were utilized in such a fashion. While the majority (324) tended to be held by religious or Salvation Army (44) groups, there were forty places devoted to political meetings, and over seventy where both political and religious assemblages occurred.[55] The Social Democrats, for example, had continued through the late 1880s and early 1890s to hold open-air meetings. Half of their twenty-nine meetings in April 1888 were outdoors, and in November 1889, twenty-six of their sixty-five weekly meetings were.[56] Before Black Monday, Hyde Park had been favored ground, attracting twenty-eight major and many minor meetings in the nine-year period from 1877 to 1885.[57]

In addition, street processions remained popular, with twelve hundred in 1889, fourteen hundred in 1888, and two hundred in a three-month period at the end of 1887.[58] General Booth reportedly said in 1888 that nine thousand Salvation Army processions took place weekly in the nation with a sizeable proportion in London.[59] Demonstrations increased as working-class groups found them an effective tool of expression. Although by 1895 there were only six major demonstrations in central London, the right to meet had become firmly embedded in local life. Ironically, only after free meeting and speech had ceased to be a major issue was this right assured.

The ban on Trafalgar Square meetings was a sore point for everyone. Informal "conversazione" were held as a way of getting around the ban, to provoke the police into making arrests, which did not happen. For protestors, these "discussions" gave "umbrage to the autocrat of Scotland Yard" and made the struggle appear to be one of the People versus the Police.[60] The effect of all this was to give Trafalgar Square the reputation of being the great washing ground of the homeless, the hungry, and the loudmouthed.[61]

"Washing ground" was literal, as D. R. Plunket, first commissioner of H. M. Works acknowledged in the Commons on a question of public health. He said the fountains were used for daily ablutions, and things both animate and inanimate were left there. The benches, placed there for the poor by Lord Brabazon, were washed down every morning. Plunket revealed more than the sanitary habits of Londoners, as he told members of Her Majesty's government the bottom line about Trafalgar Square and its temporary inhabitants: "I have not the power, even if I had the will—and I certainly have not the will—to banish these unfortunate creatures from the Square altogether."[62] Plunket was reluctant to ban people from public spaces.

Police tried to discourage meetings but folded in the face of public pressure. A bylaw was passed in 1888 forbidding collecting money on Clapham Common, a practice common during public meetings; Annie Besant challenged it and the bylaw was withdrawn.[63] In 1889, the Metropolitan Works Board prohibited meeting on Peckham Rye and Southwark Park, eliciting a strong protest against this arbitrary move, and the board was forced not only to reinstate the right to meet there but also to add Finsbury Park to its list of permitted areas.[64]

The issue of collecting money emerged again in 1896, when two men were prosecuted for collections in Hyde Park. The unusual arrests were made under an obscure law forbidding collections at performances, recitations, or representations, except with permission. The reaction of Whitehall reveals the bureaucratic haze: Police Commissioner Bradford said he regretted the action had been taken against the mendicant, but since it had progressed so far there was little to do but go ahead and finish the prosecution.[65]

The police tried various means to limit meetings, knowing there were not many good options. A few were stopped, including a June 1888 Anti-Compensation demonstration and three SDF meetings. There was a fracas in January 1889 with a Thames Embankment procession, and a man was arrested in Lambeth.[66] Hyde Park meetings resumed, and a February gathering of thirty thousand sponsored by the Metropolitan Radical Association and socialists went on peaceably despite an attempt to prevent it. Police hoped to shift responsibility to the Metropolitan Board of Works to intervene, pointing out they had not given permission for the meeting. The Works Office shot back that no such permission was needed under Rule 10, unless a vehicle was to be taken onto the grass.[67]

Increasingly after 1887, the Parks and Public Works departments were drawn into the public-meeting issue in the broadest possible way. To avoid charges of politicization, the focus was shifted to one of order: the need for clean streets and squares and for uncongested thoroughfares for vehicles and pedestrians could be used to stop assemblies. The argument was not specious, for there was genuine concern for keeping things moving on the congested streets. That played a parallel role next to the police efforts to shift responsibility for controlling meetings away from themselves, as they became concerned over their public image.

THE POLICE FALLOUT

Promoting a former army officer to police commissioner in 1887 was not in and of itself a problem for the police. By selecting a lawyer and a colonel as the first commissioners, Peel had created a balance with the Januslike nature of the force: on the one hand, it was to interact with the populace and foster beneficial living conditions; on the other, it was to administer laws and create order. The administrative and intellectual powers of Mayne, a lawyer, combined with the military order and discipline of Rowan, the retired colonel, made a model that politicians after Peel failed to follow.

Warren's appointment had been a disaster. His ousting in November 1888 and replacement by James Monro, a career police officer, did little to repair public faith. What finally pushed him out was a criminal case, the unsolved Jack the Ripper murders, which showed the public that crowd control was not enough if the police couldn't catch a madman.[68] Warren's insistence that he be in absolute control led to his ultimatum that unless the government dismissed the second in command, Monro, he would resign.[69] Warren had bitterly complained that "whereas he had been saddled with all the responsibility, he has no freedom of action, and in consequence daily his position had become more unbearable."[70]

Monro had a difficult time. Public demonstrations expanded with the start of labor agitation on a broad scale. In 1889, one hundred thousand dockworkers picketed, but London was singularly calm. Labor leader Ben Tillett viewed the strike as labor's call to the nation: "Not before in the history of industrial conflict had striking bodies of workmen in the Metropolis taken measures to advertise their discontent by daily demonstrations on Tower Hill."[71] Interestingly, Tillett characterized the relationship between strikers and police as pleasant.

Relations between Monro and the Home Office deteriorated in the spring of 1890, with meetings and processions a source of irritation in their relations. In May, Monro reiterated his policy that processions were an infringement of the right of free passage, as a crisis arose over postmen and gas stokers' processions. A sensitized Commons questioned Matthews on his attitude toward processions and possible political bias in banning them. When asked why the Lord

Mayor's Day parade was allowed, he defended it by saying it was of immemorial standing, but added, "if it had to be considered de nuovo, I do not know what view might be taken."[72] On May 15, the Home Office said there was no reason to stop the postmen's meeting, which Monro had been dead set against; he could only regulate the route.[73]

With MPs and the press questioning meeting policies,[74] Munro was shocked to discover that the Home Office did not support him. The Home Office made it clear it backed full rights for marchers, who were under no obligation to inform police of their actions. Monro drew the symbolic line in the sand, demanding full legal power to maintain what he viewed to be all facets of law and order. Otherwise, he said, "I am not prepared to fulfill the function allotted to me." The commissioner, he said, "must possess all the powers which *he* thinks necessary for the safety of the Metropolis." This was not, he wrote, "the case of the English law."[75]

Monro's relations with the Home Office remained rocky for several years. He insisted on intricately controlling procession routes, despite the government's insistence that processions were innately legal. A "monster" labor procession slated for June 7, 1890, led to another crisis.[76] In theory, the police commissioner did facilitate the public procession as he had been ordered to by the Home office; his actions are reminiscent of those police forces take in current times. A detailed thirteen-page police order explained what steps the police were to take, such as stopping the procession from time to time to let traffic pass and immediately reporting any problems. More than three thousand police were stationed at various points along the routes leading into London, either to Hyde Park or Victorian Embankment, the two major points of convergence.

What Monro failed to understand—and what plagues police today—is that the regulation of procession routes must be done with the cooperation and understanding of the participants.[77] Demonstration committee head F. N. Charrington lambasted Monro, saying that the route was "universally admitted to have been objectionable." Monro was faulted for "disallowing suggested subsidiary routes ... and after they finally devise new plans only to have them cancelled and replaced."[78] Demonstrators were infuriated at the police assertion that traffic would be given preferential treatment and the procession neither protected nor allowed to progress without pauses for traffic. The organizing committee characterized the police response as arbitrary and a "needless irritation and provocation of hostility" that could only lead to an eventual withdrawal of all public-meeting rights.[79]

That demonstration proceeded without major incident, Monro was convinced of "the wisdom of the policy pursued,"[80] and the Home Office called police behavior "praiseworthy."[81] But the Home Office's increasing sensitivity to negative public perceptions of police and repression of public meetings led to a major shift. Permanent Undersecretary Sir Godfrey Lushington assumed the mantle of public-meeting advocate, asserting Home Office authority. "However advantageous it might be to the convenience of the Metropolis, [limiting public meetings] would arouse strong popular objections," Lushington wrote. "It would be a new departure: would be entirely beyond the competence of the Commissioner to introduce: and I feel sure the Secretary of State himself would not authorize it without much consideration and consultation with his colleagues."[82]

It was too much for Monro, who resigned a few days after this demonstration, on June 12. Home Secretary Matthews admitted that "differences of opinion have arisen between him and myself in respect to questions of administration and legislation affecting the Metropolitan Police."[83] When asked to elucidate this, Matthews read the resignation letter, in which Monro stated: "My views as to police administration, unfortunately, differ in many important respects from those held by the Secretary of State."[84] The ostensible reason for the break was the disagreement over the police bill that was resting in Parliament concerning superannuation and other administrative matters, but the veneer was thin.[85] On June 16, Harcourt implied in the Commons that the bill was just an excuse for the clash. Nor did Matthews sit back and let the matter rest. On June 20, when asked about a rumor reported in the *Standard* that Prime Minister Lord Salisbury would attempt to conciliate differences between the two men, Matthews announced the appointment of Sir E. R. C. Bradford as the new commissioner.[86] Bradford, another military man of the stalwart type (he had lost one of his arms to a tiger), lasted a few years but also clashed with the Home Office.

Trafalgar Square was once again the subject of the dispute. In 1892, Liberals assumed control of the government and wanted clear public-meeting policies. It was significant that the new Home Secretary was Lord Asquith, who had so eloquently defended public-meeting advocates Graham and Burns in 1888. When the Metropolitan Radical Federation proposed a torchlight procession to Trafalgar Square in November 1892, Whitehall realized that it had to articulate policy, and on November 2, 1892, issued a crucial memorandum defining new Trafalgar Square meeting regulations. Asquith brokered a deal with the Board of Works, which administered the square, allowing meetings during daylight hours on Saturday and Sundays. While asserting the right to meet, Asquith attempted at the same time to qualify it, warning that "many people are ready to anticipate the worst and fright is very contagious."[87] He said he wanted to avoid the debacle of 1886–1887, and he established that all applications to meet in the square would be handled by the Home Office. The government was delighted by this move and by public support: "To have pleased *The Times* and the *Star* and indeed everybody may rank with the achievements of Hannibal crossing the Alps or of Orpheus charming his miscellaneous congregations. No one rejoices more sincerely than [I]," wrote the Earl of Roseberry, who was foreign secretary and who became prime minister in 1894.[88]

Not that the Home Office decisions were always in favor of allowing all assemblies. The Fair Trade Club request for blanket permission for meetings every possible Saturday, Sunday, and holiday in December, January, and February 1892–1893 was granted only for December.[89] A year later, Scotland Yard refused the application of anarchists to hold a Trafalgar Square meeting after sending the application to the Secretary of State and receiving a negative reply.[90] When the anarchists attempted to meet regularly anyway on three following Sundays, there was little in the way of conflict. The crowds were small, some socialist newspapers were sold, and the weather was bad. A few constables kept order and prevented people from loitering. At the third meeting, on December 17, about two thousand people turned out, and when a man who refused to comply with a police request to move on was arrested, a groaning crowd starting hustling police, who quickly sent for reinforcements and quelled the crowd.

The Home Office's sensitivity over meetings lasted to the end of the century. In late 1892, the Home Secretary asked the police commissioner to determine "if any, and if so, what, assistance from the military force is required."[91] Torchlight processions, at first tolerated, were banned by the end of 1892, as "on the present occasion there seems to be a dangerous element in the announcements of the promoters."[92] Even so, the Home Office was aware there was no legal backing for such a decision. Permanent Undersecretary Lushington, responding for the Home Secretary, acknowledged that the prohibition was extra-legal. "But such a procession," he wrote Bradford, "is plainly dangerous.... I feel very sure the Magistrates would make no difficulty in punishing as far as resistance to the Police those who resisted when putting out the torches.... If a procession is allowed to take place the consequences may be very serious indeed."[93]

Yet overall, inflammatory rhetoric left the Home Office unruffled. In February 1894, Home Secretary Matthews was informed by the law officer that socialist John Williams's Tower Hill speeches at an unemployed demonstration had breached the law. The Home Office decided not to pursue legal action, as Permanent Undersecretary Lushington feared Williams would become a martyr.[94] Even Scotland Yard tolerated public meetings, no matter how radical the speeches. Police could control them without too much problem, they pointed out, and they were not to be interfered with, even though "the language of their leaders . . . is objectionable in the highest degree." It was language that "has been made use of over and over again in Hyde Park and elsewhere."[95]

The confidence from both public and government that the Metropolitan Police had gained was evidenced by the 1894 Interdepartmental Committee Report on Riots. Among other things, the report was a watershed in recommending that police determine when it is appropriate to involve the military in riots. Asquith's committee established the principle that the "calling out of the military to aid in the suppression of rioting should never be resorted to except as a last expedient when there is serious ground for believing that the resources of the civil power will be insufficient."[96] Short of armed or mass uprising, there was little need to call up the troops.

The 1890s marked the legitimization of public meeting everywhere, including Trafalgar Square. Government maintained control through regulation. Trafalgar's symbolism as London's meeting capital was established. The surest sign of the legitimacy of meetings there was in February 1894, when the Bermondsey vestry held a meeting at the square to protest the House of Lords' treatment of the Local Government Bill. "It is a new departure," reported the *Times*, "for a local governing body to organize a popular demonstration such as that which was held in Trafalgar Square yesterday."[97] Such meetings were not common, but the fact that one could occur at all indicates the open use of the square.

Despite the reopening of Trafalgar Square as a public meeting ground in 1892, it never became, as Annie Besant had attempted to rename it, "Our Square"; it continued to be used, but less frequently and with increasing restrictions. The legal right of public meeting was widely assumed. Socialists used Trafalgar Square for occasional meetings but never attempted again to make it the focus of their activities. As it became less a stage for revolution and more one for reform, it receded as a demonstration ground and rose as a social one. Although it never became a garden, at the end of the twentieth century it became a pedestrian plaza closed to traffic. It was in many ways a fulfillment of the utopian vision William Morris had projected.

PT
3

VIOLENCE AND CONTROL IN THE EMPIRE CITY

NEW YORK BEFORE 1870

A scene of white chaos filled Washington Street in downtown New York on a cold February day in 1837. Not snow but flour filled the streets, as a mob of five thousand emptied barrel after barrel of the "staff of life" from the five-story Eli Hart and Co. warehouse. As little boys filled bags with flour to take home to hungry families, assaults on other flour warehouses were averted by merchants savvy enough to negotiate with the crowds. Even though it was a time of economic depression and crisis, police constables were nowhere in evidence.

The fracas was the unfortunate end of the otherwise peaceful protest against "exorbitant" prices held earlier that day. More than twenty thousand had assembled in City Hall Park to voice their anger at the "life against Death" situation of the working classes. "Hunger and cold" were pitted against "avarice and usury." The "illegal" violence that erupted was blamed on frustrated protestors, crooks in the crowd, and the failure of the authorities to prevent disruption, and people demanded punishment for disorder.[1]

Still, claimed the press, "do not punish the right of opinion—the liberty of speech—and the freedom of the people to hold public meetings." Popular reaction to the event was strongly sympathetic to the demonstrators because of "the terrible condition of the times and grasping arts of the extortioners during the last year." Only firm leadership and an end to greed could extinguish the possibility of more disorder.[2]

As wealth in nineteenth-century New York became concentrated in fewer hands, the notion of popular justice was appealing. Flinging flour in the streets reflected unease with the rising merchant elite and their monopoly over business and local governments. Three-quarters of the City Council consisted of merchants, businessmen, attorneys, and professionals, 15 percent were retailers, and only 10 percent were artisans.[3] Public protest was viewed as a healthy and necessary outlet for popular discontent, a way of keeping the young republic on track.[4]

What was not healthy was the destruction of property and death. Raucous expression of discontent was a hallmark of Jacksonian America. New York's 1837 flour riot was part of the tumult of the antebellum period, when the city was a staging ground for protests that often led to riots. These early American riots were reminiscent of European riots of previous centuries—bread riots in particular were symptomatic of preindustrial societies, and the 1837 riot was an illustration of the "ways in which traditional cultural forms and expectations helped shape lower-class behavior."[5]

Was this a legitimate expression of citizen democracy, even if it led to violence? From the 1830s to the 1860s, city life was marked by numerous public disturbances occasioned by ethnic, racial, economic, and religious issues and tied to poverty, hunger, unemployment, crowding, and unsanitary conditions. Election riots often elicited violence and death, as exemplified by those in Baltimore in the 1850s. That city is where a new and defining type of riots emerged in the early nineteenth century.[6]

This distinctively American form of collective violence "revealed the tensions and strains of communities being torn asunder by divisions and enmities."[7] Days of rioting were marked by a new level of physical violence on persons so vehement it was "almost unknown in the eighteenth century." Perhaps this was a manifestation of a new egalitarianism, which made competition that much more intense, with everyone grabbing for a piece of the pie. Such focus on individuality raised both the propensity and tolerance for violence.[8] Neophyte city governments were untested at the start of the century and unprepared in the middle of it.

The tumult in New York from the 1830s through the 1860s effected a change in the perception of what was tolerable given the ramifications of population growth. In 1830, the city had two hundred thousand residents; by 1850, it had a half million. To sustain economic viability, daily life had to be made safe. If riots could occur at the drop of a hat—and their precipitant factors were often modest—then the city could easily be destabilized. Sound institutions, a stable infrastructure, and safety were necessary to achieve to wealth.

Disruption and violence would impede New York's transformation into the "London of the New World." No other city in the expanding country competed with the money and power that coalesced in the "Empire City," whose middle classes "served as gatekeeper of America's most important outpost in the Atlantic economy."[9] The city's formidable growth was accelerated by the opening of the Erie Canal in 1825, which drastically reduced the cost of transporting goods from the East Coast to the interior and back, promoting both domestic production and exports. Within ten years, New York real-estate values had tripled and the city had consolidated its dominance of America's banking and business. Buildings and streets seemed to spring up overnight. With private investment booming, the city invested heavily in improvements and infrastructure that would facilitate growth and eliminate endemic problems such as cholera,[10] fire, and a lack of clean water. New York ambitiously addressed the water problem by constructing the world's best aqueduct at the time, the Croton water system, opened in 1842, which ensured plentiful and safe water for residents.

Despite their swelling numbers, opportunities abounded for newcomers. The old Knickerbocker elite gave way to the rising merchant class, which catered to the needs of entrepreneurs and consumers. Businessmen built empires from humble beginnings. The small-scale merchant and aspiring artisan could accumulate capital and rise in wealth and status, as exemplified by John Roach, who went from a dollar-a-day molder in the New York Iron Works to the owner of his own foundry.[11] In small workshops, artisans and skilled workers made books, boots, carriages, and pianos; unskilled workers laid paving stones for streets, forged iron, and made sugar; peddlers sold food and trinkets on the streets to workers; merchants transformed New York into America's emporium.[12]

Into this mix entered a huge influx of foreigners, predominantly Irish and German in the first half of the nineteenth century. In 1850, more than half the population was foreign born, and of that, 80 percent were Irish and German.[13] Of the Irish workers, more than half were laborers and cartmen,[14] and they were largely employed as glassworkers, stonecutters, blacksmiths, masons, bricklayers, umbrella makers, plumbers, and coopers. Germans worked as gunsmiths, shoemakers, tailors, bakers, locksmiths, cabinetmakers, turners, and carvers. In general, crafts, manufacturing, and construction constituted half of New York's workforce in 1855.[15] Newcomers increasingly banded together in work associations united by ethnicity. These labor organizations became unusually active in the 1830s, producing numerous demonstrations and strikes, many of which ended in violence.[16]

Expanding opportunities, an enlarging population, and a heady influx of ethnic, religious, and racial groups made for a potent brew of rivalries, competition, and violence. Newcomers sought wealth, but first they needed to survive. As easily as one could rise, one could fall. In 1817, New York's prosperous formed the Society for the Prevention of Pauperism to deal with the city's fifteen thousand indigent (of a total population of around 93,000). Voluntary associations proliferated in the next three decades to cope with what was perceived to be the substandard moral values of foreigners. The New York Association for Improving the Condition of the Poor was a major organization formed in 1843 to discourage poverty, considered at this point self-induced.

Not surprisingly, New York also became a maelstrom of xenophobia, racism, and factionalism. The native-born white population, increasingly a minority, resented foreigners, particularly the Irish. Foreigners were blamed for riots, drunkenness, prostitution, crime, and even dirt. The so-called bad elements in the Flour Riot, including "colored" and foreigners, were branded traditional European riffraff or "canaille."[17] Morals reformers took delight in pointing to the ethnic stew as the source of many evils, including self-perpetuating poverty. Their endeavors to abate drinking and enforce Sabbath observance were inducements for disruptive demonstrations and riots protesting temperance organizations and restrictive legislation.

Resentment of African Americans contributed to antiabolitionism and later the Draft Riots. While the percentage of African Americans in the city fell through the 1860s, they remained a simmering irritant to many, including those who felt that blacks were taking away work from them. From a little more than ten thousand in 1820, the number of African Americans grew to about sixteen thousand by 1840 (5.2 percent) but then declined by thirty-five hundred by 1860, representing only 1.5 percent of the population.

Popular protest and disorder was hardly new. Colonial and Revolutionary War–era protests were sparked by food shortages, epidemics, "bawdyhouses," impressment, customs enforcement, and arbitrary authority. One such event in New York City was the 1788 Doctors' Riot. A mob attacked a medical school, incited by the discovery that students had desecrated graves to get corpses. Two days of violence resulted in three deaths, and the militia had to be called out.

These eighteenth-century disturbances had little about them that was distinctively American, but rather they "were remarkably single-minded and discriminating," like most English and French protests of the era.[18] But American tumult rarely resulted in death or much destruction, and the absence of large cities in the United States was a factor in this. In the seventeenth and eighteenth centuries, the line between rebellion and riot was often unclear. This changed in the young republic as Baltimore, Philadelphia, and Boston became settings for protest and confrontation in an urbanizing America.

Public speech and assembly experienced significant shifts in nineteenth-century New York, leading to a series of changes that redefined public order by the 1870s. First, the frequency and number of gatherings, protests, and disturbances increased. Evidence abounds that hundreds of disruptions occurred every year. This violence continued in America's nineteenth-century cities, but New York grew intolerant of it by the 1860s.

Second, the increasing diversity of the city's population, new labor activism, and economic fluctuations were key factors causing this increase of public activity. In the previous century, colonial rebellions had usually been triggered by larger political and ideological issues. Even though the city's growth meant that jobs were always opening, the competition was intense, as the sheer number of immigrants was so large. The unprecedented ethnic and racial mix that defined New York added to this tension considerably. And while America's economic growth was equally extraordinary in this era, severe recessions and market fluctuations affected labor adversely. Gotham was home to scores of America's new millionaires, but it was also home to a vast new class of the extremely poor, who scraped by on daily subsistence wages.

Third, public disturbances were likely to be precipitated by simple triggers that often masked longstanding, complex issues. An unpopular actor, a mysterious shot, a rumor flying through a crowd, the denial of a drink, a street fistfight, or an insult to a woman by a cartman could start a rush to madness. Behind this was usually a more compelling long-term issue; certainly racism was a pervasive factor in most of the disturbances. This is a classic and continuing profile of such events: often no one ever knows what starts the melee.

Fourth, crowds grew more unruly, more violent, and less controllable in this era. Most disorder occurred in the most densely populated neighborhoods. Poor and crowded areas such as the Five Points were difficult for authorities to access. The opposite was also true: widened, straightened, and paved city streets facilitated the movement of large assemblies, processions, and protests. As crowds grew larger, so did the likelihood that minor incidents could escalate into injury or death. Not surprisingly, elected officials and the business elite became less tolerant of disruption and more concerned with safety. They had little in the way of a preventative framework to discourage disruption. The increased awareness of the negative consequences of disorder led to an increase in press reportage, arrests, and prosecution for disorderly acts.

Fifth, this led to the realization that a permanent and reliable police force was needed for the city. The combination of peace officers, constables, night watches, magistrates, and marshals that was used earlier to maintain order was casual and uncoordinated. Even the presence of professional enforcers of the peace did not always work. The number of men available to keep watch over Gotham was insufficient, there was no central authority or rules, pay was often based on rewards, and political appointments predominated. The example of London's police, formed in 1829, reinforced the awareness that New York's policing phalanx was flawed. The lack of police resulted in dependence on the National Guard, an all-volunteer force, to assist the police in controlling the worst episodes of violence from the 1830s to 1871.

Up to the 1830s, many issues could induce mayhem. In 1799, an anti-Irish mob resulted in one death; in 1806, avenging a murder by an Irishman resulted in a fracas; in 1824, an anti-Irish riot occurred. In 1801, 250 African Americans attacked a slave trader; in 1819, a melee erupted in the streets as black food vendors were attacked; other episodes of street violence occurred in 1822 and 1825. Sailors staged protests at the docks in 1802, and in 1829 the fiery speaker Francis Wright scandalized the city with her speeches, eliciting angry protest at the idea of a woman addressing the public. More than five thousand anti-Sabbatarians protested in City Hall Park in 1821. Unhappiness over English actors produced theater riots in 1825, 1831, and 1832; typical was the riot at the Park Theater in October 1831, triggered by actor Joshua Anderson's anti-American remarks. A youth riot erupted after an unsatisfactory fireworks display in 1826. That same year, a fracas erupted after the New York Magdalene society charged that the city was a hotbed of prostitution, typical of the sporadic brothel disturbances that erupted in these decades. Street and tavern riots peaked in the late 1820s, as did disruptions from New Year's Eve revelers. Several churches, particularly Baptist and Methodist ones, were the scenes of riots.[19]

As issues became more complex in the 1830s, violence increased. Jacksonian democracy found a firm footing in New York, where it was "open, bold, and genuinely, radically democratic."[20] *Evening Post* journalist William Leggett inspired breakaway Democrats to form the Locofocos, one of the groups involved in the 1837 Flour Riot. New York became an intellectual center for spreading "Young Republic" ideals through its expanding daily press and its place as home to an important generation of American writers.[21] Proliferating labor associations began marching and meeting in public spaces; New York's thoroughfares became the setting for protest speeches and strikes. In November 1833, four thousand members of the General Trades Union, including cabinetmakers, stonecutters, bakers, tailors, saddlers, glasscutters, carpenters, and hatters marched down Broadway and the Bowery. Typical was a labor meeting of thirty thousand in June 1836 in City Hall Park, the same year stonemasons rioted to protest the use of prison labor to cut stone for the construction of New York University. The militia was called up to deal with waterfront violence in 1836, which followed labor action on the docks in 1825 and 1828.

Violence was particularly notable in 1834 and 1835. The 1834 Election Riots created chaos during several days in April, resulted in one death and many wounded, and highlighted increasing tensions with the Irish. Rioters broke into the state arsenal, and twenty thousand National Guard were called out. The participation by an Irish guard unit added to the melee. After the violence was put down, the perception was that the legality of elections had been ensured:

the outcome was a "signal triumph of good principles over violence, illegal voting, party discipline, and the influence of office-holders."[22]

That summer, the National Guard was again called out, along with one thousand special constables, to quell an antiabolitionist riot around Chatham Square. In July, a mob attacked African American churches and homes in Five Points and the home of the prosperous silk merchant and abolitionist Arthur Tappan.[23] In August, a stonecutters' protest against the use of Sing Sing prison labor to cut stone resulted in four days of mayhem, requiring the Twenty-seventh Regiment to be called out.[24]

Chatham Square, a thriving business and entertainment center, was a locus for numerous disturbances. It bordered Five Points, the seething center of poor immigrants, ethnic gangs, dilapidated housing, and epidemic disease. An angry crowd assembled there in 1834 to protest the formation of the Anti Slavery Society of New York and the presence of William Lloyd Garrison. In June 1835, a nativist protest, the Five Points Riot, broke out over an Irish National Guard unit, and one man was killed by the mob.

Not all public meetings ended in violence. More than twenty thousand gathered at City Hall Park in February 1834 in support of a national bank; there were no problems. Similarly, at an antiabolitionist meeting in August 1835, crowds were warned that abolitionists were outside agitators. Following the Flour Riot in 1837, thirty thousand met in the Park in March to discuss the economic crisis, and in May, five thousand met on the same issue. A large 1842 meeting in the Park concerning the use of federal troops in Rhode Island proceeded with no incident: "It was the most quiet, orderly, dignified, and respectable assemblage of men that perhaps has been seen in New York for the last ten years, and that is saying a great deal."[25] Until the construction of the Post Office on the site, the Park was New York's major meeting place in the nineteenth century, and dozens of assemblies peaceably collected there.

Throughout the 1840s and 1850s, public speech and assembly produced even more tumult, and with it some of the worst violence of the century. The advent of a professional police force did little to stem the tide of ethnic, racial, and labor agitation. The 1849 Astor Place riots resulted in twenty-two dead, and the 1857 Bowery riots claimed twelve victims. In between, ethnic gangs, labor agitation, migration, abolitionism, and population growth meant increased disruption. "Recreational" rioting of the "fire b'hoys" was endemic to rival volunteer fire companies. That was the case in 1841, when a Houston Street clash left one dead.[26] Attempted European revolutions in 1848, the year Karl Marx and Friedrich Engels published *The Communist Manifesto*, infused German immigrants with zeal for change; two tailors were killed and many wounded in an August

1850 strike.[27] Strikebreaking itself sparked much mayhem, as the plentiful supply of new immigrants diminished the chance of success for labor action. Violence was common when scabs appeared, as was the case in 1855, when striking Irish dockworkers were replaced by African Americans.

In 1849, when cholera killed more than five thousand (a quarter of all deaths in the city), the Astor Place riots underscored New York's ethnic rivalries, fierce political battles, divide between rich and poor, and new policing presence. It provided a foretaste of what could happen when authorities failed to control disorder. The catalyst was an irritating English actor, William Macready, who alienated his audience at the newly opened Astor Opera House. Instead of the "kid-glove" audience that was anticipated, the hall was filled with a more plebian crowd. Macready's rivalry with fellow actor Edwin Forrest turned into an anti-English, pro-Irish battle. The city had known its share of theater riots, but nothing like this. Escalation was inevitable because the new mayor called up the militia to ensure that peace be maintained. The effect was disastrous: the Seventh Regiment, light artillery, hussars, horse troops, and police surrounded the theater and neighboring streets. With a crowd of more than ten thousand dissolving into chaos and pushing into the theater, the military fired, killing eighteen immediately and wounding dozens.[28]

The city remained in a state of siege the next day as a mass demonstration was held at City Hall Park, but in the end, the crowds backed down and order was restored. Law and order had been maintained only "at a terrible sacrifice."[29] The swiftness with which good men turned into uncontrollable creatures stunned people, and the use of the militia was considered both necessary and extreme. Some speculated that a more civilized means should be found to maintain public order.

That more civilized method was supposed to have been the new police. Established in 1844, they reflected the growing acceptance of a permanent and accountable civil force to prevent crime, quell disturbances, ensure stability, and protect property. It would also calm fears of rising crime; sensational murder cases, such as that of Mary Rogers, increasingly grabbed the attention of the press and the public. A little more than a decade later, New York's cops became entangled in a thirteen-year fight over who held authority over them. Following intense political wrangling, a second force, the Metropolitans, was created in 1857, reporting to the Republican-dominated state legislature in Albany. The impetus was to take political patronage from the city's Democratic power base, Tammany Hall, and to lessen political and police partisanship in ethnic New York. The city's local elite, including the Association for Improving the Condition of the Poor, endorsed this move as a means of diminishing the influence of the Irish and of closing brothels, gambling houses, and saloons.[30]

In the midst of an economic recession and public demonstrations by unemployed, the Democrats reacted against such a transfer of authority by denying it existed. The mayor insisted that the municipal police force remain and report to him. Not surprisingly, the result was confusion:

> New York presents . . . the disgraceful spectacle of confirmed anarchy . . . an ignominious conflict between two sets of individuals for the control of the police . . . a Mayor vainly striving to avert an open conflict with deadly weapons between two sets of guardians of the public peace; hardened politicians making merry over the prospect of the subjugation of the city; every where anarchy, confusion, disorder, and contempt for laws.[31]

The immediate manifestation of the internecine police war was the Dead Rabbits–Bowery B'hoys riot in July 1857, in which twelve died and three dozen were injured. The Metropolitans could not quell the Irish-nativist battle, which went on for hours in the streets. They proved to be "totally insufficient even to protect themselves from the fury of the mobs," and only the intervention of the National Guard ended the bloody confrontation.[32] In the years following, the Metropolitans proved as inadequate in controlling crime and as subject to political influence as the municipals. The courts temporarily resolved the dispute in favor of the state, but Democrats regained control in Albany, and the Metropolitans faded into history in 1870.

It was the Metropolitans, though, who in 1863 had to deal with the worst civil violence in American history. The Draft Riots resulted in the greatest manmade destruction of life and property ever known in the city. What started out as "a spontaneous outburst of popular passion, primarily at the draft," ended up as a "Carnival of Fire and Blood" in which America's largest city was savaged.[33] For five days, July 13 through 17, life in New York was suspended as "a saturnalia of pillage, murder and rapine threatened again and again to set in upon the commercial metropolis of the Union."[34] The provocation was the Conscription Act and its exemption clause, which provided that a man could replace himself or pay $300 to avoid service. The act was, of course, biased against the working man, and it let loose an immeasurable fury.

In stifling summer heat, the rumor spread that the Black Joke volunteer fire company would protest the loss of their conscription exemption by destroying records in their local draft office on July 13. Soon thereafter mobs took over Manhattan's streets, attacking and killing people at will, looting and burning hundreds of buildings and displaying insensate ferocity. The skyline of smoldering fires could be seen from Brooklyn, and for three days, a person couldn't risk buying milk without inviting attack. Public transportation ground to a halt, mail wasn't delivered, and telegraph wires were cut. In the end, there were at least 119 dead, hundreds wounded, and hundreds of buildings destroyed or damaged.[35]

Only the downtown business district escaped the looting, ransacking, and burning that engulfed the heart of Manhattan. Children were stripped of clothing on the streets, and more than two hundred orphans fled from a besieged Colored Orphan Asylum. Old-age homes, homes for unwed mothers, and other charitable institutions, such as the Five Points Mission and the Magdalene Asylum, were not spared. Railroad tracks were torn up, newspaper offices such as the *Tribune* attacked, stores such as Brooks Brothers looted, an armory and gun stores broken into, food taken from restaurants, barrels of whiskey consumed, and houses ransacked and set on fire. Travelers in vehicles were blocked by crowds demanding money before allowing passage. Home and business owners begged rioters to spare them, offering money and goods, which did not always work.

Particular violence was directed at African Americans, who tried to find temporary shelter at police stations (seven hundred went to the Central Station) or barricade themselves at home. Men, women, and children were pulled out of houses or savaged on the streets, and what little property they had taken or destroyed. Interracial couples faced particular venom, and the hanging and burning of one black man was especially vicious. The police, and occasionally the militia, tried to protect African Americans but were too weak to be consistently effective. Compensation for damages in the riots was not great, but for African Americans, it was virtually nonexistent. After the riots, employers were loathe to rehire them for fear of retaliation by whites, and incidents were reported of harassment in public places. So devastating was the effect of the riots that perhaps 20 percent of the African American population left the city, returning to the 1860 level only in 1870.[36]

This brutality reflected a profound breakdown of order. Never before had New York descended into such chaos, nor did it ever do so afterward. City streets became battle zones, with bullets and clubs flying, innocent bystanders targeted, and all civil order suspended as mobs, police, and militia fought for control. Fueling the riot was the fact that no one appeared to be in charge; the city was one big free-for-all. The failure of authorities to rein in mobs on the first day of the riot, Monday, July 13, resulted in its continuation for the next four days. Despite valiant efforts, police proved incapable of controlling the disorder without backup. Minimal federal and state forces were available, and they were cobbled by inefficiency, confusion, and at times stupidity. Whatever lines of communication that existed among police, soldiers, and politicians were terrible. The growing sense of desperation by the second day drove local authorities to place ads in the newspapers seeking volunteer assistance to put down the riots, and 1,200 responded.

Many questioned the role of the police. They had been outnumbered and unprepared for catastrophic events and hardly stood a chance of stopping the progress of destruction on the first day. Yet on closer inspection, each of the mobs they needed to put down was not large, roughly consisting of one hundred to two hundred people, which should have been controllable. But there were many of these scattered all over the city, and the New York Metropolitans could not muster a sufficient force to cover the whole city. Police were viciously attacked and even left naked on the streets, illustrating the primitive rage consuming the crowd.

Contributing to the chaos was the presence of an unprecedented range of weaponry on the streets. City authorities responded with whatever force they could find, including howitzers, rifles, carbines, muskets, cannon, pistols, and "hand grenades," some of which fell into the hands of rioters, who were already using bricks, stones, axes, and sticks. Arsenals and gasworks had no special protection. In the absence of effective policing, homeowners, businesses, and government agencies made their own security arrangements. Wall Street mobilized with defensive measures ranging from bombs to sulfuric acid, and money, bullion, and notes were sent to Governor's Island. Business owners gave employees firearms and set booby traps in their stores; some formed vigilante posses. Wealthy homeowners were said to have armed servants.

Nor was there any preparation for emergency situations such as this. Amazingly, there was no protocol for calling out the National Guard, which for the first two days was not deployed adequately or correctly. This reflected poor leadership, political partisanship, and bad communications. Only by the third day of the riot was this corrected. Federal troops were used as early as the end of the first day, but their numbers were small and their deployment entangled with that of the state militia. When the riot peaked on Wednesday of that week, there was no force in control. It took the bitter lesson of the Draft Riots for New Yorkers to learn the lesson the English had known for years: once a riot starts, it is hard to stop, and therefore it had best be prevented before starting.

What finally did quell the fury of the marauding groups of working men, youths, protestors, and rabble was a combination of the political and the practical. By Thursday, July 16, word had gotten out that the Conscription Act was suspended; at the same time, politicians scrambled to pass legislation to provide money for workingmen to buy their way out. Also that day, large numbers of militia started arriving in New York, so that by Friday, there were six thousand troops present. By Monday, when gunboats filled New York's harbor, there were thousands of soldiers providing a quiet but convincing presence in the city.[37] By Thursday, streetcars started running, the mobs came under control, repairs were started, and critical targets such as munitions works carefully guarded.

Just as quickly as the riots started, they wound down, and a week later all was quiet in the city. But burned-out buildings and soldiers patrolling the streets were a reminder of the hell the city had been subjected to. Perhaps a desire to forget the horror of the week contributed to the flattening of public interest and the quickness of public officials to dispense with the event. Certainly there was little in the way of full justice delivered to victims of the riots. Authorities found it difficult to arrest and convict rioters. Only eighty-one out of more than four hundred identified rioters went to trial, and only sixty-seven of those were convicted, receiving relatively light sentencing for the most part. Crimes against property were punished as severely, if not more, than those against persons; only one man was severely punished for attacking African Americans, and no one convicted of their murder.

No public investigation of the Draft Riots was ever mounted, and the one modest suggestion for improvement, the formation of a riot squad, was ignored. As far as material damage was concerned, about $1.1 million was paid out under an 1855 law that provided for state compensation for such damages, which was believed to be a modest percentage of the real cost. Most of the official claims were underpaid; many never received compensation. Some people may have had private insurance, but many had no recourse to claims. How much money was spent for rebuilding and repairs for the hundreds of damaged or destroyed buildings is unknown, as is the amount of money lost when commerce was suspended and wages lost.

The legacy of the Draft Riots was imprinted not only on those who experienced them but also on all future generations in New York. The riots presented a dystopian vision that ran counter to the one of progress and prosperity that energized Gotham's residents. Those living in the city that 1863 summer week felt as though the world were disintegrating. Life in Civil War–era New York was sufficiently challenging without mobs paralyzing streets, burning buildings, and wantonly killing. The psychological impact of events that July week was the creation of a behemoth, with grossly exaggerated figures of the number of dead (from eight hundred to fourteen hundred) and a polarized and politicized perspective of its causes. Rifts widened, hatreds were cemented, and blame placed on the Irish, African Americans, Southerners, labor agitators, politicians, rowdies, and crooks, on class warfare, and even on wanton women. Expanding democracy received its share of the blame for creating the heterogeneous society that was the cornerstone of the nation.

The riots stand out as a last vestige of primitive mob behavior, one typical of centuries past but not practical for the modern city. For New York, the lesson was well learned: no similar event would ever occur there again. Other American cities were less fortunate. Detroit, Los Angeles, New Orleans, and Newark experienced mob violence with terrible consequences well into the late twentieth century. Ironically, the rioting of the 1960s is most reminiscent of the Draft Riots: problems associated with race, youth, economic stratification, and urbanization produced violence marked by similar hatred and destruction. By then, suburbanization had pushed protest violence almost exclusively into cities.

Foremost, the Draft Riots underscored the need to protect commerce and the value of stability. Whatever had to be done to achieve this end would be prioritized, so that during the next few years, as will become apparent in the following chapters, local authorities created a structure to contain future riots, and to that end they crafted laws, formed agencies, and constructed policies that the populace honored because they afforded protection.

The riots also highlighted the need for the police to be local, numerous, and empowered. In 1870, the Albany-run Metropolitan Police was replaced by a municipal force, and power was reinstated in the hands of city authorities, making New York the first state to take power over a local police force and the first to relinquish it. The unhappy experiment was not repeated. The force was expanded, modernized, and reorganized in the next several decades, bringing it closer to the professional model that London had created.

As the police became dominant in maintaining public order, New York shifted away from the use of soldiers in disruptions. During the riots, even though the military was deployed, there was resistance to the idea of martial law, fearing a surrender of authority to an external source. Many maintained that local control was central and that it was preferable to leave power in the hands of the governor, whose proclamation "unlocks every arsenal of strength" without unleashing the military tiger. The presence of an armed and uniformed militia on the streets at the end of the riots reassured residents that control was once again imposed, but the sight of soldiers also had disturbing implications. America, like Great Britain, had no love for the sight of the military patrolling its city streets. It was widely believed that bringing in soldiers at the start of disruption would escalate a conflagration rather than calm it. From this point on, Gotham's police were charged with preventing tumult from developing into full-blown riot. With the exception of the Orange riots of 1870 and 1871, the militia was not deployed again during civil disturbances in New York City.[38]

The Draft Riots also established the accountability of municipal officers for maintaining order. "The abject surrender of this great city for two successive days into the hands of a reckless and passionate mob will be a lasting stain upon the history of its municipal executives," predicted the *World*, two days after the riots started. This led to the development of extensive regulations for daily life and new parameters for what was acceptable public behavior. It also led to a contraction of free speech and assembly. After the Civil War era, public meetings and protests were based less on a populist, free-expression platform than on a class-based one identified with radical politics and connected to broad ideological or national issues.

The legacy of 1863 is apparent in New York's last riot in which large numbers were killed. The 1871 Orange Riot served as a symbolic bridge between the old and new patterns of public-protest violence. This ethnic clash was rooted in Irish internecine feuding and a bitter religious divide. By this time, Irish Catholics dominated the Democratic political machinery, but ethnic rivalries and xenophobia persisted.[39] The Orange Riot reinforced the belief that to maintain order, the city had to take preventive action in all cases, have capable leaders, employ the police, and avoid using the militia. The Orange Riot also highlighted the public's intolerance for street violence, their demand for accountability, and their acceptance of the police as arbiters of order.

Long-term antagonism between Protestant and Catholic Irish had erupted the year before, during an annual ethnic parade gone awry. It was unclear what triggered the melee on the upper West Side of Manhattan on July 13, 1870, but the result was clear—three dead and seventeen injured. No special preparation had been made by the police, who had not anticipated trouble. There were always numerous parades and demonstrations in the city: just a few months before, without incident, thousands of African Americans had marched down Broadway to celebrate the Fifteenth Amendment.[40] There was widespread perception that the riot was a "breach of the public peace, and . . . a violation of public rights which cannot be justified or tolerated in this country." While awash in biased judgment and anti-Irish sentiment, the press nonetheless acknowledged that individuals had a right to speak and assemble for any reason, and the police had to protect this. On the other hand, violence could never be tolerated. "We want no winking or blinking at rioters of any creed, race or place."[41]

Local authorities tried to heed the clear warnings a year later, when the same Orange parade promised to produce another scene of chaos. Tensions had been growing for weeks, as Protestants and Catholics engaged in inflammatory rhetoric. This time authorities made extensive preparations, utilizing large numbers of police and calling out the militia. But for forty-eight hours before the event, a melodrama played out among city and state politicians. Probably under the orders of New York City Mayor Oakey Hall, Police Superintendent Kelso, "sponging the perspiration from his brow," banned the parade on Monday. Such a ban was almost unprecedented. His announcement asserted that the public streets belonged to everyone, that there was no right to march, and that a procession "inflicts a great deal of inconvenience, including interrupting traffic and disturbing sick people and students."[42]

Both the mayor and the police commissioner insisted that processions were not a matter of right but privilege, ensuring a fusillade of negative press reaction and fodder for their later condemnation. New York's dailies demanded that citizens' rights be upheld along with preserving order. The public was entitled to the "full liberty to hold meetings, picnics or parades in the street. . . . This is the very spirit of our institutions and our glorious birthright."[43] To do otherwise, it was asserted, would be to destroy the principles of the republic. Moreover, to ban the procession would be to give in to "foreigners" and prevent the police and National Guard from enforcing the rule of law. We cannot become victims of threatened lawlessness, the *Herald* said—after all, what would be next, "advising decent people to keep off the street cars because their platform is in the possession of pickpockets?"[44] The public debate was unusual in its strong cognizance of civil liberties, a phrase not common for the time.

The "struggle for civil rights" was punctuated by Governor John T. Hoffman's sudden and unexpected reversal of the ban on Tuesday.[45] Hoffman's motives are suspect—some suggested he was jockeying for votes or in battle with New York's mayor—but public anger over the cancellation was clear. The city's banking and merchant community strongly protested the very idea of submission to the mob implied by the mayor's proposed ban, which represented a "flagrant violation of every American's sense of freedom and fair play."[46] Unquestionably, negative perceptions of Irish Catholics and the rising anti-Tammany tide contributed to the support of the Orangemen to parade.[47] Veiled and overt references to religion reminded readers that, like Rome, New York's rise and fall could be tied to religion.[48] Yet the rhetoric in support of the parade from all quarters emphasized "civil rights" and free speech, pointing out that America's varied ethnic and religious constituency meant all points of view should be represented.

Amid the fierce rhetoric supporting liberty and rights, it was asserted that "in no other period of our ninety-five years' history of independence has so serious a question arisen. . . . Republics in all ages have marked their progress to recognized supremacy by popular outbreaks, which resulted in the extension of the first conceived idea of freedom."[49] That those in favor of stopping the procession were Irish Catholics was considered significant.

The governor's reinstatement of the procession had caught city officials off guard and caused great embarrassment. Allegedly, he and the mayor had not spoken to each other in a month, after a quarrel over a bill in the state legislature. Hoffman had been in New York on Monday but only learned of the ban on Tuesday from the press (although the police claimed they sent him a telegram Tuesday afternoon). In apparent fury, he took a special train back to New York on Tuesday night to meet with city officials and explain his position in countermanding the police ban. Despite their "anxious" faces, City Hall officials assured the public that the police could certainly handle any possible disturbance. The president of the police board grumbled that civic parades served "no good purpose, obstruct travel," and caused immense loss to business, "from three to five millions of dollars."[50] With the memory of the Draft Riots and the recent Paris Commune pressing on their minds, city officials had quietly mobilized the National Guard, although they publicly denied this.

While the Orangemen had at one point on Tuesday said they would cancel the parade, they didn't. The parade did occur, and it was a bloodbath, the second worst in the city's history after the Draft Riots. Sixty-two were killed and more than one hundred injured after National Guard troops fired on the crowd; the provocation was unclear. Outnumbered by thousands of demonstrators, about 100 to 150 Orangemen had been protectively surrounded by the Seventh, Twenty-second, Eighty-fourth, Sixth, and Ninth Regiments, with the police in the rear. In addition to throwing stones, the crowds had lined the Eighth Avenue parade route starting at Twenty-third Street, hanging out of buildings and firing occasional shots. At some point, the Eighty-fourth felt it was being attacked and fired back. Virtually all of the dead and mortally wounded were hit within minutes. Horrific newspaper reports described heads and limbs shattered. A quarter of the victims were under twenty, and four females, including a twelve-year old, were killed; two National Guard soldiers died. Daily reports described the decomposing dead bodies at Mount Sinai and Bellevue hospitals. Many victims had been shot more than once, and numerous amputations were reported.

Blame for the carnage was placed on politicians and the mob, but not the National Guard's furious shooting. Some felt the "lust for votes" had led to the mayor's and governor's vacillation, which in turn led to an out-of-control mob. As "The Blue Coats trump[ed] the Orange and the Green," the press extolled the triumph of law and liberty, in particular the rule of the First Amendment. New Yorkers could be comforted with "the assurance that the American people mean liberty for all, and will not permit the rights of any, be they strong or weak, to be trampled upon." There was a singular downplaying of the high fatality rate—potential anarchy was put down "with scarcely a commotion," as the dead became martyrs to freedom on the streets.

More than a hundred people were arrested but none tried for the bloodshed. The militia's actions were generally defended, and the inquest did little to shed light on what had happened.[51] The National Guard in the end escaped any serious charges, and its leader, Major General Alexander Shaler, who later led the charge for new armories, defended his men as upholders of law and order. But the massacre turned public opinion against the use of the National Guard, and this marked the last time the militia was deployed to prevent civil disturbance in the city.[52]

This "militia riot"[53] brought public fury down on city government and a consciousness of democratic principles to the public. On the one hand, order had to be maintained; on the other, there should be no harm to liberty or prejudice to subjects. "Shall law prevail, or shall mob violence hold sway in New-York?" asked a citizen, adding that when "the question is between law and anarchy, the strong arm of the law must be felt." Another New Yorker criticized "our truculent municipal authorities" who were "inefficient and incapable of right action in an emergency." As debate opened over who had the legal right to parade, the critical question remained "has an angry mob, or any number of private citizens, a legal right to say that they shall not?" Citizens should be able to "walk the streets without interference from the police," but only until the public peace is threatened.[54]

It would be many decades before the courts addressed this question, but there was one stunning result of the 1871 Orange Riot. The Police Board proposed that all processions be regulated with the exception of funerals and those of the military. They set up a special committee to get legal advice and make a report, suggesting a new law following that of the street-preaching ordinance, which banned that practice in an effort to control street traffic. The proposal wound up in Albany, where it was voted into law the following year, establishing the first-ever regulation of processions in cities across New York State.[55] With this new mantle of responsibility codified, New York City asserted its control over access to streets, parks, and squares, and citizens endorsed that decision, in the belief that never again would anyone die in the expression of public speech.

THE BATTLE OVER TOMPKINS SQUARE

In a bitter winter afternoon in January 1874, a straggly column of forty men, flanked by fifty policemen, shuffled down First Avenue, a sight unusual even for New York. This strange procession of prisoners, accompanied by throngs of relatives and friends of the prisoners, was headed for the Essex Market police court.[1] The station house was in a virtual state of siege, as mounted police attempted to control hundreds of protestors, and police armed with truncheons held back attempts by the crowd to liberate the prisoners. As the column of men arrived at the court, a startled police magistrate realized "something of unusual importance was before him."[2] Charged with a variety of offenses and bound over for arraignment and trial, the bulk of the men could not make bail of $1,000 or more. They spent the first of what would be many nights in jail.[3] As the city's usual noises were muffled by a half foot of snow that Tuesday night, the press reported hearing the prisoners sing the Marseillaise to keep their spirits up. Headlines the next morning declared that the communists had been defeated, the reds had been routed.

Had the Paris Commune finally arrived in Manhattan after a four-year transatlantic journey? In reality, the prisoners had been participants in the January 13 "Blood or Bread Riot," as the 1874 Tompkins Square riot was called. Although no one was killed and it is not a particularly well known event, it was a landmark one, demonstrating the triumph of order in the city.

The Tompkins Square riot illustrates how the modern public meeting came into being. What emerged was a new mode of democratic public discussion, and it marked the establishment of the concept of the authorized meeting. Prior to the Tompkins Square riot, city government had displayed neither the ability nor the desire to stop public gatherings. After 1874, authorities aimed to control events *before* they happened. This new concept opened a debate on the role of meetings regulation, a good twenty-five years before a national discussion of such rights and a half-century before the matter was handed over to federal courts, which is where final legal jurisdiction rests today.[4]

All this gave the police a new profile and identity. The New York force had struggled in its first quarter-century to establish responsibilities and boundaries. In 1844, the department had started as enforcers of a vague concept of public order, with broad but not clearly defined discretionary powers; by 1874, the force was the self-assured definer of order. The Tompkins Square riot both marked a new relationship between the police and the public and served as a turning point in defining the place of free expression in the city. The Tompkins Square Outrage, as some would later call it, sheds light on how municipal government dealt with the rights of citizens in using urban public spaces. It shows how pressure to maintain an orderly city dominated governmental decision making and established a precedent for tolerating police violence when the public peace was threatened. Public protests in New York underwent a transformation after the Civil War, and democratic ideals were put to the test, decided not by courts but by the police, press, and politicians.

THE ORIGINS OF TOMPKINS SQUARE PARK

In 1834, John Jacob Astor sold ten and a half acres of swamp used for snipe hunting to the city, following condemnation proceedings, for $93,000.[5] The unattractive parcel of land, designated as space for a public market in the 1811 grid plan for Manhattan, was soon selected to be a park, propelling it into a half century of controversy and abuse. The act of setting aside the space for a park was unusual: after all, commercial development was what New York was about, in what was a "reassertion of commercial functions as the basis for urban form and culture."[6]

The park, Tompkins Square, would see more than its share of controversy over the next two centuries, including a ferocious battle in the 1990s over homeless squatting and the definition of appropriate park activity.[7] In the nineteenth century, it became a stunning example of how economic and political pressures redefined the landscape, how municipal authorities set public policy, and how neighborhoods exerted influence over decisions affecting their well-being. At one point, the city literally destroyed it. Too often, it was, in the words of both the mayor of New York and the Department of Public Parks commissioner, a "beautiful frame missing a picture."[8]

The Tompkins Square neighborhood, known before the Civil War as the Dry-Dock, began as an area slated for upper-income occupancy. Located between

Seventh Street and Tenth Street and between Avenue A and Avenue B, it was one of the most eastern sections of the island, and the recipient of residents pushing north in search of housing. Just before the park's development, from 1825 to 1830, the area around it, the Eleventh Ward, witnessed the second largest population growth in New York and the second highest rise in assessed value of lots (67 percent in 1825 through 1830; the first was the Ninth Ward, at 102 percent).[9] As construction boomed and the area became denser and more populated by immigrants, its appeal to the very prosperous cooled. In 1833, it ranked eleventh in real-estate assessment, out of fifteen wards. From 1834 through 1842, the Eleventh Ward witnessed the greatest amount of new building construction in all of New York.[10] By midcentury, when its western area was split off into the new seventeenth district, these two districts constituted the densest area in Manhattan, with 18 percent of the island's inhabitants (112,527).[11]

By 1840, density also spelled an end of hope for a high-rent district. The Tompkins Square neighborhood had clearly changed into a solid working-class neighborhood, composed of Irish shipbuilders, who attended St. Brigid's on the northwest corner, and newer German immigrants, who constituted the new Seventeenth Ward, known popularly as the "Kleindeutschland." While the north side of the square was then, as it is now, the "better" side, with more expensive housing stock, it never attracted the wealthier set, who were already migrating toward the center of the island. Unlike European cities, where parks and squares promoted high-end residences, Tompkins Square never realized its early potential. While Gotham's leaders recognized in the nineteenth century that open spaces would improve the city's image and raise real-estate values, they were also reluctant to risk any loss of commercial property.[12]

The very existence of Tompkins Square Park was defining in a city that sorely lacked significant public green spaces and was loathe to convert any decent land into a park.[13] The 1811 plan, with its emphasis on commercial development, failed to designate areas for parks or squares,[14] though it did provide for a reservoir, marketplace, and parade ground. Only five public squares (and one private square) existed in the city in 1834, and the number rose only to eleven by midcentury, constituting sixty-three acres in total below Forty-second Street, a quarter of the size of one of the large parks in the city of London.[15]

Tompkins Square served as a recreational refuge in its first two decades. Shortly after the square opened on June 1, 1834, the Common Council approved a resolution that it be "filled up to the city regulation, and enclosed with a good and sufficient fence," with the generous sum of $20,000 appropriated for the work.[16] Trees, shrubbery, walkways, a fountain, seats, and fencing were added in the 1840s and 1850s, following requests from property owners for improvements. Children and courting couples regularly flocked there.

But events in 1857 foreshadowed a less optimistic future. Economic depression and the concomitant unemployment crisis that year brought thousands to the square for public meetings. There were then few accessible venues for public expression. Up to midcentury, City Hall Park was the main forum for such public assemblies, but Tompkins Square was in the heart of one of the densest districts, and it became an increasingly popular spot.

The square's denouement began in the 1860s, when the military moved into it full time. A parade ground had been considered in the 1811 grid, but the appropriation of valuable real estate for such a purpose proved undesirable to city officials. Occasional military parades in the square and a Civil War encampment there were a prelude to an 1866 State Law (ch. 593) in which the square was declared a "public parade ground for the use of the First Division of the State of New York." Further, the street commissioner was ordered on July 1 "to remove all trees and other obstructions" and "level and grade the surface." But there wasn't much to remove: the square was such a mess that it was "almost useless for the purposes for which it was intended, and the citizens in the immediate vicinity are duly complaining of the filthy condition of the same."[17] The park was closed for repairs, but at this point the state had already decided to create a public parade ground—during the same five-year period that a million new immigrants arrived in New York.

For the next decade, Tompkins Square was embroiled in a continuous battle that pitted the city against the state, politicians against citizens, military enthusiasts against park lovers, and demonstrators against the police. All this took place amid the rise and fall of the Tweed political machine, the reformulation of city government, the creation of a parks department, soaring levels of immigration, and the 1870s economic depression. The square itself was physically devastated; in an 1870 photo, it appeared very much like the "sand baren [sic] . . . now frozen past indentation of the foot of man or beast" reported by an agitated citizen.[18] An alleged $60,000 worth of Fisk concrete was laid in the square by the end of the 1860s, although later reports termed the covering two-thirds "worthless composition and the remainder left bare,"[19] as Tweed graft probably sucked up the majority of the money.

The battle over Tompkins Square centered over its use: park, parade ground, or public meeting area. The park could not serve all three purposes. In the changing political landscape of the city's new Department of Public Parks bureaucracy, it was hard to tell who advocated what position. The first annual report of the Parks Department noted the paving of the square in compliance with the military parade ground law, but it also said there had been a number of improvements indicative of usual parks usage, including the planting of three rows of deciduous trees, a grass plot forty feet wide inside of the sidewalk, and a promenade sidewalk twenty-five feet wide. Run-off basins, drinking-water lines, a music stand, two iron urinals, and tool sheds for the two keepers were indicated.[20] Ball playing was not permitted but "under consideration," although the report notes thousands of children used the park. Music concerts, fireworks, and military parades were held. During all this the pavement continued to severely disintegrate.

Mayor Woodhull in 1850 had been among the first politicians to acknowledge the need for open spaces to beautify the city and aid public health.[21] "They are the great breathing places of the toiling masses who have no other resort in the heat of summer or in time of pestilence, for pure air and healthful recreation." In New York, the focus fell on Central Park, which represented a culmination of European landscape ideals, utopian visions of nature, and social engineering, and which elevated real-estate values in the surrounding area. Despite its sobriquet as "The People's Park," it was inaccessible to the poor and had little immediate effect on the overcrowded neighborhoods of lower Manhattan. Unlike Central Park, there were few advocates for Tompkins Square and its park.

THE BLOOD OR BREAD RIOT

The fate of Tompkins Square Park was intertwined with politics. The riot there in 1874 temporarily shifted the focus away from leisure to the right of free speech and assembly. The disturbance began as a public protest on a cold Tuesday about the city's failure to provide relief for unemployment and starvation and to request public-works projects. The meeting's location in the square was significant. There were few venues left in the increasingly built-up city for such meetings, and City Hall Park, the favorite antebellum meeting place, was no longer an open space. As one contemporary observer noted, "City Hall, Washington, Union, and Madison are really the only public grounds, and they have been so much neglected they have lost most of their attractions."[22]

The 1874 Tompkins Square meeting was ill fated. For one thing, it was not clear who had called the meeting or who was running it. Many trade organizations, as one newspaper put it, were "warring or conflicting," not unusual for New York's fractious labor scene at the time. The groups insulted and discredited each other, slinging accusations of political treachery and viewing one another suspiciously. All this exacerbated fears that New York's labor community had been fatally infiltrated by radicals bent on fomenting revolution. As authorities deliberated, they were visited by delegations of "authentic" workingmen denouncing others as leftists.

When the ill-named Committee of Safety met that Monday with the police, they were told unequivocally the meeting would be banned, prompting at least one labor delegate to burst into tears.[23] Under New York's 1872 law, police had to approve processions and meetings by means of issuing a permit.[24] In this case, the police refused permission for either the meeting or a march to City Hall. Moreover, since 1871, parks commissioners also had to give permission for any park meetings. Permits for the Tompkins Square event had been granted and then revoked. Both the Police Department and the Department of Public Parks based their revocation of the permit on the fact "the proposed meeting would endanger the public peace."[25] Many participants did not know about the permit's revocation, which they later said was a factor contributing to the fracas. The Committee of Safety had appealed to the mayor and even the governor to reissue the permit but was turned down. The police only knew the meeting was banned, and set out to prevent it.

Many thousands of protestors assembled in Tompkins that day, and at least fifteen hundred police, representing almost two-thirds of the force, monitored events.[26] With truncheons raised, the officers charged without warning and arrested forty-four men for disorderly conduct, riotous conduct, incendiary speech, carrying concealed weapons, inciting to riot, and the most serious, assault (misdemeanor) or assault and battery, a felony.[27] One man charged with drunk and disorderly protested: "This policeman was drunk and I was disorderly," said twenty-three-year-old fruit vendor Peter Collins.[28] The young working-class crowd was heavily German, but there were also French, Italian, Irish, Polish, Swedish, and Americans among the shoemakers, tailors, painters, wood turners, plumbers, masons, waiters, machinists, brewers, hairdressers, carpenters, and stonecutters who were arrested. Almost all were unemployed, and many of them said they had not eaten in days.

Reaction to the riot was swift, emotional, and polarizing. The working classes sympathized with the demonstrators, while the "uptown" crowd endorsed the triumph of law and order, all of which reflected concern with the right to assemble; many other issues surfaced, including police brutality, the competence of municipal authorities, xenophobia, and new left-wing ideology. The riot focused attention on problems that needed to receive public airing, in particular police behavior. Contemporary characterization of their performance that day closely resembles modern critiques.

Many praised the police for keeping order: neither "defiance" of authorities nor "lawless spirit" would be tolerated, said the press.[29] The police were "a brave and efficient body of men ... and prompt and obedient,"[30] and they behaved with "energy and promptness,"[31] showing that the "exercise of terrorism" would not be tolerated.[32] The press also questioned the police's role in deciding what was to be permitted in terms of public behavior, and it criticized police violence. The use of such "extraordinary authority" required "great discretion";[33] an otherwise peaceful public meeting was turned into a melee because of "the want of judgment displayed by the city authorities."[34]

The *Herald* disgustedly pointed out that "the average policeman, running a muck [*sic*] with his locust in his hand, is not to be relied on for the exercise of much discretion" and "the use of violence on the part of the officers seemed altogether unnecessary, and therefore reprehensible."[35] Another newspaper said the police commissioners were "wanting in judgment."[36] "By their excessive zeal for order [the police] made an attack which looks despotic," said the conservative *Daily Graphic*.[37] One editorial, strongly critical of the meeting's organizers, reminded authorities that "of all the resources of the law, the locust club is the one which is to be used with the greatest discretion."[38] All the newspapers negatively described unabated police violence.

The press and public distinguished between "legitimate" demonstrators and troublemakers, and displayed sympathy for the so-called genuine workingmen. Numerous papers ran investigative pieces on poverty, and there was a significant increase in charitable donations by Gotham's wealthier citizens. The event also prompted many to question the acceptability of poverty and unemployment in a successful capitalistic society. The *Daily Graphic* pointed out "there must be something radically false in a state of society which throws one quarter of its laborers out of employ in a day at the beginning of winter and reduces the earnings of the rest from a third to a half."[39]

The press did not acknowledge the legitimacy of alternative political and economic ideologies. Socialists and communists (no distinction made between the two) were broadly condemned, characterized as agitators, demagogues, and poisonous rogues who were "knavish and cowardly." Xenophobic overtones permeated some rhetoric. Foreigners—"chiefly Germans or Irishmen"— were usually to blame for such things, as "Communism is not a weed of native growth."[40]

The press grasped that free speech was endangered, and questioned the legitimacy of government regulation of meetings. "There is no law which forbids people making foolish speeches," the *Daily Graphic* declared. "American citizens have the right to hold meetings and parade so long as they keep the peace."[41] Horace Greeley's *Tribune* was typical in pointing out "it is difficult for us to see that any serious harm would have resulted from the gathering if a calmer and more politic course had been adopted . . . the clubbing began before other means of putting an end to the demonstration had been exhausted."[42] The police had failed to distinguish between a dangerous mob and a foolish crowd,[43] and "when such suffering prevails as at present, it is natural that the unemployed should have curiosity to hear what men who profess devotion to their interests have to say.... This is not a proper way to treat American citizens."[44]

James Gordon Bennett's *Herald* waved the banner of law and order but reminded everyone that "so long as these men keep within the law they have the right to travesty the language of European socialists," and it counseled readers that movements such as these "profit by unwise efforts to suppress them."[45] Bennett excoriated the police for violence and the "questionableness of legal right on the part of the Park Commissioners to have ordered the police to prevent the holding of a meeting in Tompkins Square." He reminded readers that "the reserved and judicious use of authority is the best feature of free government."[46]

John Swinton, the *Sun*'s editor and former right-hand man to the *New York Times*'s Henry Raymond,[47] pressed the free-speech issue in newspapers and in a notable pamphlet entitled "The Tompkins Square Outrage." "I should like to know if the police of this place have the power to nullify the Federal Constitution and the State Constitution, or to deprive the people, of any of those rights which are supposed to be guaranteed to them by these instruments?" he asked presciently. More startlingly, he asked a question: is it illegal to show a red flag?

Possibly. The red flag was then the symbol of foreign perversion, and it became an object of hatred. German socialist Justus Schwab, an "uncleanly and small" mason,[48] was charged with inciting to riot and waving a red flag, possibly the first prosecution of its kind.[49] In a testy exchange, Justice Flammer asked him what the red flag meant—"The division of all property and riot and bloodshed?" "No, no," explained Schwab, it meant peace and unity for everybody. "For everybody?" asked Flammer. "Yes for everybody that works," Schwab replied. "Why we all work, everybody works," said Flammer. "No," said Schwab, "not everybody." "Are you a Communist?" asked Flammer. "Yes I am," he replied.[50]

Of the forty-odd men charged that day, most were dismissed for lack of evidence.[51] Two received stiff jail sentences. Joseph Hoefflicher, a fifty-year-old, rheumatic unemployed woodturner from Bridgeport, was found not guilty of inciting a riot but guilty of assault after raising his cane, in what he claimed was self-defense, and striking an officer on the arm twice; he received a three-month sentence. Christian Mayer, a twenty-nine-year-old painter, was given six months for simple assault and battery after two trials. He had claimed self-defense after hitting Sergeant William Berghold on the head with a hammer; the Court of General Sessions jury deadlocked over a felonious assault charge on February 3–4, but in an unusual legal move, Mayer was retried and convicted in the Court of Oyer and Terminer on April 13.[52] In the first trial, Mayer's lawyer, John C. Mott, had attempted what may be one of the first civil-liberties defenses in a New York City court, claiming his client's actions were protected by both national and state constitutions. "Any blow struck by the prisoner was a blow resisting an organized violation of a constitutional right and was also justifiable as an act of self-defense," he said.[53]

The court ignored the issue, but Mott, Swinton, and others pressed on, appealing to New York State Governor John Dix for a pardon.[54] Swinton had issued an emotional appeal to the New York State Assembly in March, asking for assurances of free speech and assembly rights and for an investigation into police misconduct.[55] Outcry for such an investigation had started immediately after the event, and a petition signed by workingmen sent to the mayor accused the police of incompetence and bias.[56] The seven-year-old Freethinker's League, headed by F. W. Lilienthal, was temporarily energized after a massive meeting at Cooper Union that focused on free speech.

At the end of the day, the New York police emerged unscathed from the criticism and appeared even stronger in their mandate to control public order. No policeman was charged with anything. During the month after the riot, they monitored workingmen's meetings held on private premises. Nerves were on edge: when a meeting was called at the Houston Street Casino, even police superintendent Matsell, "pale and nervous . . . sat in the rear room of a small cigar store kept by a lonely widow opposite the Casino." Mayor Havemeyer, who had been advised not to address the crowd of workingmen, was present when Police Commissioner Duryee told them they brought the clubbing upon themselves. The workingmen reminded the mayor they had votes, to which Havemeyer laughed and said, yes, but election was a long way off.[57]

Swinton's earlier question—was it illegal to show the red flag—received no definitive answer, but pragmatically the answer might as well have been yes. Swinton held a commemorative meeting in Tompkins Square on August 31, after police wisely decided not to repress the event. It marked the release, by governor's pardon, of Christian Mayer, two months early from his six-month sentence, and Swinton focused on free speech and assembly issues. On the eve of the American Revolution's centennial, he voiced a troubling question. "For what is the American flag?" he asked. "Is it merely a piece of bunting with so many stars and so many stripes? No, it is an idea, a principle, a vital potentiality. It is the Constitution. It is freedom."

If Swinton thought he was crossing the Rubicon of free speech, he was mistaken, for the meeting was not well attended in the time of unemployment and internecine labor strife.[58] For another fifty years, labor actions and public protest meetings in New York City would be accompanied by clashes with police. Labor slowly made its mark as a political force, but government established hegemony as the controller of public order. After Tompkins Square, decisions about public activity in streets and parks were based on politics, class, and race. Little thought was given to free speech, the issue that had so enraged Swinton and others. In general, the judicial system up to this point displayed a "general hostility to the value of free expression."[59]

The wife of the head of the Freethinkers League had watched from her Tenth Street home as police attacked demonstrators during the "Outrage." At a Cooper Union free-speech rally, she said she had fled Europe for freedom and had come to love her new country until the Tompkins Square event had shown civil rights to be little more than empty words, "like the music of a musician playing on a violin without strings in a castle in the air."[60]

RESURRECTING THE SQUARE

With Tompkins Square no longer an approved meeting ground, attention was turned to its development as a park. Increasingly, green spaces were in demand, and in the 1870s New York State appropriated hundreds of thousands of dollars for their improvement. By this point, more than a million people lived around the city population epicenter of Fourteenth Street and Fourth Avenue, just blocks from the square.[61] But first the parade ground issue had to be settled.

The idea of using Tompkins Square as a military parade ground had infuriated mayors Havemeyer, Wickham, and Ely in the 1870s, as well as New York's legislative delegation. Loathe to give up the precious few parks they had, these politicians had drafted a bill, which received its third reading in January 1875, so that the square would "be reformed with a view to ordinary park recreation and to prevent the further use of any part of it as a parade ground."[62] The city's Board of Aldermen were adamant: "We want no parade ground. We want no increase of debt for the land for it."[63]

Yet the Parks Department did not wholly back the square's restoration as a park. While acknowledging that "a popular recreation ground is much needed in [this] quarter," it was also "the only place in the City in which its military, firemen or police can be brought together in large number and practised in the simplest manoeuvres without serious obstruction to the streets."[64] Commissioner Henry Stebbins complained he had never been informed about the legislation, and made it clear the parade ground was still under consideration. His Solomonic decision was to keep and upgrade the parade ground and improve it enough for park use, but not at any large cost. Given the ruinous state of the ten-

and-a-half acre site, that meant doing little. By summer of the following year, no resolution had been found.

The standoff might have gone on indefinitely had it not been for two very different catalysts. One was Andrew Haswell Green, New York's controller, who was backed by the mayor, and the other was the local German community. Green and the Parks Department fought for several years over the cost and nature of payment to the laborers working on the square. The political infighting was vicious; motions were routinely overturned after passing, memos and newspaper reports consisted of mudslinging and accusations, work started and stopped, and workers were not paid or paid erratically. Local residents accused the parks commissioners of "political chicanery" and other residents of "lack of enthusiasm" and demanded the restoration be completed. This citizens' group formed a committee consisting of eighty-eight vice presidents and fifteen secretaries to make sure future meetings would have officers in attendance in order to protect the square.[65] Finally, in 1878, the state legislature authorized the full restoration as a park, first allotting $50,000 but then reducing the amount the following year to $25,000.[66]

Amid lanterns, music, and flowery oratory, more than ten thousand people attended the square's grand reopening celebration in September 1879. But press and public were still unhappy. "Tompkins Square does anything but smile in this bright Autumn sunshine. It is desolation, absolutely bladeless. . . . Does any one imagine that any gentleman could spend $75,000 on his private grounds to so little purpose and to such bad purpose?" The Parks Department received the full fury of the press: their work was "pernicious." "Before our parks are hopelessly disfigured," the *Tribune* asked, "it is time for the people to arouse themselves and insist upon Commissioners who can at least take an intelligent interest in the affairs of the department."[67]

Military parade grounds, and in general the role of the military in the city, remained a hotly contested issue for some time. Concurrent with the Tompkins Square debate, Controller Andrew Haswell Green had also squelched plans for buying a large amount of property in upper Manhattan to be converted into a military parade ground. A the same time, grave doubts over the construction of new armories resulted in much opposition to them (see chapter 10). Tompkins Square Park did receive regular infusions of money after 1880, mostly thanks to the reaction to an attack on another site, Washington Square. While that square had also occasionally been used as a parade ground, it was a proposal to erect an armory there that mobilized local citizens to form their own association, the Public Parks Association in 1878, and fight until their "last breath," as they put it, to block any construction in that square. "The recently unveiled plan of seizing one of our parks, then another, and all in succession, for the lounging and parading of militiamen, is anachronism," reported a physician member of the association.[68]

The parks movement by this point had developed extensive justifications for expansion and improvement, involving issues of public health. Another compelling argument was the well-publicized fact that real-estate values abutting parks and squares were considerably higher. By the 1880s, literature abounded descrying the paucity of park space in New York, which had only one acre of park for every 1,363 people, as compared to one to three hundred in Philadelphia, two hundred in Chicago, 190 in Boston, 205 in London, 235 in Berlin, and twelve in Paris. Despite the reluctance of politicians to invest money in building-free verdure, New York politicians managed to develop twenty designated parks in Manhattan by 1900.[69]

The Tompkins Square riot proved to be a marker in the establishment of clear rules for what was "acceptable" public behavior. Rather than see free speech and assembly as a healthy outlet for political dissent, a way of stemming public violence and thwarting revolution, authorities and propertied classes saw it as a conduit for that revolution, encouraging lawlessness, instability, and chaos. Officials discouraged popular use of public space except for parades, recreational use, or nonthreatening events.

The zeal for pristine parks and law and order was followed rigorously by the 1890s. Controls on free speech and assembly were clear when Frank Mason North, a prominent social activist in the Methodist Episcopal church and the corresponding secretary of the New York City Church Extension and Missionary Society,[70] was refused a meeting permit for the square. North was told by the Department of Public Parks that "a large element of socialists and anarchists live in that vicinity, and it has been frequently found necessary, in the interest of public safety, to refuse the organizations representing them the privilege of meeting there." It was not Rev. North's meeting they were worried about but the precedent it might set. "This Department is very unwilling to establish what might be considered a precedent by these people in insisting that permits be granted to them for public meetings at that point." The Parks Department did offer to give him a permit for Union Square.[71]

Even a religious ceremony was a threat to order. In April 1897, a rabbi was arrested for attempting to mark Birkat ha-hama, a ceremony of the blessing of the sun, in Tompkins Square Park.[72] His Lower East Side congregation reportedly trampled the grass, upset signs telling people to stay on the walks, and assembled without a permit. In court, facing the throng of supporters, the judge said he never heard of this ceremony. The indignant rabbi responded that "he thought the public parks were free to the people, and that a person could do as he pleased in those places as long as he was not disorderly."[73] The outcome was a draw. While the arrest was upheld as legal, the rabbi was discharged, as no disorder was intended, even if it did occur; the proviso was the rabbi would not file a complaint against the policeman.

Tompkins Square had to face another challenge. In the mid-1890s, the Committee on Public Baths and Public Comfort Stations proposed constructing a large public bath, replete with laundry and public toilets, in the square. The proposed building, a large, elegant, two-story structure, with arched windows, balconies, and a colonnade, was to be one of many structures erected to help deal with the virtual absence of baths and toilets in the Lower East Side. The committee's well-researched report was horrific in its implications: in one slum district consisting of 480 houses, only seventeen had bathrooms. They also estimated an average ratio of 10.5 people to each privy in New York.

The comfort-station proposal was doomed, thanks to the mobilization of neighborhood residents. Mayor Strong pointed out that "we have met with vehement protests from citizens of the neighborhood who fear that tramps and other undesirable persons will swarm there, to the discomfort of householders." Plans for the construction of the public baths had been prepared and arrangements made, he said, "but the people were so strong in their opposition that the matter was abandoned." Tompkins Square was spared this final indignity.[74] Real-estate developer Samuel Ruggles, who had supported a ban on construction in parks during the Washington Square controversy fifteen years earlier, would have credited the victory to divine direction: "Man makes buildings," he wrote, "but God makes space." In this case, it wasn't God but the politicians and the public.

NEW YORK UNDER CONTROL

DELMONICO'S TO DISARM DISORDER

The sweltering heat of July 1877 did not slow down the waiters from the famous restaurant Delmonico's as they lugged "big baskets and trays [of] meats, breads, and iced coffee" on "the finest French china and cut glass" to the soldiers waiting at the Seventh Regiment at Tompkins Market. The hungry men fought off the boredom of confinement with food and song, and strains of "Way Down on the Swanee River," "Sailor Boy," and "The Son of a Gambolier" emerged from the "sapient throats of the men."[1]

The volunteer soldiers were awaiting what had been forecast to be the siege of New York. "The anxiety and apprehension which pervaded New York City on Monday morning the 23rd of July, 1877," wrote the regiment's chronicler, "were greater than they had ever been since the dread days in the summer of 1863, when the city was actually powerless in the hands of a mob." The impetus for the state of siege: railroad workers across the northeast were engaged in "the most spectacular and widespread strike in American history," the first labor/management action of its kind.[2]

The 1877 strikes were potent, and "for the first time in America the head of labor revolution was raised."[3] To the surprise of the public, "unorganized or poorly organized workers mounted strikes and other forms of industrial action" to make their voices heard in every major city in America.[4] From Martinsburg, West Virginia, to Baltimore, Philadelphia, Chicago, St. Louis, San Francisco, Washington, D.C., and a host of smaller cities, lethal antagonism erupted from workers angry at slashed salaries, scab replacement labor, and management intent on keeping the railroads running. The massive violence left dozens dead and millions of dollars of damage in its wake.[5]

The mainstream press universally decried the violence that ensued from the strike and the cost to business and human life. "Insurrection! A Day and Night of Blood and Horror at Pittsburg" the New York *Herald* reported, referring to "a Savage War" and "Wholesale Pillage."[6] Strikers were not looked upon favorably, but sympathy for the average workingman did exist, fueled by perceptions that there were "good" and "bad" working people. In Great Britain, such a distinction had begun to fade as poverty had already been identified less as a personal failure than a societal one. In the United States, "the equation of work and virtue continued to pervade the nation's thinking long after the context in which it had taken root had been all but obliterated."[7] The "bad" were identified as communists, "demagogues and mischief-makers," or rabble involved in an "outbreak of idleness and vice."[8] That so many were foreign born just added to the mix, a reinforcement of the stereotype they were "not as decent as the brutes."[9]

"Good" workingmen, on the other hand, were characterized as victims. "This is not a struggle between Labor and Capital, but, in fact, a conspiracy against the unemployed," said a New York newspaper.[10] Sympathy for the unemployed lingered since the hard economic times of the early 1870s. As the number of immigrants swelled, so did urban poverty and the number of unemployed. As one observer noted, "If there is to be any demonstration of public or private sympathy in this matter, let it go out towards the poor fellows who are out of work."[11]

Yet many questioned why workers earning $1 to $1.50 a day should complain. That poverty was self-induced was a common belief in the United States. "Now the man whose children cry for bread when he is earning even one dollar per day spends money in other ways and neglects his children." Give up cigars and beer and you'll have money for bread, it was suggested, a standard not applied to the railroad owners.[12]

The prevailing reaction that, no matter how difficult the situation, "Labor" and "Capital" could work things out strengthened the conviction that any threat to order was external and conspiratorial, which justified the use of force to stop it. "Liberty and order are simply incompatible unless we can have local Governments strong enough to cope with any such emergency as those under which they are, one after another, hopelessly breaking down,"[13]—a typical sentiment. "The question of the highest importance, the one that overshadows all others," advised the *Daily Tribune*, "is whether we shall have order or chaos." If riot should result, "there is no safety for life nor security for property."[14] Fears of rising food prices because of shortages prompted the *Herald* to say, "It is of very great importance to all classes, but particularly to the working people, that the peace of this great city shall not be disturbed or even threatened at this time . . .

immediate and terrible suffering would fall if we should have any public disturbance."[15] The daily pleaded, "Let us have peace and order in New York."[16]

"Security for property" lay at the heart of the concern. The belief that "every striker made war upon all civilized society when he countenanced the stopping of trains" was backed up by daily reports of the riots' financial damage.[17] One morose headline warned "A Long Sunday In Trade—Business almost at a standstill and salesmen lying idle."[18] "Anxiety," "uneasiness," and "uncertainty" were favorite words to describe the city's mood. "Little work was in progress," was the report from the dry-goods district. To affect the economy so fiercely was a crime: "The man who wantonly lights an incendiary fire in a crowded city, or bears the seed of pestilence into a crowded hall is not guilty of a more clearly defined crime against society than he who blocks up the channels of transportation upon which all commerce and industry depend," asserted the *Daily Tribune*.[19]

New York was a transportation center but not the national rail hub. That was Chicago's title. Still, fear that "a reign of anarchy and plunder" would spread to Gotham was enough to induce cautious citizens to tuck their families "in the quietude of the country," safe from the "speeches which were firebrands."[20] After all, if "the wealthiest city of the Union, and one of the great financial centres of the world" fell, could America be far behind?[21] The implications were clear: "The failure of the metropolis to maintain the cause of law and order would simply have loosened the keystone of American society."[22]

The Great Fear, as it was called, raised the specter of bringing New York to its knees, or worse, convulsed in flames, much as it had been during the Draft Riots of 1863. "Not since the days of the Rebellions . . . has there been such universal excitement in this city," wrote the *Tribune*.[23] Newspapers envisaged the possibility of a city on the verge of collapse, with "bloodshed, pillage and arson." "Where will it end?" they asked, considering the possibility of disruption of the tide of commerce. "Will business grind to a halt, ferries stop running?"[24]

Politicians and police decided to issue a permit for a labor protest in Tompkins Square, despite the fact they legally could have disallowed it. Justus Schwab, the workingman's hero of the 1874 riot there, had applied for the permit himself, prompting Parks Commissioner William Martin to rush to City Hall for advice. After waiting most of the day to speak to Mayor Smith Ely, Martin was told by Smith and Board of Police President Gen. William F. Smith that they "could not see any impropriety in holding the meeting, so long as it was proposed to conduct it peaceably."[25] Mayor Smith told one reporter that the police had assured him they were "entirely competent to maintain the peace of the city," and while the meeting was "ill-timed," he had "no expectation that there will be any riotous demonstration whatever."[26] The local press grumpily agreed that is was for the best:

> Workingmen and all men, including the demagogues, whose business it is to stir up strife and increase alienations, have a right to free speech in all places which are properly accessible to them. This does not include the right to use a public park for harangues which are certain to be inflammatory and may be dangerous. . . . But, considering all the elements of the question, their concession was probably judicious. There are ten chances to one that speakers at the meeting will injure their own cause.[27]

Schwab had asked that police not attend the meeting because "the crowd would be apt to resent surveillance," and offered to set up a self-policing force with red badges. The police turned that down, reminding him that "the custom of sending policemen to preserve order and await contingencies . . . would not be departed from."[28] The mayor warned Schwab to behave himself and make sure things didn't get out of hand, as they had in 1874. Schwab assured officials: "If the Police and Militia leave us alone there will be no trouble, for if any of our own men become disorderly we will make them behave themselves."[29] Posters warned "Don't unloose the tiger," urging people not to provoke the police.[30] Schwab even promised to return the American flag borrowed from the Parks Department "without a stain."[31]

Painted by the press as a communist gathering, the rally was endorsed by the cigarmakers, cabinetmakers, machinists, and blacksmiths. The press reminded city officials that any resultant disaster would be their fault: "It is to be hoped that the Mayor, the Police Commissioners and the Park Commissioners among them, have a distinct sense of the responsibility which they have assumed to the people of this city in turning over Tompkins square. . . . It is a pretty serious step to throw open a public park on a summer night to a miscellaneous multitude of idle men."[32]

Although Smith "was confident that his force could cope with any disorder that might arise" and that "the Militia would only be called upon to assist the civil authorities if the trouble assumed a serious aspect,"[33] the National Guard was mobilized after the governor declared martial law. "If the authorities could stem the outbreak, the insurrection would receive its death blow"[34] was the idea that fueled the rare calling up of more than thirty-five hundred troops from the city's First Division, including such famous regiments as the Fifth, the Seventh, the Eighth, the Twelfth, the Twenty-second, and the Seventy-first, led by General Alexander Shaler. In addition, men readied from Brooklyn's Second Division, Albany's Third, and the Fourth through Eight Divisions upstate.

The volunteer soldiers represented a wide socioeconomic diversity, from workingmen to elite businessmen. The elite Seventh Regiment were "knights of the rueful countenance" and "business and professional men called in from comfortable homes," romantically characterized as "rudely recalled from dreams of love to deeds of war."[35] Accustomed to dress parades and social events, the volunteer militias were surprised by the call-up. One newspaper joked: "Private soldier in crack regiment, reading order to rendezvous to receive ball cartridges and march to a distant city: 'See here! This is an outrage! This ain't wot I enlisted for. Fightin! With real bullets! The ideah! I feel my 'ay fevah comin' on!' "[36]

The bullets were indeed real: two hundred thousand rounds of seventy-caliber ammunition were stored in the State Arsenal at Thirty-fifth Street, with another ten thousand rounds at the Thirteenth Regiment in Brooklyn.[37] After all, said a colonel, "no blank cartridges will be fired." In the riots in 1863, he noted "as soon as it was discovered that we were not shooting with ball, the mob hung men to the lampposts every few moments."[38] Additional soldiers from Voernors Island, Bedloe's Island, Fort Wadsworth, Fort Lafayette, and Fort Hamilton were ordered onto steamboats with two hundred rounds of ammunition and six days rations each, and another seven hundred men were held in reserve. In addition, the militia had four Gatling guns, "a number of six-pounder smoothbores," and several hundred stand of rifles and small arms.

Militia officers were told they would only act if the police failed. The marksmen of the Seventh were given the power to fire without orders. Such a "hazardous" strategy—along with the forty rounds of ball cartridges issued to each man—was only to be used if the situation became dire. "We look to New York State now for serious trouble. New York City is the critical point, and I believe tonight trouble is likely to develop," said Major General Scofield, who had overseen troops in Pennsylvania and had reported to the president. "There is a large idle element in New York. . . . But the New York Police are very strong, and the Militia in New York belong to a very different class of society from that to which the strikers do, and there will be no sympathy between the two."[39]

To "show their nonchalant confidence in their power to maintain order,"[40] all police leaves were cancelled, and a thousand police were stationed at and around Tompkins Square and at the three nearest police stations.[41] Mounted police waited at the Eighteenth Ward Market at East Seventeenth Street, and 150 men in civilian dress were scattered among the crowd "to look for pickpockets." The Steamboat Squad watched the riverfront. Police lines were set up to prevent crowds from going beyond Houston, East Fourteenth Street, or Second Avenue. Detectives reported on "the temper of the working classes and their allies,"[42] and telegrams reported every move on the streets from 5 p.m. onward.

The 1877 events marked the introduction of a new role for New York City police that they would not relish—policing labor unrest and strikes. During the next two decades, there were more than five thousand strikes in New York, affecting more than thirty-three thousand establishments and almost a million employees.[43] While work actions were common, "no moves were taken to suppress strikes, boycotts, or unions" until there was a shift to the public arena: "once labor activity spilled out of the workplaces into community resistance, reaction came swiftly."[44] Unlike England, which had absorbed labor into mainstream political movements in the last quarter of the nineteenth century, there was considerable hostility toward unions in the United States. In the late nineteenth and early twentieth centuries, American courts, law, and legal violence "played a crucial, irreducible part in shaping the modern American labor movement,"[45] and the police became inextricably bound up in this triad.

The anticipated fight never came that July 25. The Fear turned into a "fizzle," a "fiasco," and "failure." Forces of law and order outnumbered demonstrators, heads were level and property preserved: "Nobody left town." The ferries ran regularly and life was normal: "Nobody had the white lips which Byron described as in Brussels on the night before Waterloo."[46] The collective sigh of relief was sounded: "New York breathes freer this morning.... The meeting was a failure: of feeling, tame, and of influence, insignificant. Another demonstration or two of the same sort would make the question of New-York sympathy for this whole wretched business utterly ridiculous. Everybody must now see superfluous steam."[47]

With crowds estimated as large as fifteen thousand, the meeting was orderly and calm; a police inspector and captain even shook hands with one of the speakers.[48] The *Sun* reporter John Swinton, who had earned his free-speech stripes at the 1874 riot, was one of the many who addressed the crowd from the fifteen-foot platform in the middle of the square, whose railing was draped with the American flag. In various corners of the square, German and French speeches served non–English speaking immigrants. A minor fracas erupted at the rally's dissolution, when police said a group had pelted them with bricks and stones on Eighth Street. They responded with clubs, but only one major injury was reported and two people arrested.[49] Law-and-order fans pointed out with pride the "whack, whack, whack" of the police locusts nipping things in the bud.[50]

The militia never actually deployed. "Happy as a clam" and "lovely as a rose," they went home a few days later, without seeing action. The Seventh Regiment enjoyed a week of revelry as "the boys kept the carnival of fun going all day long."[51] The tensions of a nation under siege and a city taut with tension provoked one young soldier to answer the call of his heart. "Spooney," he had plunged over the brink when forced to join his regiment, and in the face of danger proposed to his fiancée. The "saucy young woman" who landed the man of her dreams could only say of the entire 1877 episode "J'aime le militaire!"

For the rest of New York, the overwhelming verdict was that communism was dead. "It was neither imposing nor impressive," said the papers, and, more damning, "as a demonstration of laboring men in support of and sympathy with the strikers on the railways it was a gross and insulting burlesque." Some pointed out that it showed the victory of free speech, no matter how "vapid, vague, and incoherent" that might be. "Everybody must now see how much better it was to let our Communist and other crack-brained folk blow off superfluous steam ... we commend their utterances to the candid consideration of impartial readers."[52]

The city should have breathed a sigh of relief. Instead, the establishment press was disappointed that the authorities gave permission for the demonstration to occur in the first place. This "delusion" that public protest was legitimate was attacked by the *New York Times*, which typified the most conservative but predominant view at the time:

> Any concourse which impedes free locomotion in a public street is necessarily illegal, because it defeats the purpose for which a thoroughfare exists. A public square or park being intended for purposes of ornament, health, and recreation, as well as for purposes of free locomotion, it is equally obvious that any assemblage which interferes with the ends for which it was acquired must also be of an illegal character.[53]

Even worse, the *Times* warned that giving permission to one group would set a dangerous precedent as other groups would demand to use Tompkins Square. The "folly and weakness of the local officials" would lead them to regrets later: "The City will not always to able to spare half its Police force and four Militia regiments to keep watch over the 'peaceable assemblage' of a set of fools fanatics, and adventurers."[54] Thus, "the mere apprehension of riot had the effect of stripping half the City of its usual force of Police, and of leaving thousands of empty houses at the mercy of thieves."[55]

The pattern for order was being set. New York was, by 1877, perfecting the mechanisms to ensure the security of business and the safety of it inhabitants. Streets were to be accessible, lines of commerce were to be undisturbed, parks were to be open, and property was to be protected. If this meant compromising the rights of free speech and assembly, so be it. Police, who generally met their share of criticism, displayed "admirable conduct" at the Tompkins Square meeting and deserved "three or four days' extra pay," said the *Herald*. So what if a cop "now and then uses his club like a ruffian"—the police were "a splendid organization."[56]

NIMBY TO THE ARMORY

A city preparing for siege is not the typical view of Gilded Age New York, whose history is rooted in the mansions of Fifth Avenue, the tenements of the Lower East Side, and the buildings of Wall Street. Such growth and prosperity was nurtured by a sense of security that enveloped the last quarter of the century, which enabled people to go about their daily lives without fear or unusual risks. But security was a dominant concern in the nineteenth century. Fear was increasingly internal: threats from outside had migrated into America and had to be dealt with. The articulation of such fears was less clear, and it emerged in some unusual ways.

One of those ways was the construction of armories for the National Guard, the civilian volunteer militia that was founded in the young republic and provided auxiliary service in times of need.[57] The name "National Guard" was used exclusively by the Seventh Regiment until 1862, when New York State adopted it for all companies, the National Guard of the State of New York (NGSNY). There were six National Guard companies in the Empire State in 1825, ten by 1826. Such quasi-military units were supported mostly by private funds, with rents for headquarters usually paid for by public funds. In 1874, New York City was home to the First Militia Division, which consisted of the First Brigade (Twelfth, Twenty-second, Sixty-ninth, Seventy-first, and Seventy-ninth Regiments), the Second Brigade (Fifth, Sixth, Eleventh, Eighty-fourth, and Ninety-sixth Regiments), and the Third Brigade (First Battalion, Seventh, Eighth, and Ninth Regiments), commanded by Major General Alexander Shaler;[58] the Washington Grays cavalry; and the B, C, G, and K Batteries.[59]

Until the 1870s, most units had only temporary, rented quarters. The facilities were unsatisfactory and complaints were fierce, starting in the 1870s. "To deprive the assignment of suitable quarters, after having so long struggled under the disadvantage of being practically without an Armory, and after so long an effort to better its conditions that respect cannot but have a most pernicious effect upon its welfare and prosperity," the Eleventh Regiment bitterly responded when told they would have to leave their Centre Market armory.[60]

TEMPORARY/RENTED HEADQUARTERS OF
NATIONAL GUARD REGIMENTS THROUGH THE 1870S

FIRST MILITIA:

Sixty-Ninth (Irish or Highlanders) Regiment, at the Essex Market (Delancey) until 1857, and then at Twenty-third Street between Sixth and Seventh Avenues

Eleventh (German) Regiment, which moved into the Essex Market at Chrystie and Delancey until it disbanded

Fifth (German or Jefferson Grenadiers) Regiment, which was to move from a saloon on Hester Street to stables at Ninth Avenue and Twenty-seventh Street

Seventy-ninth Regiment, on the fifth floor at Greene and Houston Streets

Ninety-sixth Regiment, which moved from Germania Hall in the Bowery to Centre Street

Sixth Regiment, at the top of Tammany Hall at Fourteenth Street

First Regiment, over a stable at Thirty-second Street

Twelfth Regiment, at Broadway between Forty-fifth and Forty-sixth Streets

Twenty-second Regiment, at Fourteenth Street and Sixth Avenue

Seventy-first Regiment (consolidated with the Thirty-seventh) at Broadway and Sixth Avenue

Eighty-fourth Regiment at Broadway and Fourth Street

THE THIRD BRIGADE:

Eighth Regiment, at the Excelsior Building at Twenty-third Street between Seventh and Eighth Avenues

Ninth Regiment, over a stable at West Twenty-sixth Street

Seventh Regiment, Tompkins Market

Washington Grays, at Broadway and Forty-fifth Street

First Cavalry, at Forty-sixth Street and Broadway

Third Cavalry, at the Bowery

B, C, G, and K Batteries, which shared the City Arsenal on Elm Street

In 1874, the Seventy-first Regiment voiced "intense indignation" at orders to leave its Thirty-fifth Street and Broadway site for the fourth floor in a building at Ninth Avenue and Twenty-seventh Street.[61] "Unsafe" was the judgment of the colonel in charge, as it was above stables, a hayloft, and paint storage, and it emitted an "annoying" effluvia. Major General Alexander Shaler told the Board of Supervisors that such an action would "cripple them or discourage the

'Esprit Du Corp.'" Moreover, he pointed out the *strong, tactical position and accessibility to many of the public routes of travel; it should never be abandoned as a military rendezvous except for another in the immediate vicinity.*[62] In other words, the new location was inconvenient for members. Convenience was one of the reasons given by the Ninth Regiment in 1876 for protesting an ordered move from its ten-year home at 221 West Twenty-sixth Street to Ninth Avenue and Twenty-seventh Street. "Entirely inadequate" was the verdict: the room "wholly insufficient," "not pleasant.... And the surroundings are very disagreeable."[63]

The sudden storm over National Guard headquarters emanated from the political drama of the time. When Tammany Hall boss William M. Tweed fell from power in 1871, a group of prominent and wealthy New Yorkers designated themselves the Committee of Seventy and stepped in to rein in city finances. Andrew Haswell Green, who became comptroller in September 1871 and remained in this key position for five years, was told to reduce the city's debt, which had risen dramatically under Tweed. With the Board of Supervisors at his side, he began a tough campaign of frugality. City workers went without pay, streets deteriorated, and every expenditure was audited.

High rent for the armories was a particularly volatile issue, as were cost overruns for their maintenance. In 1873, rents, repairs, and furniture for armories and drill rooms ran $108,152.51, an overrun of $8,152.10.[64] Another $50,434.83 went for repair bills. The press had a field day looking at the exorbitant charges. In one estimate, the rents were triple market rate. And the Sixth Regiment, housed at Tammany Hall itself, paid an annual rent nine times the appropriate charge. Similarly, the Twelfth Regiment paid almost four times the reasonable rent, and for the First Infantry the overcharge was about eight times.[65] On the 1874 budget for departments under the Board of Supervisors, armories were the second most expensive item at $300,000, after judiciary salaries at $700,000.[66]

Arguments over militia headquarters were fierce and political. While Green tried to control costs, they continued to run high, a legacy of Tammany Hall deals. In 1875, another audit of all armories showed that of the quarter of a million dollars spent on rent, a fourth of the money was for properties not even being used. When the Seventy-first was asked to move, it was pointed out that the new rent was a scandal at $12,500, "three times what it was worth," because the lease was obtained by "fraud" and it was a bad location.[67] In 1876, Mayor William Wickham allowed the Ninth to stay put; the Board of Supervisors gave in on the $20,000 rent for the Twenty-second, stating that "it is not possible to procure an armory in a proper location for a Regiment on more reasonable terms."[68]

But politics played a role in all this. The New York governor's office could be called upon to help sway a decision. Adjutant General John Rathbone advised

Mayor Havemeyer "The 71st Regiment is one of the best in the First Division," he wrote, "and which, in case of disturbance or riot, would be among the first to be called out. If the Board of Supervisors persists in making this change it will be disastrous in its effect upon the regiments, and will be the means of breaking it up."[69]

Green was outspoken in both cutting spending on armories and opposing construction of all new ones. He led the city government's disinclination to support such expenditures. Although the armory-building boom in America in the last quarter of the nineteenth century may have been fueled by fear of uprising, in municipal New York, at least, the ruling elite felt the city was secure, police in control, and the money could be used more wisely elsewhere. They were concerned about wasting valuable real-estate assets on armories. Upstate constituents were apparently more worried about rebellion, and the New York State legislature passed a law in 1873 establishing a board of commissioners of armories and drill rooms for the First Division, with broad power to purchase or take public land, spending up to a half million dollars a year; the money was to be raised through personal and real-estate taxes, and additional money could be raised by floating bonds.[70] Green was furious.

The drive to construct new armories in New York City came from the militia companies themselves and the lingering effects of the Draft Riots.[71] The companies felt they deserved bigger and better-furnished spaces as a reward for past service and as an inducement for recruiting. Most regiments had served in the Civil War, and a few had been called up during the 1863 Draft Riots. In the peaceful post–Civil War era, when it seldom saw fighting, New York City's National Guard developed a strong social profile, with entertainment, leisure, and dress parades foremost. "The 'citizen-soldier' never forgets that he is a good deal more citizen than soldier—soldier perhaps two weeks in the year and citizen the other fifty," a contemporary militia booster wrote. "He feels his service to be a favor to the State, for not only is it voluntary, but he bears the bulk of its expenses, which are often heavy, since so much is laid out in parade and frolic."[72] More incentive to join the militia was tied into the idea of reward for the voluntary service:

> And if the politicians now will think of what we have done,
> In quelling all disturbances between here and Washington,
> They'll give us what we're waiting for, and think it only right
> That when we can the better drill we can much the better fight.[73]

At the same time that the National Guard supported the construction of more armories, questions arose over the size of the force, and the state legislature began reducing the size of the state militia. In 1868, Governor John T. Hoffman cut it to thirty thousand from fifty thousand, saying "my aim is to reduce ... military expenses of state."[74] The next year it was cut back to twenty-five thousand and then twenty thousand, returning to twenty-four thousand in 1870. In New York City, National Guard membership increased slightly from the near ten thousand level in 1873: in 1882, it reached 12,495, dropped to 11,687 in 1884, and returned to 12,480 in 1888. As the number of National Guard declined, the armory itself became an inducement for membership, with its clubhouse facilities and huge and well-appointed interiors. And as Shaler noted in 1888, "all the organizations are quartered in suitable armories, except in the city of New York."[75]

Gotham's residents apparently did not care. They wanted lower taxes. The basic premise was why waste money on armories? Six publicly funded armories were constructed in Manhattan from 1872 through 1895, and one privately funded one;[76] in the rest of New York state, twenty-one were built.[77] They were established despite angry public protests over costs, fear of property devaluation because of the presence of an armory, massive delays, and the realization that New York City property was so valuable that commercial development was preferable to civic development. City Hall found it had a symbolic gun pointing at its head over this. The regiments lobbied fiercely for new quarters and the state legislature mandated first that quarters be built. But Albany did not provide the money, so the city got stuck with the bills.[78] In particular, the construction of the Eighth, Ninth, Twelfth, and Twenty-second Regiment armories exemplified the continued reluctance to invest in such high-priced ventures.

As early as 1874, still cleaning up after the Tweed mess, the city was overruled by the state, when it tried to eliminate the commissioners for the erection of armories and drill rooms. Mayor Havemeyer claimed there were enough drill spaces, that new ones would be too expensive, and that no sites were available. Repeal would have let the city off the armory hook, but Governor John Dix refused to nullify the law.[79]

The story of the privately funded Seventh Regiment Armory illustrates the ambivalence of New Yorkers to the entire idea.[80] The "Silk Stocking" militia raised half a million dollars to construct its castellated Upper East Side headquarters, which became home to the city's most famous art exhibitions and social soirees. It lush interiors and upper-crust architecture became the envy of all the other regiments and influenced the selection of architects for later projects. With its privileged connections, the Seventh began lobbying in the early 1870s for a state law providing for its own new armory; it had earned particular distinction because its Twenty-first Street headquarters had been destroyed by the angry mobs in the Draft Riots.[81] The first "uptown" armory, the Seventh, was built on two acres on Park Avenue between Sixty-sixth and Sixty-seventh, the site of what was once part of Hamilton Square, but only after years of fighting for sites in other areas of the city. As rich and well-connected as this regiment was, it took almost two decades and many dead ends before the armory was constructed.

When the Seventh Regiment tried to get Reservoir Square (now Bryant Park) for its new armory in the mid-1870s, horrified city officials pointed out the land alone was worth $1.5 million, and that with a new building, the expense would exceed $2 million. The City Controller said that "residents of the vicinity were opposed to having an armory there, and some of them appeared to think that . . . it would . . . depreciate the value of their property."[82]

The next proposed site, Washington Square, elicited a fury that made the Reservoir Square battle seem tame. "Tax Payers and Workingmen," as local property owners described themselves, were already unhappy at the physical neglect of the square, and in 1877 petitioned the city to put it "in a proper and healthy condition."[83] The armory would have taken over a portion of the park, leaving space for a parade or drill ground. When the armory was proposed, locals argued that a park was more important for a crowded population. The argument was plausible. Dr. Edward Seguin, member of the New York Academy of Sciences and a leader in the new parks movement, warned that "to save our parks will save hundreds of children." Nothing could justify encroachment: "All nations now send their militia to the field of maneouvre every year, and excuse them from the painful duty of frightening the servant girls and their babies in the square—a drill sufficient to dress the bloody gendarmes of Paris, or operatic soldiers, but insufficient to initiate young men in modern warfare."[84]

The parks movement may have caught the public ear with health concerns, but the "wonderful effect of Central Park on Real Estate values" caught the public purse. The New York Park Association, a group of well-heeled and civic-minded businessmen, pointed out what was obvious to any savvy observer at the time: that the cost of the park was paid for many times over because of the increase in the value of land and taxes: $21 million more than the initial outlay. "But for the existence of Central Park, a very considerable part of the tax paid by the enhanced real estate in the Twelfth, Nineteenth and Twenty-Second wards would be imposed upon the rest of the city."[85]

The Public Parks Protective Association, another lobbying group—perhaps the first NIMBY ("not in my backyard") group in American history—led the opposition against the proposed Washington Square armory. While the mayor reminded everyone that in "periods of turmoil and excitement nothing inspires our community with so much confidence as the presence of our citizen soldiery," the public remained unconvinced, and hardboiled New Yorkers were unimpressed by the threat of an undelivered revolution.

Another illustration of public resistance to armories is that of the Sixty-ninth Regiment, which fought for two decades for satisfactory headquarters. Colonel Emmons Clark, who took the helm from General Shaler in the late 1880s, tried saber rattling to gain support—"in case the civil authorities and the municipal police are unable to protect the lives and property of the people and maintain public order," their uptown headquarters would be too far from the business and population centers to be effective. Yet even a brigadier admitted it was rare for "the National Guard [to be] called upon to aid the Municipal authorities."[86] And local law barred any park or public place from being made into an armory, which meant the Hall Place site near Tompkins Market would not be appropriate.[87] Despite further wrangling and continued pressure from the armory board, the Hall Street site was instead used to enlarge Tompkins Square Market, and the Sixty-ninth wound up at an acre-and-a-half site at Lexington Avenue between Twenty-fifth and Twenty-sixth, in 1899. That move was not without a bitter fight: Gramercy Park residents fought the issue for years, with the Twenty-third Street Protective Association objecting to the blight the armory would bring; they were backed by former Mayor Abram Hewitt.

The elimination of the Washington Square site had other ramifications. It marked the end of establishing any drill ground downtown, and it underscored the absence of such a space on the island of Manhattan. Even the New York Park Association, always promoting open spaces, admitted "there is not a spot on Manhattan Island to which one citizen soldier can resort for purposes of drill or military."[88] Andrew Haswell Green made sure the public knew just how expensive such a ground would be, at $1.5 million for the land and $125,000 in maintenance costs, forcing Mayor Wickham to side with him in the midst of an economic depression.[89] But the absence of parade grounds did not diminish the era's steady stream of National Guard dress parades in New York City, which were celebratory civic occasions attended by city officials and the public.

To bolster its chances for armories to be built, the National Guard lobbied fiercely, and in 1884, the Armory Board of New York City started operations. The board consisted of New York City's mayor, the commissioner of public works, the commander of the First Division, and three guardsmen, and was later expanded.[90] This law was the symbolic bullet in the gun pointing at the city's head. The New York State legislature mandated the construction of armories and even paid for most of them around the state, but New York City had to pay for its own.[91] The city, for its part, did everything it could to delay or deter such construction, leading to furious correspondence over the years concerning the board's failure to act on various issues in a timely fashion.

In 1884, the Armory Board succeeded in getting the Sinking Fund to authorize $2 million in bonds in order to start the purchase of sites for new armories for the Eighth, Ninth, Twelfth, and Twenty-second Regiments. Fierce opposition arose immediately, and the controller only authorized the first $800,000, for the Eighth, Twelfth, and Twenty-second sites.[92] Controller Loew blocked the money for the Ninth. General Shaler pleaded: "Suppose that a bag of dynamite were placed on the Brooklyn bridge as it was on the London structure," Shaler said, by way of pressing for the immediate bond issue. "Wouldn't there be a good deal of alarm?" Recorder Smyth's answer was classic New York: "Then we would issue the bonds at once."[93]

The battles for armories for the Ninth, Seventy-first, and Sixty-ninth Regiments each raged for more than a decade and typically included charges and countercharges of corruption, malfeasance, and foot dragging. Taxpayers complained about higher taxes, property owners complained their property was being infringed on, and displaced business owners fought against eminent domain or eviction. The Ninth Regiment cited its valor at Gettysburg and the fact that "neither the City or State have ever testified their appreciation of the sacrifice made, nor created a monument in testimony of their faithfulness."

Their frustration was apparent in their lobbying: "If neglect, unjust treatment and the poorest accommodations for improvement could have broken up an organization, it would now be but a memory ... it only asks ... that it shall have fair, just and honorable treatment at the hands of the authorities." In disgust, one stalwart of the Ninth, a ten-year member and "solid democrat," wrote to Mayor Hugh Grant in 1891 that their "dilapidated structure" is "one of the worst in the City: houses of the worst reputation are all around it, and a lady can not be asked to take any part in the receptions to which they hold there." The smell was so bad, he said, that uniforms could not be left in the armory. The urgency was lost on the city—it would not move into its Fourteenth Street home until 1897.

Finances were paramount. When a new state law in 1889 would have placed yet more financial burden on the city to pay for armories outside of it, Mayor Grant objected, with support from the House and Real Estate Owners Association of the Twelfth and Nineteenth Wards. Such a law would prove "detrimental to the economy of every business man and the taxpayer at large."[94] When the Ninth and Seventy-first Regiments battled over a site for a new armory, the Sinking Fund Commissioners turned down the recommendation of the Armory Board to acquire a site for the Seventy-first, preferring to wait for a peaceful—and cheaper—solution.[95] The Seventy-first didn't get its East Thirty-third Street home until 1894.

The new home for the Eighth Regiment should have opened for Christmas in 1889, but didn't, because the Armory Board was haggling over bids for interior work, most of which exceeded the limits imposed by the Sinking Fund.[96] The palatial nature of the new armory overwhelmed the *New York Times*: "The limits of a newspaper article are inadequate to convey a just conception of the magnitude and striking architectural characteristics of the new armory." It noted that bowling alleys would be added, so that the building "conserve the social as well as the military side of National Guard life."[97] Delays in opening were not surprising, given the fact that these projects took so long. Even when armory construction finally began, it went slowly. "I deem it my duty to report on the slow progress of the work on the 71st regiment armory. The iron work is at a standstill, and so with brick work," reported the clerk of the works to the Board of Armory Commissioners in 1892.[98]

An efficient and prosperous city was a far greater concern than military prowess. In the fall of 1885, sensational hearings were held over transactions by the Armory Board. The issue was that "a great deal more was paid for armory property than it was worth ... and there was very extensive dickering in that matter."[99] The Gibbs Commission was set up to look into "defects" in municipal administration, excessive taxes, excessive salaries, noncompliance with laws, and questionable armory land deals. Testimony came from a variety of city officials, including those of the Armory Board, docks, fire, street cleaning, excise, and parks; issues ranged from disbursements to tax-exempt property, ordinance enforcement, and purchasing.

The Gibbs testimony revealed huge profits from real-estate deals involving land for armories. Implicated was Alexander Shaler, New York State National Guard First Division head, who was indicted, much to the horror of his National Guard. Two trials ended in hung juries, but Shaler resigned in disgrace from both the Armory Board and the Board of Health. That Shaler had sat on both the Armory Board and the Sinking Fund had clearly been one of the most damning parts of the case against him.

In addition to the six armories built before 1900, another four were built in Manhattan after that, three between 1901 and 1911, and one, the 369th, the Harlem Hellfighters, in 1932. Not only in New York but across the nation, armories were not only homes to the National Guard but also "community centers," "used very frequently and often as public meeting places, civic centers," a resource for towns during emergencies.[100] Their construction was mired in controversy, as the National Guard they housed had limited military action. In New

York, most were torn down, some burned down, and a few still stand, including the Seventh, which enters the twenty-first century with a decidedly unmilitary use: it is to be renovated for use as a cultural center. While the military may have served many purposes, one of them was not to occupy the streets of Gotham. When it came to preserving order, New York relied on its police, bureaucracy, and laws to keep the peace.

ARMORIES BUILT IN MANHATTAN

AFTER START OF ARMORIES BOARD IN 1872 UNTIL THE END OF CENTURY[1]

PLACE AND UNIT	LOCATION	DATE OPENED	DATE CLOSED	STYLE
1. Seventh Regiment[2]	643 Park Ave.	(1877–1881) 1880	still used	medieval[3]
2. Twelfth Regiment[4]	Columbus/ 61–62nd Sts.	1887	1958[5]	medieval
3. Eighth Regiment[6]	Madison Ave. & 94th St.[7]	1889–1890	1966[8]	medieval
4. Twenty-second Regiment[9]	Broadway/ Columbus & 67–68 Sts.	1889–1892	1929	fortress
5. Seventy-first Regiment[10]	Park Ave. & 33–34th Sts.	1892–1894[11]	1972	medieval
6. Squadron A	E. 94–95 Sts.	1894–1896	1966[12]	medieval
7. Ninth Regiment[13]	West 14th St.	1894–1897	1969	medieval

MANHATTAN ARMORIES BUILT IN THE TWENTIETH CENTURY

PLACE AND UNIT	LOCATION	DATE OPENED	DATE CLOSED	STYLE
8. First Battery[14]	West 66th St.	1901	in 1980, became ABC TV headquarters	Gothic
9. Sixty-ninth Regiment	Lexington Ave. & 26th Sts.[15]	1904–1906	still armory	Beaux Arts
10. Twenty-second Regiment[16]	168th & Ft. Washington	1909–1911	used for other purposes	
11. 369th Regiment[17]	142–143 Sts. & Fifth Ave.	1932	still armory	Art Deco

UNIT	LOCATION	DATE
Twenty-third Regiment	Clermont Ave.	1872–1873 (remodeled in 1911 for First Battalion, Field Artillery)
Forty-seventh Regiment	Marcy Ave.	1883–1884
Twenty-third Regiment	Bedford Ave.	1891–1895
Thirteenth Regiment	Sumner Ave.	1892–1894
Fourteenth Regiment	Eighth Ave.	1891–1895

ARMORIES BUILT IN THE TWENTIETH CENTURY OUTSIDE OF MANHATTAN

UNIT	LOCATION	DATE
Second Battery	Franklin Avenue, Bronx	1908–1911
Eighth Coastal Artillery District	Kingsbridge Rd., Bronx	1912–1917 (largest in America to 1940)
101 Cavalry Squadron	Manor Rd., Staten Island	1922
Second Signal Corps	Dean St., Brooklyn	1909–1911
Troop C	Bedford Ave., Brooklyn	1903–1907
Brooklyn Arsenal	Second Ave.	1924–1926
Seventeenth Separate Comp.	Northern Ave., Flushing, Queens	1904–1905
Fourth Regiment	168th St., Jamaica, Queens	1936 [18]

[1] There were six armories built in Manhattan before the 1870s, of which only the Central Park one still exists.

[2] Also known as the "Silk Stocking Regiment." This was originally the Twenty-seventh Regiment, 1834–1847. With ties to the socially prominent, the regiment began in 1868 to lobby for new headquarters, as affluent members moved uptown. They turned down an offer by William Tweed to get a free site in Reservoir Square and connection with the New Armory Fund. By 1881, they had $237,000 in private subscriptions pledged for a new headquarters.

[3] Usually refers to the castellated style of the building.

[4] The first armory funded by the Armory Board.

[5] Site used for Lincoln Center.

[6] Funded by the Armory Board. In the twentieth century, it moved to the Bronx.

[7] Shared space with Squadron A.

[8] Became I.S. 29.

[9] Funded by the Armory Board.

[10] Originally leased quarters at Broadway and Thirty-first Street.

[11] It burned down in 1902 and was replaced in 1905.

[12] Towers and walls were retained.

[13] They had rented on West Twenty-sixth Street. This was the last armory erected before 1901; the National Guard built a new one for the Forty-second Division—Forty-second Division HQ 1970–1971.

[14] Also known as Battery K, First Regiment of Artillery; later housed other units.

[15] This became the 165th Infantry around World War I.

[16] This became the 102nd Engineers.

[17] The "Harlem Hellfighters" was an African American regiment. It was originally the Negro Regiment, then the Fifteenth, before it became the 369th.

[18] Todd, *New York's Historic Armories.*

Sources: Landmarks Preservation Commission Designation lists 164, 259, 245; *Official Deliberations*, Armory Board of the City of New York (1884 created) (1880–1913); *Annual Reports*, The New York City Armory Board 1884–1911 (1912); Fogelson, *America's Armories*; Ann Beha Associates, *The Armory*; *New York Times*, July 8, 1871; April 4, 1874; November 2, 1879; December 29, 1888; February 5, 12, 18, 19, 21, 24, 26, 27, 1878; March 6, 1878; July 8, 1871; *The Daily Tribune*; Molineux, *Riots in Cities and Their Suppression*; Wingate, *History of the Twenty-second Regiment of the National Guard*; Clark, *History of the Seventh Regiment of New York, 1806–1889*; New York Historical Society: Emmons Clark to NY County Board of Supervisors, September 15, 1873; Seventh Regiment Archives, *The New Armory of the Seventh Regiment, N.G.S.N.Y.* (1875); "Protest of the Eighth Regiment NGNYS against the Action of the Board of Aldermen in Assigning them to the condemned building, corner Ninth Avenue and Twenty-seventh St.," dates 1877 but probably 1879; *Proceedings of the Commissioners of the Sinking Fund of the City of New York*, September 4, 1884; Investigation of the Departments of the City of New York by a Special Committee of the Senate of the State of New York (1885)—(Gibbs Committee Investigation); Israel, "NY's Citizen Soldiers"; Reinders, "Military and Public Order in Nineteenth-Century America."

FIGURE 0.1 The massive Iraq war protest in Hyde Park, London, February 2003. *Source*: AP Images.

FIGURE 0.2 Brian Haw in discussion with the Metropolitan Police in front of Parliament. Note policeman videotaping discussions with protesters. *Source*: Photo by author.

FIGURE 2.1 Regent's Street, London, in the nineteenth century. *Source*: Hulton-Deutsch Collection, Corbis.

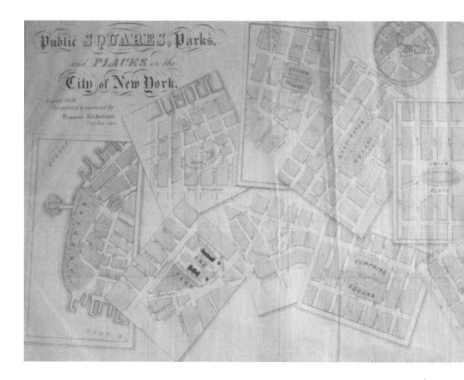

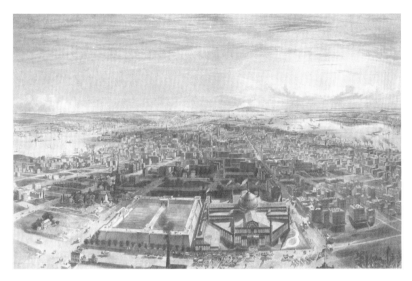

FIGURE 2.2 New York, looking south from Forty-second Street and the Reservoir, 1855. *Source:* NYPL Digital Picture Gallery.

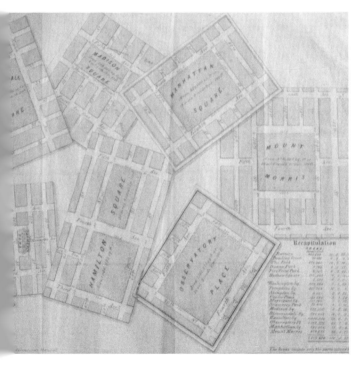

FIGURE 2.3 Evaporating spaces: the squares of New York, 1838. *Source:* Author's collection.

FIGURE 2.4 A typical London bobby, 1860s–1870s. *Source*: Mary Evans Picture Library.

FIGURE 2.5 Sir Richard Mayne, Metropolitan Police Commissioner. *Source*: Mary Evans Picture Library.

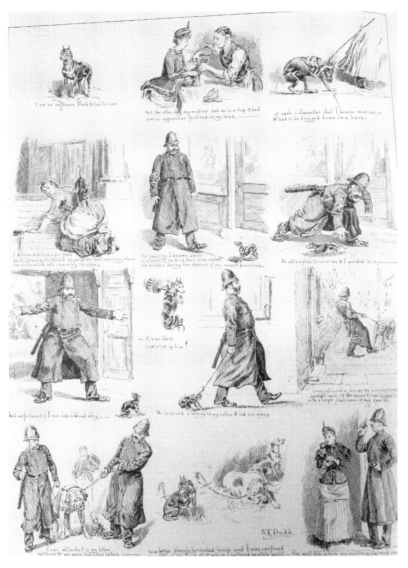

FIGURE 2.6 Animal handling was one of the London police's diverse responsibilities. *Source*: *Illustrated London News*, January 2, 1887.

FIGURE 2.7 Giving directions to a city full of newcomers was a typical activity for the New York police in 1899. *Source*: NYPL Digital Library.

FIGURE 3.1 The 1833 Coldbath Fields Riot tested the London police's ability to maintain order. *Source*: Mary Evans Picture Gallery.

FIGURE 4.1 Legislation banning commercial activity on Sundays was the impetus for the Sunday Trading Bill Riots in 1855. *Source*: Mary Evans Picture Gallery.

FIGURE 4.2 Home Office Secretary Sir George Grey handled Chartists and helped set policy for public meetings. *Source*: Mary Evans Picture Gallery.

FIGURE 5.1 The young George Bernard Shaw gained fame as a street orator in the 1880s (1892). *Source*: Bettman/Corbis.

FIGURE 5.2 Demand for electoral reform prompted the tearing down of fences in Hyde Park in the 1860s during the Reform Bill Riots. *Source*: Mary Evans Picture Library.

FIGURE 5.3 By the 1860s, Trafalgar Square was on its way to becoming an important meeting ground. *Source*: Mary Evans Picture Library.

"KICKED OUT." (?)

FIGURE 5.4 Following election as an MP, Charles Bradlaugh refused to swear an oath and was kicked out of Parliament. This prompted him to advocate free-speech issues. *Source*: Mary Evans Picture Library.

FIGURE 5.5 Trafalgar Square reshaped central London (1850). *Source*: Mary Evans Picture Library.

FIGURE 5.6 Artist and writer William Morris took up the Socialist cause in the 1880s and challenged free speech and assembly restrictions. *Source*: Mary Evans Picture Library.

FIGURE 6.1 Sir William Harcourt, free-speech advocate. *Source*: *Illustrated London News*, March 7, 1885.

FIGURE 6.2 A bitter winter and deepening depression contributed to sleeping "rough" on the streets of London. *Source*: *Illustrated London News*, October 29, 1887.

FIGURE 6.3 For Sir Charles Warren, Metropolitan Police Commissioner, order was primary. *Source*: *Illustrated London News*, May 1, 1886.

FIGURE 6.4 Socialists clashed with police during meetings in Trafalgar Square in 1887. *Source*: Mary Evans Picture Library.

FIGURE 6.5 "The Riots in London on Sunday, Nov. 13: Defence of Trafalgar Square." *Source*: *Illustrated London News*, November 19, 1887.

FIGURE 6.6 Orators tried their best to be heard over the din of the large crowds at Hyde Park on Sunday, November 20, 1887. *Source*: *Illustrated London News*, November 1887.

FIGURE 7.1 The indomitable Annie Besant, one of the founders of the Law and Liberty League. *Source*: Mary Evans Picture Library.

FIGURE 7.2 The fiery labor leader John Burns. *Source*: Mary Evans Picture Library.

FIGURE 7.3 Trafalgar Square in 1890. *Source*: Mary Evans Picture Library.

FIGURE 7.4 "Squared!": —'Wot! Allowed to meet in Trafalgar Square on Saturdays, Sundays and Bank 'olidays, are we!' —'Then we just won't go!'

Two unemployed men complain about limitations of meetings in Trafalgar Square.

Source: Mary Evans Picture Library.

FIGURE 8.1 The militia fired on demonstrators at the Astor Place Riot, 1849. *Source*: NYPL Digital Gallery.

FIGURE 8.2 The wanton violence of the Draft Riots of 1863 had long-lasting effects on New York's handling of public-order issues. *Source*: NYPL Digital Library.

FIGURE 8.3 The 1871 Orange Riots resulted in sixty-two deaths and legislation requiring permits for public assemblies and processions. *Source*: Bettmann/Corbis.

FIGURE 9.1 By 1870, Tompkins Square had become not a park or parade ground but a vast wasteland awaiting repair. *Source*: New York City Municipal Archives.

FIGURE 9.2 "The Communist Riot" and the "Blood or Bread Riot" were two descriptions of the meeting in Tompkins Square on January 14, 1873. *Source*: *The Daily Graphic*.

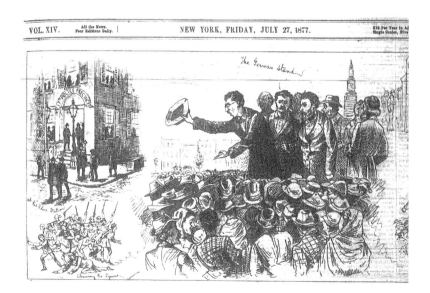

FIGURES 10.1 (PREVIOUS PAGE, LOWER) AND 10.2 Tompkins Square was packed for the July 1877 meeting that authorities allowed to be held despite a general ban on meetings there. *Source*: *The Daily Graphic*.

FIGURE 10.3 The Seventh Regiment lobbied fiercely for years for a new armory. *Source*: NYPL Digital Gallery.

FIGURE 10.4 The Ninth Regiment Armory was one of a handful built in New York City during the last quarter of the nineteenth century. *Source*: NYPL Digital Gallery.

FIGURE 10.5 New York City Comptroller Andrew Haswell Green opposed expenditures for the armories. *Source*: NYPL/Miscione.

INCIDENTS OF THE STRIKE

FIGURE 11.1 National Guard joined police in trying to keep order during the violent transit strike in Brooklyn in 1895. *Source*: *The Herald*, January 15, 1895.

INSULTING HIS MAJESTY.   CAUGHT IN THE ACT.

A CASE IN HAND.   ON THE DEAD BEAT.

NEW YORK POLICE SCENES. (See Page 78.)

FIGURE 11.2 Dealing with children was one of the many responsibilities of the New York police (1871). *Source*: NYPL Digital Gallery.

FIGURE 11.4 (OPPOSITE PAGE) "Duties of a Sergeant." The New York police try to regularize responsibilities. *Source*: New York Municipal Archives.

FIGURE 11.3 For many years, police stations served as "flophouses" for the homeless (1877). *Source*: NYPL Digital Gallery.

DUTIES OF A SERGEANT,

OF THE POLICE DEPARTMENT, CITY OF NEW YORK.

AND THE TIME IN WHICH HE PERFORMS THEM.

THE DUTIES OF A SERGEANT VARY EACH DAY FOR FOUR CONSECUTIVE DAYS AND THEN REPEAT THEMSELVES.

	DESK DUTY.	PATROL DUTY.	RESERVE DUTY.	MEALS.	OFF DUTY.
LONG DAY,	6 a.m. to 8 a.m. 1 p.m. to 6 p.m. 12 mid. to 6 a.m.	9.40 a.m. to 12 noon.	7.40 p.m. to 12 mid.	8 a.m. to 9.40 a.m. 12 noon to 1 p.m. 6 p.m. to 7.40 p.m.	None.
	13 Hours.	2 Hours, 20 Min.	4 Hours, 20 Min.	4 Hours, 20 Min.	None.
DAY OFF,		6 p.m. to 12 mid.			6 a.m. to 6 p.m. 12 mid. to 6 a.m.
		6 Hours.			18 Hours.
SHORT DAY,	8 a.m. to 1 p.m.	2.40 p.m. to 6 p.m. 12 mid. to 6 a.m.	7.40 p.m. to 12 mid.	1 p.m. to 2.40 p.m. 6 p.m. to 7.40 p.m.	6 a.m. to 8 a.m.
	5 Hours.	9 Hours, 20 Min.	4 Hours, 20 Min.	3 Hours, 20 Min.	2 Hours.
DAY OFF,	6 p.m. to 12 mid.		12 mid. to 6 a.m.		6 a.m. to 6 p.m.
	6 Hours.		6 Hours.		12 Hours.
FOUR DAYS,	24 Hours.	17 Hours, 40 Min.	14 Hours, 40 Min.	7 Hours, 40 Min.	32 Hours.
ONE DAY,	6 Hours.	4 Hours, 25 Min.	3 Hours, 40 Min.	1 Hour, 55 Min.	8 Hours.

FIGURE 11.5 The "Bicycle Policemen" helped deal with traffic mania in the city. *Source*: NYPL Digital Gallery.

FIGURE 11.6 "Idiotic raptures" outlawed. *Source*: *The World*, August 5, 1900.

FIGURE 12.1 By the mid-nineteenth century, Union Square had become a park at the conjunction of streets in the heart of New Yorks' population center. *Source*: NYPL Digital Gallery.

FIGURE 12.2   The IWW, better known as the Wobblies, tested the limits of free speech in Union Square in the early decades of the twentieth century (July 14, 1914). *Source*: Bettman/Corbis.

FIGURE 12.3   May Day celebrations attracted large crowds in the 1930s in Union Square. *Source*: Bettman/Corbis.

FIGURE 12.4 Communisits demonstrated in Hyde Park in 1931. *Source*: Mary Evans Picture Library.

FIGURE 12.5 A crowd of 350,000 people gathered for a Diana Ross concert on the Great Lawn in Central Park in July 1983. *Source*: AP Images.

Nº
11

THE REGULATED CITY

"SUPPRESSING RASCALITIES"

Truncheons and cries of "scab" flew fast and furious in the January cold during the most violent strike ever to occur in Brooklyn. Two years after the Panic of 1893, which brought with it unemployment (an estimated fifty thousand in Brooklyn alone), homelessness, outdoor relief, and labor protest, the Brooklyn Surface Railroad workers said they could not live on their $2 daily wages.[1] More than seven thousand National Guard filled the streets of Brooklyn, which was still an independent municipality across the East River from New York City. This was one of the few times the militia was called out in the post–Civil War era, and one of the rare times the National Guard fired on demonstrators. At a cost of a half million dollars, they assisted the police in trying to keep the trolleys running and control strikers determined to prevent that.

"They can't win. ... The police will protect the companies. ... The public has to have its cars. ... They've got the militia on their side," predicted George Hurstwood, Theodore Dreiser's fictional strikebreaker in *Sister Carrie*. Hurstwood's pessimism was not unwarranted. Brooklyn was like "an armed camp, or as in the midst of a civil war," according to Edward Morse Shepard, a prominent Brooklyn lawyer and Democratic reformer who was influential in New York politics. Shepard told a sympathetic audience at the Board of Trade dinner at Delmonico's on January 23 to pay attention to "the condition out of which the disorder has arisen," the misery of the unemployed. Disorder, he reminded the businessmen, produced inconvenience that focuses attention on public issues. However compelling the cause, Shepard warned, disruption was unwarranted and unacceptable: "Public order should be made the first consideration and inexorably." Shepard struck the interesting balance of the liberal of the turn of the century: "We must first have law, but with law public sentiment ought to require that there shall go right."[2] The bitter two-week strike, which cost the rail companies $15,000 a day, did little to help the workers, who were forced to call it off in the end.[3] Confidence that New York could provide such a balance was the product of three decades of creating an ordered city. Disruptions of this nature since 1870 had been minor and had not required such draconian force. Shepard was typical of business and civil leaders at the time, who recognized that different constituencies had to be satisfied to make the city work effectively. They had worked to establish a city in which commerce could function smoothly, services could be delivered in a consistent way, and culture and leisure possibilities provide enhancement to daily life. In principle, this was a city open to all.

Efficient transportation was important to a well-ordered city. By 1900, a million people per day used the city's rail lines, horsecars, ferries, and bridges. Any breakdown of this complicated network could bring the city to its knees and endanger order. Without dependable transportation, business would lie idle, merchants languish, banks come to a standstill, and the economy halt. As had been the threat in 1877, the prospect of the city grinding to a halt struck terror in the eyes of even the most liberal citizens. By 1900, as Shepard was about to run for mayor of the newly consolidated greater New York, he would remind people that "the security of property is an integral and sacred part of personal liberty."[4]

An earlier transit strike had occurred in 1886, when streetcar workers protested sixteen-hour workdays and created chaos. As would happen in 1895, much popular sympathy existed for the strikers, which resulted in people obstructing tracks with debris and harassing police. The Central Labor Union called a general strike, which suspended much of the city's transit on March 5, 1886. Police fought back and cleared the tracks without National Guard help. Unions replied through the ballot box: they supported their own candidate for mayor, Henry George, under a new United Labor Party, aimed at consolidating the political strength of unions. After George failed to win, however, union membership dipped for three decades. Strikes and labor actions continued in large numbers, but not until the 1920s did union membership coalesce and strengthen as activism increased.

The transit strikes of 1886 and 1895 elicited fierce reaction from both civil authorities and the public.[5] The strikes reflected high unemployment, large pools of immigrant labor, and increasing polarities of wealth and poverty. Sympathy for strikers could cross class lines. Propertied classes were sympathetic to the distress of poverty, and sometimes police and the National Guard were loathe to act against strikers, as had been the case in various places during the

1877 railroad strikes. In *Sister Carrie*, Dreiser had described the conflict of the policeman in 1895, who may have hated the scab but "felt the dignity and use of the police force, which commanded order."[6] Those unsympathetic to labor identified labor movements as radical and foreign, and strikes only hardened their positions.

Whatever the political viewpoint, strikes obviously disrupted daily life, and this could not be tolerated in a thriving city. An important urban dynamic emerged in the post–Civil War era, in which the desire for order took precedence over personal liberties. The public accepted this as normative, as a means for achieving success and prosperity. The increasing division between private and public life translated into public life becoming more controlled.

From 1870 to 1900, the city defined what the public could and could not do in public spaces. It developed infrastructure to support an efficient, workable, and expanding metropolis, ensuring what we have come to call the "quality of life." In this period, public space was defined so that the public knew what it could and could not do in those spaces. The policies established then would lay the framework for future generations of New Yorkers. European cities also grappled with these issues, but they could fall back upon a historical legacy in which basic structures and services were present. In America, neophyte cities had to create from scratch the structures and services necessary for the ordered city.

To regulate life, streets, parks, and squares had to be created, maintained, and defined for usage to facilitate navigation and commerce; utilities, including water, sewage, lighting, and fuel supplies, had to be developed and built; crime and disorder had to be controlled; transportation, mostly in private hands, had to be facilitated and integrated into the public domain. To create an acceptable quality of life, public-decency standards had to be set and preserved. The health and welfare of the individual was at stake, and therefore the success of the city. To further that success and control the excesses of the city, many believed there needed to be a "moral" environment, an elusive concept that proved most controversial in application. Both regulation and quality-of-life concerns are hallmarks of the modern city and help define the divergence between city and country. As Americans migrated to cities in the late nineteenth and twentieth centuries, expanding population necessitated extensive regulation.[7]

The establishment of order as a priority brought with it new civic authority and new bureaucracy to carry it out. It involved the idea that the municipality had a public mandate for looking after the welfare of its inhabitants.[8] New York was typical of American cities in that its authority derived from the state, which passed necessary laws and controlled revenues. And Albany kept the city on a short leash, producing negotiation and concession between city and state.

As the largest, richest, and most important of American cities, New York by the last quarter of the nineteenth century became the model for America. Requests constantly arrived at the mayor's desk for information about how to construct this new civic order. Whether it was how to inspect steamboilers, clean streets, run electricity, raise taxes, extinguish fires, regulate theaters, or control coal supplies, New York was seen as the expert on all things municipal.[9]

What had to be done to construct the ordered city was staggering. New York, a grid plan on paper, was transformed into a grid of cobblestones and macadam as streets were created. Once made, they had to be cleaned from muck, snow, live and dead animals, and vagrant people. The city decided what was to be allowed to happen on these streets, including how they should look, what signs and decorations were permitted on them, and how to let the public use them. Infrastructure required massive investment and construction; gas and electric lines, sewers, bridges, streetlamps, and fire hydrants defined the new public-works projects.

People's conduct, well-being, and behavior could negatively affect the city and thus became the object of control during this thirty-year period. New laws and regulations defined what was acceptable and unacceptable, including issues relating to health, pollution, food, markets, waste, gambling, prostitution, juvenile delinquency, beggars, peddlers, entertainment, lotteries, scams, and parks. Municipal agencies oversaw all this: police, fire, parks police, sanitation, and city officials became the designated agents of order. The mayor of New York became the most significant public official to deal with all these changes, as he initiated, endorsed, opposed, and battled for policies, laws, and ordinances. The police became the primary agents for both carrying out policies as well as determining them on a de facto basis. All this was amended and refined in the twentieth century, built upon this basic nineteenth-century framework.

Before the Civil War, New York had a plan for streets and a basic outline for commercial activity, including ordinances relating to docks, water, and real estate.[10] After 1865, the sketch became an intricate painting with every detail attended to, and by the end of the century, an ideal vision of the city had been created. The "City Beautiful" movement is an example of this, and reflected at the end of the century a vision of the city that was both well functioning and attractive. In turn an attractive city would be a magnet for "a desirable class of residents" and would "increase the value of real estate."[11]

Mistakes were made, there was gross inefficiency, graft and corruption did exist, and costs skyrocketed, but the city experienced an upward trajectory of improvement. When the Committee on the Affairs of Cities in the State Assembly criticized the New York City police for a "culpable want of efficiency and lack of skill, system and economy" in keeping the streets clean, Mayor Havemeyer pointed out that "A great City should not be left to any hazard in so important a matter as this." His answer was to shift responsibility from the Police Department's Scavenger Bureau to a street-cleaning bureau.[12] Priority was placed on the order.

The public wanted efficiency and recognized that city government bore primary responsibility in this area. The municipality had to keep order, and when things went awry, it had to fix things. "I have carefully watched your manly, honorable course in suppressing rascalities of all kinds in this city," wrote one citizen to Mayor Hewitt. "For all your efforts I thank you most heartily."[13] "Order-loving people," asserted Henry Bergh of the American Society for the Prevention of Cruelty to Animals, can't bear the city's disorder: "I sicken, at the bare contemplation of the innumerable nuisances, which have been allowed to fasten themselves upon this great City . . . [they] have become odious in the sight of order loving people."[14]

Licenses for various public activities became even more widespread and lucrative to help control potential chaos and bring in revenue. Licenses had been in use for some time: in 1828, for example, seven thousand licenses were issued to butchers, grocers, tavern keepers, cartmen, pawnbrokers, and inspectors.[15] The licensing served to restrict numbers doing the work, limit access to work opportunities, and create a privileged class. Revenue was less likely to wind up in city coffers than in someone's pocket. The licensing in the post–Civil War era was very different. The "Street permits" that became common from the 1870s onward were formal, city issued, and encouraged activity as well as revenue that would benefit the city. Every kind of daily activity could require purchasing a permit, including junk shops ($20), junk carts ($10), pawnbrokers ($50), gunpowder renewal (50 cents), charcoal ($2.50), dog carts ($1), kindling wood ($2.50), porter ($1), chimney sweep ($3), boarding house ($10), vender ($5), and public carts ($2).[16]

Citizens became active participants as the city laid out its map for order. Democracy could be asserted and accountability sought for a penny postcard. Thousands of them poured into the mayor's office every month, detailing every shadow of woe from great to small. The complaint process became formalized, with investigations, reports, and responses for each date-stamped query.[17] Even when the complaints could not be verified, they were investigated and responses sent out, with municipal authorities spending much time following up.

Dirty or obstructed streets were a common complaint of the last quarter of the century. Decades earlier, the City Inspector had blasted rag pickers, the miserable souls of New York, who cleaned all sorts of matters from the streets.[18] In

1875, licensed scavengers were replaced by municipal street cleaners. Competing concerns with health and appearance fueled citizen complaints. Streets had to be sprinkled with water regularly to keep dust and effluvia down.[19] Taxpayer groups complained constantly. The North Side Association wrote to Mayor Cooper in 1879 about streets and sewers.[20] In 1893, the Taxpayers Health Protective Association complained about waste paper in the streets.[21] Business and property owners on East Fourteenth Street between Avenue D and the East River petitioned the Common Council in 1880 to clean and repair obstructed sidewalks after pleas to do so had been ignored. A woman who fell on the sidewalk at Sixth Avenue asked that police ensure sidewalks be free from snow and ice in 1881. Neighbors balked at a West Forty-eighth Street store owner's manure in barrels on the sidewalk.[22]

Standards kept rising: not only did the city have to remove nuisances, it had to clean streets on a regular basis. A resident of East Sixty-ninth street complained about the "failure of the street-cleaning bureau to properly remove ashes and garbage," and said once a week was necessary. "Workingman and Taxpayer" requested the mayor "designate the streets cleaned on the 1st of every month and from where to where," adding, "why can't they have proper sized carts with very low bodies to collect ashes . . . instead of having to lift barrels?"[23] The mess from not cleaning a gutter could result in a fine, as it did for a Wooster Street resident in 1893.

Hard-pressed city budgets meant that citizens had to actively participate in beautifying their streets. By the 1880s, the proliferation of fire hydrants made it impossible for all of them to be cleaned by city employees, and Mayor Grace said it was not the police's responsibility to remove the snow but rather the citizens'.[24] During the depression of the 1870s and 1890s, street cleaning along with park maintenance was a favorite suggestion for unemployed workers. Colonel George Edwin Waring Jr., socialite and Civil War veteran, revolutionized sanitation work in the 1890s. The twenty-seven hundred white-suited workers of his new department, founded in 1881, produced cleaner streets and fewer obstructions. This marked the end of official river dumping and the start of an elementary recycling effort.

Attractive visual vistas were equally important. "The most unsightly things in this city are the ash barrels and boxes that array the sidewalks of brown stones and tenements alike," complained one man in 1879.[25] In 1876, a man wrote that "our curb stones [are] disfigured by the posting of bills."[26] The same year, an ordinance for awnings and side curtains on storefronts was put into effect: for $1 a year one could get a permit to maintain or erect an awning with permission from the building owner.[27] Mayor Hewitt nixed a proposal for the city's first sandwich-board advertising man, saying that if a stationary advertising sign was an obstruction, a peripatetic one was even more so.[28]

It was not just dirt and snow that was a problem—people were, too. Complaints against peddlers were common, though often they emanated from storeowners annoyed at the competition. Peddlers blocked traffic, left garbage, obstructed store entrances, and annoyed people. One man, fined $10 in 1875 on a charge of disorderly conduct, complained: "is it by law of this City prohibited to sell on the street merchandises as: Handkerchiefs?"[29] Loafers of "low character" hung out on the Harlem bridge.[30] Shop owners put their signs in places that blocked other store signs. Fruit vendors plying their trade from morning until midnight in the public square at Division, Market, Forsyth, and Bayard Streets were deemed such a hazard because of their refuse that they were arrested in June 1887.[31]

Yet New York was a peddler's heaven, where a successful stand could stave off starvation or bring its owner modest fortune. City authorities acknowledged that both the posh shops and the peddlers had rights, and if their customers clogged the streets, that was all the better for commerce. Regulations for street business had been brought to America from European roots, where public markets were the essential life of the towns. In New York, the markets declined as street-peddler sales increased with immigrant traffic.[32]

The issuance of peddling licenses legitimized the trade and brought in revenue, and only when there were extreme conditions were violations issued. This changed as traffic surged in the early twentieth century, and given the pressure from storeowners and real-estate interests, it was not surprising that pushcarts were essentially prohibited. In the nineteenth century, they represented commercial success. A complaint about "peddlers vending their wares . . . and the congregating of people in front of show-windows" elicited an interesting response from police. "West Fourteenth Street is one of the greatest and most attractive thoroughfares in this City—People from neighboring cities and our own citizens throng it daily," reported J. B. French, president of the police board. "That they have the right to do so cannot be questioned, and it is to be presumed that [complainants] Mrs. Sherman and other tradespeople of that neighborhood are satisfied, and pleased, with their present location for business purposes." Licensed peddlers, he said, "have also the right at proper times, to sell their wares."[33]

And then there were the animals. An 1874 ordinance prevented goats from running around the city, and subsequent ones provided for removal of mad dogs and for restrictions on loose cows.[34] An epidemic of horse disease in the early 1870s prompted similar legislation for dead horses; in 1880, for example, fifteen thousand dead horses had to be removed. Horses also created significant sanitary problems, with each animal producing from fifteen to thirty-five pints of manure per day and a quart of urine (in 1900 there were an estimated 130,000 horses in the city).[35] This provided impetus for a slew of public complaints about animals. The stray-dog problem became so acute it elicited a sharp exchange between city politicians regarding the solution.[36] A dead horse festering at Union Square got the mayor and police chief involved.[37] Stray cats were so numerous as to produce an ordinance to eliminate them; even the mayor had to deal with a dead cat complaint.[38]

Traffic congestion and speeding drivers drove exasperated police to a radical solution in the 1890s: bicycles. Organized in December 1895 with four men, and then two men four months later, they became great traffic regulators, making 321 arrests in five months, 90 percent for fast riding and driving on public streets, bringing in $921 in fines. Police Treasurer Avery Andrews pointed all this out to the mayor in a request for funds to purchase cycles; the "wheels" they were using were on loan from manufacturers and dealers "for extended test."[39]

Licensing was mandatory for vehicles but not uniformly enforced, as fines show. Overnight and Sunday parking regulations, the subject of many a driver's ire today, were born in complaints in the 1880s by locals who didn't want vehicles parked in their neighborhoods.[40] These parked vans brought bad smells and flies and blocked her store window, complained one owner.[41] A particular problem was loading trucks—businesses complained constantly they were being harassed. "Persecution" by police and "rigid and autocratic orders" hampered efforts by the Hill Brothers Company to load raisins at the Washington Market in 1894.[42] By this time, vehicles had to have lights to make them visible to other drivers—a light seen from the front and side one hour after sunset to one hour before sunrise, visible at two hundred feet, white in front and colored on the sides.[43]

Visibility on the street was not just for vehicles. Lighting sidewalks was acknowledged as a major factor in preserving order. Months after the Draft Riots of 1863, hundreds of lamps, posts, and fittings were replaced for the ones destroyed, costing tens of thousands of dollars. Gaslight was necessary for police to "afford that protection to the property, which its great value and exposed condition demand." Without it, "intoxicated persons and strangers" would plunge into the river, and thieves would "skulk in dark recesses."[44] Yet the large number of streetlights was so costly that the city tried to cut down the number, leading to an 1877 ordinance requiring permits for calcium or Drummond lights to prevent their "indiscriminate use."[45] The year before, in a cost-cutting measure, Mayor Havemeyer removed some of the "extra" 1,348 lamps in front of churches, schools, restaurants, saloons, clubhouses, and officials' houses.[46] In general, more lighting was normal, although distribution was not equal across New York's neighborhoods.[47]

If public spaces were to be safe, they also had to be tolerable in terms of personal thresholds. Freedom from noise and smell was a nineteenth-century theme. Loud music was a constant problem in the densely populated city; even the use of a mechanical machine to trim horse hairs on a Sunday would elicit a complaint by "Many Good Citizens."[48] The Taxpayers' Health Protective Association complained about "the most obnoxious fumes and gases which pollute the atmosphere for at least six blocks on both sides" of an artificial manure factory and fat-rendering establishment. "Our freedom from the affliction or our suffering depends entirely on the direction of the wind. ... Sometimes it is comparatively light ... sometimes intense and overpowering."[49] Uncleaned sidewalks could produce odors that "are at times extremely unpleasant and almost nauseating."[50]

Odors and noises were part of the quality-of-life issues that made public order a priority. Such rules reflected social and economic class, moral biases and prejudices, cultural sensitivities, and political pressures of the period. "This city is yet far from being civilized when a law abiding citizen can not, except at the risk of his life, perform the duties of a citizen," Mayor Hewitt was told in 1889. Hewitt, a dynamo when it came to citizen complaints, was acutely aware of the "rascalities" plaguing a great city.

In the era dominated by Anthony Comstock, a morals crusader, and Tammany graft, it is not surprising that coping with vice was a major preoccupation. Dives, panel houses, dance halls, and scams provided plenty of fodder for complaint. While the police always followed up, there was a suspicious preponderance of dropped cases due to lack of evidence. When an engraved calling card for Miss Nellie Dunscombe was sent to the police for investigation—the card read "At Home—Sundays, Monday, Tuesdays, Wednesdays, Thursdays, Fridays and Saturdays"—police responded that they were trying to get evidence.[51] Often complaints came from out-of-towners "rolled" by prostitutes. One man reported how he was unable to get away from two girls, even though "I said I did not want to [go with them]." When they "began to feel around in the most vulgar manner"—the police report noted the two girls were naked while he was in a chair—the Pittsburgh native was relieved of $100.[52]

"Sporting men and women of doubtful character" were part and parcel of city life.[53] The new accountability meant that every complaint, including those of morals crusaders like Comstock, Henry Ward Beecher, and Charles Parkhurst, had to be responded to. "A Mother and Troubled Wife" reported a billiard saloon;[54] unlicensed dealers, gambling and faro operations, policy shops, "carousing," and drunks falling into the river were par for the course. More often than not the police would not be able to substantiate claims of misconduct: typical was a report on "one of the lowest and crookest Dives in this City," to which the police captain reported that it is "occupied by persons whose moral character is not the best" but "there is no disorderly conduct or anything that would warrant police interference."[55] Two ministers living across the street verified this.[56]

Arrests occurred when bad behavior spilled out into the streets. Frequently, they were dismissed in court or fines paid with no effect on the operation. "An American Citizen" counted pitchers of beer going in and out of a store on a Sunday; the store owner was arrested but later discharged. Mayor Hewitt insisted the police were doing all they could to arrest Sunday law violators, gamblers, and prostitutes. Veteran police captain Anthony Allaire detailed his efforts—delusionally—to control vice: "I raided and drove from this precinct all gambling houses 7 years ago, and that no faro, poker, or other game of change exists in this precinct." Plainclothes details of five men on the 6 p.m. to midnight shift, another five on the midnight to 6 a.m., and four during the day—fourteen every day—checked his Eleventh Precinct daily for vice. Allaire proudly pointed out that in the eight years of his command from 1879 to 1887, there were 57,672 arrests for all offences by a precinct force that averaged sixty men.[57] Despite this, continuing complaints over vice operations lent credibility to assumptions the police "looked the other way." Letters constantly refer to payoffs to officers, and the 1895 Lexow Commission found truth in much of this.

Scams in New York could be complex and artful, which prompted legitimate businesses to complain angrily. The Louisiana lottery was illegal; the Craig Medical Clinic was bogus; foreign bonds were fake; the European Musee of Anatomy an outrage or swindle, with "all manner of flimsy pretexts the to-be-coerced patron is made to pay."[58] Opium dens were raided, "glove fights" interrupted, and river bathers stopped.[59] Con artists were a particular irritation to the public and the police. Store owners planted people on the street to entice customers into shops, but even plainclothes cops had difficulty proving this.[60]

Whatever the laws, police judgment was crucial in creating the moral compass of New York. They stopped a passion play whose producer did not have a permit, decided that a performance in the Egyptian Hall had a "rude" character, determined a "can'can dance" immoral, and debated over whether to allow a bullfight.[61] When it came to deciding if a Chinese performance was indeed a "sacred concert" as its producers maintained, the police went to great lengths, including hiring a translator and interviewing locals to find out what was going on.

And then there were children. Ball playing, bean shooting, assaulting pedestrians, and just being obnoxious produced plenty of complaints. An indignant citizen wanted the police to control boys annoying passengers on the Chatham Street elevated railway: what, the officer asked, did the man expect him to do, "remain there all the time?"[62] "Is there no reformatory they can be sent to and *kept* there?" asked one annoyed New Yorker after being harassed. The police sanguinely responded, "there is no law to prevent young boys engaging in that business."[63] Sabbatarian fury was turned on Sunday ball playing, but police tended to let that infraction pass uncorrected.

In 1894, police ordinances clarified that the first duty of the force was to preserve the public peace, then to prevent crime. This reflected the reality in these decades. Police responsibilities embraced a broader range of activities than would be familiar to us in contemporary times. Police were charged with finding missing people, finding and caring for lost children, and lodging the homeless in precinct stations. During the Draft Riots, the Twentieth Precinct gave refuge to two hundred kids from the Colored Orphan Asylum, while police headquarters sheltered seven hundred African Americans.[64] The mayor acted as welfare bureau and a human lost and found. From time to time, police succeeded in finding lost people; such was the case of Miss Lizzie Cox of Yaphank, looking for "my father I have not seen him for 12 years."[65] No such luck for a "broken harted [*sic*] wife" looking for her husband, nor for the family of a man from Kansas City, nor the family of Evan Mintzer, who sent a picture of an angelic-looking child whom they thought might have joined the circus.[66]

Until 1896, foundlings were brought to local police stations, taken to Central Office and kept by the matron overnight, and then taken to the Department of Charities, before winding up in Bellevue hospital. The resultant high mortality rate caused the police board to finally send babies directly to a hospital. At the same time, the police board eliminated another longstanding and oft-used custom, accommodating the homeless in station houses. A typical case was that of sixty-year-old Hannah Harris and six-year-old James Gowan, who had been living on the sidewalk at Mulberry Street. "In the name of humanity and civilization," wrote a New Yorker to the mayor, "I appeal to you to have something done in the matter as it is a disgrace and shame to our city." They wound up in the Fourth Precinct station house.[67] The 1896 elimination of police lodging was seen as a way of stemming "the spread of disease and filth" and ending "an institution that was of no good whatever to the persons it was intended to benefit viz. the deserving but unfortunate poor who would not accept the hospitality on account of the filth and dirt of the persons who habitually resorted to them."[68]

At the end of the century, the New York police chief could report that the force had created a regulated city and had insured the quality of life within it. His optimism may have been naïve. "I have never seen [in my twenty-nine years of service] such effective measures taken by the police to enforce the Excise Law," he wrote President of the Board of Police Commissioners Theodore Roosevelt. "There is no such thing now in the city as public gambling of any kind," he asserted, and "pool rooms are things of the past." Prostitution was limited to "persons who are very well known to the proprietors of the places."

As police became the arbiters of authority, they gained the power to demand correction without arresting the violator. This produced a significant decline in ordinance fines; in the nineteen months after June 1895, they declined by thirty thousand. The improvement is "apparent to any person who in his walks through the streets of our city will take the trouble to make any observations in this regard."[69] The new bicycle squad, started in December 1895, gave police an edge among the "daily and nightly large gathering of bicycle people" and prevented accidents caused by this new traffic mania.

Police pride might well have reflected relief at the bullet dodged from the Lexow Commission in 1895. The commission had investigated police corruption and had produced scathing testimony and a report, but in the end there was little in the way of substantive change. The commissioner's report noted that double the number of officers were dismissed in the year after Lexow, and that the Board had "striven ... to impress unworthy members of the force that they will be more severely dealt with."[70] New York was on the verge of consolidation, and the larger city would mean more problems of order. In 1898, the charter of consolidation gave control of public improvements to its own board, and by 1901, the city charter was amended so public improvement fell under the control of borough presidents.

That the regulated city had been established was clear, but where the rules would take residents was not. In 1900, in the newly consolidated greater New York, the Brooklyn Rapid-Transit Company issued new rules, following a complaint, to regulate behavior on public transport. No more hugging and kissing by "spooning" couples, no "pawings, caresses and fulsome endearments ... at times accompanied by an idiotic rapture of countenance that would make angels weep." Station Master O'Keefe said such behavior was disorderly or offensive, and "if anyone tries that sort of thing ... he will have to quit it or walk."[71] Perhaps that's why New Yorkers are great walkers.

EPILOGUE

Nº
12

THE TRIUMPH OF ORDER

A sea of spokes had swirled down the late-night New York city streets once a month for years without incident until the hot evening of August 27, 2004. Red lights and yellow cabs didn't stop the thousands of cyclists, but the police did. They decided the monthly "bike power" event was really political protest and the staging ground for disorder. Police arrested 264 people for obstructing governmental administration, unlawful assembly, and disorderly conduct.[1]

The cyclists belonged to Critical Mass, a group which had been holding monthly rides for more than ten years in cities across the United States and the world. Their rides brought attention to environmental issues and the rights of cyclists and pedestrians. They said they had no organization, no membership, no scheduled program, no route, and no political agenda; they described the events as "pro-bike celebration."[2]

What transformed this bike run into a headline-grabbing event was the Republican National Convention in Manhattan, and the perceptions that the cyclists were protestors: "Extremists have hijacked the bike ride," said Police Commissioner Raymond Kelly in newly hardened rhetoric.[3] Suddenly, the cyclists, who once were ignored by squad cars, had become a menace to public safety. And because Critical Mass had failed to obtain a permit, police said, its participants were violating the law.

Critical Mass urged New Yorkers to join their protest against the bicycle crackdown and to support freedom of movement and expression. "Come out of your homes and come out of your stalls, / To the streets which are here for the use of us all!" said a Critical Mass blogger.[4] It was not just Critical Mass that was targeted. During the Republican convention, a massive Central Park demonstration was banned and meetings across the city restricted. Since

2004, the city has continued to prevent, or control, the bike rides. They have arrested hundreds of people, enforced minor traffic regulations, blocked potential routes, and placed undercover agents with video cameras among the cyclists for surveillance purposes.[5]

By contrast, in London, Critical Mass cyclists steeled themselves for the worst in the fall of 2005, when a new law created a one-kilometer restricted protest zone around Parliament Square, requiring six days' notice of demonstrations and establishing controlled conditions for protests. Failure to comply would mean arrest for "unlawful demonstration" under the new Serious Organised Crime and Police Act (SOCPA), which had become law in April of that year.[6] Despite the insistence of Critical Mass that they were neither organized nor a protest group, the Metropolitan Police notified them on September 30 that for their next ride they must observe the new law.[7]

With tensions increased by the July 7, 2005, terrorist bombing of the London Underground, twelve hundred cyclists convened to the beat of samba music on October 28, 2005. Twenty cycle police and one police van watched but did not interfere, except to placate irritated drivers. One blogger reported that "the police had reconsidered their authoritarian stance, and provided a truly excellent and sensible facilitation of the ride."[8] Another reported "all was lovely" as the police acted as traffic wardens.[9]

That a crackdown hadn't taken place was credited to the fact the new law was a "folly," the effect of the waves across a very dark pond. "Sadly, the Met seems to be copying the NYPD's crackdown on Critical Mass ... a ritualistic game of cat and mouse between cops and massers has taken place ever since [the Republican Convention]—a costly lesson in how little can be achieved by pointless macho policing."[10] A group of ten who were the first to be arrested under SOCPA pointed out that the net effect of such a law would be to allow police to organize protests and effectively challenge free speech. Even the prime minister, they said, would object, referring to his 2002 declaration that "I may not like what they call me, but I thank God they can. That's called freedom."[11]

Some saw Blair's remark as disingenuous, as the popular prime minister backpedaled on an earlier campaign promise and endorsed a national identity card system. Slated to start in 2008, it has been plagued by problems and delays, but its extraordinary cost has been deemed acceptable in return for the security it would add.[12] The ID card elicited unprecedented furor from both sides of the bench. The system was prohibitively expensive, with setup costs estimated to range between 5.7 billion pounds over ten years to 19.25 billion, and annual running costs of more than 500 million pounds; the per-person cost of the card would range from £93 to £300. The card could contain sensitive biometric information, which elicited a maelstrom of protest: "The idea that civil liberties are not inhibited by [ID cards] introduction is no longer advanced by any sensible person."[13] The bill squeezed through Parliament in February 2006 by thirty-one votes, and the public was left stunned: "Britain needs a hard-nosed defence of our security and freedom. Instead, all we get from the Government is ineffective authoritarianism."[14] Yet opposition had weakened a year later, when the Identity and Passport Service explained to the public that these cards were essential to protect the public, family, and community, and that they would make "life easier."[15]

By 2008, freedom had become even more restricted in the streets and parks of London and New York. The modern urban dweller is ensconced in the world of surveillance, with each person monitored in public; free speech is even locked out of "exclusion zones," areas of the city that are off limits for public usage. Two late twentieth-century technologies, the computer and the closed-circuit television (CCTV), have increased the power of government to peer into the private spheres of individual action, including travel, phone calls, purchases, medical information, banking, and street movement. These innovations have served many beneficial purposes, but with the increase in terrorism threats into the twenty-first century, they have ensnared every aspect of our lives.

None of this is recent. In the world's two most important cities, freedom eroded in the nineteenth century, as order trampled free speech and assembly. This choice was endorsed by the majority of people, to accommodate economic, political, and social demands; our toleration of limits has changed over time. Viewed over the last 150 years, even with allowance for the growth of certain personal and civil liberties, the broader construct of liberty has contracted and that of order has increased.

The case of the Critical Mass cyclists reveals how endemic this contraction has been. Under the public radar until 2004, the story moved into the spotlight following the Republican convention and highlights the contradiction shared by the public and government over the shift to order. It raises philosophical and pragmatic questions as people realize the implications of curtailing the simplest of activities.

That the cyclists became more provocative with time is clear. "Corkers" were known to block cross-town traffic in advance to facilitate the flow of the riders in San Francisco, Buffalo, and Portland. But it was during the 2004 Republican Convention that Critical Mass deviated from its origins as a grassroots environmental group. New York police enforced demands for a parade permit for each ride, seized bicycles, and arrested cyclists. "We can't let a bunch of kids regulate city traffic . . . it's only a matter of time before things get ugly," a city official said. An irate pedestrian on Park Avenue expressed her frustration: "Any chance of crossing the street tonight?"[16]

In Solomonic fashion, in December 2004, Federal Judge William H. Pauley III rejected both the city's request that the cyclists get permits and the Critical Mass demand that they be allowed to go "wherever their wheels take them," sending the case to a state court.[17] In February 2006, State Supreme Court Justice Michael D. Stallman agreed that the seizure was illegal but acknowledged the "danger" of the bike rides and asked that the routes be agreed upon by both sides ahead of time, rejecting the Critical Mass policy of no set ride route.[18] The parade permit law has never been successfully challenged since it started in the nineteenth century.[19] By spring 2007, a federal court once again reasserted the right of the police to require permits for groups of fifty or more cyclists.[20] This bolstered the confidence of New York Police Commissioner Raymond Kelly, who a few weeks earlier had called the 2004 Republican National Convention "perhaps the finest hour in the history of the New York City Police Department," citing the fact only eighteen hundred were arrested and only sixty-seven civilian complaints filed.[21]

By early 2007, a revelation hit the press: undercover police had monitored potential protestors across America, Europe, and Canada, collecting voluminous information on anyone who might participate in a demonstration. Such wide-scale surveillance was justified as central in preventing disruption during the Republican National Convention.[22] This followed a later disclosure that Critical Mass events were secretly videotaped. A forensic video analyst turned over pictures of the undercover officers to the press, and the police union sued the city, charging that the tactics "were so heavy-handed and intimidating that their First Amendment rights were violated." Officer Walter Liddy accused the city of "criminalizing dissent," bizarrely echoing the comment of protest organizer Leslie Cagan in 2004, when New York tried to prevent anti–Iraq War marchers. The undercover agents asked demonstrators questions to elicit political opinions and were considering using "proactive" techniques such as misinformation to minimize disruption at public events.[23]

As this book has shown, the use of undercover police dates back to the middle of the nineteenth century. Concerns that surveillance violated liberty's framework were not sufficient then (or now) to stop it. Since 9/11, U.S. courts have made such methods easier by chipping away at the Handschu settlement, a 1980s federal case reducing the scope of surveillance. It set limits for investigating political organizations. In loosening these limits, the federal court pointed out "perils sufficient to outweigh any First Amendment cost." Such a statement shows how attitudes toward order have been shaped "by the politics of the moment and the perception of public safety needs."[24]

Attempts to restore Handschu parameters have not succeeded. In June 2007, Federal Judge Charles S. Haight Jr. reversed his own decision and reaffirmed the police right to videotape, based on "new information" that suggested unlawful activity did occur.[25] A few months earlier, second thoughts about the potential effects of unlimited videotaping had led him to give police a rap on the knuckles. In February, he had said that police videotaping was only allowable if there were indications that unlawful activity would occur; he also said that videotaping does not automatically qualify as an infringement of First Amendment rights. When New York police fought back, bringing the issue to court again, the judge sided with the authorities. The decision awaits broader tests outside of New York and possibly in higher courts, where the "politics of the moment" might produce other results.[26]

Videotaping might be a new wrinkle for the United States, but not for the United Kingdom. The use of CCTV there is the most extensive in the world, with four million cameras, one for every fourteen people in 2007. In London in 2007, one is "captured" on video an average three hundred times a day; six thousand cameras monitor the Underground alone, London's eighty-five hundred buses are said to have a dozen cameras each, the shopping center of Oxford Street has thirty-five, Parliament has two hundred and sixty, railway stations have eighteen hundred, and there are hundreds more monitoring streets. Private places that accommodate large amounts of public traffic, such as hotels, stores, and theaters, use thousands more cameras. Another six hundred cameras read cars' license plates to enforce central London's congestion-fee system. As one writer has pointed out, "it is now possible to spend a day in London being digitally photographed from the minute you arrive until the second you leave."[27]

In a world of webcams and *Big Brother*—the television show's title borrowed from George Orwell's futuristic novel 1984—satellites can capture images of where we are and what we are doing from thousands of miles up. In the city, surveillance has become the key to order. This tactic was of course used often in the past, with spies filing written reports. Jeremy Bentham, the great nineteenth-century Utilitarian philosopher, proposed the Panopticon, an all-seeing method to monitor prisons. The idea that there would be a system to monitor and collect information has floated for decades, but not until recent technological innovations was the potential fulfilled. CCTV was launched in Great Britain as a method for crime reduction, and experts report that just the consciousness of knowing one is being watched contributes to a reduction of crime.[28]

The concept of monitoring public space is rooted in the nineteenth-century need for public behavior to conform to the needs of an orderly metropolis. Cities protected private behavior, gave lip service to rights, and demanded order for the public polity. The legacy has been powerful. In Britain, few people view

CCTV as an infringement on civil liberties; no doubt the country's long battle with Irish terrorism was a factor. In the United States, resistance to television monitoring in public, long entrenched, has changed since September 11, 2001. The Department of Homeland Security created a security initiative that placed cameras across the nation. In 2006, Chicagoans learned that the Crown Fountain, a piece of public art with human faces on it, included surveillance cameras. After public outcry in which the monitoring was called "Orwellian," the cameras were removed from the fountain, but they remain in other areas of the city.[29]

CCTV and identification cards challenge basic Anglo-American concepts regarding liberty. Experts in both countries have warned that both present the possibility of eroded civil liberties and the "systematic failure to protect the privacy of its citizens."[30] The surprisingly sanguine public reaction in Great Britain is credited to fear of crime and concern for security, which may account for the fact that in the late 1990s, little opposition was mounted to expanded surveillance laws, with the exception of special-interest groups such as Liberty and Privacy International. By the start of 2008, support for compulsory ID cards had grown to 54 percent from 37 percent a decade earlier. One expert calls this the "boiled-frog syndrome"—the saucepan grows hot so slowly that the frog fails to jump out, fooled by the slow heat buildup and unaware of the danger.[31] The far-reaching implications of these shifts in urban centers strikes at the heart of Western values: "The city center itself . . . is not simply governed through freedom but also the curtailment of freedom and quality of life for particular groups and categories." In the eyes of many, CCTV has ensured the maintenance of order in the modern city.[32]

Public acceptance of CCTV along with what might be called the "salami-slicing of civil liberties"[33] reflects historical influences, contemporary pressures, and technological innovations. In Britain, longstanding trust in government is one factor. Another is the relief that surveillance has aided crime reduction. And while terrorism has an older legacy in Great Britain than in the United States, the new violence of international terrorism has added to the balance in favor of surveillance. Revolutionary changes in the technology landscape may have contributed to the public's lack of understanding of what was transpiring. The recent Freedom of Information Act in Great Britain has contributed to growing public cognizance of possible misuse of information. Still, experts say the balance is shifting: "There is more discussion on security than liberty these days . . . but the issue is to try to balance things, and in the end, individual nation-states have to make their own decisions—security appears more important."[34]

In New York, where sensitivity to breaches of civil liberties remains high, a general loathing for homeless persons, panhandlers, and squeegee men prompted Mayor Rudolph Giuliani to mount an offensive against such "obnoxious" behavior in the 1990s. The success of that campaign met with public approval, even though such actions violated basic tenets of liberty of person. Giuliani used the idea of "quality of life" improvements much the way it was used in the nineteenth century. No doubt, his administration made the city more livable: less crime, cleaner streets, fewer peddlers, less visible homelessness, efficient transportation, "decency standards," and better-enforced regulations. Prostitutes, drug dealers, and pornography almost disappeared. Michael Bloomberg, his successor, continued these policies, even creating an umbrella complaint bureau, "311," to respond to citizens' needs.

In 1850, the Jeffersonian idea that "a little rebellion now and then is a good thing" seemed reasonable; 150 years later, that idea has lost its luster and become tempered by pragmatic considerations. London and New York had struck a balance between order and freedom. In both cities, the right to use public space was qualified and regulated. The price paid for making the resilient city was the creation of sanctioned speech: that is, assemblage determined not to be harmful or dangerous by officials. Unfortunately, judging the content of speech is subjective.

The legacy of the nineteenth century was a new structure for public order, in which liberty was expendable. Great Britain and America retained a framework for free speech and assembly, but democracy as an ideal became tempered by realities of city life. The principles and practices established in the nineteenth century yielded long-lasting societal parameters affecting public space, free speech, and assembly. These parameters can be assessed in four overlapping areas: (1) who utilizes public space and what kind of ideas and opinions are expressed, (2) where in public this speech and related events are played out, (3) how the public behaves when participating in democratic processes, and (4) how authorities act and what influences their decisions.

In 1850, the public expression of dissent, including civic pride, was legitimated as a natural outcome of democratic processes. As this book has argued, by 1900, officials questioned the legitimacy of that expression, branding it as nonconformist or adversarial. New voices tested freedom by expressing discontent, speaking out for the underrepresented, and advocating ideas that competed for mainstream ones. In both London and New York, labor emerged as one of the most aggressive public voices; others advocated socialism, racial equality, women's suffrage, or birth control. Free speech was not necessarily pleasant speech.

Although Americans have loudly boasted of "the land of the free" and although New Yorkers think that they live in the most tolerant place on earth, the truth is more complicated. In general, the United Kingdom has been more respectful of free speech and assembly than the United States, and London has typically provided greater opportunities for public expression of dissent than the great metropolis on the Hudson River. But the trajectory of both cities has been similar, and one must admit that London and New York have been remarkably successful in projecting an image of freedom within a framework of safety and order. Not by accident have they remained atop the urban pyramid.

It is remarkable how this pattern played out in the twentieth century. In America, labor began an aggressive campaign to represent working-class interests, two decades after it had shifted into the mainstream political scene in England. Thwarted in public demonstrations, labor revitalized itself on the streets of New York in the two decades after 1900, fueled by the open-air rhetoric of the Industrial Workers of the World, better known as the Wobblies. During that period, demonstrators had contentious relations with the authorities, relations not helped by incidents such as the bomb blast in Union Square in 1908.

One spectator in the densely packed square was killed by a bomb allegedly aimed at a group of police. With "Haymarket" figuring prominently in newspaper headlines, all decried the violence. But the central issue was whether the meeting of socialists and unemployed should have been permitted. The parks commissioner had at first granted a permit and then cancelled it, showing "timidity" of the authorities. Is it "better to prevent such danger in its inception," or will such a "repressive policy only stimulate the spirit of riot"—after all, people can just blow off steam. In London, "the authorities permit such demonstration . . . with no worse results than occur from the opposite policy in this city."[35]

After this, the city ordered a large police force at every meeting, and the free use of clubs led one orator to comment, "let us remove Madam Liberty from Bedlow's island and put there instead Inspector Schmittberger with his Club."[36] The day of the explosion, Schmittberger had "held out his nightstick" and said, "this, at times, is over the Constitution."[37] Demonstrators, cognizant of civil-liberties issues, disagreed. "I stand on my rights under the First Amendment," said B. L. Zimm, an event organizer. Wealthy activist Robert Hunter, who knew the meeting had been banned, came anyway because "it seemed to me a violation of the Constitution" and that the "best plan . . . was to be arrested for speaking and to test the matter in the courts." As he never took the platform, the challenge never occurred.[38]

Union Square meetings continued, only with permits and subject to limitations and rules imposed by authorities. Labor Day rallies and marches shifted into acceptance as a celebration of labor, not a challenge to the establishment.

Radical politics were identified with May Day. A year after the 1908 bomb, the New York press sounded relieved when rain dampened the spirit and attendance at the "red flag" event. There were as many American flags as red ones, it was noted, and the fact that a third of the marchers were women changed the tone and tenor of the day. Even the presence of ten thousand shirtwaist makers, only a year after the bitter Triangle Shirtwaist Factory strike, seemed positive. In the same month, a police parade and a suffrage parade were large and celebratory.

Official policy reflected perceptions of the causes at hand at these events. Meetings in Union Square were for the most part legal, with police issuing permits, such as the one in 1910, attended by more than one hundred thousand. The Wobblies' demonstrations were contentious, and police monitored content carefully: "if anybody here reflects on the glory of the American colors and the priceless liberty those colors stand for, I will arrest him," a sheriff told Big Bill Haywood, IWW leader.[39] By the eve of World War I, these demonstrations had become routinely raucous and prone to dispersion, as police were incapable of handling them. A sanctioned meeting in 1914 resulted in a melee after police confiscated two black flags, one of which said "Hunger." By 1914, police were smashing "soap-box forums" and arresting speakers on charges of inciting to riot.

There was a brief respite during the tenure of Police Commissioner Arthur Woods, the first Harvard-educated police official. He brought a new attitude to the treatment of public assemblies. Believing that immigrants were affected by memories of police brutality in the old country, he tried to convince demonstrators that the police were not out to harm them—that a new government of freedom would not treat them as the old government of oppression did. Non-uniformed police were to stay on the periphery of the demonstration, not in it; moreover, not only were they not to interfere with the meeting, they were to protect participants from those who would disrupt it.

Woods convinced his men in 1914 that even if the content of the speech was distasteful, they had to respect the speech as long as it did not provoke violence. In our country, he said, people "have a constitutional right of free assemblage and of free speech ... it is the duty of the police, not merely to permit this, but to protect people in the enjoyment of free speech and assemblage."[40] The caveat was that the meetings couldn't annoy others, obstruct streets, or produce violence. Provocative speech, still under local jurisdiction, had been defined by New York Chief Magistrate and former police commissioner McAdoo "as inciting to riot if it was 'provocative of immediate violence,'" which left a lot of room for interpretation.

The qualification disturbed Gilbert Roe, first-generation civil-liberties attorney. While complimenting Woods on reducing the use of force, he questioned when interference was warranted:

> If it is merely a question of what is expedient, the answer will vary as the personnel of the officers charged with the enforcement of law varies. One police chief will direct the use of the club, and another will not. One will rely upon intimidation. . . . Another will wait until life or property is actually in jeopardy. The very differences in the rules applied bring the administration of the law, and the law itself, into disrepute.[41]

The idea that justice was relative in its application is one that has lasted until the present time.

Roe pointed out that if police were sympathetic with demonstrators they would be lenient. Such was the case when thousands of women marched in suffrage parades, even though crowds both cheered and jeered; in 1910, a massive car parade filled New York's streets and the suffragettes filled Union Square for five hours. Another "benign" event was that of five thousand students protesting cuts to evening schools in 1916. In both cases, the police were helpful, not combative.

Such a sanguine attitude evaporated when unpopular stances were advocated and when sensitive issues such as race arose. The century had started inauspiciously, with the first major race disturbance New York had witnessed since the Draft Riots. In reaction to the fatal stabbing of a policeman by an African American, ten thousand people rioted on August 15, 1900, covering a fifteen-block area in the Tenderloin district on Manhattan's west side. The injuries and general ugliness of the incident was intensified by charges that police indiscriminately clubbed blacks. Under public pressure, an investigation was mounted, even as the press accurately predicted that "there is no probability that any one will be punished for this cowardly assault."[42] President of the Board of Police Commissioner Bernard J. York piously wrote to complainants that he agreed "fully that the color of a man's skin should not be the index of his character or ability; nor should the color of his skin have anything to do with the conduct of the investigation now under way."[43] Despite contrary testimony, police were exonerated. As York said, in order to preserve the peace police had to act vigorously.[44]

The reaction to the riot reveals the degree to which order was a priority. The press squarely condemned police behavior, comparing their "wild joy" in misusing their clubs with a slave trader's "frenzy for bruises and blood" directed at African Americans.[45] Police behaved in a "disgraceful and disgusting" manner, and although both "negroes" and whites behaved badly, the *World* said, only negroes were attacked. The press was most distressed at the notion that police had allowed the city to disintegrate into chaos. The duty of police was to "put down the rioters, scatter the mob and arrest those guilty of assaults ... without regard to race or color. Anything short of this will bring disgrace to the city."[46]

The specter of the Draft Riots and the Orange Riots reappeared and reminded everyone they did not want a return of the nineteenth-century disordered city. "Since that time the elements of organized lawlessness have gradually faded away and the police force has been developed to such a fine pitch of efficiency that the possibility of such scenes as those of 1863 and 1871 seems very remote," the press commented.[47] The days when blood "Baptized the Streets and Many Lives Have Been Lost" was replaced by how "The City Nowadays [is] a Model of Good Behavior by Comparison."[48] The Draft Riots were a reminder to people in 1900 not to follow the "wretched failure of the wearers of the uniform to suppress the disorder," and that the "pit of shame" of the police was the breach of order, the failure to maintain a riot-free city.[49] Such an event, wrote one citizen, disgraced New York City, "the metropolis of enlightenment, as well as commerce."[50]

Public assemblies and processions as well as widespread utilization of public spaces in London and New York continued into the twentieth century, tested by new causes. The 1906 Open Spaces Bill in England regulated these activities but did not stop or significantly limit them. Women's suffrage proved to be a brutal test, as British suffragettes commonly engaged in confrontation with police. Their desire to be arrested, the cat-and-mouse pattern that emerged, and the sensational forced feedings they endured shocked the public and tested authority. Unlike New York, speech content was unlikely to affect police behavior toward demonstrators. Highly unusual was the decision by the Home Office to disallow a Good Friday meeting in Trafalgar Square requested by the Archbishop of Canterbury in 1915.[51] In general, even the stress of war did not tear the fabric of toleration of public speech and assembly.

That fabric met its most severe test two decades later with the rise of fascism, which prompted laws limiting public-place usage. Custom and public policy had established broad permissibility of meetings and marches. The 1882 *Beatty v Gilbanks* case, for example, which supported the broad right to demonstrate in public, had determined that a legal procession was not made illegal because others caused disruption or because there was a potential for disruption, and it served as an important precedent for half a century.

The erosion of *Beatty* started with *Duncan v. Jones* in 1936, which challenged the established principle that police interference could only occur in a public event after a breach of peace had occurred.[52] Instead, *Duncan* established broad discretion on the part of officials to deal with public obstructions. The arrest and conviction of a woman on charges of obstruction was interpreted as expanding the discretionary powers of police: "It would appear that the Common law of England, which rightly penalized the speaker who persists in insulting language and behavior (*Wise v. Dunning* 1902) has ceased to protect the speaker who merely desires to give expression to his opinion without causing any obstruction or committing, inciting or provoking any breach of the peace."[53]

The shift was completed when Sir Oswald Mosley and his British Union of Fascists, a modest number of marchers, and large numbers of anti-Fascists pushed police to their limits. By the mid-1930s, several thousand Metropolitan police were deployed at such events to prevent disorder. The resultant 1936 Public Order Act, sweeping in change, enabled police to impose conditions on or ban processions in order to prevent disorder, and it provided punishment for offenders. Its grounding principle was that officials could do what was necessary to ensure order. But demonstrations were never banned: even when violence was deemed likely to occur, such as the Union Movement meetings of fascist Sir Oswald Mosley in Trafalgar Square, the government did not ban it. Such a ban, said the government, would amount to censorship.[54]

The second parameter in the new structure of public order concerns space. In the last three decades of the nineteenth century, London allowed any of hundreds of public spaces to be used for assemblies and processions; no space was disallowed outright. In New York, the opposite was the case, as space after space was closed to the public for nonleisure purposes. London's Hyde Park and Trafalgar Square continued to be used for meetings in the twentieth century. In nineteenth-century New York, Central Park was never used for demonstrations, and by 1900, only Union Square was a main gathering point for both political and celebratory events. Increasingly, even that fell out of use.

Union Square was intended to be a park, not a center for public assemblage. Named after the conjunction of streets that met at Fourteenth Street, the square started as a potter's field and by the 1840s had been transformed into a gathering place with fountains and walks. Prominent real-estate developer Samuel Ruggles pushed for improvement of the square, originally called Union Place, and it opened as a 3.5 acre park in 1839.[55] In the mid-nineteenth century, the square was the geographical heart of New York and a logical place for celebrations. It was the scene of "the frequent erection of temporary stagings, booths, tents, flags, staffs and lighting apparatus" to facilitate spectators' ease, but was not to be a parade or military ground.[56] Union Place, as one of the only open spaces in the growing city, increasingly became used as a meeting and parade center, replacing downtown City Hall Park (known as the Park), which became the site of a huge post office.

Thousands celebrated the opening of the Croton water system in 1842 in Union Square. More than one hundred thousand gathered to support the Union cause in 1863, and two decades later, on September 5, 1882, the nation's first Labor Day was celebrated in the square, establishing its connection with the city's working class. By that point, all public events in New York had to be sanctioned by city permit. With the closing of Tompkins Square in the 1870s as an official meeting place, Union Square became the most used site in Manhattan. As the square became the center for working-class residents and businesses, numerous demonstrations and celebrations caused constant interruptions. War, as was argued earlier, brought out the worst, with speech and assembly restrictions mostly likely to occur as considerations of national security triumphed.

Union Square's status as a battleground for free speech and assembly in the twentieth century is a stunning reminder of the difference between American and English attitudes. While massive demonstrations were tolerated in London, no matter what the cause, in New York they often fell victim to the desire to control unpopular speech. While several generations proudly recall going to the square to rally or protest, the reality does not match the myth. Authorities in New York limited demonstrations while nominally skirting First Amendment infringement and often banned demonstrations and parades when public-order disruption was a projected outcome. Larger issues of the time, including war and economic depression, were also likely to affect the toleration of free speech and assembly. Union Square changed from a radical protest space to a patriotic declaration ground.

The case of annual May Day celebrations and rallies illustrates this. In 1930, the shift to "legitimize" activities in Union Square and make them mainstream was marked by the allowance of two rallies, one by the Veterans of Foreign Wars and one by "communists," which described a wide spectrum of interests. A thousand policemen allowed "color and noise" but no disorder. But two months before, "communists" were refused permission to meet there, resulting in forty injured, when police broke up the forty thousand who had gathered there anyway. That year had started with refusal to grant a permit for a funeral cortege for a strike picketer shot by police; Police Commissioner Whalen didn't want a parade "'all over town' [as] Business interests must not be annoyed."[57] By March, the city was mobilizing for a Union Square demonstration as if it were a foreign invasion. In August, a peaceful gathering turned violent when police charged the crowd. By 1932, a packed Union Square was "black with people," but the crowd was subdued by heavy rain and the hopelessness and hunger brought about by the Great Depression, resulting in a "Gentle Red Festival" marked by "perfect order."[58]

While May Day remained England's (and Europe's) most important vocalization of labor prominence and dissatisfaction, by 1933 in the United States it was on its way to becoming a generic holiday, a "political picnic on the pavements," when one hundred thousand gathered peacefully in Union Square. In 1937, it was "the biggest, best humored and most orderly May Day parade since Lenin made little hammers and sickles."[59] The eight-hour parade may have been "gay," but speakers were not allowed at Union Square. In 1939, it was recast as a labor event, a "celebration to mark the beginning of the eight-hour day movement in 1886," with four "celebrations."[60] The transformation was complete by the end of World War II, when Loyalty and May Day events were combined "to recapture from leftist groups the May Day Parade" and reassert it as a workingman's event.[61] By the mid-1950s, as the nation writhed under McCarthyism, New York officials were focused on a "rededication of Union Square to Americanism" and God.[62]

But there was no rededication to free speech. When Mayor William O'Dwyer banned a peace rally in the square by "communists," the New York Civil Liberties Committee accused him of overzealousness.[63] Under NYCLC pressure, a compromise allowed them ninety minutes in the square. The Fourteenth Street Association, a merchants group, was issued a permit to occupy the square for six hours of "fun and games" (and a few years later this was increased to eight hours).

Authorities had flatly refused the New York Labor Conference for Peace a meeting permit in July 1950, citing possible disorder and what New York Supreme Court Justice Eugene L. Brisach referred to as the "right of the balance of the public."[64] Thousands went to the August demonstration anyway, but not in Union Square. The effect of this was to mobilize demonstrators to fight back, and in October the Ad Hoc Committee to Reestablish the Right of Public Platform for Peace Groups won a Supreme Court reversal of the Parks Department ban on their meeting. By 1953, May Day parades were banned completely, because they "would create a potential riot-laden situation."[65]

That ban could have led to the eradication of free speech and assembly rights but for a compromise brokered by Robert Moses, parks commissioner, and pressure by civil-liberties groups. He allowed a limited rally in Union Square. A decade earlier, the New York City Civil Liberties Committee had accused Moses of harming free speech by requiring permits for meetings. Moses angrily responded that permits had always been required, and that during his tenure, there had never been "a single instance in which up to this time an application has been denied for a permit to speak in Union Square or any other place designated for public meetings."[66]

Yet parades, celebrations, and rallies that represented mainstream or popular causes were never banned or stopped no matter how large or disruptive. George Washington's oath reenactment in 1932 filled Bryant Park, a site rarely used for protest; the 1939 World's Fair preview paralyzed Gotham for two days as a million spectators filled the streets; the Spanish Civil War and fascism were "acceptable" subjects of protest; and the usual panoply of civic or celebratory parades and marches filled avenues with throngs of spectators. By the 1960s, the mood shifted along with the nation's politics: an attempt to ban a Nazi rally in Union Square was ruled illegal, although folksinging and loudspeaker bans in Washington Square Park were upheld in court. Popular causes, including protesting the nuclear bomb and the Vietnam War, won widespread support in New York in this era, when numerous protests occurred. Union Square was popular as the center for burning draft cards and discharge papers as war protests. Overall, the 1960s were the exception to the rule, with many of these events occurring without permits.

In the 1950s, Union Square had become a "graveyard of memories," as a former demonstrator saw it, with the cold war and McCarthyism freezing public speech. The square was filled with ghosts for aging activist Isidore Wisotsky, who saw World War II as the death knell for meetings there. Permission to meet in Union Square was rarely asked for and rarely given after the war, he said, and he wondered "about the fears some people have about the supposed danger in free speech symbolized by the old Union Square," where nothing happened that "ever damaged the nation's institutions." The square served as an outlet for "emotions which otherwise channeled, or bottled up, might have caused serious harm." Wisotsky looked longingly across the Atlantic at Hyde Park, where "anyone with something to say and a will to say it may speak in perfect safety from everything but hecklers."[67]

A few years earlier, an American professor in London wondered whether New York needed a Hyde Park, a place where public speech would be tolerated without limits. "The relaxed attitude of the British toward the sedition expressed every day in Hyde Park would reduce an American superpatriot to apoplexy," he wrote during the chilly McCarthy-style political atmosphere of the time. The British were pragmatic about their free speech, while Americans had tied themselves "into a legal and constitutional tangle." Impressed by their "common sense" arrangement, he wondered if Americans could negotiate spaces for their soapbox speakers like the British. A central location and "friendly and cooperative" police were the essential elements for a workable solution to this fundamental democratic institution.[68]

The absence of such a place created problems in the 1960s and 1970s, as New York's political meeting and procession places were increasingly limited—although civic and celebratory public events remained abundant. In London, there were still dozens of places to hold meetings. London always had open space for public assembly in the city center. New York never did, and even when it became possible to gain such spaces in the late twentieth and twenty-first centuries, the city failed to do so. As large-scale construction projects reshaped Gotham, laws afforded private developers additional building rights on the condition they maintain some open space on building sites. These "private/public" spaces, numbered at more than five hundred in 2000, mislead the public into thinking they are public, but in fact they are legally private. The owner of the building can restrict who gathers there and for what purpose. They are not subject to First Amendment protection.[69]

The trenchant issues then (and now)—war, racial equality, free speech, feminism, nuclear disarmament, gay rights—provided focal points for national public demonstrations. The era of "demonstration democracy," as one scholar has called it, flourished in the 1960s, leading to a heady but false sense that "demonstrations are becoming an integral part of our democratic way of life."[70] As Americans and Europeans searched for "harmony and understanding" in the age of Aquarius (as the hit Broadway show *Hair* called it), they took to the streets in record numbers. Some see the 1960s as the era launching "America's last great experiment in democratic idealism."[71] This outburst of public expression, from San Francisco to New York, Paris to Prague, seemed an ideal democratic platform, but the accompanying violence tarnished the image of free speech and assembly. Los Angeles in 1964 and Newark and Detroit in 1967 were scenes of wanton destruction. In Europe, activism by anarchists and the left rose to new levels and was accompanied by much violence.

That violence and an increase in terrorism polarized public perception of demonstrations and alienated authorities even further from tolerant or conciliatory positions. In the formative nineteenth century, police displayed a mixture of aggression and hesitance when it came to controlling the public, making up their own guidelines or waiting for officials to make them up. To their credit, they lowered crime, made judicious decisions, and preserved the tenets of personal liberty. Had they been provided with consistent and better guidance, learned from their mistakes, and been removed from political influences more quickly, which was more often the case in London, they might have been able to learn how to handle crowds effectively. The public, for its part, alternated between using the police to uphold those aspects of public order that made their lives better and falling prey to an inbred hostility to authority.

By the twentieth century, public meetings and processions had become linked with violence, with both public and police bringing deeply felt antagonism to the public spaces of cities. Official inquiries and commissions in the 1960s took pains to separate demonstrations from violence, arguing that such events were healthy and could be safe. The President's National Commission on the Causes and Prevention of Violence had investigated disturbances in American cities, and a subgroup, the Task Force on Demonstrations, Protests, and Group Violence, argued that demonstrations were not inevitably violent and were vital to a free society. They counted 216 demonstrations in one month from September 16 to October 15, 1968, a year tarnished by the assassination of Martin Luther King Jr. and Robert Kennedy, and noted that only about a third of them resulted in riots.[72] But a third was too high for public sensibilities. The nineteenth century had taught that the compelling reason to curtail public-space usage was to preserve order. From public meeting to riot seemed to many to be a short route, so precautions to stop this were compelling.

Whether violence can ever be eliminated totally from public events is dubious, but demonstrations and marches declined after the 1970s. Politics played a role in allowing events. A sympathetic Mayor John Lindsay in 1967 allowed hundreds of thousands of anti–Vietnam War protestors in Central Park;[73] a few years later he joined an Earth Week march through the park. But his parks commissioner, August Heckscher, saw things differently, banning the use of Central Park for political assemblages. Under pressure from the mayor, he said applications would be judged on "practical merits," but the die was cast. Even the liberal *New York Times*, branding Heckscher's ruling a "ukase," agreed that "parks are not for politics" and that Union Square would be a better place for gatherings, with the occasional large group allowed to use the Sheep's Meadow.[74] One of the last great gatherings in the park was in 1982, when an anti–nuclear arms rally, with Mayor Ed Koch participating, brought upward of a half million together.

Few suggested banning cultural events in Central Park after the 1967 antiwar march, even as political events there thinned. A Barbra Streisand concert left a colossal waste dump, requiring three days of cleanup, but Heckscher insisted that such events would continue. For political events, police followed the principles set down a century before: elaborate preparations, large numbers of men, and better communications. A 1968 antiwar demonstration of an estimated eighty-seven thousand had police on edge and resulted in 160 arrests but caused little commercial disruption for a Saturday, a key barometer in assessing the effect of marches on the city. In 1967, the press reported three thousand police monitoring a march, but by the following year, the police department declined to announce the number of police assigned, a practice it has usually followed to the present time. Following the violence of Stonewall in 1969, gay marches to Central Park were relatively peaceful, but they involved only a few thousand demonstrators. A march of ten thousand feminists spread out beyond police barricades and tied up traffic on Fifth Avenue down to Bryant Park but caused little commercial disruption.

Disruption was more likely in London, where hundreds of demonstrations, from small to massive, occurred regularly, with large police presence and numerous arrests the norm. A 1956 Trafalgar Square demonstration against the invasion of the Suez was peaceful until the thirty thousand that had gathered tried to disperse. In the 1960s and 1970s, large turnouts involving tens of thousands were common for issues including the Campaign for Nuclear Disarmament, Vietnam, and Ireland; a perception that "riotous crowds" were out of control in the mid-1980s led authorities to question whether "normal" policing methods were adequate to maintain order.[75] Public demonstration remained strong in these decades, and by the early twenty-first century, anti–Iraq War protests brought hundreds of thousands to Trafalgar Square and Hyde Park.[76] As in New York decades earlier, the presence of a sympathetic local politician, left-wing mayor of London Ken Livingstone, lent an air of approval to these demonstrations.

The dearth of spaces in New York makes it all but impossible to hold major outdoor meetings, demonstrations, or processions of a noncelebratory nature. By the end of the last quarter of the twentieth century, Union Square had been redesigned and relandscaped to make large meetings physically impossible. The fact that protestors during the 2004 Republican Convention could not get a meeting permit (discussed in the introduction) illustrates how difficult it is to hold a political street event. Central Park was deemed unusable by city authorities because of potential damage to the grounds, a reason used previously to deny permits. It would appear that lawn maintenance fazes the British far less than the Americans: concerns for grass did not stop the use of Hyde Park, where "the people gather in the mud amid the rising smell of trampled grass."[77] Destruction of the grass was one of the prime factors cited by the Central Park Conservancy in opposing granting a permit for the 2004 meeting.

The role of the Central Park Conservancy in preventing meetings in the park is significant and represents an important shift in the way parks and public spaces are run and used. Formed in 1980, the conservancy viewed itself as the savior of the park, which had "succumb[ed] over the years to New York's 'tough love' only to be saved by the unique public/private partnership." The conservancy took over maintaining and running the park, and in 2006 signed an eight-year agreement providing for total day-to-day care and public programs. While the City of New York "retains control and policy responsibility" and the Parks Department provides "advice and consent," the high-powered board of trustees raises money (which runs in the tens of millions annually), initiates capital improvements, and exerts major influence through its oversight of the park. The sixty-member board consists of two city officials ex-officio (the parks commissioner and the Manhattan borough president), five trustees appointed by the mayor, and the remainder are the cream of Gotham's business and banking industry, many of whom live near the park. The original backers of the park had a similar profile.[78]

Although the conservancy says the park "will continue to be a forum for large events, including political demonstrations," there is little evidence of that. Political demonstrations are not allowed, and restrictions announced in 2005 reduced the use of the thirteen-acre Great Lawn to six cultural events per year, with none over fifty thousand. The last large event there was a Dave Matthews concert in 2003, which had eighty thousand in attendance. The Parks Department admitted the new limitations were formalized after the 2004 protest fight. "You have two choices," said Adrian Benape, parks commissioner. "You can have unlimited, large-scale events, or you can have nice grass, but you can't have both."[79] In January 2008, the Parks Department announced it was mounting a study of the potential use of the Great Lawn following a lawsuit brought by a group denied a demonstration permit. This study, to be submitted by July 2009, will rely on the findings of a panel of experts "to determine whether the Parks Department's regulations governing large events should be re-examined, loosened, or tightened." The experts were to be appointed by the city and the findings nonbinding.[80]

The motivation for this "public/private" shift is the financial vise that grips modern cities, a result of pressured city budgets and rising costs. It also exists in London, where oversight for the vast green spaces remains in the public domain. Financial support comes from either central or local government, depending on the status of the land. Perhaps inspired by New York, the London Parks and Green Spaces Forum was formed in 2001 to assist the funding crisis of open spaces. It seeks to "promote the regeneration, management and sustainable future" of these parks and advocate for more funding. As an advocacy group, however, there is no issue of management or determination of usage of spaces.[81]

In neither London nor New York are public meetings forbidden outright. The ban is de facto in Central Park. Throughout the city, every potential event is subject to municipal permission, which is not often given for political events. When permission is given, it is only after intense negotiation and with many restrictions. In London, decisions about allowing events are left to the local authority, in the case of commons and local parks, and to the central government for major and royal parks. There are plenty of meetings of a political nature in these places. The disparity between the attitude of New York and London authorities to grant permission to demonstrators reflects the traditions that were established in the nineteenth century. Fear of damage to the grass is an interesting excuse. Well-manicured lawns are hardly urban, but they are a standard of financial success, especially for the well-heeled living around parks. According to the model established more than a century ago, in New York disruption is bad, traffic is a priority, commerce is critical, and free speech and assembly are expendable. In London disruption is tolerable, traffic is significant, commerce is important, and free speech and assembly rights are critical.[82] In both places crowds are unpredictable, potentially violent, and prone to make messes.

What is and isn't allowed on the streets of London and New York still reflects political bias, the national zeitgeist, and longstanding custom. On a warm May Day, 2001, hundreds of New York's Finest surrounded the perimeter of Union Square and spilled out onto the surrounding streets, blocking parking and causing traffic congestion. Inside the local Starbucks, police officers were already looking weary at 10:30 in the morning. The massive police presence was caused by the fact that "there are going to be a lot of protests today," according to a young Latina officer, "something to do with May 1."[83] There was neither a protestor nor a placard in sight in Union Square.

That same Tuesday evening, BBC World TV flashed images of Europe's main cities convulsed with violent demonstrations in honor of May Day. Protestors were anarchists, Trotskyites, and a host of fringe and mainstream groups, protesting issues ranging from politics to hunger to environmentalism. London, chilly and grey, received extensive television coverage: moving images revealed angry confrontations between protestors and police in Oxford Circus, the mercantile heart of the metropolis, and much fury was directed at property. Damage estimates approached millions of pounds, and as the camera panned in on angry, contorted faces, the commentator dolefully intoned, "Free speech does not come without a high price."

In the same May week that Union Square remained empty of demonstrators, New York hosted six street festivals, three street fairs, one parade, and a forty-two-mile bicycle race. All required closing public streets, banning parking, rerouting traffic, controlling crowds, and providing additional sanitation and police presence. This translated into considerable expense. An avenue street fair can close off to traffic from five to twenty blocks, which means police must carefully control side-street traffic access to avoid peripheral street clogging. Impenetrable human "walls" combing merchandise booths for bargains block vehicle access, including ambulances and fire trucks. All these street activities are publicly sanctioned, and each festival, fair, and parade receives official permission from city agencies. From October 2006 through November 2007, there were 366 street events across the city, including parades, charity walks and races, and street fairs of a celebratory or commercial nature, requiring permits from the city; only four were political in nature.[84] None had to contend with public objections that would have forced them to go to court to seek legal sanction to proceed.[85]

Moreover, the pattern established in the nineteenth century regarding public order repeats itself over and over, reinforcing differences in the two nations. Despite a major but thwarted bombing attempt in central London in late June 2007, life went on as planned in the next few days: a charity race in city center, a major rally in Trafalgar Square, and a Princess Diana memorial concert close to the city. No activity was cancelled or changed. And while police cleared a "peace camp" set up across the street from the House of Commons in the summer of 2007, they allowed a protest march a few months later despite the fact it was technically illegal. The British press pointed out it was the Chartists all over again, with the victory of the right to protest.[86]

In New York, on a pleasant September 2007 weekend, New York closed Sixth Avenue to a street fair, Fifth Avenue to an ethnic parade, and the West Side Drive and the East River Drive, the city's main arteries, to a charity bike tour. Yet political demonstrations and marches are routinely denied permits because they are perceived to be security threats or termed impediments to street access. In the beginning of the twenty-first century, New York authorities controlled or blocked dozens of events ranging from union rallies to the Million Man March to the Amadou Diallou rally. Ethnic or holiday parades are not immune from such restrictions if they embrace political ideologies that cause controversy or fail to conform to mainstream civic standards. New York's St. Patrick's Day parade was long the magnet for politicians until a division over gay participation resulted in politicians opting out. While Gotham's annual gay-pride parade is a positive sign of street usage, the barricades and heavy police presence remind us it occurs only with the sanction of authorities, recent converts to tolerance of diversity.[87]

London, too, has tightened its rules. Over the past half century, numerous laws were enacted to extend police ability to control disorder, including the 1953 Prevention of Crime Act, the 1964 Police Act, the 1980 Highways Act, and the 1986 Public Order Act. This last law extended police authority and discretion to interfere with an assembly, instead of waiting for a breach of peace or obstruction to passage; police can ban processions for this reason but cannot ban assemblies. In these laws, police gained the right to demand that they be notified three to seven days in advance of an event in order to impose conditions including date, starting time, and route, and to know the name of the organizer. Section 44 of the Terrorism Act of 2000 gave police the right to stop anyone in certain areas for cause.

Parades and processions throughout history were public statements in which societies validated religious, cultural, or social beliefs. They were the rare instance in which all people, including the disenfranchised, outsiders, and women, were afforded the opportunity to make public statements, even those not endorsed by the authorities. Subsumed under Christian practices, these public activities retained a pagan element, as an aura of festivity permeated even the most solemn events, such as Mardi Gras. When public parades and processions adopted a nonbenign mode of public expression, usually entailing political or economic issues or violence, then they were not tolerated, and public-order mechanisms were mobilized to restore order. But until the modern period, few societies banned benign modes of public expression. The evolution of the use of public space for free expression reveals the increasing complexity of that expression.

Whatever the issue or cause, each assembly, procession, or parade is a reaffirmation of the right of free expression. Flags, Statue of Liberty floats, and burning Guy Hawkes effigies are common symbols that have come to represent national identity, unity, and freedom. Every time we walk down a street en masse we voice our civic expression in a way that would have been unknown two centuries ago. This has given material form to freedom, and we have defined the parameters of it for everyday life. The ideal of freedom, however, is less defined and certain. In 1874, after the Tompkins Square riot, journalist John Swinton tried to remind people the American flag was not "merely a piece of bunting with so many stars and so many stripes" but "an idea, a principle, a vital potentiality. . . . It is freedom." That we should both treasure a national flag for the freedom it symbolizes and be able to destroy it as a sign of freedom of speech remains an unresolved but ongoing controversy in the United States.

The police served then and now as the guardians of that freedom by allowing or disallowing its expression and by honoring or abusing the law that protects it. Their authority was cemented in the nineteenth-century city: for better and for worse, they are the enforcers of order. At times they succeed brilliantly and at other times are fallible; even in the latter case, they rarely are subject to more than harsh criticism or a slap on the wrist. Police powers in New York are in theory regulated by law, but as the nineteenth century showed, they were subject to other forces, especially politics. Police in both cities became agents of government, and in New York, they were subject to an especially confusing set of legal guidelines after 1925. They followed local law until then, but after the *Gitlow* decision, federal courts had jurisdiction over free speech and assembly. Since *Gitlow*, the courts have established a broad legal framework for public meetings and processions. The rules appear simple: meetings and processions must be allowed, but they are subject to restrictions by municipal authorities based on the time, place, and manner of the events, in order to maintain order. Such restrictions are subject to a vast array of possible interpretations, which affect the right substantially.

English common law was not subject to such interpretation. Prior to *Gitlow*, the American civil-liberties lawyer Gilbert Roe warned that no one in America knew the law because "the old common law has been so far modified by the statutes of the various states that it is no longer a safe guide on the subject."[88] In order to rein in common law, the English have had to create new laws to enable police to have more authority. The most interesting of these laws is the most recent, the 2005 Serious Organized Crime and Police Act, which may prove to have the most sweeping effects yet. It remains to be seen whether the strong nineteenth-century tradition will be maintained in the face of the new threats of terrorism. The potential cost of freedom could be high: the British "have a strong rhetorical attachment to liberty, as something for which a certain price in danger and disorder is worth paying," said David Blunkett, the former Home Secretary who created antiterror legislation.[89]

A certain price is at the heart of the debate. The nineteenth-century regulated city sought to make life amenable to those who would make it prosper. The twenty-first-century city zealously guards against those who would throw it into disorder by bolstering itself against terrorism. Its denizens want a place of residence and work that is safe, with trustworthy mechanisms and transparent policies to ensure this. Yet they don't want all this at the cost of a human life or the infringement of basic rights. What price is too much to pay to ensure order be maintained on our city streets? That remains to be negotiated. New Yorkers and Londoners are not ready or willing to follow the Singapore model and permanently give up freedom for order.

In nondemocratic or totalitarian states, order has always been prioritized, with no question of guarding individual rights. These states have used the need for political stability, economic development, and social equalization as justification for their regimes. But there is little evidence that the price for achieving all this is abandonment of liberties. For states steeped in democratic traditions, it is disturbing to think they would abandon their foundational beliefs in liberty when challenged. The chipping away of liberties is evident in the increase of free-speech arrests, surveillance, intolerance for criticism of government, intrusion on privacy, and police powers.

The playwright Alan Bennett portrayed this devastating message at the start of *The History Boys*. As Irwin, government functionary, tells MPs, they will introduce a bill to abolish trial by jury and presumptions of innocence. The strategy rests on the idea that

> the true liberty of the subject consists in the freedom to walk the streets unmolested, etc., etc., secure in the knowledge that if a crime is committed it will be promptly and sufficiently punished and that far from circumscribing the liberty of the subject this will enlarge it. . . . Paradox works well and mists up the windows, which is handy. "The loss of liberty is the price we pay for freedom" type thing.[90]

We now face a twenty-first-century future in which public behavior is monitored and restricted. When we cross a street against the light, should we be arrested? When we walk in a public place, are we comfortable with cameras monitoring our movements? If we wish to express an opinion in public, should that voice be tempered to conform to community restrictions? Should we need to adjust the content of our public speech to suit commercial demands? In both England and America, we assume that freedom cloaks us, shapes our lives, and gives rise to the trenchant individualism that defines our societies. Yet what is freedom and what are its boundaries? On closer inspection, we have surrendered considerable freedom in return for control and security.

The timeliness of this argument is apparent as threats to security confront London and New York in the twenty-first century. Terrorism, which is not new, has gained increased destructive potential. Concepts that were previously unthinkable have entered into the public discourse. Skyscrapers can be blown up, "dirty" bombs can render unusable a city area without destroying it, and a neutron bomb can kill large numbers of people without collateral damage to buildings. Individuals face a nonviolent but equally destructive threat in the form of identity theft, in which perpetrators create a living hell for victims. Many have questioned whether too much freedom has allowed new threats to emerge; many fear permanent abridgement of freedom under these threats. Could our treasured concept of freedom be subjugated to rigid intellectual and material conformity for the sake of security?

A legal scholar has reminded us that "the danger of repression is greater than the danger of debate."[91] The British prime minister reminds us the key is "the right balance" between freedom, protection of privacy, and public safety and security.[92] Neither London nor New York has tipped the scales irrevocably when it comes to how they weigh freedom. It remains to be seen if the balance between order and freedom can be maintained, and if the de facto public-order contract will become a one-way street. Metal barricades are routinely used to channel people on city streets and squares, and fences are used to define green spaces. The hope is that the barricades and fences will be used to limit, but not end, the places we can go.

ACKNOWLEDGMENTS

Nothing about writing this book was conventional, nor are the people who contributed their advice, assistance, and support. I owe far more than thanks to all of them.

The author expresses appreciation to the University Seminars at Columbia University for their generous help in publication. Material in this work was presented to the University Seminar on the City. Thanks to Bob Belknap, Alice Newton, and Michelle Salerno. The author expresses appreciation to the Gilder-Lehrman Institute for a grant at the start of this research.

Material in this book was presented in papers delivered at the following: the Centre for Urban History, University of Leicester; Urban History Association Conference; Organization of American Historians Annual Conference; American Historical Association Annual Conference; and the Society for American City and Regional Planning History/Urban History Association Conference.

Heartfelt thanks go to many others. In Athens, Mrs. Tsakona of the Benaki Museum. In London, Sean Waterman of the Museum of London; Mark Vivian, of the Mary Evans Archive. In New York, Kim Strong of CORBIS; John Tauranac, an exceptional cartographer. At Columbia University Press, to Peter Dimock, for his great support and assistance, and Kabir Dandona, for his patience and help. Thanks to Michael Haskell and Rob Fellman for their diligence and assistance with the manuscript. At Purchase College: Pat Callahan, library director, who brought the library into the twenty-first century; Carrie Eastman, Angela Messina, and Leah Massar Bloom, research genius. In CTS, Bill Junor and George Liao, who helped bring me into the technological twenty-first century. Colleagues and friends Owen Gutfreund, Tim Gilfoyle, Nancy Kwak, Barnett Schechter, Albert Fried, Clyde Griffin, Virginia Breen, Trevor Dawes, Nina

Keller, Tania Mather, Olga Broumas, and Marv Lipman. Each was supportive at just the right time.

In a class by himself: Ken Cobb, archivist extraordinaire and good friend of every New York City historian.

To those who are the vertebrae in the spine: Tony Wohl, my inspiration for thirty-five years; dear hearts Rosalie Reutershan, Alison Yarrington, John Rigos, and Stavroula and Aspasia Pantazopoulou; Paul McNeil, dean of wit; Gari La-Guardia, who ensures every day has sunshine; and Ken Jackson, who made the project a demand and a joy at the same time.

To my mother and father, for a lifetime of support: this book is dedicated to my father, who did not live to see its publication.

To Saky Yakas, whose unconditional love and support carried me through all, and to Benjamin Yakas, who carries my heart in his pocket with his loose change and who must grapple with the issues in this book.

NOTES

PREFACE

1. Because municipal boundaries and population statistics are notoriously unreliable and determined by different factors, I have used the metropolitan boundaries of the metropolitan police district in London and of the Metropolitan Board of Health in New York as the units of analysis. London's suburbs at this point are within the city, New York's outside, for the most part, but both are large physical areas. For most of the nineteenth century, "New York City" refers to Manhattan. After 1874, the Bronx was added in stages; by 1898, Queens, Brooklyn, and Staten Island had joined greater New York. "Greater London" includes the area of the Metropolitan Police district. The City of London is a small area in the very center of London and is not included in much of this discussion, as it has its own legal jurisdiction and police.
2. Jacobs, *The Death and Life of Great American Cities*, 30.
3. Lesoff, *The Nation and Its City*, 273.
4. From 1882 until 1972, a federal law imposed severe limitations on demonstrations, public speech, and parades. Those that did occur required federal permission. See Barber, *Marching on Washington*.

INTRODUCTION: A PERFECT STORM OF PEOPLE

1. *Observer*, February 16, 2003. The extensive press coverage from mid-January to early March provides excellent information about the march. See the *Observer*, the *Guardian*, the *London Times*, and the *Daily Telegraph* for this period. Estimates for the size of the march ranged from 750,000 by the London police to the organizers' claim of 1.5 million.
2. *Daily Telegraph*, February 5, 2003; see also the *London Times* and *Daily Telegraph*.
3. *Independent*, February 15, 2003.
4. Quoted later in the *Guardian*, December 9, 2005.

5. *New York Times*, August 30, 2004. Crowd size ranged from 120,000, according to the Associated Press, to a half-million, according to event organizers.

6. *Atlanta Journal-Constitution*, August 30, 2004.

7. *New York Times*, August 28, 2004.

8. *New York Times*, August 17, 2004.

9. The 2004 Republican Convention protest was disallowed in the park for this reason. The official size limit at this point was eighty thousand. It was lowered to fifty thousand in January 2006.

10. Editorial, *New York Times*, February 22, 2007. In June 2008, the Supreme Court ruled that prisoners at Guantanamo Bay, Cuba, have a right to be heard in federal court, reversing a 2007 federal court decision. As of 2007, debate over the Patriot Act continued as revelations concerning its use unfolded. FBI director Robert S. Mueller III, for example, told officials that the information was improperly obtained. *New York Times*, March 10, 2007.

11. *New York Times*, August 12, 2004.

12. Spain, also an ally in this war, experienced a rail terrorist attack in Madrid in 2004.

13. See David Beetham, "Political Participation, Marr Protest, and Representative Democracy," *Parliamentary Affairs*, October 1, 2003; and David Sanders, Harold Clarke, Marianne Stewart, and Paul Whitely, "The Dynamics of Protest in Britain, 2000–2002," in *Parliamentary Affairs*, October 1, 2003.

14. See Matthew Rothschild, "Protestor = Criminal," *Progressive*, February 2004; "A Generation Finds Its Voice," *Newsweek*, June 2, 2003; Maria Margaronis, "Britain," *The Nation*, April 14, 2003; "The Perils of Protest," *Time*, April 14, 2003; "The New Face of Protest," *The Nation*, March 28, 2005; "No Banners on My Land," *The New Statesman*, November 1, 2004; *The New Statesman*, October 4, 2004; June 7, 2004; September 13, 2004; August 16/23, 2004; August 1, 2005; June 13, 2005; "Restrictions Overreach," *USA Today*, May 27, 2003; "The War Over Peace," *Rolling Stone*, October 20, 2005; "Is Iraq Another Vietnam?" *The CQ Researcher*. Ironically, the law did not retroactively apply to Haw.

15. Eric Foner, "Not All Freedom is Made in America," *New York Times*, April 13, 2003.

16. Berlin, *Two Concepts of Liberty*, 10.

17. Janis Joplin, "Me and Bobby McGee," *Pearl*, 1971.

18. In February 2006, WNYC (New York Public Radio) offered as a promotion during its annual fundraising drive a pocket-size U.S. Constitution with comments, saying it hoped the document would help people understand basic ideas.

19. *New York Times*, March 13, 2006.

20. Eric Foner, "The Idea of Freedom in the American Century," The Lawrence F. Brewster Lecture in History XXI, East Carolina University, Greenville, North Carolina, available online at http:/www.ecu.edu/history/brewster/bl102.htm. See also Foner, *The Story of American Freedom*.

21. Tchen, *New York Before Chinatown*, xviii.

22. Mill, *On Liberty*, 59.

23. Ibid., 63.

24. Breyer, *Active Liberty*, 16.

25. See Tilly, *Popular Contention in Great Britain, 1758–1834*.

26. Bachin, *Building the South Side*, 11.

27. Schuyler, *The New Urban Landscape*, 6.

28. Hartog, "The Constitution of Aspiration and 'The Rights That Belong to Us All,'" in Thelen, *The Constitution and American Life*, 354.

29. Mill, *On Liberty*, 71.

30. See Stone, *Perilous Times*; Sunstein, *Why Societies Need Dissent* and *Democracy and the Problem of Free Speech*; Stone, Epstein, and Sunstein, *The Bill of Rights in the Modern State*.

31. Ackerman and Fishkin, *Deliberation Day*.

32. The Power Inquiry, which issued a Report in 2006, was set up to improve participation in popular politics. See http://www.makeitanissue.org.uk.

1. THE ELEMENTS OF DEMOCRACY:
FREE SPEECH, FREE ASSEMBLY, AND THE LAW

1. Weber, *The Growth of Cities in the Nineteenth Century*, 439.

2. An extensive historiography exists on 1848; some argue, as did historian G. M. Trevelyan, that it was the "turning point at which modern history failed to turn," while others support the notion that it laid the foundation for all modern nations today.

3. *Justice*, October 10, 1885.

4. Petition submitted on August 26, 1877, by T. E. Tomlinson, to Committee of Arts and Sciences, Mayor's Papers, NYCMA.

5. *New York Times*, July 25, 1877. See Meiklejohn, *Free Speech and Its Relation to Self-Government*.

6. See Novak, "The Pluralists' State," and Connolly, "Progressivism and Pluralism," in Gamber, Grossberg, and Hartog, eds., *American Public Life and the Historical Imagination*.

7. Finley, *The Legacy of Greece*, 27.

8. Hades, introduction to *Complete Plays of Aristophanes*, 9. The Pnyx is the background for the Aristophanes comedy *The Knights*.

9. Dunn, *Democracy: A History*.

10. Finley, *The Legacy of Greece*, 24.

11. See Finley, *Democracy Ancient and Modern*; Moore, ed., *Aristotle and Xenophon on Democracy and Oligarchy*; Jones, *Athenian Democracy*; Plato, *Dialogues*.

12. See Nippel, *Public Order in Ancient Rome*; Millar, *The Crowd in Rome in the Late Republic*; Brunt, *Italian Manpower 225 B.C.–14 A.D.*; Brunt, "The Roman Mob"; Vanderbroeck, *Popular Leadership and Collective Behavior in the Late Roman Republic*; McClelland, *The Crowd and the Mob*. The various writings of Cicero, Sallust, and Livy are particularly valuable.

13. Millar, *The Crowd in Rome in the Late Republic*, 175.

14. See Ozment, *Magdalena and Balthazar*.

15. See Bellamy, *Crime and Public Order in England in the Later Middle Ages*; Wall, *Power and Protest in England, 1525–1640*; Collison, *Public Order and the Rule of Law in England, 1688–1720*; Tilly and Tilly, *The Rebellious Century*; Quinault, *Popular Protest and Public Order*; Fletcher and Stevenson, *Order and Disorder in Early Modern England*; Palmer, *Police and Protest in England and Ireland, 1780–1850*; Stevenson, *Popular Disturbances in England*.

16. Another exception to this is the Gordon Riots of 1780, in which 285 people were killed. This was significant, but it was also an anomaly, as there were few cases of such violence in British public-order history.

17. Keller, "Powers and Rights," in Thelen, *The Constitution and American Life*, 17, 24.

18. Hartog, "The Constitution of Aspiration and 'The Rights That Belong to Us All,'" in Thelen, *The Constitution and American Life*, 354.

19. Mill, *On Liberty*, 59–71.

20. See chapter 5; Shaw, *The Fabian Society (Fabian Tract 41)*, 9; Elton, *England Arise*, 120; and *Justice* for estimates of numbers. Another famous application of Shaw's lesson was performed by suffragettes.

21. Special committee, State Assembly, *Report*, March 14, 1884, as cited in Phelps Stokes, *Iconography*.

22. New York State took the early lead in passing restrictive legislation. See, for example, Laws of 1872, chap. 590, "An Act to regulate processions and parades in the cities of the State of New York."

23. Smith, *Sunshine and Shadow*, 180–181.

24. Child, *Letters from New York*, 1849.

25. *The Daily Graphic*, January 14, 1874.

26. 1832 Special Commission, "Reprint of an Address by Chief . . . ," 321.

27. Much discussion exists regarding the nature and intent of the Constitution. See, for example, Keller, *Affairs of State*; Godkin and Keller, *Problems of Modern Democracy*; Kammen, *A Machine That Would Go of Itself*; Kelly, Harbison, and Belz, *The American Constitution*. A discussion of law and history is in Reid, *The Ancient Constitution and the Origins of Anglo-American Liberty*.

28. *Gitlow v. New York*, 268 U.S. 652 (1925).

29. The best discussion of this topic is in Rabban, *Free Speech in Its Forgotten Years*.

30. The basis for most English law can be found in Sir William Blackstone's *Commentaries*. Dicey remains the primary nineteenth-century legal scholar on this topic: Dicey, *Introduction to the Study of the Law of the Constitution*. See also Barendt, *Freedom of Speech*; Pollock and Maitland, *The History of English Law Before the Time of Edward I*; Brewer and Styles, ed., *An Ungovernable People*.

31. Dicey, "On the Right of Public Meeting," *Contemporary Review*, April 1889.

32. Street, *Freedom, the Individual, and the Law*, 48.

33. Lord Plunket, *Hansard* 41, 129–130.

34. *Stephen's Commentaries*, vol. 3, 186; *Hawkins Pleas of the Crown*, 1787, 6th ed., vol. 1, book 1; and *Wise on Riots and Unlawful Assemblies*.

35. *Hawkins Pleas of the Crown*, 297.

36. See Brownlie, *The Law Relating to Public Order*, for a discussion of the most significant cases.

37. The major statutes that dealt with riot and rules for setting them up were 25 Ed. III c. 2 (Treason); 34 Ed. III c. 1 and 15; Rich. II c. 2 (justices' responsibility); 1 Geo. I Stat. 2 c. 5 (the Riot Act); 57 Geo. III c. 19 s. 23 (the Seditious Meetings Act, meetings while Parliament sits); 7 Will. IV and 1 Vict. (dispersion of riots); and 49 and 50 Vict. c. 38 (the Riot Damages Act). The foremost treason statute was 25 Ed. III; sedition was covered by 37 Geo. III c. 123 and 52 Geo. III c. 104. Another significant but short-lived law was the Seditious Meetings and Assemblies Act, 60 Geo. III and 1 Geo. IV c. 6, which made it illegal for meetings of more than fifty persons to be held in London, which would cause terror, confusions, and calamities; this expired five years after being passed (1819). A second tier of supportive law also existed: 13 Chas. II c. 5 (Stat. 1) (Tumultuous Petitioning); 1 Will. & Mary (sess.2) c. 2; and 24 & 25 Vict. c. 97 (Malicious damage to buildings); 1 Anne (St. 2) c. 21; 36 Geo. II c. 7, ss.1 & 6; 57 Geo. III c. 6, s. 1; and 5 & 6 Vict. c. 51 s. 3. Another statute, 1 & 2 Will. IV c. 41, dealt with appointing special constables during disturbances, but only after two or more justices took testimony from credible and sworn witnesses that tumult, riot, or felony would take place and that only interference could preserve the peace.

38. PP 1839 XXXVIII, Russell to Rolleston, June 3, 1839.

39. Thomas Hall, Chief Police Magistrate, Mepol 2/59 and HO 45/252 (ff1–36).

40. Mepol 2/248 and HO 48/53.

41. LOO 280, HO 45/9472.

42. Mepol 2/248, "Memorandum on Public Meetings in the Metropolis," 1889.

43. 10 Geo. IV c. 44 and 2 & 3 Vict. C. 47.

44. In 1865, it was noted the police were not technically authorized to act on commons because legally there was no interest of the public on commons and the police could only act where there was public interest. PP 1865 VIII.

45. Mepol 7/28 and 7/132, Works 16/794 for issues regarding police in the parks.

46. Cited by Sir Charles Russell, *Hansard*, March 1, 1888. There is no direct statement in *Hansard* 1848. Grey himself referred to this statement in 1866. See also the *Diary of John Evelyn Denison*.

47. PP 1886 XXXIV, appendix VII. The returns omits the 1866 Reform League meeting.

48. Taylor, "Post Chartism: Metropolitan Perspectives on the Chartist Movement in Decline, 1848–80," in Cragoe and Taylor, *London Politics, 1760–1914*, 86. See also Taylor, "Commons Stealers, Land Grabbers, and Jerry Builders."

49. Whipple, *The Story of Civil Liberty in the United States*, 264.

50. Among the many historians who address this are Fischer, *The Revolution of American Conservatism*; Appleby, *Capitalism and a New Social Order*; Kammen, *Spheres of Liberty*;

Levy, *Legacy of Suppression*; Anderson, "The Formative Period of First Amendment Theory, 1870–1915"; Eldridge, *A Distant Heritage.*

51. There is an extensive body of scholarship addressing this in reference to particular wars. For an overview, see Stone, *Perilous Times*; Foner, *The Story of American Freedom.*

52. Neely, *The Fate of Liberty*, estimates from 13,000 to 38,000 arrests. Foote, *The Civil War*, 360, gives newspaper estimates.

53. Levy, *Liberty and the First Amendment: 1790–1800*, 35.

54. Some cases dealt with new obscenity laws that fell under federal jurisdiction through postal regulation, such as the Comstock Act (1873). There were also cases concerning labor injunctions.

55. See Hartog, *Public Property and Private Power*; Teaford, *The Municipal Revolution in America.*

56. Bassiouni, ed., *The Law of Dissent and Riots*, 333.

57. Steffens, *The Autobiography of Lincoln Steffens*, 214. Steffens was a member of the board of directors of the Free Speech League. See below.

58. Anderson, "The Formative Period of First Amendment Theory, 1870–1915."

59. Ibid.

60. Rabban, *Free Speech in Its Forgotten Years*, 39, 52. See the Theodore Schroeder Papers in the Southern Illinois University Library.

61. There is an extensive body of scholarship dealing with the Wobblies.

62. Chafee, *The Blessings of Liberty*, 70.

63. The National Civil Liberties Bureau predates this. It was founded as part of the American Union Against Military, a 1916 antiwar movement. There are numerous histories of the ACLU, including Walker, *In Defense of American Liberties*; Johnson, *The Challenge to American Freedoms*; Baldwin, "Recollections of a Life in Civil Liberties."

64. *Hague v. Committee for Industrial Organization*, 307 United States Reports 496 (1939).

2. THE WORLD OF THE GREAT CITY

1. Poe, *Doings of Gotham.*

2. Dickens, *Martin Chuzzlewit*. Dickens wrote *Chuzzlewit* following his 1842 grand tour of the United States, and the novel is partially set in America.

3. In 1850, Paris came in second at 1 million, followed by Leeds at 700,000, St. Petersburg, 485,000; Naples, 449,000; Vienna, 444,000; Berlin, 419,000; Liverpool, 376,000; Moscow, 365,000; Glasgow, 357,000; and Manchester, 303,000.

4. Mitchell, *European Historical Statistics, 1750–1970*; Rosenwaike, *Population History of New York City*. See also Lees, *Cities Perceived.*

5. Infant mortality, always high, barely changed in the nineteenth century, declining only after World War I.

6. Schneer, *London 1900.*

7. There is an extensive body of work on Victorian London. For a variety of perspectives, see Olsen, *The Growth of Victorian London*; White, *London in the Nineteenth Cen-*

tury; Schwarz, *London in the Age of Industrialization*; Hitchcock and Shore, eds., *The Streets of London*; Nead, *Victorian Babylon*; Inwood, *A History of London*; Whitfield, *London: A Life in Maps*.

8. Select Committee on Metropolitan Communications, 1854–1855, cited in Owen, *The Government of Victorian London, 1855–1889*, 102.

9. London and Birmingham (1837), London and Southampton (1838), London and Croydon (1839), Northern and Eastern (1840), London and Blackwall (1840), London and Brighton (1841). London Bridge served as the terminus. A horse-drawn railway ran from Wandsworth to Croydon in 1803. Many of the railroads consolidated with others. Railway construction was estimated to have resulted in the evictions of 120,000 people from houses that were destroyed. See Shepherd, *London 1808–1870*; Barker and Robbins, *A History of London Transport*; White, *A Regional History of the Railways of Great Britain*; Robbins, *The Railway Age*; Dyos, *British Transport*; Kellett, *The Impact of the Railways*.

10. Olsen, *The Growth of Victorian London*, 318.

11. Shepherd, *London*, 148–149; Shapiro, "Urban Utilities in London and New York," 138, citing *London Statistics* 24 (1914): 477, in Harris, ed., *Civil Society in British History*; Barker, *London Transport*.

12. Dickens, *Bleak House*, 220. See Wohl, *The Eternal Slum* and *Endangered Lives*.

13. Owen, *The Government of Victorian London, 1855–1889*, 33.

14. The Local Government Act of 1888 finally created the County of London, excluding the City. Davis, *Reforming London*, 11, citing Hansard, CXXXCIII 16 March 1855; Edwards, *London Street Improvements*; Jephson, *The Sanitary Evolution of London*.

15. Phelps Stokes, *Iconography*, citing Chamber, *Things As They Are in America*.

16. Phelps Stokes, *Iconography*; *Valentine's Manual* (1850); *New York Illustrated* (1870).

17. Arnold, *Culture and Anarchy*.

18. Dickens, *Our Mutual Friend*, 6.

19. Smith, *Sunshine and Shadow*, 36.

20. McCabe, *Secrets of a Great City*.

21. Smiles, *Self-Help*.

22. Willis, *Open-Air Musings in the City*.

23. There is a wide variety of materials across the disciplines addressing this. For example, see de Certeau, *The Practice of Everyday Life*; Sennett, *The Fall of Public Man*; Kasitz, *Metropolis*; David Harvey, *The Condition of Postmodernity*; Nead, *Victorian Babylon*. See also Schivelbusch, *Disenchanted Night*.

24. Dickens, *Our Mutual Friend*, 318.

25. See Sexby, *The Municipal Parks, Gardens, and Open Spaces of London*; Waters, "Progressives, Puritans, and the Cultural Politics of the Council, 1889–1914," in Saint, ed., *Politics and the People of London*.

26. There are numerous other small parks, including Victorian Tower Gardens, Royal Hospital Chelsea, Wapping Recreation Ground, King Edward Memorial, Archbishop, Geraldine Harmsworth, Vauxhall, Myatt's Fields, Ruskin, Horniman Gardens, Mayow, Biggin Wood, Norbury, Morden Hall, John Innes, Mostyn Gardens, Wimble-

don, King George's, Wandsworth, Hurlingham, South, Bishops, Tabard Gardens, Newington Recreation Ground, Deptford, Telegraph Hill, Hillyfields, Ladywell Recreation Ground Forster Memorial, Sutcliffe, Avery Hill, Maryon, Highbury Fields, Downshill, Lordship Recreation Ground, Avenue House, Golders Hill, Hendon, Sunny Hill, Gladstone, Roundwood, Welsh Harp, Barham, Barn Hill, Norethwick, Pinner, Headstone Manor, Bentley Priory, Ravenscourt, Walpole, Elthorne, Brent Lodge, Cranford, Hanworth, Valentines, Springfield, Bedfores, Dagham, Parsloes, Central, Ayersbrook, Havering Country, and a host of others developed in the past twenty years. See Forshaw and Bergstrom, *The Open Spaces of London*; and see Parliamentary Papers, "Copy of Ordnance Survey of Commons and Open Spaces within the Metropolitan Police District," 10 August 1866 [531].

27. Schuyler, *The New Urban Landscape*, 20.

28. Cook, *A Description of the New York Central Park*, 17.

29. Despite a general ban, sports were played in the park, including baseball, officially banned. Tennis, archery, tennis, lacrosse, football, and roller skating were played in the 1880s with permission. See Blackmar and Rosenzweig, *The Park and the People*.

30. See Blackmar and Rosenzweig, *The Park and the People*; Reed, *Central Park*; Cranz, *The Politics of Park Design*.

31. *Atlantic Monthly*, April 1861.

32. Homberger, *Scenes from the Life of a City*, 292.

33. Rosenzweig and Blackmar, *The Park and the People*. Even a proposed parade in Central Park of the popular Seventh Regiment met with fierce opposition: it was said that it would not only damage the park but set a bad precedent. Protest from the City Club of New York, Gilroy 13, NYCMA.

34. Documents, Board of Assistants, I: 153–161, cited in Phelps Stokes, *Iconography*, 1705.

35. New York Park Association, *More Public Parks*.

36. The Sinking Fund and the New Parks, City Revenue and the Constitutional Amendment, *What is the Debt of the City*, n.d. [1886?].

37. City of New York, *Report of Committee on Small Parks*.

38. See Habermas, *The Structural Transformation of the Public Sphere*.

39. Bachin, *Building the South Side*, 11. See also Ethington, *The Public City*.

40. Upton, "The Empire City," lecture at the Metropolitan Museum of Art, November 4, 2000.

41. Ryan, *Civic Wars*, 16.

42. See Lefebvre, *Critique of Everyday Life* and *The Survival of Capitalism*; Debord, *The Society of the Spectacle*.

43. Melville's haunting midcentury tale "Bartleby, the Scrivener" is considered one of the finest examples of life alone in the city. Morrison's end-of-the-century novel *Child of the Jago* painted a bleak view of the corrosive city.

44. See Plotz, *The Crowd*.

45. See Rude, *The Crowd in History*.

46. See also Chevalier, *Labouring Classes and Dangerous Classes*; "The Fear of Mobs," *The Spectator*, February 13, 1886; Knollys, "Mobs and Revolution," *Fortnightly Review*, December 1, 1886; Roberts, "Mobs," *Cornhill*, June 1867.

47. See Chesterton, *Revelation of Prison Life*; Holmes, *Pictures and Problems from London's Police Courts*; Archer, *About my Father's Business* and *The Pauper, the Thief, and the Convict*; Peek, *Social Wreckage*.

48. Booth, *Life and Labour of the London Poor*.

49. Park called crowd psychology "a new science" at the start of the twentieth century. Park, *The Crowd and the Public and Other Essays*, 5.

50. See Countryman, *A People in Revolution*; Wood, "A Note on Mobs in the American Revolution"; Maier, *From Resistance to Revolution*.

51. See, for example, Stott, *Workers in the Metropolis*; Wilentz, *Chants Democratic*; Weinbaum, *Mobs and Demagogues*; Gilfoyle, "Strumpets and Misogynists," in Mohl, *The Making of Urban America*.

52. See, for example, Moody, *The Astor Place Riots*; Headley, *The Great Riots of New York, 1712–1873*; Bernstein, *The New York City Draft Riots*; Cook, *Armies of the Streets*.

53. See, for example, Rude, *Paris and London in the Eighteenth Century*; Bohstedt, *Riots and Community Politics in England and Wales, 1790–1810* and "The Moral Economy and the Discipline of Historical Context."

54. See, for example, Mather, *Public Order in the Age of the Chartists*.

55. See, for example, Tilly, *Popular Contention in Great Britain, 1758–1834*; Stanley Palmer, *Police and Protest in England and Ireland, 1780–1850*; Boyer, *Urban Masses and Moral Order in America*; Gilje, *Rioting in America*.

56. Thompson, "The Moral Economy of the English Crowd in the Eighteenth Century."

57. Canetti, *Crowds and Power*.

58. See Canetti, *Crowds and Power*; Rude, *The Crowd in History*; Hobsbawm, *Primitive Rebels* and *Bandits*; Hobsbawm and Rude, *Captain Swing*; Smelser, *Theory of Collective Behavior*; Tilly, *Popular Contention in Great Britain, 1758–1834*; Tilly, Tilly, and Tilly, *The Rebellious Century, 1830–1930*; Park, *The Crowd and the Public and Other Essays*; Thomis, "The Aims and Ideology of Violent Protest in Great Britain, 1800–1848," in Mommsen and Hirschfeld, *Social Protest, Violence and Terror in Nineteenth- and Twentieth-Century Europe*.

59. See, for example, Gilje, appendix to *The Road to Mobocracy*.

60. Connolly, "Progressivism and Pluralism," in Gamber, Grossberg, and Harton, eds., *American Public Life and the Historical Imagination*, 50.

61. Useful discussions of the transfer of power under nineteenth-century democracies are in Montgomery, *Citizen Worker*; Ryan, *Civic Wars*; Thompson, *The Making of the English Working Class*.

62. Schlesinger, *The Crisis of Confidence*.

63. Shoemaker, *The London Mob: Violence and Disorder in Eighteenth-Century England*; Slack, ed., *Rebellion, Popular Protest, and the Social Order in Early Modern England*; Brewer and Styles, *An Ungovernable People*.

64. See Jones, *O Strange New World*; Hofstadter and Wallace, *American Violence*; Graham and Gurr, *Violence in America*; Brown, *Strain of Violence*; Brown, *Violence in America*; Gilje, *Rioting in America*.

65. Hofstadter, *American Violence*, 6.

66. See Hofstadter, *American Violence*; Graham and Gurr, *Violence in America*; Fogelson, *Violence as Protest*; *Kerner Commission Report*; Farmer, *Civil Disorder Control*; Bordua, ed., *The Police*; plus studies on Los Angeles, Newark, Detroit, New York, Rochester, Philadelphia, Nashville, Boston, Cincinnati, Milwaukee, and Buffalo. Fogelson (12–13) argues that the 1960s riots "were attempts to alert America, not overturn it."

67. Brown, *Strain of Violence*, vii.

68. The major exception to this is anti-Irish bias, but London disorders are not noted for this issue.

69. See Bernstein, *The New York City Draft Riots*; Cook, *The Armies of the Streets*.

70. *Times*, July 2, 1855.

71. See Disraeli, *Sybil*; Mayhew, *London Labour and the London Poor*; Jones, *Outcast London*.

72. New York Association for Improving the Condition of the Poor, *Annual Report* [1864], 30.

73. Ibid.

74. Foster, *New York by Gaslight*, 124–125.

75. *Herald*, February 13, 1837.

76. For an overview of the military's role, see Babington, *Military Intervention in Britain*.

77. The return of the jilted and unhappy Queen Caroline to England in 1820 after exile on the Continent was the occasion for the calling out of troops and mass popular protest in her favor.

78. Historian Eric Monkkonen strongly denies that rising crime or class or ethnic conflict motivated the formation of the police: see *Police in Urban America, 1860–1920* and *America Becomes Urban*. See also Emsley, *The English Police* and *Gendarmes and the State in Nineteenth-Century Europe*; Reith, *A Short History of the British Police*; Miller, *Cops and Bobbies*; Critchley, *A History of Police in England and Wales, 1900–1966*; Philips and Storch, *Policing Provincial England, 1829–1856*; Hart, *The British Police*; Taylor, *The New Police in Nineteenth-Century England*; Hay and Snyder, eds., *Policing and Prosecution in Britain 1750–1850*; Petrow, *Policing Morals*. Colonial forces are said to have been built on the Anglo-Irish model. See Jeffries, *The Colonial Police*. Palmer, *Police and Protest in England and Ireland*; Richardson, *The New York Police*; Lardner and Reppetto, *NYPD*; Fogelson, *Big-City Police*; Dubber, *The Police Power*.

79. These forces were established in 1855, as was Chicago's. Other forces established in that decade include those of New Orleans, Baltimore, Cincinnati, and Newark.

80. There is a vast archive of material available on London's Metropolitan police, because they were under Home Office jurisdiction. Most of the papers are located in Kew at the National Archives, formerly the Public Records Office. New York's police papers met a less kind fate: they were sold off for scrap around World War I. Any surviving documents are in the Mayor's papers in the New York City Municipal Archives.

81. Urban riots in America, such as in Newark, Detroit, and Los Angeles, highlight the conflict that National Guard usage engenders.

82. Poe, *Doings of Gotham*.

83. Dickens, *Oliver Twist*. Bow Street Runners are in the novel; they are forerunners of London's Metropolitan Police.

84. See Tobias, *Crime and Industrial Society* and *Crime and Police in England, 1700–1900*; Monkkonen, *America Becomes Urban*.

85. Among the most famous of these private forces were the Bow Street Runners, run by novelist Henry Fielding and his brother John. See Harris, *Policing the City*; Reynolds, *Before the Bobbies*.

86. Metropolitan Pavement Act 1817, 57 Geo. III, c. XXIX. The City Lighting Act (1736) and Westminster Paving Act (1762) were intended to bring more order by having less trash on the streets to throw at people.

87. The London Metropolitan police are generally considered the model for most civilian urban police forces. See Emsley, *Gendarmes and the State in Nineteenth-Century Europe*; Jeffries, *The Colonial Police*; Palmer, *Police and Protest in England and Ireland*; Anderson and Killingray, *Policing the Empire*; Brewer et al., *The Police, Public Order, and the State*.

88. This discussion does not include the City of London police, which had its own private, complex, and confusing system. In the nineteenth century, the number of residents living in the City declined drastically.

89. Cobb, *The First Detectives*, 44.

90. Mepol 8/2.

91. Mepol 1/44, May 26, 1836.

92. Problems in recruiting police and military because of the prevalence of recruits of substandard height and weight drew attention to broader health and nutrition issues, which became the focus of much reform in the second half of the nineteenth century.

93. Erhardt, "The Duties of a Policeman."

94. Hewitt 26, NYCMA.

95. Richardson, *New York Police*, 70–71, citing Board of Alderman IIXX, No. 43 and 45; Ernst, *Immigrant Life*. The mayor's report noted that police ethnicity corresponded with that of each ward.

96. This is for Manhattan. 90 SWL 45 NYCMA, and Erhardt, "The Duties of a Policeman."

97. Strong 90 SWL 45, NYCMA.

98. Andrews, "The Police Systems of Europe." Andrews was a former police commissioner of New York. The London population figure excludes the city of London; New York had added Brooklyn.

99. *Staats-Zeitung*, March 24, 1855, cited in Callow, *The Tweed Ring*, 64. Callow notes that the figure may not be completely accurate but it certainly reflects political patronage patterns.

100. Callow, *The Tweed Ring*, 146.

101. See reports from the Lexow Commission 1894–1895, New York State Senate Documents 1895, no. 63; the Mazet Committee; the Committee of Fifteen; the 1897 Charter Revision Committee; the Citizens Committee of 9, on reorganization of the New York Police Force (1905–1906).

102. PP Police (Metropolis) Increase of Pay, (HO) Return, January 27, 1890. Other pay ranges were sergeant, 34–40s; station and clerk sergeant, 45–48s; Inspector, 56–64s; sub-divisional inspector, 70s; chief inspector, 83s.

103. Andrews, "The Police Systems of Europe."

104. See reward certificates in NYCMA.

105. *New York Herald*, May 16, 1857. Equally contentious was the battle from 1857 to 1858 over the position of streets commissioner.

106. Letter from Alexander Piper, Second Deputy Police Commissioner, March 20, 1903, MSColl Chrystie Family, Columbia University Rare Book and Manuscript collection.

107. Browne, *Stop That Clubbing*, 10.

108. Wickham 1261 (225), NYCMA.

109. *Mazet Committee, Lexow Committee*, 1894–1895.

110. Wickham 1264 (261), NYCMA.

111. Strong 90 SWL 45, NYCMA. The mayor had no replacement for him but wanted him on "on receipt of this." The matter did not end with the letter, however; Parker refused to resign.

112. The Metropolitan Police issued detailed annual statistics. Many scholars question the reliability of crime statistics. The overall sense of most studies, regardless of argument over specifics, is that the rate declined.

113. Rates per 100,000. Monkkonen, *Murder in New York City*.

114. Grace 97, NYCMA.

115. 90 SWL, NYCMA.

116. See NYCMA, Mayor's Papers for New York, and H.O. Annual Reports and Mepol files for London.

117. PP Metropolitan Police Annual Report 1882; Edward Cooper 156, NYCMA.

118. Mommsen, "Non-Legal Violence and Terrorism in Western Industrial Societies," in Mommsen and Hirschfeld, *Social Protest, Violence, and Terror in Nineteenth- and Twentieth-Century Europe*.

119. Hale, *Sunshine and Shadow*, 558, 706.

120. Whitman, *Leaves of Grass*, 638.

121. Dickens, *A Tale of Two Cities*, 2.

122. Donnelly, *Caesar's Column*.

123. Ibid., 36–43.

124. Ibid., 95.

125. Gissing, *The Netherworld*, 280.

3. LONDON BEFORE 1850

1. Editorial, *Times*, May 15, 1833.
2. Thurston, *The Clerkenwell Riot*; PP 1833 XIII, Select Committee on Coldbath Fields.
3. PRO Mepol 7/1 & 2, Police Orders 1830, Public Records Office (PRO) (now known as the National Archives).
4. PP 1833 XIII, 7.
5. PP 1833 XIII, 49.
6. PP 1833 XIII, 59.
7. Radzinowicz, *English Criminal Law*, 4:166.
8. *Rex v. Fursey, State Trials* 1891 n.s., vol. 3, 1315.
9. At two subsequent trials for the stabbings of the other two policemen, the court ruled that although an illegal meeting may be dispersed, Lord Melbourne's notice did not mean the meeting itself was illegal. The purpose of the meeting had been to support the National Convention, which would have changed the laws of the country, and therefore was clearly illegal.
10. Prior to the formation of the Metropolitan Board of Works in 1855, only the Metropolitan Police had authority extending over all of London.
11. L. & P. Acts, 40 Vict. C. viii (Metropolitan Board of Works Act, 1877). Some acts prior to this, which had added on land to the Works Office control, were Finsbury Park Act 1857 (20 & 21 Vict. C. cl); Thames Embankment Act 1863 (26 & 27 Vict. C. lxxv); Southwark Park Act 1864 (27 Vict. C. iv); Hampstead Heath Act 1871 (34 & 35 Vict. C. lxxvii); Metropolitan Commons Supplemental Act, Blackheath (34 & 35 Vict. C. lvii); Metropolitan Commons Supplemental Act, Shepherd's Bush (34 & 35 Vict. C. lxiii); Metropolitan Commons Supplemental Act, Hackney Common (34 & 35 Vict. C. xliii); Thames Embankment Act 1872 (35 & 36 Vict. C. lxvi) and 1873 (36 Vict. C. vii); Metropolitan Commons Supplemental Act, Tooting Bec (36 & 37 Vict. C. x); Metropolitan Board of Works Act 1875 and 1876, Tooting Graveney and Thames Embankment (38 & 39 Vict. C. clxxix and 39 and 40 Vict. C. lxxix).
12. Affected were Finsbury and Southwark Parks; Victorian, Albert, and Chelsea Embankment Gardens; Hampstead Heath; Blackheath; Leicester Square Gardens; Shepherd's Bush Common; Totting Bec and Tooting Graveney Commons; Hackney, Plumstead, Eel Brook, and Peckham Rye Commons; Wormwood Scrubs, Brook, Parson's Nunhead, Shoulder of Mutton, and Goose Greens. Some of these names were later changed.
13. Shorthand writers at times were employed by the police. Mather, *Public Order in the Age of the Chartists*, 192, cites a £986.6.3 bill paid in 1848 to Gurney and Sons, a firm of shorthand writers, for their coverage of the Chartist Convention.
14. H.O. 45/102.
15. See the classic study by Mather, *Public Order in the Age of the Chartists*. Goodway, *London Chartism, 1838–1848*, is mostly a rehashing of material contained in my 1977 PhD thesis. In Mepol 2/59, a note from Chief Clerk Yardley underscores the fact that re-

ports were solicited by the Home Office, and most of these files are Home Office files, not Mepol.

16. PP 1833 XLLI, 3.

17. See, for example, Campion, "Policing the 'Peelers,'" in Cragoe and Taylor, *London Politics: 1760–1914.*

18. Mather, *Public Order in the Age of the Chartists*, 198.

19. Mepol 2/59, May 15, 1839.

20. Linton, *Memoirs.*

21. HO 61/24 contains many letters from people offering information. In 1839, of 380 people confined on a variety of charges of sedition and libel in England, thirty-five were in London, and of that number twenty-six were discharged after a short period of retention. PP XXXVIII, 1840.

22. As Reith, *A New Study of Police History*, 158, pointed out, Home Office policy "was deliberately designed to curry public favour by continuing to show official disapproval of them."

23. Mepol 7/8, September 21, 1842.

24. Mayne and Rowan had requested two inspectors and eight sergeants but were granted only six sergeants.

25. HO 45/1107, December 1845. The newspaper reports came from the *Morning Advertiser* and the *Times.*

26. Mepol 7/8, December 10, 1845.

27. Mepol 1/44, October 16, 1830 (Confidential Outletter Book).

28. Mepol 7/8, September 21, 1842 (Daily Order Book).

29. HO 45/43313 and HO 45/1889.

30. HO 45/1889, October 16, 1847.

31. Mepol 1/45, 1836.

32. See, for example, the letter book from 1843–1846, which is mostly assault by police, with some complaints of failure to arrest of carry out the law. Mepol 4/6.

33. PP 1849 XLIV. Charges included neglect of, violation of, and refusal to do duty; assault; offensive language; improperly taking into custody; drunkenness; and felony.

34. Mepol 2/60, November 1830.

35. Mepol 1/45.

36. For example, in 1839, police officially observed forty-four meetings from January through August. HO 44/52 (ff1–245) and Mepol 2/59; 1840–1841, 8 [HO 45/10]; and in 1848 35 (HO 45/2410).

37. HO 61/24.

38. HO 61/24.

39. See HO 61/25 and the *Times*, January 1840.

40. Mepol 7/8, Order Book August 16, 18–20, 1842.

41. Mepol 7/8, August 22, 1842.

42. HO 45/252, August 21, 1842; Mepol 7/8, Order Book August 18, 20, 1842. The provocative nature of language during any sort of public disturbance is well known. On Au-

gust 20, 1842, the *Times* reported a constable to have said "You blackguard Chartist," most likely the most printable of the language.

43. Mepol 7/8, Police Order Book 1842–1843.

44. This account, as are the other descriptions of events during demonstrations and marches, was compiled from many contemporary sources, including newspapers such as the *Times, Standard, Morning Post,* and *Northern Star;* police reports; and Chartist histories.

45. See Creighton, *Memoir of Sir George Grey.*

46. The then seventy-nine-year-old Wellington remains in a class by himself in British politics. Extraordinarily popular and outside any defined political circles, he represented a singular national pride. His leadership in the 1848 event was a brilliant maneuver by the government, as his presence helped assure the public that things were well under control.

47. Lord John Russell to Prince Albert, April, in Benson and Esher, eds., *Letters of Queen Victoria,* 2:198.

48. Ibid., 2:200.

49. *Standard,* April 11, 1848.

50. Frost, *Forty Years' Recollections,* 135–136.

51. Duncombe, *The Life and Correspondence of Thomas Slingsby Duncombe,* 378.

4. THE SUNDAY TRADING BILL RIOTS

1. H.O. 45/6092, October 31, 1855.

2. Mepol 7/14, June 15, 1848, Caution to Superintendents.

3. Mepol 2/66. There tended to be a lot of inconsistencies on both sides when accusations of excessive force were made. There were also files of letters of appreciation, many of which might have been solicited. Mepol 2/67.

4. Mepol 2/59 and HO 45/3136.

5. Karl Marx, "Anti-Church Movement—Demonstration in Hyde Park," in *Marx and Engels on Britain.*

6. See Harrison, "The Sunday Trading Bill Riots of 1855," for a good discussion the riots in relation to Sabbatarian legislation. The issue of allowing commerce on Sunday remains a debated question, although by the start of the twenty-first century, both London and New York allowed and promoted Sunday business.

7. PP 1831–2 VII, Select Committee on the observance of the Sabbath and Sunday Trading, 3.

8. Mepol 4/6.

9. PP 1850 XIX, Select Committee on the Bill to Prevent Sunday Trading, Q 1492.

10. Mepol 1/45, November 29, 1839.

11. PP 1850 XIX, Select Committee on the Bill to Prevent Sunday Trading, Q 1515.

12. PP 1851 X. This report consisted mostly of police reports of activities in respective districts.

13. Hansard 138, 1928, 1913.

14. Mepol 4/6.

15. Mepol 1/45, November 29, 1939.

16. HO 61/25, February 1840.

17. The bill was drastic. It would have made it illegal to sell any goods, chattels, effects, or things in London and the City on Sunday, punishable by a summary conviction and a 5s fine for the first offence, up to 40s after. Exempted were medicines, milk (except from 9 a.m. to 1 p.m.), newspapers (except before 10 a.m.), fruit and prepared victuals (except from 10 a.m. to 1 p.m.), meat, poultry, fish (in summer only and only before 9 a.m.), and pubs and food shops. PP 1854–5 VI.

18. Newspaper reports range from a low of 50,000 to a high of 250,000. The *Times*, which usually gave a conservative estimate, put the crowd at 150,000.

19. Hansard 139, 79, 159.

20. HO 45/6092.

21. Of the seventy-two arrested, twenty-nine were discharged in their own recognizance or unconditionally, twenty-four charged for riot or throwing stones, twenty for riot or assault on the police, eighteen for obstructing the police in the execution of their duty, and ten as thieves and pickpockets. PP 1856, IX.

22. Hansard 139, 369.

23. Hansard 139, 369, 530 (MP Dundas).

24. Hansard 139, 370.

25. Hansard 139, 526.

26. Hansard 139, 452.

27. *Illustrated London News*, July 7, 1855. The normally staid publication, which published an engraving of the crowd thronging the drive and unsettling carriages, backed the inquiry.

28. The *People's Paper* had been a Chartist publication. Historian Brian Harrison had pointed out that there was a link between Chartists and the Sunday riots, but neither the police nor the Parliamentary investigation made any links. Harrison, "The Sunday Trading Bill Riots of 1855."

29. HO 45/6092.

30. Duncombe, *The Life and Times of Thomas Slingsby Duncombe*, 118; and *People's Paper*, July 14, 1855.

31. HO 45/6092.

32. Boase, *Modern English Biography*. The Recorder is a judicial official.

33. See HO 45/6092 and PP 1856.

34. PP 1856, 69, 116.

35. Rude, *The Crowd in History*, 240.

36. PP 1856, 134, 507–508, 103.

37. See PP 1852–3 XXIII.

38. PP 1856, 13, 88.

39. See Wroth, *The London Pleasure Gardens*; Sexby, *The Municipal Parks, Gardens, and Open Spaces of London*; and contemporary newspapers and guidebooks.
40. The Metropolitan Commons Act of 1866.
41. Cruikshank and Wight, *Sunday in London*, 42.
42. This included the high-end prostitutes of London.
43. Smith, *Sketches of London Life and Character*, 186.
44. Gronow, *Reminiscences and Recollections of 1810–1860*, 57.
45. Baedeker's *London* (1883), 249.
46. Gibbs-Smith, *The Great Exhibition of 1851*, 64.
47. HO 45/6092.
48. PP 1856, 51.
49. PP 1856, 163.
50. Mepol 2/248. The date was November 18, 1856.
51. Mepol 2/248 and Works 16/790.
52. PP 1856, 226–230.
53. PP 1856, xxxi.
54. HO 45/6092.
55. PP 1856, 349.
56. PP 1856, 53.
57. I have referred only to truncheons, because most of the injuries to civilians were caused by them. Staves were drawn. Superintendent Hughes had authorized this, which was severely criticized by the Commission. Police rules said staves were only to be used to prevent rescue of prisoners or in self-defense, and only flourished to show power.
58. PP 1856, 352, 502–505.
59. In thirteen cases where the aggrieved parties testified against known policemen, eight favored police. In the twenty cases of witnesses complaining of misconduct of known policemen without the injured party being present, fourteen were decided for the police.
60. PP 1856, xxx.
61. PP 1856, xii.
62. HO 45/6092.
63. PP 1856, various testimony. It was noted that the force was English (less than 10 percent were Scottish or Irish).
64. HO 65/20.
65. Officer Bewlay's defense included a memorial signed by about two hundred taxpayers of Marylebone, asserting that "for the last twelve years (they) have been daily witnesses of the indefatigable and efficient manner in which the officer has executed the most arduous duties in this part of the parish." HO 45/6092.
66. HO 45/6092.
67. HO 45/6092.

68. HO 65/20.
69. See Vogler, *Reading the Riot Act.*
70. PP 1856 453.

5. PRELUDE TO BLACK AND BLOODY

1. Shaw, *The Fabian Society*, tract 41, 9. Shaw noted the method was hard on the martyrs who suffered but received no compensation and little thanks. Shaw himself was peeved because his own repeated attempts to be arrested resulted in failure.
2. The group was named after a Roman general, Quintus Fabius Maximus, known for his deliberative battle strategies. Later members included Bertrand Russell, John Maynard Keynes, Emmeline Pankhurst, H. G. Wells, Harold Wilson, Ramsay MacDonald, and Tony Benn. There are an estimated five thousand members in existence today.
3. Classic works on the 1867 Reform Bill include Gertrude Himmelfarb, *Victorian Minds*; Harrison, *Before the Socialists*; and Smith, *The Making of the Second Reform Bill.*
4. Mepol 7/28 and 7/132.
5. HO 45/6794.
6. Mepol 2/69.
7. HO 45/6794.
8. HO 45/6094.
9. Mepol 2/248, October 11, 1862.
10. PP Primrose Hill Report, 1864.
11. Hansard 184, 1074–1075.
12. Mepol 2/248; Hansard 184, 1391–1398. Mayne's order was issued July 23, 1866.
13. Works 16/793, July 28, 1866. This file, which contains similar information to some Home Office files, contains the actual legal opinion, which is not in other files.
14. PP 1888 LXXII; Annual Register 1866, 98.
15. Mepol 2/59.
16. Harrison, *Before the Socialists*, 96.
17. HO 48/53 (LOO 179), also in Mepol 2/248.
18. Mepol 2/248.
19. The "Parks Regulation Bill." This was the second of two bills. The first, "Meetings in Royal Parks Bill," limited the right of meeting in Hyde Park. The second bill widened that to all Royal Parks, except with Her Majesty's permission, and parks under the Metropolitan Board of Works. Summary conviction was highly discretionary, and fines up to £10 were approved.
20. Hansard 184, 1588.
21. Hansard 188, 1890.
22. Hansard, July 29, 1867, 396, 394.
23. Hansard, August 15, 1867, 1573.

24. The 1872 Royal Parks and Gardens Act (35 & 36 Vict., c. 15) also included St. James, Green Parks, Kensington Gardens, Primrose Hill, Greenwich Park, Kew, Hampton, Richmond Park and Green, Bushy, Victoria Parks, Parliament Square Gardens, Kennington, Battersea, Holyrood, and Linlithgow Parks. In 1887, Battersea, Kennington, and Victoria Parks were transferred to the Metropolitan Board of Works.
25. *Bailey v. Williamson* L.R. 8 Q.B. 122, 125.
26. 1872 Royal Park and Gardens Act, revised 1896. The area specified was the "open part of the Park which is bounded by the Horse Ride running from Marble Arch to Victoria Gate and thence to the Powder Magazine and by the Carriage Drive running from Powder Magazine along Serpentine to Hyde Park Corner and thence to Marble Arch."
27. PP1886 XXXIV, Appendix VII. Victoria and Battersea Parks also hosted meetings, but they were removed from Board of Works jurisdiction by 1896.
28. Hansard 12, 907.
29. Cole and Postgate, *The British Common People*, 377.
30. *Justice*, May 17, 1884.
31. Winsten, *Salt and His Circle*, 64.
32. Bax, *Reminiscences and Reflections of a Mid and Late Victorian*, 88–89.
33. Snell, *Men, Movements, and Myself*, 101.
34. Shaw, "Who I Am, and What I Think," 111–112.
35. Lansbury, *My Life*, 86–87.
36. *Justice*, February 21, 1885.
37. *Justice*, July 5, 1884.
38. Tsuzuki, *H. M. Hyndman and British Socialism*, 69.
39. Besant, *An Autobiography*, 312.
40. *Justice*, April 11, 1885.
41. *Commonweal*, October 1885.
42. Elton, *England Arise*, 120.
43. Attendance estimates from *Justice*. Even allowing for some exaggeration, these were enormous crowds.
44. *Daily News*, September 22, 1885; also in Thompson, *William Morris*. Morris was up on disorderly conduct charges.
45. Morris, *William Morris*, 227. She says the delegation was headed by a Free Church leader, Dr. Clifford.
46. *Justice*, October 3, 1885.
47. See the *Times*, *Daily News*, *Standard*, and *Daily Telegraph* for the week of September 28, 1885.
48. Cole, *John Burns*, 9, writes that some early police attempts to stop open-air meetings were at the initiative of the Metropolitan Board of Works.
49. This continues to be the case now. Both cities have spaces that are called public but are really private. See chapter 12.

50. See also chapter 2 and chapter 5 for specific regulations. The Highway Act (5 & 6 Will. IV c. 50 s. 72); 2 & 3 Vict. C. 47 s. 54 cl. 13 and ss. 52 and 54.

51. PP 1865 VIII, iv (2) and v.

52. The 1866 Metropolitan Commons Act, which was later amended. PP 1868–9, IV.

53. L. & P. Acts, 40 Vict. C. viii (Metropolitan Board of Works Act, 1877). Some acts prior to this which had added land to Works Office control were Finsbury Park Act 1857 (20 & 21 Vict. C. cl); Thames Embankment Act 1863 (26 & 27 Vict. C. lxxxv); Southwark Park Act 1864 (27 Vict. C. iv); Hampstead Heath Act 1871 (34 & 35 Vict. C. lxxvii); Metropolitan Commons Supplemental Act, Blackheath (34 & 35 Vict. C. lvii); Metropolitan Commons Supplemental Act, Shepherd's Bush (34 & 35 Vict. C. lxiii); Metropolitan Commons Supplemental Act, Hackney Common (34 & 35 Vict. C. xliii); Thames Embankment Act 1872 (35 & 36 Vict. c. lxvi) and 1873 (36 Vict. C. vii); Metropolitan Commons Supplemental Act, Tooting Bec (36 & 37 Vict. c. x); Metropolitan Board of Works Act 1875 and 1876, Tooting Graveney and Thames Embankment (38 & 39 Vict. C. clxxix and 39 and 40 Vict. C. lxxix).

54. Affected were Finsbury and Southwark Parks; Victorian, Albert, and Chelsea Embankment Gardens; Hampstead Heath; Blackheath; Leicester Square Gardens; Shepherd's Bush Common; Totting Bec and Tooting Graveney Commons; Hackney, Plumstead, Eel Brook, and Peckham Rye Commons; Wormwood Scrubs, Brook, Parson's Nunhead, Shoulder of Mutton, and Goose Greens. Some of these names were later changed.

55. 1880, 5 Q.B.D. 155.

56. *DeMorgan v. Metropolitan Board of Works* 5 Q.B.D., 158.

57. PP 1888 LXXXI.

58. PP 1888 LXXXI.

59. PP 1888 LXXXI, August 25, 1883. In court, the taxpayers said they had understood that Harcourt had in effect given permission for the meeting by stating that orderly meetings could not be prohibited. Harcourt said this was a misinterpretation of what he had said, adding that their action would have to wait until the laws were changed, as he could not sanction law breaking. *Times*, August 29, September 1, September 3, 1883.

60. PP 1888 LXXXI, November 12, 1884.

61. PP 1888 LXXXI. Harcourt himself was responsible for a meeting of 120,000 people in Hyde Park in support of a bill reforming London's government. Increasingly unpopular, the Board of Works was one of the targets of local government reform. The London County Council took over many municipal functions after the passage of the Local Government Act of 1888.

62. PP 1886 XXXIV, appendix VII. The return omits the 1866 Reform League meeting.

63. Cited by Sir Charles Russell, Hansard, March 1, 1888; 1885. There is no direct statement in 1848 Hansard. On July 24, 1866, Grey referred to statements he made previously, probably in 1848, in which he affirmed the legality of the Trafalgar Square

meeting. Hansard 184, 1406. See also *Diary of John Evelyn Denison*, for Grey's statement concerning law Hansard, March 1, 1888, 1885.

64. Mace, *Trafalgar Square*, 31, citing "First Report to His Majesty's Commissioners for Woods, Forests and Land Revenues," London, 1812. See also Olsen, *The Growth of Victorian London*.

65. 53 George III, c. 121 and 7 George IV c. 77.

66. 7 & 8 Vict. c. 60. See Mace, *Trafalgar Square*, 40; and PRO Crest 40/83; Crest 26/152; L.R. 1/268–9.

67. 14 & 15 Vict. c. 42.

68. See "Crown Builds," *Architectural Review* (1953).

69. Mace, *Trafalgar Square*, 34; and Crest 26/188; also "Report from the Committee on the Petition of the Tradesmen and Inhabitants of Norris Street and Market Terrace," PP 1817 (79) iii.

70. Mace, *Trafalgar Square*, 87; and Works 20/2–1, April 6, 1841.

71. Hansard, March 1, 1888, 1884.

72. See discussion of Chartists in chapter 4, and similar modern meeting limitations in chapter 12.

73. Mepol 2/248.

74. Hansard, March 1, 1888, 1904.

75. *The Letters of Queen Victoria*, February 13, 1886.

6. BLACK MONDAY, BLOODY SUNDAY

1. Booth, *In Darkest England and the Way Out*.

2. Mearns, *The Bitter Cry of Outcast London*.

3. See Roberts, *Victorian Origins of the Welfare State*.

4. *Beatty v. Gilbanks*. See chapter 7.

5. Classic discussions of London politics in this period include Thompson, "Liberals, Radicals and Labour in London 1880–1900"; Thompson, *Socialist, Liberals, and Labour*; Pelling, *The Origins of the Labour Party*.

6. Lecture diaries are contained in the socialist newspapers, with place, date, and name of speaker given. *Justice* and *Commonweal* are the best sources for this information.

7. See Jones, *Outcast London*, appendix 2, table 11. At the end of August 1885, there were 85,301 Londoners on relief (34,082 outdoor); by the end of January 1886, there were 99,266 (41,516). *Pall Mall Gazette*, February 10, 1886. See Jones, *Outcast London*, esp. part 3, chap. 16, for a well-documented account of the recognition of the problems of the residuum and urban degeneration. There is an enormous body of both contemporary and modern social history about London.

8. See Owen, *English Philanthropy*; Wohl, "The Bitter Cry of Outcast London."

9. Pelling, *A Short History of the Labour Movement*, 217.

10. Harris, *Private Lives, Public Spirit*, 116.

11. The mean winter temperatures were the coldest London had seen in some time, 38.7 degrees Fahrenheit in December, 36.3 in January, and 33.9 in February. Jones, *Outcast London*, table 12.

12. *Justice*, January 30, 1886.

13. Lansbury, *My Life*, 88. Bradlaugh later accused a Labourers' League organizer named Peters of accepting a large sum of money from prominent conservatives via the Fair Trade League to support the demonstration and agitate the unemployed. Peters denied the accusation, which was made in the Commons, but declined Bradlaugh's challenge to a formal investigation. Bradlaugh claimed he had traced one of the checks to Salisbury, who denied it in a letter to the *Times*, December 2, 1886. But Salisbury gave no response when Bradlaugh offered to have the matter investigated before a House Committee. Peters then began a libel action against Bradlaugh, which became a complicated affair. An account of it is in Bonner, *Charles Bradlaugh*.

14. Hyndman, *Record of an Adventurous Life*, 401.

15. Memorandum, February 10, 1886, P.P. 1886 XXXIV, appendix IV.

16. See testimony in P.P. 1886 XXXIV, concerning the confusion of the message.

17. See newspaper accounts for week of February 8, as well as Mepol 2/182 and Mepol 2/174.

18. Mepol 2/182.

19. *Times*, February 11, 1886.

20. *Times*, February 9, 1886.

21. Thompson, *William Morris*, 357.

22. *Standard*, February 9, l886.

23. "Topics of the Day . . . The Riots of Monday," *Spectator*, February 13, 1886.

24. *Pall Mall Gazette*, February 9, 1886.

25. Arnold, *Culture and Anarchy*, 76–77.

26. Ibid., 203–204.

27. *Times*, February 9, 1886.

28. *Justice*, February 13, 1886.

29. *Times*, February 10, 1886.

30. *Letters of Queen Victoria*, 3rd series, 1:51–52.

31. *Times*, February 15, 1886, contains a list of claims of £30 and over. Of 340 claims, two hundred were over £30.

32. *Pall Mall Gazette*, February 11, 1886. The *Spectator* (February 13, 1886) exaggerated the damage to £50,000.

33. The *Times* and the *Morning Post* interpreted things at their worst, though the *Morning Post* felt the mob to be fanatics and thieves. The *Morning Advertiser* and *Daily Chronicle* blamed the SDF and Gladstonian Liberalism; the *Standard* blamed the police. The *Daily Telegraph* felt London was disgraced, but the *Daily News* stood alone in calmly stating there was nothing to be alarmed about. Although there was some sympathy for the unemployed, law and order was what all this amounted to. Historians' ver-

dicts also reflect such bias. Thompson, *William Morris*, 481, called the riot a "bit of a bust-up."

34. *Times*, February 9, 1886.
35. *Pall Mall Gazette*, February 9, 1886.
36. P.P. 1886 XXXIV, 486.
37. P.P. 1886 XXXIV, appendix II.
38. Elton, *England Arise*, 124.
39. *Times*, February 12, 1886, letters to the editor.
40. *Times*, February 9, 1886.
41. *Justice*, February 13, 1886.
42. Shaw, *The Fabian Society*, 8.
43. *Commonweal*, March 1886.
44. Thomson, *England in the Nineteenth Century*, 228.
45. *Times*, February 16, 1886.
46. Hyndman said the Lord Mayor received £75,000 within forty-eight hours. George Lansbury said it was £100,000 in a few hours. Shaw said the fund jumped to £79,000.
47. *Times*, February 12, 1886.
48. "The No-Police Riots," 219.
49. *Pall Mall Gazette*, February 9, 1886.
50. *Pall Mall Gazette*, February 11, 1886.
51. *Justice*, February 13, 1886.
52. Childers, *The Life and Correspondence of Hugh C. E. Childers*, 238–239.
53. *Times*, February 15, 1886.
54. Hansard, 302; 605 (Commons, February 18, 1886).
55. Hansard, 302, 600.
56. Hansard, 302, 602–603.
57. During the course of the Select Committee Investigation, Henderson said he had found pencil notes from Sir Richard Cross to Capt. Harris on June 3, 1875. P.P. 886, Question 2341.
58. Childers, *The Life and Correspondence of Hugh C. E. Childers*, 242.
59. Ibid., 243.
60. Ibid., 244.
61. Hansard, 302, 569 (Lords, February 18, 1886).
62. The Select Committee on the "Origin and Character of the Disturbances ... " P.P. 1886, XXXIV.
63. P.P. 1886 XXXIV, report, viii.
64. Croker, *Correspondence and Diaries of John Wilson Croker*, 2:18 (September 26, 1829). Cited in Radzinowicz, *A History of Criminal Law*, 4:170; and Reith, *A New Study of Police History*, 146. Peel had hazily acknowledged this: "No doubt 3 shillings a day will not give me all the virtues under heaven, but I do not want them ..." October 10, 1829.

65. P.P. 1886 XXXIV (Committee on … Administration and Organization), 504. Previous committees in 1868 and 1879 had suggested decentralized control but had been ignored.

66. Mepol 2/182.

67. Some felt the Home Secretary got off too easily. The *Times*, *Standard*, *Morning Post*, *Daily Chronicle*, and *Daily Telegraph* concurred in supporting the report's conclusion of blaming the police. The only dissenter was the *Pall Mall Gazette*, which felt it was too sweeping in its denunciation of Scotland Yard and Henderson. See these newspapers for February 24, 1886.

68. *Letters of Queen Victoria*, 64.

69. See Mepol 2/182 for letters.

70. Under 7 & 8 George IV cap. 31 sec. 2, compensation rights provided by 57 George III cap. 19 sec. 33, based upon 1 George I cap 5 sec. 6, had been repealed by 7 & 8 George IV cap. 27.

71. Gissing, *In the Year of Jubilee*, 259.

72. *Times*, February 10, 1886.

73. See H.O. 45/9662. There were the usual bureaucratic delays associated with compensation, which necessitated clarification of procedures. See also P.P. 1886 III and P.P. 1886 I.

74. Childers's decision was made after consultation with Mr. Monro (the head of the CID), the Treasury Solicitor, and Sir Henry James (Attorney General in the previous Liberal government). Hansard 302, 598–599 (February 18, 1886).

75. Besant, in the *National Reformer*, February 21, 1886.

76. *Pall Mall Gazette*, February 10, 1886.

77. Burns, *The Man With the Red Flag*, 7, 11. This was a pamphlet of the speech. Burns later said he considered the trial to be a lucky escape. Burgess, *John Burns*, 26.

78. Shaw, *The Fabian Society*, 8. The jury did, though, consider the language inflammatory.

79. *Justice*, April 17, 1886.

80. *Justice*, April 24, 1886.

81. Pease, *The History of the Fabian Society*, 53.

82. Marx and Engels, *Correspondence*, 447 (no. 200, February 15 and March 18, 1886, to Bebel).

83. Baedeker, *London and Its Environs* [1894], 273. The name "Speaker's Corner" had not yet come into popular usage.

84. Mill, *On Liberty*, 75–85.

85. "Topics …", *Spectator*, February 13, 1886.

86. Childers, *The Life and Correspondence of Hugh C. E. Childers*, 241, letter to his son Francis, March 18, 1886.

87. The SDF later accused Home Secretary Matthew, a Catholic, of repressing socialists following an encyclical by Pope Leo XIII. *Justice*, September 11, 1886.

88. *Letters of Queen Victoria*, 110.

89. Mepol 2/182.

90. Hansard, 322 and 323, March 1, 2, 1888.

91. Mepol 2/182, report of C. Howard.

92. Besant, *An Autobiography*, 323.

93. Morris, *William Morris*, 241.

94. Mepol 2/182.

95. Socialist presses estimated the crowds at 100,000 to 200,000; nonsocialist presses at 50,000 to 75,000.

96. The *National Reformer*, February 28, 1886. The man was named Walter Hamilton.

97. *Commonweal*, July 31, 1886.

98. *Justice*, June and July 1886.

99. Morris's satire of the trial, *The Tables Turned: or, Nupkins Awakened*, featured the judge, Peter Edlin, as Nupkins. Morris also parodied police testimony, which he considered contrived and contradictory.

100. *Justice*, August 21, 1886.

101. *Justice*, November 6, 13, 20, 27, 1886; *Times*, November 1, 2, 3, 5, 6, 7, 10, 16, 18, 19, 20, 22, 1886.

102. Only socialists were arrested. See *Justice* for April and May, as well as the *Times* and *Commonweal*. This is similar to what occurred when Salvationists were attacked by the Skeleton Army.

103. *Justice*, May 7, 1887. The next day, an Easter Monday Anti-Coercion Bill meeting brought fifty thousand to Hyde Park with no arrests. *Times*, April 12, 1887. *Justice*, April 16, 1887, reported 250,000, an unusually large discrepancy for the London press. But it was a sunny bank holiday, when Hyde Park would have been filled anyway.

104. Hansard 314, 1746–1779.

105. This became a significant legal bone of contention in the twentieth century in both England and the United States.

106. Hansard 314, 1757, May 12, 1887.

107. Bradlaugh had been active in public demonstrations since 1866 in Hyde Park, including one in 1875 to protest grants to the Prince of Wales. He also held two meetings in 1881 in Trafalgar Square.

108. Gissing, *In the Year of Jubilee*, 50.

109. Ibid., 64.

110. Morris, *William Morris*, 24.

111. Tschiffely, *Don Roberto*, 237.

112. Lambeth Conservative MP Arter and the *Daily Telegraph* correspondent Bennett Burleigh. *Justice*, November 12, 1887.

113. *Pall Mall Gazette*, October 18, 1887. Sentences related to public-meeting disorder, especially for assaulting police, were always stiff by British standards, carrying a minimum two to three months, with hard labor.

114. "The Set Against the Police," *Spectator*, August 20, 1887.

115. *Commonweal*, May 14, 1887.

116. See, for example, *Reynolds* and *Pall Mall Gazette*.

117. *Justice*, October 22, 1887.

118. Mepol 7/49, police orders 1887.

119. *Pall Mall Gazette*, November 10, 1887.

120. Mepol 2/174.

121. *National Reformer*, October 16, 1887.

122. *Pall Mall Gazette*, November 11, 1887.

123. Scott, *The Life and Death of a Newspaper*, 148–149. Stead wanted to attend the November 13 rally but was told by his boss he would have to resign if he went. Stead remained active in the cause through editorial policy and his work in the Law and Liberty League. The *Gazette* was the publisher of the pamphlet "Remember Trafalgar Square."

124. *Daily Chronicle*, November 11, 1887.

125. *Pall Mall Gazette*, November 12, 1887.

126. Shaw, *The Fabian Society*, 9–10.

127. *Times*, November 14, 1887.

128. These figures are from the *Times*, November 14. Other sources give different figures. Thompson, *William Morris*: seventy-five arrests and two hundred injuries. Tsuzuki, *H. M. Hyndman and British Socialism*: sixty hospitalized and 150 detained by police. Morris, *William Morris*: 150 arrests with seventy-five charges. During the period of November 13, 1887 through January 2, 1888, according to figures given by Matthews in Hansard (March 1, 1888), 126 were brought before a summary magistrate for public-meeting offences, of whom twenty-seven were discharged, twenty-two appealed to Sessions, and two convictions quashed.

129. Of the fifty arrested, twenty-five were identified in the Police Court report in the *Times* by age and/or occupation. They include a laborer, 44; an electrical engineer; an MP; a socialist leader; two basket makers; a solicitor; a sailor; a warehouseman; a fiber dresser, 31; an ostler, 18; a bootmaker, 33; a painter and decorator; a coachbuilder; a carman; a baker, 37; a laundryman; a tailor; a mineral-water manufacturer; and men aged 22, 29, 19, 38, 23, and 16. Those treated in the hospital came from Whitechapel, Bermondsey, Peckham, Fulham, Battersea, St. Luke's, and other areas. See the various newspaper reports of the week.

130. Burns had been forewarned by his wife's uncle, a policeman, that he would be arrested if he came to the square, but "Burns pushed his bowler firmly onto his head and his hands in his reefer jacket pocket and stepped into the roadway; the police faced him and he then pounded them in the chest once or twice—it was only a token assault—and they walked him off." Kent, *John Burns*, 28–29. It is interesting to note that Burns, who became an Independent Radical MP a decade later, described the Metropolitan Police as "the best" in the world, in Parliament in 1900. Hansard, LXXXV, 1559, July 13, 1900.

131. *Commonweal*, November 19, 1887.

132. *Justice*, November 19, 1887.

133. Besant, *An Autobiography*, 324.

134. Snell, *Men, Movements, and Myself*, 110.

135. Morris, *William Morris*, 248.

136. Pearson, *Bernard Shaw*, 83; Hulse, *Revolutionists in London*, 93.

137. Police orders 1887, in Mepol 7/49.

138. *Illustrated London News*, November 19, 1887. Punch ran parodies of the special constables.

139. *Commonweal*, November 26, 1887.

140. *Punch*, November 26, 1887.

141. *Times*, November 15, 1887, letter to the editor.

142. There is disagreement as to the date of Linnell's injuries. Tsuzuki, *H. M. Hyndman and British Socialism*, gives November 13, as does Mackail, *William Morris*. Elton and E. P. Thompson are correct in citing the date as November 20, 1887.

143. Besant, *An Autobiography*, 327.

7. TAKING BACK TRAFALGAR

1. Morris, *News from Nowhere*, 34.

2. *Link*, February 4, 1888.

3. The *Link* ceased publishing in November 1888, its funds lacking and support waning. The league's assets in February 1888 were £680, but its liabilities were almost as much. Ironically, its last page was devoted to "Trafalgar Square Outrages."

4. See chapter 12 for similar tactics engaged in a century later by Critical Mass.

5. *Daily Telegraph*, *Daily Chronicle*, and *Morning Post*, January 19, 1888.

6. *Times* and *Globe*, January 19, 1888.

7. *Daily News*, January 19, 1888.

8. *Pall Mall Gazette*, January 19, 1888.

9. *Justice*, February 25, 1888. Other good accounts appear in the *Link*, *Commonweal*, and Thompson, *William Morris*, 582–583.

10. Hyndman, *Record of an Adventurous Life*, 324.

11. Thompson, *William Morris*, 583.

12. *Link*, July 21, 1888.

13. Hansard 322 and 323, March 1 and 2, 1888.

14. Participants included the Attorney General, Sir Richard Webster and Secretary of State Matthews, and MPs Reid (Dumfries), Hall (Camberwell), Howell (Bethnal Green), Burdett-Coutts (Westminster), Bradlaugh (Northampton), William Harcourt (Derby), Murdoch (Reading), Firth (Dundee), Whitmore (Chelsea), Lawson (St. Pancras), Baumann (Peckham), Stuart (Shoreditch), Jesse Collings (Birmingham), Lockwood (York), Sir Henry James (Lancashire), and Cunninghame Graham (Lanark).

15. Hansard 322, 1899.

16. Hansard 323, 131.
17. Hansard 323, 125.
18. Hansard 323, 79.
19. Hansard 323, 39.
20. Hansard 323, 69.
21. *Justice*, March 10, 1888.
22. *Link*, March 10, 1888.
23. P.P. 1888 VII and P.P. 1889 VIII (not printed). Many of the provisions were enacted as local regulations in the twentieth century.
24. P.P. 1888 VI.
25. Hansard 328, 1419.
26. Hansard 328, 1423.
27. Hansard 330, 1241.
28. Hansard 336, 1132; Hansard 339, 173.
29. Hansard 337, 553.
30. Hansard 344, 1858.
31. Hansard 344, 1862.
32. Childers, *The Life and Correspondence of Hugh C. E. Childers*; Hansard, 1874.
33. *R. v. Cunninghame Graham* 1888, 16 Cox C.C. 430. Mr. Justice Charles. The criminal liability issues appear to be a corollary of 1 & 2 Will IV c. 41, making it mandatory for magistrates to take action upon sworn testimony.
34. Ibid.
35. *Ex parte Lewis* L.R. 1888 Q.B.C. 21. A similar ruling was in *Homer v. Cadman*, 1888 Cox C.C. 51.
36. Ibid.
37. Works 20/110. The laws that governed Trafalgar Square were defined in 53 Geo. III, c. 121, and 7 & 8 Vict. c. 60.
38. Hansard 322, 1895; 323, 125, 64, 61.
39. Hansard 322, 1900; 323, 72, 47.
40. 11 Adolphus and Ellis, 877.
41. *Forbes v. Ecclesiastical Commissioner*, Law Report 15 Eq.
42. The case concerned a march of one hundred thousand in regard to the Tichborne claimant. An old law, 13 Chas. II c. 5 s. 1, Tumultuous Petitioning, made it an offence for more than ten persons to present a petition, complaint, remonstrance, or declaration to the King or Parliament. Mepol 2/248, Memo. The LOO also recommended the application of 34 Ed. III, c. 1, s. 2, empowering justices to restrain rioters and take sureties of good behavior. The problem at the time was less the procession than the demonstration in Palace Yard.
43. *Law Journal* 16 (October 15, 1881): 480.
44. *McClenaghan v. Waters . . .* ; *Times*, July 18, 1882.
45. *Beatty v. Glenister*, 51 L.T. 304.

46. *Beatty v. Gilbanks*, 9 Q.B.D. 313, 314. Beatty remained the guiding principle until 1936 (see chapter 12). Beatty was criticized in *O'Kelly v. Harvey*, 1883, 15 Cox C.C. 435, and in Bodkin and Kershaw, *Wise on Riots and Unlawful Assemblies*.
47. *Hansard* 337, 1254.
48. *Homer V. Cadman* 1888 Cox C.C. 51. Also *Hawkins Please of the Crown*, 8th ed., book 1, chap. 32.
49. Goodhart, "Public Meetings and Processions."
50. Mepol 2/248.
51. Works 20/110.
52. Mepol 7, 48–57. See also appendix. By "major" is meant demonstrations warranting a special police order.
53. P.P. 1866 LIX.
54. P.P. 1892 LXV.
55. P.P. 1892 LXV.
56. *Justice*, April 15, 1888, and November 23, 1889.
57. P.P. 1886 XXXIV.
58. Hansard 344, 1871–1872. There were seventeen major ones in 1887, thirteen in 1888, and sixty in 1889.
59. *Link*, April 7, 1888.
60. *Link*, July 7, 1888.
61. *Contemporary Review*, December 1887.
62. Hansard 320, 1804.
63. Nethercot, *The First Five Lives of Annie Besant*, 25.
64. *Justice*, June 15, 1889.
65. Mepol 2/231b. The precedent for the case had been the prosecution in 1892 of a mendicant who claimed to be a lecturer.
66. *Justice*, January 5, 1889.
67. Mepol 2/231a.
68. *Times*, November 13, 1888.
69. Warren was reputed to resent Monro's control of the newly separated CID.
70. *Times*, November 13, 1888.
71. Tillett, *Memories and Reflections*, 125.
72. Hansard 344, 1281. The case was legally complicated because of Post Office regulations that said Post Office servants must refrain from holding meetings outside of a Post Office building, but the constitutionality of such an order was questionable.
73. HO 45/9718.
74. See, for example, the *Daily Telegraph*, May 10, 1890. The Home Office was furious at the leak and ordered an investigation.
75. H.O. 45/9718A51563, May 13, 1890. The Secretary of State's responses were penciled in the margins in what is likely Permanent Undersecretary Godfrey Lushington's handwriting.

76. "Monster" was used by demonstrators and police to rouse interest, excitement, and reaction. In reality, only twenty thousand attended. This was an Anti-Compensation procession, protesting the compensations clauses for the surrender of licenses in the Local Taxation Bill of 1890.

77. The changes would have placed the procession on streets less likely to afford large crowds and therefore lessen the effectiveness of the demonstration.

78. Mepol 2/250, June 7, 1890.

79. Mepol 2/250.

80. Mepol 2/250.

81. Mepol 2/250.

82. H.O. 45/9816, May 3, 1890.

83. Hansard 345, 735.

84. Hansard 345, 846.

85. Monro was annoyed at the bill's inadequacies in regard to benefits. In addition, he hinted that Matthews was guilty of patronage in considering the appointment of a friend to the post of assistant commissioner over that of veteran Chief Constable Howard. Matthews finally did appoint Howard, but this may have been as rebuttal to Monro's charges.

86. Hansard 345, 1504.

87. Mepol 2/174, November 2, 1892.

88. Spender and Asquith, *Life of Hubert Henry Asquith*, 82.

89. *Times*, November 28, 1892.

90. A meeting had been permitted on November 12, 1893, during which a miniature gallows had been set up. *Times*, November 28, 1893.

91. Mepol 2/174. Secretary of State to Police Commissioner, November 14, 1892.

92. H.O. 45/9861:13077A.

93. H.O. 45/9861:13077A.

94. H.O. 45/9861:B13077C.

95. H.O. 45/9861:B13077C.

96. Mepol 2/360. Also in P.P. 1895 XXXV.

97. *Times*, February 19, 1894.

8. NEW YORK BEFORE 1870

1. *Herald*, February 12–25, 1837. Much of the material in this chapter is culled from contemporary newspaper accounts.

2. *Herald*, February 20, 16, 1837.

3. Pessen, "Political Democracy and the Distribution of Power in Antebellum New York City," 23. In 1845, 1 percent owned half the wealth in the city, and 4 percent owned 80 percent.

4. Interestingly, in 1893, during "widespread distress," the Charity Organization Society, in a letter to Mayor Thomas Gilroy, endorsed the offer of a milling company to

donate twenty-thousand bags of flour to the city. The COS was usually reluctant to offer such direct aid. Gilroy 12, NYCMA.

5. Gutman, *Work, Culture, and Society in Industrializing America*, 60.
6. See, for example, Gilje, "The Baltimore Riots of 1812 and the Breakdown of the Anglo-American Mob Tradition"; Olson, *Baltimore*.
7. Gilje, *Rioting in America*, 63.
8. Monkkonen, *Murder in New York City*.
9. Beckert, *The Monied Metropolis*, 4. See also Blumin, *Emergence of the Middle Class*; The Metropolitan Museum of Art, *Art and the Empire City*.
10. Cholera epidemics occurred in 1832, 1834, 1849, 1851, 1854, and 1866.
11. These were the Etna Iron Works. Beckert, *The Monied Metropolis*, 53.
12. See for example Wilentz, *Chants Democratic*.
13. Rosenwaike, *Population of New York City*.
14. Wilentz, *Chants Democratic*, 110.
15. Ernst, *Immigrant Life in New York City, 1825–1863*.
16. See also Stott, *Workers in the Metropolis*; Le Blanc, *A Short History of the U.S. Working Class*; Moody and Kessler-Harris, *Perspective on American Labor History*; Mohl, *Poverty in New York*.
17. See the *Evening Star*, *Journal of Commerce*, and *Sun* for the week of February 12, 1837.
18. Maier, "Popular Uprising and Civil Authority in Eighteenth-Century America," in Friedman and Scheiker, *American Law and the Constitutional Order*, 75. Maier cites Rude's classic *The Crowd in History*.
19. See Gilje, *The Road to Mobocracy* and *Rioting in America*; Weinbaum, *Mobs and Demagogues*; Feldberg, *The Turbulent Era*; Grimsted, *American Mobbing*; Gilfoyle, "Strumpets and Misogynists"; Stansell, *City of Women*; and contemporary newspaper accounts.
20. "The Democratic Review," December 1839, as cited in Widmer, *America: The Flowering of Democracy in New York City*.
21. Widmer says by 1850 there were more than one hundred publications in New York.
22. Cited in Phelps Stokes, *Iconography*, 1726.
23. The incident began over the whether a black choir had rights to use the church over a white choir. As the mob surged into Five Points, it was said that whites were told to put candles in their windows to ward off attackers. Among the targets were St. Philip's Church on Centre Street, which was ruined; Chatham St. Chapel, the Bowery Theater, Dr. Cox's church and house, Zion Church, St. Phillips Church, and the African Baptist Church.
24. See also Headley, *The Great Riots of New York*.
25. *Herald*, May 18, 1842.
26. Feldberg, *The Turbulent Era*, 76.
27. Bruce Levine, *The Spirit of 1848*.
28. See also Moody, *The Astor Place Riot*.
29. Ranney, *An Account of the Terrific and Fatal Riot at the New York Astor Place Opera House*, 31.

30. Montgomery, *Citizen Worker*. See chapter 2 for police background.

31. *Harper's Weekly*, 1:338.

32. *Herald*, July 6, 1857.

33. *World*, July 18, 14, 1863.

34. *World*, July 14, 1963.

35. This figure comes from Adrian Cook, *Armies of the Streets*, 1974. The number of dead has been the subject of much controversy. Cook says 105 died immediately, three were missing, three died in falls, two died later; including questionable deaths, the figure comes to 119. There were thirty-five soldiers and thirty-two police seriously wounded, thirty-eight soldiers and seventy-three police lightly wounded, and 128 civilians hurt. Estimates of the number of dead ranged from several dozen to several thousand. See also Schechter, *The Devil's Own Work*; Bernstein, *The New York City Draft Riots*; Spann, *Gotham at War*. Most of this discussion is based on newspaper accounts.

36. The number of African Americans stayed low through the nineteenth century, reaching only 23,601 out of a total population of 1.5 million in New York in 1890 (this does not include Brooklyn). Rosenwaike, *Population History of New York City*, 77.

37. This included the 26th Michigan Volunteers, 152nd New York Volunteers, and the 74th Regiment. Other companies that came included the 20th New York Battery, 65th Regiment, 16th New York Cavalry, 15th New York Artillery, 8th United States Infantry, the Citizens Guard, the 11th Regiment, the 22nd Regiment, and the 37th Regiment. By Saturday, joining them were Battery C of the 5th United States Artillery, the 8th Regiment, and the 71st Regiment. Reported en route to New York on Monday, July 20, were the 22nd and 37th Regiments. All information comes from newspaper accounts. Contrary to popular myth, there were no troops from Gettysburg.

38. Immediately following the destruction of the Twin Towers of the World Trade Center on September 11, 2001, three battalions of the National Guard were deployed in New York City. The were the 1st Battalion of the 69th Infantry Regiment (Manhattan), the 1st Battalion of the 258th Field Artillery Regiment (Jamaica, Queens), and the 101st Cavalry Squadron (Staten Island). By September 18, approximately 4,500 to 5,000 men were mobilized. By mid-October, that number declined to an estimated 2,700. *New York Times*, September 18–October 17, 2001. In the twentieth century, the National Guard moved toward becoming "an instrument of rescue and relief," with the exception of the urban riots of the 1960s and 1970s. See Rich and Burch, "The Changing Role of the National Guard," 702. The National Guard was deployed during the 1895 Brooklyn transit strike, but at that time Brooklyn was an independent municipality and not yet part of New York City.

39. See Hershkowitz, *Tweed's New York*; Mandelbaum, *Boss Tweed's New York*.

40. Quigley, *Second Founding*, 73–74.

41. *Herald*, July 14, 1870.

42. *Herald*, *Tribune*, *World*, July 9–11, 1871.

43. *Herald*, July 10, 1871.

44. *Herald*, July 12, 1871.
45. *Tribune*, July 12, 1871.
46. Ibid.
47. Tammany Hall head William "Boss" Tweed, New York's most potent political leader, was on his way out, facing indictment for corruption.
48. This is a reference to Edward Gibbons's *Decline and Fall of the Roman Empire*, which argued that Christianity was a major factor in the empire's collapse.
49. *Herald*, July 12, 1871.
50. *Tribune*, July 12, 1871.
51. The foreman of the Grand Jury at the Court of General Sessions was Theodore Roosevelt (Senior); his son, the future U.S. President, later was police commissioner in New York City.
52. They were used in Brooklyn, still a separate city, in 1895, during the transit strike.
53. Gordon, *The Orange Riots*, 151.
54. *New York Times*, July 16, 1871.
55. Laws of 1872, chap. 590, "An Act to regulate processions and parades in the cities of the state of New York," passed May 7, 1872.

9. THE BATTLE OVER TOMPKINS SQUARE

1. This chapter is based on contemporary newspaper accounts from the *Herald*, *World*, *Evening Post*, *New York Times*, *Tribune*, *Sun*, and *Daily Graphic*. The men had left the Fifth Street police house in the seventeenth precinct. Newspapers and court documents indicate a significant involvement of women in the events. While no women were arrested, they were at the courts, on the streets, bailing out men, and attending public demonstrations. As one woman was to say, "they share the indignation of the men" (Mrs. F. W. Lilienthal, *The Sun*, January 31, 1874). This came at a time when women's participation in public and political activities was increasing.
2. *Herald*, January 14, 1874.
3. This was absurdly high for the offense. Typical bail at the time: after stabbing his wife three times, John Biesbacher's bail was set at $1,000. The same day, a man who stole $53 had bail set at $2,000. *Herald*, January 27, 1874.
4. Meetings on Sunday, usually the only day off for many workingmen, were forbidden completely. Law of 1872, ch. 590.
5. The land was assessed at $89,418, the whole of the amount, with $6,000 costs and charges, was imposed upon and paid by the private owners of 3,552 lots. Ruggles memorial, New York State Assembly Doc. 99, 1878.
6. Schuyler, *The New Urban Landscape*, 17.
7. See chapter 12.
8. Parks Dept. Memo and Mayor Havemeyer Annual Message to the Common Council, June 1871, NYCMA.

9. These two areas also had the largest number of vacant lots. Blackmar, *Manhattan for Rent*, table 4 (from Board of Assistant Aldermen Doc. 1, no. 37 and no. 4, Dec. 5, 1831).

10. There were 1,118 new buildings, plus 570 in the Seventeenth Ward, after 1837; the next highest was the Sixteenth Ward, with 1,092. See Blackmar, *Manhattan for Rent*. Also see Homberger, *The Historical Atlas of New York City*.

11. New York State Census of 1855. In 1836, real-estate assessment in New York rose 62 percent, the single greatest rise in the 1817–1850 period.

12. See Blackmar, *Manhattan for Rent*.

13. Washington Square had been a potters field; Madison Square had been laid out as a potters field.

14. See Valentine, *Corporation Manual*.

15. January 1850 Mayor Woodhull address to Board of Aldermen. Proceedings of the Board of Aldermen of the City of New York, 1850, Vol. XXXVIII.

16. Mayor, II, 211, Proceedings of the Board of Aldermen of the City of New York, 1834, Vol. VII.

17. Preamble and resolution relative to repairing Tompkins Square, Board of Councilmen, January 22, 1866. Board of Aldermen, February 12, 1866, Committee on Lands and Places, NYCMA.

18. Letter from Bronson Murray, January 1874, Mayor's Papers, NYCMA.

19. 1868 Laws, ch. 853. Parks Dept. Memo, "Tompkins Square: A Historical Sketch."

20. "First Annual Report," Dept. Public Parks, New York.

21. "Address to Board of Aldermen," New York, January 1850.

22. Browne, *The Great Metropolis*, cited in Spann, *The New Metropolis*, 172.

23. *Tribune*, January 13, 1874.

24. As discussed in chapter 8.

25. S. B. Wales, president of the Department of Public Parks, *Herald*, January 15, 1874.

26. Estimates of crowd size varied. The *Herald* said 6,000; the *Times* 3,000; the *World*, 7,000–8,000.

27. Gutman reports forty-six men. The *Herald* reports forty-four; other papers have different figures. But not all the arrests occurred in the square, as some men were apprehended after the dispersal of the crowd. According to the *Herald* (January 14), of the forty-four men, twenty-one were German, eleven American, four French, three Irish, two Poles, two Italian, and one Swede, though at least two of the Americans have German-sounding names. For bills of indictment, see NYCMA.

28. *Herald*, January 14, 1874.

29. *New York Times*, January 13, 1874.

30. *Evening Post*, January 14, 1874.

31. *Tribune*, January 14, 1874.

32. *Herald*, January 13, 1874.

33. Ibid.

34. *Sun*, January 16, 1874.

35. *Herald*, January 14, 1874.

36. *Evening Post*, January 14, 1874.

37. *Daily Graphic*, January 14, 1874.

38. *Tribune*, January 14, 1874.

39. *Daily Graphic*, January 14, 1874.

40. *New York Times*, January 14, 1874.

41. *Daily Graphic*, January 14, 1874.

42. *Tribune*, Jan. 14, 1874.

43. *Evening Post*, January 14, 1874.

44. *Sun*, January 16, 1874.

45. *Herald*, January 13, 1874.

46. *Herald*, January 14, 1874.

47. He ran for mayor in the fall of 1874 on a labor ticket.

48. *World*, January 14, 1874. Schwab had been arrested two years before, during an attempted Internationale parade, also in defiance of police orders. He had lived in the United States for four years, though he was not a citizen; when asked by the court if he were, he replied he was a citizen of the world.

49. Schwab also figured prominently in the 1877 attempted demonstration in Tompkins Square that fizzled. He had earned the sobriquet "red-flag man" and visited the Seventh Regiment as it prepared to defend the city against a siege. See "Who was G. W.?", 1879.

50. *Tribune*, January 16, 1874. Schwab had been lucky to have been bailed out by Swinton, who also gave him dinner and found him a lawyer. Schwab and others were rearrested January 30 following discovery of a "defect" in their commitment papers, and they had to rebail, at which time Frederick W. Lilienthal bailed him and another prisoner out for $1,000 each. The others rearrested were George Deerbecker, bailed by Philip Stubenwall for $1,000; Charles Dees, bailed by Peter Disch, $1,000; and Thomas McGrann, bailed by Arthur McQuaide, $300. Schwab and five others were eventually discharged, "as they were too poor to furnish bail" (although Schwab had already received bail) and "as the evidence against them was slight." *Herald*, February 14, 1874.

51. Benedict Smith was released after he showed a bankbook proving he had $10,000. Others were released because of poverty. Some were allowed to go free on their own recognizance with no reason provided. The cases dragged on for weeks, many of them unresolved until mid-February.

52. There is some confusion about Mayer's plea. In the first case, the police court record indicated a guilty plea from him. He admitted striking Officer Berghold, but said it was in self-defense. In the second trial he pleaded not guilty.

53. *Sun*, February 4, 1874.

54. The Governor's Office issued a formal request for all papers connected with the case on April 27, 1874. New York County District Attorney Indictment papers, NYCMA.

55. Swinton, *The Tompkins Square Outrage*, March 25, 1874.

56. The document is a letter that indicated the signers represent thirty workingmen's societies, but the actual signatories are not with the letter. NYCMA, Havemeyer Papers 1237.

57. *World*, January 14, 1874.

58. Crowds were estimated at between two to three thousand people.

59. Rabban, *Free Speech in Its Forgotten Years, 1870–1920*, 175.

60. *Sun* and *Herald*, January 31, 1874. She is described by the *Herald* and "tall, stout" and speaking in a faint voice and by the *Sun* as "bright-eyed, pleasant," "attired in plain black with a white ruffle around her neck," and speaking "clearly and distinctly without looking at her notes."

61. Report of the Supt. of Building for 1870 and 1871, New York (1872).

62. Wickham 1262:246, NYCMA.

63. Board of Aldermen, August 17 and 28, 1876, NYCMA.

64. Board of Aldermen, August 17 and 28, 1876, NYCMA.

65. *Tribune*, June 3, 1876.

66. See also Wickham 1256, 179, NYCMA.

67. *Tribune*, September 29, 1879.

68. Edwin Seguin, *Our Parks, to Be or Not to Be, by a Physician*.

69. It had also closed a number of very small parks.

70. *Dictionary of National Biography*. See Lacy, *Frank Mason North*.

71. Charles Burns, secretary, Department of Public Parks, June 27, 1895, to Rev. Frank Mason North. 90 SWL 43 Parks, NYCMA.

72. Rabbi Moses Wechsler of Temple Brith Solam. Performed every twenty-eight years, it is supposed to occur at the exact moment of the sun cycle as at creation, and worshipers must see the sun at that moment. Given the crowded tenements in the Lower East Side at this time, it would have been impossible to have seen the sun at that morning hour from anywhere but a large open space.

73. *Evening Post*, April 7, 1897.

74. Report on Public Baths and Public Comfort Stations by the Mayor's Committee of New York City, 1897. *Tribune*, May 22, 1897.

10. NEW YORK UNDER CONTROL

1. "Who Was G. W.?" 27–29. This was a pamphlet reprint of articles from *The World*.

2. Gilje, *Rioting in America*, 117.

3. Ware, *The Labor Movement in the United States*, 48. Also see Yellowitz, *Industrialization and the American Labor Movement, 1850–1900*; Pessen, *Most Uncommon Jacksonians*; Leab, *The Labor History Reader*; Dubovsky and Van Tine, eds., *Labor Leaders in America*; Montgomery, *Beyond Equality*.

4. Moody and Kessler-Harris, *Perspectives on American Labor History*, 129. Also see Wilentz, *The Rise of the American Working Class*.

5. See Foner, *The Great Labor Uprising of 1877*; Bruce, *1877: Year of Violence*.

6. *New York Herald*, July 23, 1877.

7. Rodgers, *The Work Ethic in Industrial America, 1850–1920*.

8. *New York Daily Tribune*, July 23, 1877.

9. Smith, *Sunshine and Shadows*.

10. *New York Daily Tribune*, July 24–25, 1877.
11. *New York Daily Tribune*, July 25, 1877.
12. *New York Daily Tribune*, July 24, 1877.
13. *New York Times*, July 25, 1877.
14. *New York Daily Tribune*, July 23, 1877.
15. *New York Herald*, July 24, 1877.
16. *New York Herald*, July 25, 1877.
17. *New York Daily Tribune*, July 25, 1877.
18. *World*, July 25, 1877.
19. *New York Daily Tribune*, July 21, 1877.
20. "Who Was G. W.?" 12, 5.
21. Martin, *The History of the Great Riots*, 281.
22. *World*, July 27, 1877.
23. *New York Daily Tribune*, July 24, 1877.
24. Martin and others.
25. *New York Times*, July 24, 1877.
26. *World*, July 24, 1877.
27. *Daily Graphic*, July 25, 1877.
28. *World*, July 26, 1877.
29. *New York Times*, July 25, 1877.
30. Other reports were "Do not arouse the 'Tiger!' referring to the laws and their penalty." *New York Herald*, July 26, 1877.
31. *World*, July 26, 1877.
32. *World*, July 24, 1877.
33. *New York Times*, July 25, 1877.
34. Martin, *The History of the Great Riots*, 293–294. Newspapers differentiate between the formal counts and the number of soldiers who actually showed up.
35. "Who Was G. W.?"
36. *Daily Graphic*, July 24, 1877.
37. *New York Times*, July 24, 1877.
38. *New York Daily Tribune*, July 23, 1877.
39. *New York Daily Tribune*, July 25, 1877. This was also a swipe at the Pennsylvania's Sixteenth Regiment, which had refused to fire on strikers at Reading.
40. *World*, July 25, 1877.
41. The Eleventh Precinct had 150 men, the Eighteenth had 190, and the Seventeenth had 348.
42. *World*, July 26, 1877.
43. "Strikes and Lockouts," *16th Annual Report of the Commissioner of Labor*. Also Harring, *Policing a Class Society*.
44. Moody and Kessler-Harris, *Perspectives on American Labor History*, 129.
45. Forbath, *Law and the Shaping of the American Labor Movement*, 3.
46. Martin, *The History of the Great Riots*, 296.

47. *New York Daily Tribune*, July 26, 1877.

48. While the *Tribune* placed crowds that night at Tompkins Square at four thousand and the *Times* at five thousand, the *World* more accurately put it at fifteen thousand, a figure backed up by the *Daily Graphic* engraving.

49. Arrested were Charles Miller for throwing bottles at an office and John Miller, carpenter, for assaulting a man on a stoop. *World*, July 26, 1877. Injured was Michael Folz, "a German of middle age" at East Eighth Street, who was sitting in his front yard when a policeman struck him with a revolver on the neck and severely wounded him. He tried to leave and was again clubbed, injuring his knee. *New York Daily Tribune*, July 26, 1877.

50. "Who Was G. W.?" 54.

51. Ibid., 57.

52. *New York Daily Tribune*, July 26, 1877.

53. *New York Times*, July 21, 1877.

54. *New York Times*, July 27, 1877.

55. *New York Times*, July 26, 1877.

56. *New York Herald*, July 27, 1877.

57. In 1792, the Militia Act established militia in every state, constituted by white males between eighteen and forty-five years of age. The militia was to act against domestic or foreign adversaries but was under the control of the state. The act was ignored and the butt of jokes. By the 1840s, it had been replaced by volunteer militia. See Cunliffe, *Soldiers and Civilians*.

58. Shaler's influence in city politics was substantial. He became a police commissioner in 1877 and later a member of the Armory Board and the Board of Health. He also served on the New York Park Association. He was later involved in scandal resulting from the Gibbs commission.

59. Information on the armories is compiled from an extensive list of sources, including Landmarks Preservation Commission Designation lists 164, 259, 245; *Official Deliberations, Armory Board of the City of New York*; *The New York City Armory Board 1884–1911*; Fogelson, *America's Armories*; Ann Beha Associates, *The Armory*; *New York Times*, July 8, 1871; April 4, 1874; November 2, 1879; December 29, 1888; February 5, 12, 18, 19, 21, 24, 26, 27, 1878; March 6, 1878; *New York Daily Tribune*; *World*, January 19, 1874; Molineux, *Riots in Cities and Their Suppression*; Wingate, *History of the Twenty-second Regiment of the National Guard*; Clark, *History of the Seventh Regiment of New York 1806–1889*; New-York Historical Society: Emmons Clark to N.Y. County Board of Supervisors, September 15, 1873; Seventh Regiment Archives; *The New Armory of the Seventh Regiment, N.G.S.N.Y.*; City Clerk files, NYCMA; Proceedings of the Commissioners of the Sinking Fund of the City of New York, September 4, 1884; Todd, *New York's Historic Armories*; Everett, *Historic National Guard Armories*; Joint Hearing Before the United States Senate Committee on Military Affairs, 74th Congress, "National Guard Armories," April 17, 1935; and various newspaper and magazine articles.

60. City Clerk, Armories, 1873, NYCMA. They had been at 22 Delancey at Chrystie Street, which was deemed untenantable, and were given the Centre Market location, which was repaired for their tenancy in 1872. Another regiment was then given rights to the Centre Market site, and the Eleventh then ordered to be moved to 37–39 Bowery, which was at that point occupied by the Third Cavalry, who also did not want to move.

61. *Daily Tribune*, April 1, 1874.

62. City Clerk, Armories, 1875, NYCMA. It is not without some irony that four years later, the building collapsed, due to rain leaks, bad maintenance, and general deterioration. *New York Times*, February 4, 1878.

63. City Clerk, Armories 1876, NYCMA. The petition notes the improvements cost $117,000 and the company themselves put in another $18,000–$20,000.

64. City Clerk papers, Armories, NYCMA.

65. The Sixth Regiment paid $36,000 for premises worth $4,000; the Twelfth Regiment rooms were worth $4,000 but rent was $15,000; the First Infantry rent was $16,500 but was worth $2,000. *New York Times*, July 8, 1871. The scandal did not stop Tammany Hall from sending a letter to the Board of Supervisors on September 2, 1872, asking them to have the armory vacate the premises for lack of rent payment. City Clerk, Board of Supervisors, 72, NYCMA.

66. City Clerk, Board of Supervisors, September 1, 1875. These were followed by executive salaries and election expenses, each $200,000.

67. The previous annual rent, paid for five years, had been $23,000. City Clerk, 1875, Armories, NYCMA. The 1871 Report of the Joint Investigating Committee of Supervisor Alderman and citizens. The Ninth had spent $117,000 on fixing up the building.

68. City Clerk, Board of Supervisors, NYCMA.

69. City Clerk, Armories, 1874, NYCMA. The Board of Supervisors, in an exculpatory move, noted that the mayor had received the communication regarding Governor Dix's disapproval of the move "*many days ago.*"

70. Ch. 429, Laws of New York State, May 7, 1873. Excluded from this list were Central Park, Reservoir Square, Union Square, and Madison Square.

71. City Clerk, Armories, 1873 NYCMA. As of December 1873, there were 23,360 New York National Guard. *Adjutant General Annual Report*, 1874. As of April 28, 1873, there were 9,733 men in the First Division under Shaler, of whom 6,846 were privates, 1,554 noncommissioned officers, 811 musicians, and 522 commissioned officers.

72. *New York Times*, July 26, 1877.

73. Van Winkle, "The New Armory of the Seventh Regiment," *Seventh Regiment Scrapbook*, 1875, Seventh Regiment Archives, New-York Historical Society.

74. *Public Papers of John T. Hoffman, Governor of New York*, "1869 Report."

75. *Adjutant General Annual Reports*, 1874–1888. Brooklyn was not yet part of New York City.

76. There is no reliable source on the total number of new armories built in the United States in this period. In *America's Armories*, Fogelson says hundreds were built, mostly in the Northeast and Midwest.

77. There were at one point 125 armories and arsenals throughout New York State, of which sixteen were in Manhattan, fourteen in Brooklyn, and two in the Bronx. Of these, forty-four no longer exist. In New York City, of the six that were built in this era, only one survives as an armory; there are currently seven armories and arsenals in Manhattan now in existence. Todd, *New York's Historic Armories*.
78. The Laws of 1857, ch. 630, provided for the sale of state arsenals to New York City.
79. Havemeyer papers, Box 1220, file 2, NYCMA. Laws of 1873, ch. 429. See also Laws of 1870, ch. 80.
80. See the vast Seventh Regiment Archive in the New-York Historical Society.
81. Cooper 136, Armories, NYCMA. At the start of the twenty-first century, the Seventh is once again embroiled in controversy over who owns its holdings, as it plans to renovate the building and expand its use in cultural activities. It received public funding in 2007 to proceed.
82. *New York Times*, January 12, 1878; February 5, 1878. See Laws of 1873, ch. 431; Laws of 1879, ch. 57.
83. City Clerk 1977, Petitions, NYCMA. See *Sweet's Real Estate Record and Building Guide* for soaring prices. See Rosenzwieg and Blackmar, *The Park and the People*, for a history of Central Park.
84. Seguin, *Our Parks: To Be or Not to Be, by a Physician*.
85. New York Park Association, *More Public Parks*, 16.
86. Grant 88, NYCMA. Brigadier General Louis Fitzgerald.
87. Corporation counsel Henry Beekman cited the Laws of 1887, ch. 330. Grant 88—April 9, 1889, NYCMA.
88. *More Public Parks*, 19.
89. *New York Times*, May 12, 1875; June 26, 1875.
90. After 1886, also on the board were the President of the Department of Taxes and Assessments and another high-ranking military official. Laws of 1883, ch. 299. It was later amended by Laws of 1886, ch. 412; Laws of 1884, ch. 91.
91. About two dozen armories built from 1886 to 1900, paid out of state coffers, were built mostly upstate with the exception of Brooklyn's (Kings County) Twenty-third and Forty-seventh. Kings County had to finance the Thirteenth and Fourteenth armories. Brooklyn was its own municipal entity; consolidation with New York did not occur until 1898.
92. *New York Times*, December 2, 4, 18, 1884; June 27, 1884.
93. *New York Times*, December 18, 1884.
94. Grant 88-GHJ-1, Armories NYCMA. Bills 875, 784, June 4, 1889.
95. *New York Times*, February 5, 1889.
96. *New York Times*, October 18, 1889.
97. *New York Times*, December 2, 1889.
98. Grant 88-GHJ-1, Armory, NYCMA.
99. *New York Times*, September 10, 1885. State of New York no. 105, In Assembly. Communication, March 6, 1884; No. 172, May 15, 1884.

100. These characterizations were provided by various National Guard commanders testifying before the United States Senate Committee on Military Affairs, 74th Congress, at a Joint Hearing on "National Guard Armories," April 17, 1935. An inventory showed there were 866 armories in 810 towns across America, with 1,740 looking for homes. The National Guard was seeking federal funding to build headquarters for the homeless companies.

11. THE REGULATED CITY

1. During the Depression of the 1870s, public-works projects paid between $1.50 and $2 a day.
2. Edward Morse Shepard, Uncatalogued Correspondence, January–May 1895, Columbia Rare Books and MS.
3. *New York Times*, January–February 1895.
4. *World*, August 21, 1900.
5. Similar reactions were elicited by the transit strikes of 1969, 1980, and 2005.
6. Dreiser, *Sister Carrie*, 388.
7. For development of infrastructure in New York, see Koeppel, *Water for Gotham*; Schultz and McShane, "To Engineer the Metropolis"; Monkkonen, *America Becomes Urban*.
8. See Hartog, *Public Property and Private Power*, for a discussion of the legal implications.
9. Cooper 157, 87-HAS, Gilroy 13, Wickham 1259, NYCMA. Most of the material in this chapter is from the papers in NYCMA.
10. For a pre–Civil War view of city improvements, see Spann, *The New Metropolis, 1840–1857*; and various Laws of New York State. The New York press reported diligently on all this.
11. Kantor, "The City Beautiful in New York," in *The Physical City*.
12. Havemeyer 1238, 163, NYCMA. *New York Times*, February 12, 1874.
13. Hewitt 29, NYCMA.
14. Wickham 1259, 1206, NYCMA.
15. Burrows and Wallace, *Gotham*, 520.
16. Mayors' Papers, box 1219, no. 41, NYCMA.
17. The postcards and letters and files of investigations are contained in the extensive Mayor's files in NYCMA.
18. *Evening Post*, March 3, 1843; cited in Phelps Stokes, *Iconography*, 1779.
19. See the street-sprinkling ordinance of July 1, 1878: Ely 1226 (3), NYCMA.
20. Cooper 135–140, NYCMA.
21. 90-SWL 45, NYCMA.
22. Grace 97, NYCMA.
23. Grace 79, NYCMA.
24. Grace 97, NYCMA. By 1881, there were 6,047 hydrants.

25. Cooper 135, NYCMA. A law had been passed in April 1866 to prevent the throwing of ashes and other substances in the streets and public places of the cities of New York, Albany, Buffalo, and Brooklyn, with a $10 fine or five-day imprisonment, but as usual no mechanism for its enforcement was provided.

26. Wickham 1260 no. 227, NYCMA.

27. The ordinance was amended two years later. It did not allow awnings on Broadway, Fifth Avenue, Lexington Avenue, or Madison Avenue, and it stated that awnings had to clear the sidewalk by seven feet.

28. Proceedings Board of Alderman, 1887 (CLWWWV) 629–630, in Phelps Stokes, *Iconography*, 1992.

29. Wickham 1250, NYCMA. The alternative to the fine was ten days in prison.

30. Hewitt 31, NYCMA.

31. Hewitt 30, NYCMA.

32. See Bluestone, "The Pushcart Evil," in Ward and Zunz, *The Landscape of Modernity*. It is ironic that in the late twentieth and early twenty-first century, there has been the most severe limitation of street selling ever in relation to carts, while street "fairs" in which commercial goods are sold on weekends has increased substantially.

33. Hewitt 26, NYCMA. Also Edson 88, Cooper 156, Wickham 1260, 90 SWL 45, NYCMA.

34. Havemeyer 187 et al., NYCMA.

35. McShane and Tarr, "The Centrality of the Horse in the Nineteenth-Century American City," in Mohl, ed., *The Making of Urban America*.

36. Mayors' Papers, NYCMA 1873.

37. Wickham 1264, NYCMA.

38. City Clerk, 1880, Mayor's Office, NYCMA.

39. Strong 90 SWL, NYCMA.

40. Hewitt 30, NYCMA.

41. 90 SWL 45, NYCMA.

42. Gilroy 13, NYCMA.

43. 90 SWL 45, NYCMA.

44. Wickham 1264 no. 259.

45. April 1877. Smith Ely 1266 (2), NYCMA.

46. Havemeyer 1237, NYCMA.

47. Cooper 169, NYCMA.

48. Edson 88, 90 SWL 45, among others, NYCMA.

49. Gilroy 13, September 1893, NYCMA.

50. Hewitt 30, NYCMA.

51. Hewitt 29, NYCMA.

52. Cooper 156, NYCMA.

53. Grace 97, 1881, NYCMA.

54. Edson 89, NYCMA.

55. Hewitt 28, 1887, NYCMA.

56. Edson 84, 88, 89; HAS 26; Hewitt 28; Wickham 1260, no. 230, NYCMA.

57. Hewitt 26, NYCMA.

58. Hewitt 2, 28, 29 88, 89; Cooper 157, 161, 119, 123; Grace 97, NYCMA.

59. Grace 98, Wickham 1264, no. 259, Edson 88, 89, NYCMA.

60. Cooper 156, 1879, NYCMA; *New York Times*, February 2, 1874.

61. Edson 88, Grace 98, Cooper 157, Gilroy 89-GTF-14, NYCMA; *Herald Tribune*, September 2, 1874.

62. Cooper 156; Edson 89; Hewitt 29; 90 SWL 45, NYCMA.

63. This was from Alexander "Clubber" Williams of the Twenty-ninth Precinct, known for his liberal use of the truncheon and the cushioned lifestyle he had.

64. Walling, *Recollections of a New York Chief of Police*. Also Cook, *The Armies of the Streets*. Police chronicler Augustine Costello reprinted a *New York Herald* illustration of a policeman saving a black family.

65. 90 SWL 45, NYCMA.

66. Grace 97, 98, NYCMA.

67. 90 SWL 1897, NYCMA.

68. Chief of Police Report to Theodore Roosevelt, President Board of Police Commissioners, 90 SWL 45, January 20, 1896, NYCMA. In 1886, separate lodging houses were mandated by New York State Law (ch. 535) under the aegis of the commissioners of charities and correction; excepted were women, children, aged, and infirm men.

69. Chief of Police Report to Theodore Roosevelt, President Board of Police Commissioners, 90 SWL 45, January 20, 1896.

70. Ibid.

71. *World*, August 5, 1900.

12. THE TRIUMPH OF ORDER

1. See *New York Times*, August–December 2004; March–August 2005; *Daily News*, November–December 2004; Associated Press reports, November 2004–October 2005. See also http:/www.democracynow.org/article.pl?sid=05/03/28/1434209.

2. http://www.times-up.org.

3. Op-ed, *Daily News*, October 28, 2004.

4. http:/www.bikesummber.org/1999/zine/nightBeforeCritMass.htm.

5. Forty-nine arrested August 26, 2005; August 27, 2005, 230 arrested; Friday, April 30, 2005, thirty-four arrests.

6. The Serious Organised Crime and Police Act 2005 (SOCPA). The law became effective August 1, 2005, but the Designated Area portion, which spells out the limited area, became effective July 1, 2005. The first conviction under the SOCPA was in December 2005. In addition, new police powers came into effect January 1, 2006.

7. Letter from Superintendent Gomm, New Scotland Yard, September 29, 2005. The letter asked for six days' notice, date, time, proposed route, and name and address

of organizer. "These cycle protests are not lawful because no organiser has provided police with the necessary notification."

8. www.indymedia.org.uk/en/2005/10/326614.html.

9. http://www.urban75.org/photos/critical/28_10_2005.html.

10. *Guardian*, October 26, 2005.

11. *Guardian*, December 9, 2005.

12. In September 2007, the procurement phase of the national identity card scheme was announced. Its parameters have been modified to include a two-year trial period. The first cards to foreigners are scheduled to be distributed in November 2008.

13. *Daily Telegraph*, November 13, 2005. See also the *Guardian*, *Mirror*, *Daily Mail*, *Times*, *Sunday Telegraph*, and *Observer*.

14. *Sunday Telegraph*, February 12, 2006. In Europe, ID cards are compulsory in ten countries, including Belgium, Germany, Italy, and Greece; they are voluntary in ten countries, and not used in three others. A national ID card with biometric information was set to start in Portugal in 2007. In May 2007, a two-thousand-pound fine was set for people who did not provide new addresses for the cards. See the *Independent*, May, August, September, November 2007.

15. *Biometric Technology Today*, September 2007; "UK's national ID card procurement begins," *Card Technology Today*, September 2007.

16. In September 2005, Pauley threw out a case by five Critical Mass cyclists who claimed they were denied their First Amendment rights when their bikes were seized, but he did say that three of the five were not adequately warned and therefore denied their due process. Still, he said, the city had an interest in using streets effectively and safely. Associated Press State and Local Wire, September 30, 2005. *New York Post*, October 1, 2005; *New York Sun*, October 11, 2005; *Daily News*, December 30, 2004; *New York Times*, November 4, 2004; December 5, 2004; *Daily News*, November 5, 2004; Associated Press State and Local Wire, December 23, 2004.

17. U.S. District Court, Southern New York, *Rebecca Bray v. City of New York*, *New York Law Journal*, November 3, 2004.

18. *Daily News* and the *New York Times*, February 16, 24, 2006.

19. A city Criminal Court judge dismissed charges against the cyclists in early 2006, saying that the demand for a permit was unconstitutional but that ruling had little effect. "City's Parade Permit Law Ruled Unconstitutional," *NY1 News*, January 10, 2006. In September 2006, a Manhattan Supreme Court judge and a traffic court judge dismissed cases against Critical Mass riders, but these had no bearing on the constitutionality of the permit law. *New York Law Journal*, September 13, 2006.

20. The U.S. District Court for the Southern District denied a request by Critical Mass to prohibit the police from requiring permits on April 17, 2007. Judge Lewis A. Kaplan did not see that the permit violated basic rights, although he did sympathize with the cyclists. Cyclists must apply to the New York Police Department for a Parade Permit (Form 637-041) at the local precinct where the event starts. If a sound device will be used, a separate permit must be applied for (Sound Device Permit), also at

the local police precinct. Notarized applications are then submitted to the Police Department's Office of the Chief of Department Investigation Review Section at Police Headquarters, 1 Police Plaza.

21. Interview with Gabe Pressman, "News Forum," Channel 4 New York, April 1, 2007.

22. *New York Times*, March 25, 2007.

23. *New York Times*, December 22, 2005; February 3, 2006; March 22, 2001; March 17, 2006. The phrase "criminalization of dissent" has been commonly used in the press.

24. *New York Times*, December 22, 2005.

25. *New York Times*, June 14, 2007.

26. Associated Press, February 16, 2007; *New York Times*, February 16, 2007.

27. *Daily News*, March 26, 2006, citing Liberty, the British civil liberties organization; Andrew O'Hagan, "Watching Me Watching Them Watching You."

28. In 2007, the British government introduced "talking" CCTV, which added loudspeakers to the cameras in an attempt to tackle nuisances such as littering and vandalizing. Those monitoring can audibly address the miscreant. There is a growing body of literature on CCTV. See Gill, ed., *CCTV*; Painter and Tilley, eds., *Surveillance of Public Space*; Norris and Armstrong, *The Maximum Surveillance Society*; Rule, *Private Lives Public Surveillance*; http://www.London.gov, crime reduction, Home Office Web site; Cousens, *Surveillance Law*; Goold, *CCTV and Policing*.

29. *New York Times*, December 28, 2006.

30. Robertson, *Freedom, the Individual, and the Law*, cited in Fay, "Tough on Crime, Tough on Civil Liberties."

31. "Learning to Live with Big Brother," *Economist*, September 29, 2007; "Rights Under Foot," *Economist*, January 18, 1997; "Waning," *Economist*, January 25, 2007.

32. Coleman, *Reclaiming the Streets*, 176. For a perspective on modern issues, see Rule, *Privacy in Peril*. In November 2007, French interior minister Michele Alliot-Marie announced government intentions to triple the number of CCTV units, despite longstanding reservations over their use, citing a 78 percent public approval of their use.

33. Ash, "Killing Liberty in the Name of Security." For an overview of civil liberties, see Hewitt, *The Abuse of Power*.

34. Personal interview, Christian Kaunert, lecturer in EU politics/international relations, University of Salford, November 20, 2007. The EU has both engaged in widespread discussion of liberty and security and adopted measures to promote cooperation in security matters and facilitate exchange of information. For example, the new European arrest warrant, used to assist arrest of the 21/7 bombers, has revolutionized the extradition process in EU countries. See http://ec.europa.eu/justice_home (Freedom, Security and Justice); the Treaty of Amsterdam, 1999; the Hague programme, 2004; and European Commission measures regarding documentation for passports and travel documents. For a discussion of the current issues regarding terrorism, see Savitch, *Cities in a Time of Terror*.

35. *Daily Tribune*, March 30, 1908. The local press coverage of the event is extensive.

36. *New York Times*, April 5, 1908.

37. *Daily Tribune*, March 29, 1908.

38. *Daily Tribune*, March 30, 1908. Hunter was the son-in-law of wealthy New Yorker Anson Phelps Stokes.

39. *New York Times*, May 26, 1912.

40. Woods, "Reasonable Restrictions Upon Freedom of Assemblage," 30–31. Woods's zeal for reform under Mayor John Purroy Mitchell eventually led to his resignation from the force, following the revelation that he had conducted extensive wiretapping.

41. Ibid., 36. Roe's free-speech advocacy put him on the front lines of the new cause and took him to Washington many times to testify on behalf of civil liberties. As a Free Speech League lawyer, he defended conscientious objectors in World War I. He became active in the new American Civil Liberties Union.

42. *Evening Post*, August 18, 1900.

43. VWRA 11 (121), NYCMA.

44. *New York Times*, December 9, 1900.

45. *Tribune*, August 17, 1900.

46. *World*, August 17, 1900.

47. *World*, August 19, 1900.

48. Ibid.

49. *Tribune*, August 19, 1900.

50. *New York Times*, August 19, 1900, letter to the editor.

51. The Home Office, which had authority over the square, preferred not to be the party responsible for denying permission. Works 20/110.

52. *Duncan v. Jones*, 1936 1 K.B. 218.

53. Mrs. Katherine Duncan, member of the National Unemployed Workers' Movement, was arrested for obstructing police when she refused to move a public meeting, with police fearing a potential breach of peace. Wade, "Police Powers and Public Meeting," 178. Beatty is cited in *Stephen's Commentaries*, 13th ed. (1899), vol. 4, as a principle behind the definition of riots, routs, and unlawful assemblies. Other cases that had supported Beatty include *Beatty v. Glenister*, 51 L.T. 304; *R. v. Londonderry Justices* 1891, 28 L.R. Ir. 440 Q.B.D.; *R. v Clarkson* 1892, 17 Cox C.C. 483.

54. See press for July 22–25, 1962; *New York Times*, July 24, 1962.

55. An iron fence enclosed the park from 1849 until 1872, when a pavilion was placed at the north end. The official designation of Union Square Park was received in 1872. There have been numerous modifications and redesigns of the park and square since then. New York City Department of Parks, Arsenal archives.

56. *Third Annual Report*, Board of Commissioners, Department of Public Parks, New York, 1875, 18.

57. *New York Times*, January 28, 1930.

58. Newspaper reports of crowd size include an increasingly dramatic discrepancy between police estimates and those of organizers, with police figures usually half. *Herald Tribune*, May 2, 1932.

59. *Herald Tribune*, May 2, 1937.

60. *New York Times*, May 2, 1939.

61. *Herald Tribune*, May 2, 1948.

62. *Herald Tribune*, May 2, 1954.

63. *New York Times*, August 14, 1950.

64. *New York Times*, August 4, 1950.

65. *New York Times*, April 29, 1953.

66. New York City Parks Department Archives, the Arsenal, N-89, 1941. Moses was so furious he sent the letter to the press.

67. Wisotsky, "Echoes of the Union Square That Was," *New York Times*, October 12, 1958.

68. Carr, "Should We Have a Hyde Park, Too?" *New York Times*, August 28, 1955.

69. Kayden, *Privately Owned Public Space*.

70. Etzioni, *Demonstration Democracy*. See Gitlin, *The Sixties*.

71. Miller, *Democracy Is in the Streets*, 16.

72. About a quarter of these occurred in New York, involving mostly students and teachers. Skolnick, *The Politics of Protest*. The commission took an interpretative and relativistic view, saying that violence was "ambiguous," disruptive of a politically defined order, and not always forbidden or condemned in American society.

73. Since the nineteenth century, estimating the number of people at public events has been contentious. The police usually underestimate, event organizers usually overestimate. In the 1960s, police started using a formula based on the square footage of a site and the measure that a person occupied three square feet.

74. *New York Times*, April 15, 1967; May 1–2, 1967.

75. Babington, *Military Intervention in Britain*, 197.

76. See Driver, *The Disarmers*, regarding the campaign for nuclear disarmament; Bowes, *The Police and Civil Liberties*, suggests that police interference with the labor movement provokes violence; See Wilcox, *The Decision to Prosecute*, regarding police discretion in prosecuting.

77. *New York Times*, February 16, 2003.

78. http://www.centralparknyc.org.

79. *New York Times*, December 31, 2005. Four of the six events were to be the Metropolitan Opera and the New York Philharmonic. Other organizations created to help fund and run New York's open spaces include the City Parks Foundation and the Partnerships for Parks. They, along with dozens of "local greening groups," raise money and advocate for local parks. New York also promotes an "Adopt-A-Park" program, encouraging "businesses, community groups, or individuals to provide financial support for the refurbishment and maintenance of New York City's greenspaces." These "adoptions" run from $2,500–$7,000 for a park bench to $15,000 and up for a playground. See http://www.nycgovparks.org.

80. The fact that the findings were to be nonbinding was not formally announced but was stated by Kate O'Brien Ahlers, media and communications director for the New

York City Law Department, in a phone interview on January 10, 2008. The lawsuit was brought by the National Council of Arab Americans and the ANSWER Coalition in 2004. A press release by the NYC Law Department restated that the Parks Department and its commissioner, Adrian Benepe, believe restrictions on activities help protect the Great Lawn. All current rules stay in effect until the study is completed, except for increasing the size of crowds from fifty thousand to seventy-five thousand for the six allowed events.

81. http://www.green-space.org.uk.

82. Limitation of traffic into London's city center began in 2004 with congestion pricing, which has proven to be very successful in cutting down traffic without negative consequences and raising sufficient revenues to improve significantly the bus system.

83. Personal interview, May 1, 2001.

84. This list was gathered from the Mayor's Community Assistance Unit's monthly Events Calendar, at http://www.nyc.gov. The four events were a 1199 SEIU (United Healthcare Workers) march, March 15, 2007; a United for Peace and Justice March, March 18, 2007; a Captive Nations march (President Bush had declared the week of March 15 Captive Nations Week), July 15, 2007; and an Anti-War March by United for Peace and Justice, October 27, 2007. On December 16, 2006, the Rev. Al Sharpton organized a march on Fifth Avenue to protest the killing of an unarmed black man in Queens. No estimates were given for the size of the crowd, which was said to stretch out for ten blocks, nor is it known if Rev. Sharpton had a permit. Parade permits come directly from the police department (see note 20).

85. Street fairs, festivals, block parties, and similar events require permission from the Street Activity Permit Office (SAPO), which issues its own rules and procedures. Eligible for these permits are "community-based, not-for-profit organizations, associations, or the like which [have] an indigenous relationship to the specific street or community or both." Permits for business celebrations (individuals or commercial entities) may be issued at the discretion of the SAPO director. The application first goes to the local community board, then to the Police Department, the Fire Department, the Department of Sanitation, and the Department of Transportation. Other city agencies may also be involved, depending on the nature of the event. An appeals process exists should a permit be rejected. See http://www.nyc.gov.

86. See especially the *Guardian* and the *Independent* for the weeks of October 1 and October 8, 2007.

87. Two annual events that highlight the differences in how such events are handled in the two cities are the annual Puerto Rican Day parade in New York and the Notting Hill Afro-Caribbean Carnival in London. See the *New York Times* and the *New York Daily News* for June–October, 2000; Waddington, *Liberty and Order*, 194; Pryce, "The Notting Hill Carnival," 35–52; Edgar, "Festivals of the Oppressed," 61–76; Keith, *Race, Riots, and Policing*.

88. *Papers and Proceedings*, Ninth Annual Meeting, American Sociological Society, 1914, 36.

89. Christopher Caldwell, "After Londonistan," *New York Times Magazine*, June 25, 2006.

90. Bennett, *The History Boys*.

91. Stone, *Free Speech*.

92. Prime Minister Gordon Brown speech, *BBC News*, October 25, 2007.

BIBLIOGRAPHY

UNITED STATES

Primary Sources

PUBLIC RECORDS AND ARCHIVES

Columbia Rare Book and Manuscript Library: Sidney Howard Gay papers; Edward Kilroe
papers; William Mason Grosvenor papers; Thomas Ludlow Chrystie papers; Edward
Morse Shepard papers; Society for the Prevention of Crime papers; John T. Hoffman
papers; Community Service Society; New York Association for Improving the Condition of the Poor, *Annual Report.*

Seventh Regiment Archives, New-York Historical Society.

New York City Municipal Archives (NYCMA): Mayor's Papers, Boxes 1206–1210, 1212,
1214–1220, 1229, 1231–1238, 1240, 1242, 1256, 1259, 1260–1262, 1268–1272; Edson 6, 88–
90; Cooper 156–169; Gilroy 1, 12–14, 89; Grant 1, 37–40; Grace 5, 97, 98, 102, 103; Hewitt
26–35; Strong 1, 45, 46.

New York City Department of Parks. Archives. The Arsenal, New York.

New York State Archives. Albany. AO531–78.

DISSERTATIONS

O'Donnell, Edward. "Henry George and the New Political Forces." Ph.D. thesis, Columbia University, 1995.

Schuyler, David. "Public Landscapes and American Urban Culture, 1800–1870: Rural
Cemeteries, City Parks, and Suburbs," Ph.D. thesis, Columbia University, 1979.

NEWSPAPERS AND PERIODICALS

Atlanta Journal-Constitution
Atlantic Monthly

CQ Researcher
Daily Graphic
Evening Star
Evening Post
Harper's Weekly
Journal of Commerce
Nation
New York Daily Tribune
New York Herald
New York Times
Newsweek
Rolling Stone
Sun
USA Today
World

PUBLISHED

Adjutant General Annual Reports. New York State National Guard. 1872, 1874, 1882, 1883, 1884, 1886, 1888.

Andrews, Avery. "The Police Systems of Europe." *Cosmopolitan.* March 1903, 1889, 1893.

Annual Report of the Bureau of Statistics of Labor of the State of New York. 1884, 1885, 1890. Albany.

Annual Report of the Commissioner of Labor, 1901. Albany.

Annual Report of the Inspector General of the State of New York for the Year 1863, 1864. Albany.

Baedeker, Karl. *The United States.* New York: Scribner's Sons, 1899.

Baldwin, Roger. "Recollections of a Life in Civil Liberties." *Civil Liberties Review,* 1975.

Bellows, Henry. *Manual for Local Defense.* New York: Macmillan, 1918.

Board of Aldermen, New York. *Proceedings.* New York. 1847, 1855–1878. Vols. 33–150.

Board of Assistant Aldermen, New York. *Proceedings.* 1832–1833, 1858, 1873. Vols. 2–7, 19–20, 22–27, 31–35, 67–72, 130–133.

Board of Commissioner, Dept. of Public Parks, New York. *2nd Annual Report.* New York. 1872; *3rd Annual Report.* 1873.

Browne, William. *Stop That Clubbing.* New York (E. Kimpton, partr.), 1887.

Child, Lydia Marie. *Letters from New York.* New York: C. S. Francis, 1849.

City of New York. *Report of Committee on Small Parks.* New York: Brown, 1897.

Clark, Emmons. *History of the Seventh Regiment of New York, 1806–1889.* New York: Seventh Regiment, 1890.

Commons, John, et al. *History of Labor in the United States.* New York: Macmillan, 1918.

Compendium of the Laws and Decisions Relating to Mobs, Riots, Invasion. . . . 1864.

Cook, Clarence. *A Description of the New York Central Park.* New York: F. J. Huntington, 1869.

Costello, Augustus. *Our Police Protectors*. New York, 1885.

Davis, Gherardi. *The Establishment of Public Parks in the City of New York*. New York, 1897.

Donnelly, Ignatius. *Caesar's Column*. Chicago: F. J. Schulte and Co., 1890.

Dos Passos, John. *Manhattan Transfer*. Boston: Houghton Mifflin Co., 1953.

Dreiser, Theodore. *The Color of a Great City*. New York: Boni and Liveright, 1923.

——. *Sister Carrie*. New York: Bobbs-Merrill Co., 1900.

Erhardt, Joel B. "The Duties of a Policeman." *The City Vigilant*, May 1894.

Foster, G. G. *New York by Gaslight*. New York, 1884.

Gerard, J. W. *London and New York: Their Crime and Their Police*. New York: W. C. Bryant, 1853.

Gompers, Samuel. *Seventy Years of Life and Labor: An Autobiography*. New York: E. P. Dutton and Co., 1925.

The Great Metropolis, or New York Almanac. New York, 1854.

Headley, Joel Tyler. *The Great Riots of New York, 1712–1873*. Indianapolis: Bobbs-Merrill, 1873.

Janvier, Thomas. *In Old New York*. New York: St. Martin's Press, 1894.

Kerner Commission Report. Washington, D.C.: U.S. Government Printing Office, 1968.

Laird, William. *Consolidation of Revised Ordinances of the City of New York*. New York, 1894.

The Lexow Commission 1894–95. New York State Senate Documents 1895, no. 63.

Marsh, Luther. *History of the New Parks Briefly Stated*. New York: Burgoyne, 1886.

Martin, Edward. *The History of the Great Riots*. Philadelphia: National Publishing Co., 1877.

Mathews, J. M. *Recollections of Persons and Events Chiefly in the City of New York*. New York: Sheldon, 1865.

Mayor's Annual Message, City of New York.

The Mazet Committee. *Report. The Citizens Committee of 9 on Reorganization of the New York Police Force 1905–06*.

McAdoo, William. *Guarding a Great City*. New York: Harper and Bros., 1906.

McCabe, James. *New York by Sunlight and Gaslight*. New York, 1882.

——. *Lights and Shadows*. Philadelphia: National Publishing Group, 1872.

——. *Secrets of a Great City*. Philadelphia: Jones, Bros. & Co., 1868.

Molineux, E. L. *Riots in Cities and Their Suppression*. Providence: State of Rhode Island Adjutant General's Office, 1884.

The New Armory of the Seventh Regiment, N.G.S.N.Y. New York: Hebbeard and Munro, 1875.

New York City Mission and Tract Society, 49th Annual Report. New York, 1876 (1875), 1877 (1876).

New York Park Association. *More Public Parks*. New York, 1882.

New York State Assembly. *Documents*. 1873 (49); 1874 (122); 1875 (68); 1876 (106); 1878 (90, 99); 1879 (148); 1880 (148); 1884 (105, 125, 172, 54).

New York State Senate. *Documents*. 1867 (80, 58); 1868 (86); 1873 (23); 1882 (9); 1884 (26); 1887 (50); 1888 (42, 52); 1890 (34); 1891 (80); 1894 (27); 1895 (2, 5, 29, 49, 63).

Official Deliberations, Armory Board of the City of New York; The New York City Armory Board 1884–1911. New York, 1912.

Papers and Proceedings. Ninth Annual Meeting, American Sociological Society. Chicago: University of Chicago Press, 1914.

Poe, Edgar Allen. *Doings of Gotham.* Pottsville, Pa.: J. E. Spannuth, 1929.

Police Department of the City of New York, *Instructions for Members of the Force at Mass Demonstrations.* New York, n.d. (1971?).

Potter, Orlando. *New Parks.* New York, 1885.

Public Papers of Governor Lucius Robinson, Governor of New York. Albany: Argus Co., 1877–1879.

Public Papers of John T. Hoffman, Governor of New York. Albany: J. Munsell, 1869–1872.

Ranney, H. M. *Account of the Terrific and Fated Riot at the New-York Astor Place Opera House . . .* New York, 1849.

Seguin, Edward. *Our Parks: To Be or Not to Be, by a Physician.* New York: Brentano's Literary Emporium, 1878.

The Sinking Fund and the New Parks, City Revenue and the Constitutional Amendment. *What Is the Debt of the City.* New York, n.d. (1886?).

Smith, Matthew Hale. *Sunshine and Shadow.* Hartford: J. B. Burr, 1868.

Sorge, Friedrich. *Labor Movement in the United States: A History of the American Working Class from 1890–1896.* Translated by Kai Schoenhals. New York: Greenwood Press, 1987.

Steffens, Lincoln. *The Autobiography of Lincoln Steffens.* New York: The Literary Guild, 1931.

Stokes, I. N. Phelps. *The Iconography of Manhattan.* New York: Robert H. Dodd, 1915–1928 (repr. New York: Arno Press, 1967).

Strong, Josiah. *Our Country: Its Possible Future and Its Present Crises.* New York: Baker & Taylor, 1885.

Swinton, John. *The Tompkins Square Outrage.* 1874. Reprinted from the Albany *Argus.*

Valentine's Manual of the Corporation of the City of New York. New York, 1865, 1866.

Walling, George. *Recollections of a New York Chief of Police.* New York: Caxton, 1888.

Walling, H. F. *Route and City Guide, City of New York.* New York: Tainton Bros., 1861.

Wheatley, Richard. "The New York Police Department." *Harper's Magazine* 74, no. 442 (March 1887).

Whitman, Walt. *Leaves of Grass.* New York: Modern Library, 1892.

"Who was G. W.?" New York, 1879[?]. Reprinted from *The World.*

Wingate, George. *History of the Twenty-second Regiment of the National Guard of the State of New York from Its Organization to 1895.* New York: E. W. Dayton, 1896.

Secondary Sources: Books and Articles

Abbott, Carl. *Political Terrain: Washington, D.C., from Tidewater Town to Global Metropolis.* Chapel Hill: University of North Carolina Press, 1999.

Anderson, Alexis. "The Formative Period of First Amendment Theory, 1870–1915." *American Journal of Legal History* 24.

Ann Beha Associates. *The Armory: Armories of New York City*. New York: NY Landmarks Conservancy, 1978.

Appleby, Joyce. *Capitalism and a New Social Order: The Republican Visions of the 1790s*. New York: New York University Press, 1984.

Aronowitz, Stanley. *False Promises: The Shaping of American Working-Class Consciousness*. New York: McGraw-Hill, 1973.

Asbury, Herbert. *The Gangs of New York: An Informal History of the Underworld*. New York: A. A. Knopf, 1928.

Astor, Gerald. *The New York Cops: An Informal History*. New York: Scribner's, 1971.

Avrich, Paul. *Anarchist Portraits*. Princeton, N.J.: Princeton University Press, 1988.

Babson, Steve. *The Unfinished Struggle: Turning Points in American Labor, 1877–Present*. Lanham, Md.: Rowman & Littlefield, 1999.

Bachin, Robin. *Building the South Side: Urban Space and Civic Culture in Chicago, 1890–1919*. Chicago: University of Chicago Press, 2004.

Barber, Lucy. *Marching on Washington*. Berkeley: University of California Press, 2002.

Barendt, Eric. *Freedom of Speech*. Oxford: Clarendon Press, 1985.

Bassiouni, M. Cherif. *The Law of Dissent and Riots*. Springfield, Ill.: Thomas, 1971.

Bayor, Ronald H. *Race and Ethnicity in America: A Concise History*. New York: Columbia University Press, 2003.

——. *The Columbia Documentary History of Race and Ethnicity in America*. New York: Columbia University Press, 2004.

Bayor, Ronald H., and Timothy Meagher, eds. *The New York Irish*. Baltimore, Md.: The Johns Hopkins Press, 1996.

Beckert, Sven. *The Monied Metropolis: New York City and the Consolidation of the American Bourgeoisie, 1850–1896*. Cambridge: Cambridge University Press, 2001.

Bender, Thomas. *Toward an Urban Vision: Ideas and Institutions in Nineteenth-Century America*. Baltimore, Md.: The Johns Hopkins University Press, 1982.

——. *Community and Social Change in America*. Baltimore, Md.: Rutgers University Press, 1982.

Berlin, Isaiah. *Two Concepts of Liberty*. Oxford: Clarendon Press, 1958.

Bernstein, Iver. *The New York City Draft Riots*. New York: Oxford University Press, 1990.

Binder, Frederick, and David Reimers. *All the Nations Under Heaven*. New York: Columbia University Press, 1995.

Blackmar, Elizabeth. *Manhattan for Rent, 1785–1850*. Ithaca, N.Y.: Cornell University Press, 1989.

Blumin, Stuart. *The Emergence of the Middle Class: Social Experience in the American City, 1760–1900*. Cambridge: Cambridge University Press, 1989.

Bordua, D. J., ed. *The Police: Six Sociological Essays*. New York: Wiley, 1967.

Boyer, Paul. *Urban Masses and Moral Order in America, 1820–1920*. Cambridge, Mass.: Harvard University Press, 1978.

Brewer, John. *The Police, Public Order, and the State*. New York: St. Martin's Press, 1988.

Breyer, Stephen. *Active Liberty*. New York: Alfred A. Knopf, 2005.

Bridges, Amy. *A City in the Republic*. Cambridge: Cambridge University Press, 1984.

Brown, Richard Maxwell. *Strain of Violence: Historical Studies of American Violence and Vigilantism*. New York: Oxford University Press, 1975.

Bruce, Robert. *1877: Year of Violence*. Chicago: Quadrangle Books, 1959.

Burrows, Edward, and Mike Wallace. *Gotham*. New York: Oxford University Press, 1998.

Callow, Alexander B., Jr. *The Tweed Ring*. New York: Oxford University Press, 1966.

Carroll, Thomas F. "Freedom of Speech and of the Press During the Civil War." *Virginia Law Review* 9, no. 7 (May 1923).

Chafee, Zechariah. *The Blessings of Liberty*. Philadelphia: J. B. Lippincott Co., 1956.

——. *Free Speech in the United States*. Cambridge, Mass.: Harvard University Press, 1941.

Cook, Adrian. *The Armies of the Streets: The New York City Draft Riots of 1863*. Lexington: University Press of Kentucky, 1974.

Countryman, Edward. *A People in Revolution: The American Revolution and Political Society in New York, 1760–1790*. Baltimore, Md.: The Johns Hopkins University Press, 1981.

Cranz, Galen. *The Politics of Park Design*. Cambridge, Mass.: The MIT Press, 1982.

Cunliffe, Marcus. *Soldiers and Civilians: The Martial Spirit in America, 1775–1865*. Boston: Little, Brown, 1968.

Daum, Andreas, and Christof Mauch. *Berlin-Washington, 1800–2000: Capital Cities, Cultural Representation, and National Identities*. Cambridge: Cambridge University Press, 2005.

Dickson, Paul, and Thomas B. Allen. *The Bonus Army: An American Epic*. New York: Walker & Co., 2004.

Dubber, Markus Dirk. *The Police Power: Patriarchy and the Foundations of American Government*. New York: Columbia University Press, 2005.

Dubovsky, Melvyn, and Warren Van Tine, eds. *Labor Leaders in America*. Urbana: University of Illinois Press, 1987.

Dunn, John. *Democracy: A History*. New York: Atlantic Monthly Press, 2006.

Eldridge, Larry. *A Distant Heritage: The Growth of Free Speech in Early America*. New York: New York University Press, 1994.

Englander, David, ed. *Britain and America: Studies in Comparative History, 1760–1970*. New Haven, Conn.: Yale University Press, 1997.

Ernst, Robert. *Immigrant Life in New York City, 1825–1863*. Syracuse, N.Y.: Syracuse University Press, 1994.

Ethington, Philip. *The Public City*. Cambridge: Cambridge University Press, 1994.

Etzioni, Amitai. *Demonstration Democracy*. New York: Gordon & Breach, 1970.

——. *The Limits of Privacy*. New York: Basic Books, 1999.

Everett, Dianna. *Historic National Guard Armories*. Washington, D.C.: National Guard Bureau, 1994.

Farmer, David. *Civil Disorder Control: A Planning Program of Municipal Coordination and Cooperation*. Chicago: Public Administration Service, 1968.

Feldberg, Michael. *The Turbulent Era: Riot and Disorder in Jacksonian America*. New York: Oxford University Press, 1980.

Finan, Christopher M. *From the Palmer Raids to the Patriot Act: A History of the Fight for Free Speech in America*. Boston: Beacon Press, 2007.

Fischer, David Hackett. *The Revolution of American Conservatism: The Federalist Part in the Era of Jeffersonian Democracy*. New York: Harper & Row, 1965.

Fogelson, Robert. *Big City Police*. Cambridge, Mass.: Harvard University Press, 1977.

——. *Violence as Protest: A Study of Riots and Ghettos*. Garden City, N.Y.: Doubleday & Co., 1971.

——. *America's Armories*. Cambridge, Mass.: Harvard University Press, 1989.

Foner, Eric, "The Idea of Freedom in the American Century." The Lawrence F. Brewster Lecture in History XXI, East Carolina University, Greenville, North Carolina, available online at http:/www.ecu.edu/history/brewster/bl102.htm.

——. *The Story of American Freedom*. New York: Norton, 1999.

Foner, Philip S. *The Great Labor Uprising of 1877*. New York: Monad Press, 1977.

Foote, Shelby. *The Civil War: A Narrative 360*. New York: Random House, 1963.

Forbath, William. *Law and the Shaping of the American Labor Movement*. Cambridge, Mass.: Harvard University Press, 1991.

Friedman, Lawrence, and Harry Scheiker. *American Law and the Constitutional Order: Historical Perspectives*. Cambridge, Mass.: Harvard University Press, 1978.

Gamber, Wendy, Michael Grossberg, and Hendrik Hartog, eds. *American Public Life and the Historical Imagination*. Notre Dame, Ind.: University of Notre Dame Press, 2003.

Gilfoyle, Timothy. *City of Eros*. New York: W. W. Norton & Co., 1992.

——. "Strumpets and Misogynists: Brothel 'Riots' and the Transformation of Prostitution in Antebellum New York City." *New York History* 68 (1987).

Gilje, Paul. *Rioting in America*. Bloomington: Indiana University Press, 1996.

——. *The Road to Mobocracy: Popular Disorder in New York City, 1765–1834*. Chapel Hill: University of North Carolina Press, 1987.

Godkin, Edwin, and Morton Keller. *Problems of Modern Democracy*. Cambridge, Mass.: Belknap Press of Harvard University Press, 1896.

Gora, Joel, David Goldberg, Gary Stein, and Morton Halperin. *The Right to Protest: The Basic ACLU Guide to Free Expression*. Carbondale: Southern Illinois University Press, 1991.

Gordon, Michael. *The Orange Riots: Irish Political Violence in New York City, 1870 and 1871*. Ithaca, N.Y.: Cornell University Press, 1993.

Gottesman, Ronald, and Richard Maxwell Brown. *Violence in America: An Encyclopedia*. New York: Scribner's, 1999.

Graham, Hugh, and Ted Gurr. *Violence in America: A Report to the National Commission on the Causes and Prevention of Violence*. Washington, D.C.: U.S. Government Printing Office, 1969.

Grimsted, David. *American Mobbing, 1828–1861*. New York: Oxford University Press, 1998.

Gronowicz, Anthony. *Race and Class Politics in New York City Before the Civil War*. Boston: Northeastern University Press, 1998.

Gutman, Herbert. *Work, Culture, and Society in Industrializing America: Essays in American Working-Class and Social History*. New York: Knopf, 1976.

——. "The Tompkins Square Riot in New York on Jan. 13, 1874." *Labor History* 6 (1965): 44–70.

——. "The Failure of the Movement by the Unemployed for Public Works in 1873." *Political Science Quarterly* 80 (1965): 254–276.

Hall, Simon. *Peace and Freedom: The Civil Rights and Antiwar Movements of the 1960s*. Philadelphia: University of Pennsylvania Press, 2005.

Harring, Sidney. *Policing a Class Society: The Experience of American Cities, 1865–1915*. New Brunswick, N.J.: Rutgers University Press, 1983.

Hartog, Hendrik. *Public Property and Private Power: The Corporation of the City of New York in American Law, 1730–1870*. Chapel Hill: University of North Carolina Press, 1983.

Harvey, David. *The Condition of Postmodernity: An Enquiry Into the Origins of Cultural Change*. Oxford: Blackwells, 1989.

Hayes, Carlton J. H. *A Generation of Materialism: 1871–1900*. New York: Harper & Bros., 1941.

Heaps, Willard A. *Riots, U.S.A., 1765–1970*. New York: Seabury Press, 1970.

Hershkowitz, Leo. *Tweed's New York: Another Look*. New York: Anchor Press, 1977.

Hill, Robert B., and Robert M. Fogelson. *A Study of Arrest Patterns in the 1960s Riots*. New York: Bureau of Applied Social Research, Columbia University, 1969.

Hofstadter, Richard, and Mike Wallace, eds. *American Violence: A Documentary History*. New York: Knopf, 1970.

Homberger, Eric. *Scenes from the Life of a City: Corruption and Conscience in Old New York*. New Haven, Conn.: Yale University Press, 1994.

——. *Historical Atlas of New York City*. New York: Henry Holt & Co., 1994, 2005.

Jacobs, Jane. *The Death and Life of Great American Cities*. New York: Vintage Books, 1961.

Jackson, Kenneth T., ed. *The Encyclopedia of New York*. New Haven, Conn.: Yale University Press, 1995.

Jackson, Kenneth T., and Stanley K. Schultz, eds. *Cities in American History*. New York: Alfred E. Knopf, 1972.

Jeffers, H. Paul. *Commissioner Roosevelt*. New York: John Wiley & Sons, 1994.

Johnson, Donald. *The Challenge to American Freedoms: World War I and the Rise of the American Civil Liberties Union*. Lexington: University of Kentucky Press, 1963.

Jones, Howard Mumford. *O Strange New World*. New York: Viking Press, 1964.

Joyce, Patrick. *The Rule of Freedom: Liberties and the Modern City*. London: Verso, 2003.

Judd, Jacob, and Irwin Polishook., ed. *Early New York Society and Politics*. Tarrytown, N.Y.: Sleepy Hollow Restorations, 1974.

Kammen, Michael. *A Machine That Would Go of Itself: The Constitution in American Culture*. New York: Knopf, 1986.

——. *Spheres of Liberty: Changing Perceptions of Liberty in American Culture*. Madison: University of Wisconsin Press, 1986.

Katznelson, Ira, and Aristide R. Zolberg. *Working-Class Formation: Nineteenth-Century Patterns in Western Europe and the United States*. Princeton, N.J.: Princeton University Press, 1986.

Kayden, Jerold. *Privately Owned Public Space: The New York City Experience*. New York: John Wiley, 2000.

Keller, Morton. *Affairs of State: Public Life in Late Nineteenth-Century America*. Cambridge, Mass.: Belknap Press, 1977.

Kelly, Alfred, Winfred Harbison, and Herman Belz. *The American Constitution: Its Origins and Development*. New York: Norton, 1983.

Kersch, Ken. *Constructing Civil Liberties: Discontinuities in the Development of American Constitutional Law*. Cambridge: Cambridge University Press, 2004.

——. *Freedom of Speech: Rights and Liberties Under the Law*. Santa Barbara, Calif.: ABC-CLIO, 2004.

Koeppel, Gerald. *Water for Gotham*. Princeton, N.J.: Princeton University Press, 2000.

Kohn, Margaret. *Brave New Neighborhoods: The Privatization of Public Space*. New York: Routledge, 2004.

Kurland, Gerald. *Seth Low: The Reformer in an Urban and Industrial Age*. New York: Twayne, 1971.

Landmarks Preservation Commission: Designation List 164, 245, 259.

Lane, Roger. *Policing the City: Boston, 1822–1885*. Cambridge, Mass.: Harvard University Press, 1967.

Lankevich, George. *American Metropolis*. New York: New York University Press, 1998.

Lardner, James, and Thomas Reppetto. *NYPD: A City and Its Police*. New York: Henry Holt & Co., 2000.

Laurie, Bruce, and Eric Foner. *Artisans Into Workers: Labor in Nineteenth-Century America*. New York: Hill and Wang, 1989.

Leab, Daniel. *The Labor History Reader*. Urbana: University of Illinois Press, 1985.

Leahy, James. *The First Amendment, 1791–1991: Two Hundred Years of Freedom*. Jefferson, N.C.: McFarland & Co., 1991.

Le Blanc, Paul. *A Short History of the U.S. Working Class: From Colonial Times to the Twenty-First Century*. Amherst, Mass.: Humanity Books, 1999.

LeGates, Richard, and Frederic Stout. *The City Reader*. London: Routledge, 1996.

Lessoff, Alan. *The Nation and Its City: Politics, "Corruption," and Progress in Washington, D.C., 1861–1902*. Baltimore, Md.: The Johns Hopkins University Press, 1994.

Levine, Bruce. *The Spirit of 1848: German Immigrants, Labor Conflict, and the Coming of the Civil War*. Urbana: University of Illinois Press, 1992.

Levy, Leonard. *Legacy of Suppression: Freedom of Speech and Press in Early American History*. Cambridge, Mass.: The Belknap Press, 1960.

——. *Liberty and the First Amendment: 1790–1800*. 1962. Reprint from *American Historical Review* 68, no. 1 (October 1962).

Lightfoot, Frederick. *Nineteenth-Century New York in Rare Photographic Views*. New York: Dover Publications, 1981.

Macek, Steve. *Urban Nightmares: The Media, the Right, and the Moral Panic Over the City*. Minneapolis: University of Minnesota Press, 2006.

Maier, Pauline. *From Resistance to Revolution: Colonial Radicals and the Development of American Opposition to Britain, 1765–76*. New York: Knopf, 1972.

Mandelbaum, Seymour. *Boss Tweed's New York*. Westport, Conn.: Greenwood Press, 1965.

Masotti, Louis, and Don Bowden, eds. *Riots and Rebellion: Civil Violence in the Urban Community*. Beverly Hills, Calif.: Sage Publications, 1968.

Meiklejohn, Alexander. *Free Speech and Its Relation to Self-Government*. New York: Harper, 1948.

Menez, Joseph, and John R. Vile. *Summaries of Leading Cases on the Constitution*. 14th ed. Lanham, Md.: Rowman & Littlefield, 2004.

Methvin, Eugene. *The Riot Makers: The Technology of Social Demolition*. New Rochelle, N.Y.: Arlington House, 1970.

Miller, Benjamin. *Fat of the Land*. New York: Four Walls Eight Windows, 2000.

Miller, Wilbur. *Cops and Bobbies: Police Authority in New York and London, 1830–1870*. Chicago: University of Chicago Press, 1977.

Mohl, Raymond. *Poverty in New York*. New York: Oxford University Press, 1971.

——, ed. *The Making of Urban America*. Lanham, Md.: SR Books, 1997.

Monkkonen, Eric. *America Becomes Urban*. Berkeley: University of California Press, 1988.

——. *Murder in New York City*. Berkeley: University of California Press, 2001.

——. *Police in Urban America, 1860–1920*. Cambridge: Cambridge University Press, 1981.

Montgomery, David. *Beyond Equality: Labor and the Radical Republicans, 1862–1872*. Urbana: University of Illinois Press, 1981.

——. *Citizen Worker: The Experience of Workers in the United States with Democracy and the Free Market During the Nineteenth Century*. Cambridge: Cambridge University Press, 1993.

Moody, J. Carroll, and Alice Kessler-Harris. *Perspective on American Labor History*. DeKalb: Northern Illinois University Press, 1989.

Moody, Richard. *The Astor Place Riot*. Bloomington: Indiana University Press, 1958.

Mushkat, Jerome. *The Reconstruction of New York Democracy, 1861–1874*. Rutherford, N.J.: Fairleigh Dickinson University Press, 1981.

Nadel, Stanley. *Little Germany: Ethnicity, Religion, and Class in New York City, 1845–80*. Urbana: University of Illinois Press, 1990.

Neely, Mark. *The Fate of Liberty: Abraham Lincoln and Civil Liberties*. New York: Oxford University Press, 1991.

Papke, David. *Framing the Criminal: Crime, Cultural Work, and the Loss of Critical Perspective, 1830–1900*. Hamden, Ct.: Archon Books, 1987.

Park, Robert E. *The Crowd and the Public and Other Essays*. Edited by Henry Elsner Jr., translated by Charlotte Elsner. Chicago: University of Chicago Press, 1905.

Pessen, Edward. *Most Uncommon Jacksonians: The Radical Leaders of the Early Labor Movement.* Albany, N.Y.: SUNY Press, 1967.

Quigley, David. *Second Founding: New York City, Reconstruction, and the Making of American Democracy.* New York: Hill & Wang, 2004.

Rabban, David. "The Emergence of Modern First Amendment Doctrine." *University of Chicago Law Review* 50 (1983).

——. "The First Amendment in Its Forgotten Years." *Yale Law Journal* 90 (1981).

——. *Free Speech in Its Forgotten Years, 1870–1920.* Cambridge: Cambridge University Press, 1997.

Reader, John. *Cities.* New York: Grove Press, 2004.

Reed, Henry Hope. *Central Park: A History and a Guide.* New York: C. N. Potter, 1967.

Reid, John Phillip. *The Ancient Constitution and the Origins of Anglo-American Liberty.* DeKalb: Northern Illinois University Press, 2005.

Reinders, Robert. "Militia and Public Order in Nineteenth-Century America." *Journal of American Studies* (April 1977).

Repetto, Thomas. *The Blue Parade.* New York: Free Press, 1970.

Rich, Bennett, and Philip Burch Jr. "The Changing Role of the National Guard." *American Political Science Review* 50, no. 3 (1956).

Richardson, James. *The New York Police: Colonial Times to 1901.* New York: Oxford University Press, 1970.

——. *Urban Police in the United States.* Port Washington, N.Y.: Kennikat Press, 1970.

Robertson, Andrew. *The Language of Democracy: Political Rhetoric in the United States and Britain, 1790–1900.* Ithaca, N.Y.: Cornell University Press, 1995.

Rodgers, Daniel T. *The Work Ethic in Industrial America, 1850–1920.* Chicago: University of Chicago Press, 1978.

Rosenwaike, Ira. *Population History of New York City.* Syracuse, N.Y.: Syracuse University Press, 1972.

Rosenzweig, Roy, and Elizabeth Blackmar. *The Park and the People: A History of Central Park.* Ithaca, N.Y.: Cornell University Press, 1992.

Rousey, Dennis. *Policing the Southern City, 1805–1889.* Baton Rouge: Louisiana State University Press, 1996.

Ryan, Mary. *Civic Wars.* Berkeley: University of California Press, 1997.

Savitch, H. V. *Cities in a Time of Terror: Space, Territory, and Local Resilience.* Armonk, N.Y.: M. E. Sharpe, 2008.

Schivelbusch, Wolfgang. *Disenchanted Night.* Berkeley: University of California Press, 1988.

Schechter, Barnett. *The Devil's Own Work.* New York: Walker & Co., 2005.

Schlesinger, Arthur. *The Crisis of Confidence: Ideas, Power, and Violence in America.* Boston: Houghton Mifflin, 1969.

Schneider, John. *Detroit and the Problem of Order, 1830–1880.* Lincoln: University of Nebraska Press, 1980.

Schultz, Stanley, and Clay McShane. "To Engineer the Metropolis." *Journal of American History* (September 1978).

Schuyler, David. *The New Urban Landscape: The Redefinition of City Form in Nineteenth-Century America*. Baltimore, Md.: The Johns Hopkins University Press, 1986.

——. *Public Landscapes and American Urban Culture, 1800–1870: Rural Cemeteries, City Parks, and Suburbs*. Ann Arbor, Mich.: University Microfilms International, 1979.

Scobey, David. *Empire City*. Philadelphia: Temple University Press, 2002.

Sennett, Richard. *The Fall of Public Man*. New York: Knopf, 1977.

——. *The Uses of Disorder*. New York: Penguin, 1970.

Skolnick, Jerome. *The Politics of Protest: Report from the Task Force on Violent Aspects of Protest and Confrontation of the National Commission on the Causes and Prevention of Violence*. New York: Simon & Schuster, 1969.

Smolla, Rodney. *Free Speech in an Open Society*. New York: Knopf, 1992.

Spann, Edward. *Gotham at War: New York City, 1860–65*. Wilmington: Scholarly Resources, 2002.

——. *Ideals and Politics*. Wilmington: SR Books, 1972.

——. *The New Metropolis: New York City, 1840–1857*. New York: Columbia University Press, 1981.

Stark, Rodney. *Police Riots: Collective Violence and Law Enforcement*. Belmont, Calif.: Wadsworth Publishing Co., 1972.

Stern, Robert A. M., Thomas Mellins, and David Fishman. *New York 1880: Architecture and Urbanism in the Gilded Age*. New York: Monacelli Press, 1999.

Still, Bayrd. *Mirror for Gotham*. New York: Fordham University Press, 1956.

Stone, Geoffrey. *Perilous Times: Free Speech in Wartime*. New York: W. W. Norton & Co., 2004.

Stone, Geoffrey, Richard Epstein, and Cass Sunstein. *The Bill of Rights in the Modern State*. Chicago: University of Chicago Press, 1992.

Stott, Richard. *Workers in the Metropolis: Class, Ethnicity, and Youth in Antebellum New York City*. Ithaca, N.Y.: Cornell University Press, 1990.

Sunstein, Cass. *Democracy and the Problem of Free Speech*. New York: The Free Press, 1993.

——. *Why Societies Need Dissent*. Cambridge, Mass.: Harvard University Press, 2003.

Teaford, Jon. *The Municipal Revolution in America*. Chicago: University of Chicago Press, 1975.

——. *The Unheralded Triumph: City Government in America, 1879–1900*. Baltimore, Md.: The Johns Hopkins Press, 1984.

Tchen, John. *New York Before Chinatown*. Baltimore, Md.: The Johns Hopkins University Press, 1999.

Thelen, David. *The Constitution and American Life*. Ithaca, N.Y.: Cornell University Press, 1988.

Todd, Nancy. *New York's Historic Armories: An Illustrated History*. Albany, N.Y.: SUNY Press, 2006.

Upton, Dell. "The Empire City." Lecture given at the Metropolitan Museum of Art, November 4, 2000.

Vila, Bryan, and Cynthia Morris. *The Role of Police in American Society: A Documentary History*. Westport, Conn.: Greenwood Press, 1999.

Viteritti, Joseph. *Police, Politics, and Pluralism in New York City*. Beverly Hills, Calif.: Sage Publications, 1973.

——. *Police Professionalism in New York City*. New York: Center for Research in Crime and Justice, New York University School of Law, 1987.

Wagman, Robert. *The First Amendment Book*. New York: World Almanac, 1991.

Walker, Samuel. *In Defense of American Liberties: A History of the ACLU*. New York: Oxford University Press, 1990.

Ward, David, and Olivier Zunz. *The Landscape of Modernity*. New York: Russell Sage Foundation, 1992.

Ware, Norman. *The Labor Movement in the United States: A Study in Democracy*. Gloucester, Mass.: Peter Smith, 1959.

Warren, Mark. *Democracy and Association*. Princeton, N.J.: Princeton University Press, 2001.

Weinbaum, Paul. *Mobs and Democracy: The New York Response to Collective Violence in the Early Nineteenth Century*. Ann Arbor, Mich.: UMI Research Press, 1978.

Whipple, Leon. *The Story of Civil Liberty in the United States*. New York: Vanguard Press, 1927.

Widmer, Edward. *America: The Flowering of Democracy in New York City*. Oxford: Oxford University Press, 1999.

Wilentz, Sean. *Chants Democratic*. New York: Oxford University Press, 1984.

Williams, Lee E. *Post-War Riots in America, 1919 and 1946: How the Pressures of War Exacerbated American Urban Tensions to the Breaking Point*. Lewiston, N.Y.: E. Mellen Press, 1991.

Wood, Gordon. "A Note on Mobs in the American Revolution." *William and Mary Quarterly* (1966).

Woods, Arthur. "Reasonable Restrictions Upon Freedom of Assemblage," *Papers and Proceedings of the Ninth Annual Meeting of the American Sociological Society*, 1914 (repr. 1971).

Yellowitz, Irwin. *Industrialization and the American Labor Movement, 1850–1900*. Port Washington, N.Y.: Kennikat Press, 1977.

——, ed. *Essays in the History of New York City*. Port Washington, N.Y.: Kennikat Press. 1978.

Zeisloft, Idell, ed. *The New Metropolis, 1600–1900*. New York: D. Appleton & Co. 1899, 1900.

GREET BRITAIN AND EUROPE

Primary Sources

PUBLIC RECORDS OFFICE (NATIONAL ARCHIVES)

All references refer to research done while still the PRO.

Mepol 1 (Private and Confidential Outletters; Correspondence): 44, 45, 46, 47, 53, 59, 60, 61, 62.

Mepol 2: 1, 26, 27, 29, 32, 33, 34, 37, 46, 48, 59, 60, 61, 62, 63, 64, 66, 67, 68, 69, 130, 134, 135, 136, 137, 147, 174, 182, 191, 231a, 231b, 248, 250, 360, 411, 472, 511, 1378, 5796, 5798, 5800, 5802, 5803, 5807.

Mepol 3: 1, 3, 4, 35, 36.

Mepol 4: 1, 6, 12–30.

Mepol 5: 278.

Mepol 7 (Daily Orders): 1, 2, 3, 8, 9, 11, 14, 15, 19–60, 131–133.

Mepol 8: 1–5, 27–33.

H.O. 41: 25, 26.

H.O. 44: 52.

H.O. 45: 59, 102, 181, 247, 252, 292, 1107, 1677, 1826, 1889, 2299, 2410, 2412, 2619, 2670, 3136, 3336, 3614, 3634, 4313, 5128, 6092, 6093, 6751, 6794/5, 6794/7, 7618, 7618/4, 7618/5, 8174, 8275, 9472, 9620, 9662, 9816, 9718, 9861, 9953.

H.O. 48: L.O.O. 231/1, 231/2, 231/3, 179.

H.O. 49: 9–11.

H.O. 60: 3–7.

H.O. 61: 20–28.

H.O. 64: 8–10.

H.O. 65: 7–9, 11–51.

H.O. 66: 1, 2.

H.O. 75: 11–18.

Works 16: 473–479, 501, 790, 793, 794, 914, 996, 997, 1000, 1027, 1033, 1034, 1038.

Works 20: 70, 87, 110.

MIDDLESEX SESSIONS RECORDS

Sessions Papers
Summary Jurisdiction Records, 1855–1889
Special Minute Book—Ossultone Hundred

DISSERTATIONS

Emsley, Clive. "Public Order in England, 1790–1801." M. Litt. thesis, Cambridge University.

Keller, Lisa. "Public Order in Victorian London." Ph.D. thesis, Cambridge University, 1977.

Prothero, I. J. "London Working Class Movements." Ph.D. thesis, Cambridge University.

Summerson, H. "The Maintenance of Law and Order in England, 1227–1263." Ph.D. thesis, Cambridge University, 1975.

PARLIAMENTARY PAPERS

1833 XIII S.C. Coldbath Fields

S.C. on the Petition of Fred. Young (Popay . . .)

S.C. Metropolitan Police

1834 XVI S.C. Police of the Metropolis

XLVII Home Office and the Police

1839 XXXVIII Correspondence, Lord John Russell

1840 XXXVIII Total Confined on . . . Seditious or Blasphemous Libel Charges

XXXIX Return, Metropolitan Police

1849 XLIV Return, Metropolitan Policemen Charged Before Magistrates Return, Metropolitan Police Divisions

1851 X S.C. Sunday Trading Bill

1852–3 XXXVI Report on Police in Great Britain

XXIII S.C. Criminal and Destitute Children

1854–5 VI Sunday Trading Bill

1856 XXIII S.C. Hyde Park Riots

1864 XLVIII Primrose Hill Meeting

1881 LIII Juvenile Offenders

1886 I Metropolitan Police (Compensation) Act

III Riot (Damages) Act

XXXIV S.C. Riot of Feb. 8, 1886

Report on Administration and Organization of the Police

LIII Memo, Home Secretary, on 1886 Riots

1887 XI S.C. Public Parks and Works (Metropolis) Bill

V London Parks and Works Act 1887

1888 LXXXII Return, Injured Police, Nov. 13, 1887

Police Orders of July 21, 1866, Instructions re: the Suppression of Meetings. . .

VI Public Meetings in Open Spaces Act 1888

VII Bill for the Regulation of Meetings in Trafalgar Square 1888

LVI Report of R.C. on the Metropolitan Board of Works

LXXXI Home Office—Metropolitan Board of Works Correspondence re: Public Meetings

1889 LXI Trafalgar Square Regulations

1890–1 CXIII Home Office Correspondence

1893–4 LXXIV D.C. Report on Police

1895 XXXV Interdepartmental Committee Report on Riots

1895 CVIII Introduction to Judicial Statistics (1893 reprint)

1865 VIII S.C. Open Spaces

1868–9 IV Metropolitan Commons Acts

1876 LXI Home Office Correspondence

1860–1899 Metropolitan Police Annual Reports

1857–1899 Metropolitan Police Inspectors' Reports

1857–1892 Judicial Statistics: Criminal Returns

1830 XXIII; 1834 XVI; 1835 XII; 1837–8 XLVII; 1840 XXXIX; 1844 XXXIX; 1849 XLIV; 1852–3
    LXXCIII; 1856 L; 1867 LVII Police Returns

Selected Bills and Acts

Local and Personal Acts

HANSARD

Public Records Office, *Public Order, Discontent, and Protest in England: 1820–1850* (micro-
    film, 49 reels) (1981)

NEWSPAPERS, PERIODICALS, GENERAL REFERENCE WORKS,
AND LAW REPORTS

Annual Register

British Workman

Charity Organization Review

Christian Socialist

Commonweal

Daily Chronicle

Daily News

Daily Telegraph

Economist

Guardian

Illustrated London News

Independent

Justice

Link

London Times

Morning Advertiser

Morning Post

Nation

National Reformer

New Statesman

Northern Star

Observer
Our Corner
Pall Mall Gazette
Parliamentary Affairs
People's Paper
Practical Socialist
Punch
Standard
The Times
Today

CAMBRIDGE UNIVERSITY LIBRARY REFERENCE ROOM

Boase. *Modern English Biography*. London: Frank Cass, 1965.
Dictionary of National Biography. London.
Dod.
Hubbard's Newspaper Directory.
Halsbury's Laws. [Cambridge University Library]
Hawkins Please of the Crown (1787). [Cambridge University Library]
Stephen's Commentaries. (Multiple editions: 1950, 1925, 1922) [Cambridge University Library]

ANCIENT TEXTS

Herodotus. *The Histories*. Penguin.
Thucidydes. *The Peloponnesian Wars*. Penguin.
Aristotle. *Politics* (XX); *Athens Constitution* (XXI). Loeb Classical Library.
Cicero. *In Catilinam*; *Pro Murena*; *Pro Sulla*; *Pro Flacco* (X). Loeb Classical Library.
Livy. *History of Rome* (I–XIII). Loeb Classical Library.
Plato. *Dialogues* (I). Loeb Classical Library.
Tacitus. *Annals*; *The Histories* (III). Loeb Classical Library.
Moore, J. M., ed. *Aristotle and Xenophon on Democracy and Oligarchy*. Berkeley: University of California Press, 1975.
Hadas, Moses. *Complete Plays of Aristophanes*. New York: Bantam Books, 1971.

BOOKS AND ARTICLES

Archer, Thomas. *About My Father's Business*. London, 1876.
——. *The Pauper, the Thief, and the Convict*. London: Groombridge, 1865.
Arnold, Matthew. *Culture and Anarchy*. 1869.
Baedeker's *London*. 1883, 1894.

Bax, E. Belfort. *Reminiscences and Reflections of a Mid and Late Victorian*. London: G. Allen & Unwin, Ltd., 1918.

——, ed. *Harry Quelch: Literary Remains*. London: Grant Richards, 1914.

Beames, Thomas. *The Rookeries of London*. London: T. Bosworth, 1850.

Bennett, Alan. *The History Boys*. London: Faber & Faber, 2004.

Benson, A. C., ed., and Viscount Esher. *The Letters of Queen Victoria*. 1907.

Bent, James. *Criminal Life: Reminiscence of Forty-Two Years as a Police Officer*. London, 1891.

Besant, Annie. *An Autobiography*. London: T. F. Unwin, 1895.

Blackstone's Guide to the Serious Organised Crime and Police Act 2005. Oxford: Oxford University Press, 2005.

Bonner, Hypatia Bradlaugh. *Charles Bradlaugh*. London, 1908.

Booth, Charles. *Life and Labour of the London Poor*. London, 1902–1903.

Burgess, J. *John Burns*. London, 1911.

Burns, John. *The Man with the Red Flag*. London, 1886.

Buxton, Charles. *Memoirs of Sir Thomas Fowell Buxton*. London: John Murray, 1872.

Carpenter, Edward. *Prison, Police, and Punishment*. London: A. C. Fifield, 1905.

"Causes of Crime in the Metropolis." *Tait's Edinburgh Magazine* (June 1850).

Chesterton, G. L. *Revelations of Prison Life*. London: Hurst & Blackett, 1856.

Childers, E. S. E. *The Life and Correspondence of Hugh C. E. Childers*. London, 1904.

"City of London Police." *Blackwood's* (November 1886).

Clay, John. "On the Effect of Good or Bad Times on Committals to Prison." *Journal of the Royal Statistical Society* (December 1857).

——. "On the Relations Between Crime, Popular Instruction, Attendance on Religious Worship and Beer Houses." *Journal of the Royal Statistical Society* (March 1857).

Collins Illustrated Atlas of London. 1854 (repr. 1973, edited by H. J. Dyos).

"The Coming Ninth of November." *The Spectator* (October 23, 1886).

Croker, John. *The Croker Papers: Correspondence and Diaries of the Late Right Honorable John Wilson Croker*. London: J. Murray. 1884.

Cruikshank, G., and J. Wight. *Sunday in London*. London: Effingham Wilson, 1833.

Diary of John Evelyn Denison. [*Notes from my journal . . .*] London: John Murray, 1900.

Dicey, A. V. *Introduction to the Study of the Law of the Constitution*. London: Macmillan & Co., 1915.

——. *Lectures on the Relation Between Law and Public Opinion in England*. London: Macmillan, 1905.

——. "On the Right of Public Meeting." *Contemporary Review* (April 1889).

Dickens, Charles. *American Notes*. 1842.

——. *Martin Chuzzlewit*. 1844.

——. *Oliver Twist*. 1838.

——. *Our Mutual Friend*. 1865.

——. *A Tale of Two Cities*. 1859.

Disraeli, Benjamin. *Sybil*. Penguin.

Duncombe, Thomas H. *The Life and Times of Thomas Slingsby Duncombe*. London: Hurst & Blackett, 1868.

Edwards, Percy. *History of London Street Improvements*. London: London County Council, Truscott & Son, 1898.

Elliot, J. H. "The Increase of Material Prosperity and of Moral Agents Compared with the State of Crime and Pauperism." *Journal of the Royal Statistical Society* (September 1868).

Evans, H. "The London County Council and the Police." *Contemporary Review* (April 1889).

"The Fear of Mobs." *The Spectator* (February 13, 1886).

"The French and English Police Systems." *Cornhill Magazine* (October 1881).

Frost, Thomas. *Forty Years' Recollections*. London: Sampson, Low, Marston, Searle, Rivington, 1880.

——. *Reminiscences of a Country Journalist*. London: Ward & Downey, 1886.

Gammage, R. G. *History of the Chartist Movement, 1837–54*. New York: A. M. Kelley, 1894.

Gissing, George. *In the Year of Jubilee*. London: J. M. Dent, 1894.

——. *The Nether World*. 1889.

Greenwood, James. *The Seven Curses of London*. London: Rivers, 1869.

Gronow, R. H. *Reminiscences and Recollections of Captain Gronow, 1810–1860*. London: The Bodley Head, 1964.

Grosvenor, George. "Statistics of the Abatement of Crime in England and Wales During the Twenty Years Ended 1887–8." *Journal of the Royal Statistical Society* (September 1890).

Henderson, Philip, ed. *The Letters of William Morris*. London: Longmans, Green, 1950.

"Hyde Park Corner." *Saturday Review* (April 1882).

Hyndman, H. M. *Further Reminiscences*. London, 1912.

——. *Record of an Adventurous Life*. London: Macmillan, 1911.

Jephson, Henry. *The Sanitary Evolution of London*. London: Unwin, 1907.

Kaunert, Christian, interview, University of Salford, November 20, 2007.

Kirwan, Daniel. *Palace and Hovel*. London: Abelard-Schuman, 1870.

Knollys, W. W. "Mobs and Revolution." *Fortnightly Review* (December 1884).

Lang, Andrew. *Life, Letters, and Diaries of Sir Stafford Northcote, First Earl of Iddesleigh*. Edinburgh: Blackburn, 1890.

Lansbury, George. *My Life*. London: Constable, 1928.

LeBon, Gustave. *The Crowd: A Study of the Popular Mind*. London, 1896.

Linton, W. J. *Memories*. London: Lawrence & Bullen, 1895.

"London Larrikens." *Spectator* (August 27, 1898).

"The London Police." *The Saturday Review* (May–June 1888).

"London Police Duty." *Leisure Hour* (May 1879).

Mann, Tom. *Memoirs*. London: Labour Publishing Co., 1923.

Martineau, Harriet. "The Policeman: His Health." *Once a Week* (June 2, 1860).

Marx, Karl. *The Class Struggles in France*. London: Martin Lawrence, 1934.

Marx, Karl, and F. Engels. *Correspondence, 1846–1895*. London: Martin Lawrence, 1934.

Mayhew, Henry. *London Labour and the London Poor*. London, 1861.

Mayhew, Henry, and John Binny. *The Criminal Prisons of London and Scenes of Prison Life*. London, 1862.

Meason, M. Laing. "The London Police." *Macmillan's Magazine*. 1882 (46).

"Mobs." *Cornhill* (June 1867).

"Mobs and Revolution." *Fortnightly Review* (December 1886).

"The Modern Science of Thief-Taking." *Household Words* (July 13, 1850).

Monro, James. "The London Police." *North American Review* (November 1890).

Morris, May. *William Morris*. London, 1936.

Morris, William. *News from Nowhere*. London, 1890.

——. "Unpublished Letters of William Morris." *Socialist Review* (March–May 1928).

Morrison, Arthur. *A Child of the Jago*. London, 1894.

——. *Tales of Mean Street*. London, 1895.

Morrison, W. D. *Crime and Its Causes*. 1891.

——. "The Increase of Crime." *Nineteenth Century*. 1892.

"A Night with the Peelers." *Bentley's Miscellany*. 1854 (35).

Nott-Bower, John. *Fifty-Two Years a Policeman*. London: E. Arnold, 1926.

Owen, Edward. *Hyde Park: Select Narratives During Twenty Years' Police Service*. London, 1906.

Pease, E. R. *The History of the Fabian Society*. London: A. C. Fifield, 1916.

Peek, Francis. *Social Wreckage*. London, 1883.

"Police Mysteries." *London Society* 13.

Porter, Fitzjohn. "How to Quell Mobs." *North American Review* 141.

"Principles of Police . . ." *Fraser's Magazine*. 1837 (16).

Pugh, Giles. *Crime, in Its Relation to Religion, Education and Laws*. 1857.

"The Right to Riot." *The Spectator* (January 14, 1888).

"The Riots." *Blackwood's* (September 1842).

Roberts, Morley. "Agitators and Demagogues." *Murray's Magazine* (May 1890).

Ruggles-Brise, Sir Evelyn. *The English Prison System*. London: Macmillan, 1921.

Salt, H. S. *Company I Have Kept*. London, 1930.

Sanders, William. *Early Socialist Days*. 1908.

Scheu, Andreas. *Umsturzkeime*. Translated by H. Cohen. Vienna, 1923.

"The Set Against the Police." *The Spectator* (August 20, 1887).

Sexby, J. J. *The Municipal Parks, Gardens, and Open Spaces of London*. London: E. Stock, 1905 (1898).

Shand, Alex Innes. "The City of London Police." *Blackwood's* (November 1886).

Shaw, G. B. *The Fabian Society* (Fabian Tract No. 41). London: The Fabian Society, 1892.

——. *Shaw Gives Himself Away*. Newtown: The Gregynog Press, 1939.

——. *Sixteen Self-Sketches*. London: Constable, 1949.

"The Sketcher in London: Policeman AE." *Leisure Hour* (January 7, 1858).

Smiles, Samuel. *Self-Help*. 1859.

Smith, Albert. *Sketches of London Life and Character*. London, 1848.

Snell, Lord H. *Men, Movements, and Myself*. London: Dent, 1936.

Stuart, James. "The Metropolitan Police." *Contemporary Review* (April 1889).

Sweeney, John. *At Scotland Yard: Being the Experiences During Twenty-Seven Years' Service*. London: Grant Richards, 1904.

Taine, Hippolyte. *Notes on England*. 1872.

Tillett, Ben. *A Brief History of the Docker's Union*. London, 1910.

——. *Memories and Reflections*. London: J. Long, 1931.

Timbs, John. *Club Life of London*. London: Richard Bentley, 1866.

——. *Curiosities of London*. London, 1867.

Tindal, Nicholas. *Reprint of an Address by Chief Justice Tindal*. London: John Henry Parker, 1848.

"Topics of the Day: The Riot of Monday." *The Spectator* (February 13, 1886).

Tweedie, E. [Mrs. Alex Tweedie]. *Hyde Park*. London: E. Nash, 1908.

The Letters of Queen Victoria. 3rd series. London: Murray, 1930.

Warren, Charles. "The Police of the Metropolis." *Murray's Magazine* (November 1888).

Weintraub, Stanley, ed. *Shaw: An Autobiography, 1856–1898*. 1969.

White, Arnold. *The Problems of a Great City*. London: Remington & Co., 1886.

Wise, Edward. *The Law Relating to Riots and Unlawful Assemblies*. London: Butterworth Shaw, 1907.

"The Work of the London Police." *The Spectator* (September 7, 1882).

Secondary Sources: Books and Articles

Altick, Richard. *Victorian People and Ideas*. New York: Norton, 1973.

Anderson, David, and D. Killingray, ed. *Policing the Empire: Governments, Authority, and Control, 1830–1940*. Manchester: Manchester University Press, 1991.

Ash, Timothy Garton. "Killing Liberty in the Name of Society." *Globe and Mail*, November 15, 2007.

Babington, Anthony. *A House in Bow Street: Crime and the Magistracy, 1748–1881*. 1969.

——. *Military Intervention in Britain: From the Gordon Riots to the Gibraltar Incident*. London: Routledge, 1990.

Barker, T. C., and Michael Robbins. *A History of London Transport*. London: Allen & Unwin, 1963.

Barker, Theo, and Anthony Sutcliffe, ed. *Megalopolis: The Giant City in History*. Basingstoke: Macmillan, 1993.

Barrows, Susanna. *Distorting Mirrors: Visions of the Crowd in Late Nineteenth-Century France*. New Haven, Conn.: Yale University Press, 1981.

Beattie, J. M. "The Pattern of Crime in England, 1660–1800." *Past & Present* (February 1974).

Beetham, David. "Political Participation, Marr Protest, and Representative Democracy." *Parliamentary Affairs* (October 1, 2003).

Bellamy, John. *Crime and Public Order in England in the Later Middle Ages*. London: Routledge & Kegan Paul, 1973.

Bennett, Alfred. *London and Londoners in the Eighteen Fifties and Sixties*. London: Unwin, 1924.

Bernard, L. L. "Mob." *Encyclopedia of Social Sciences*. 1934.

Blake, Robert. *Disraeli*. New York: St. Martin's Press, 1967.

Bohstedt, John. "The Moral Economy and the Discipline of Historical Context." *Journal of Social History* (Winter 1992).

——. *Riots and Community Politics in England and Wales, 1790–1810*. Cambridge, Mass.: Harvard University Press, 1983.

Bowes, Stuart. *The Police and Civil Liberties*. London: Lawrence & Wishart, 1966.

Bradlaugh Centenary Committee. *Champion of Liberty: Charles Bradlaugh*. London: Watts, 1933.

Brewer, John, and John Styles, eds. *An Ungovernable People: The English and Their Law in the Seventeenth and Eighteenth Centuries*. London: Hutchinson, 1980.

Brewer, John D., et al. *The Police, Public Order, and the State: Policing in Great Britain, Northern Ireland, the Irish Republic, the USA, Israel, South Africa, and China*. Basingstoke: Macmillan, 1988.

Briggs, Asa. *Chartist Studies*. London: Macmillan, 1959.

——. "Middle-Class Consciousness in English Politics, 1780–1846." *Past & Present* (April 1956).

——. *Victorian Cities*. London: Odhams Press, 1963.

——. *Victorian People*. London: Odhams Press, 1954.

Brownlie, Ian. *The Law Relating to Public Order*. London: Butterworth, 1968.

Brunt, P. A. *Italian Manpower, 225 B.C.–14 A.D.* London: Oxford University Press, 1971.

——. "The Roman Mob." *Past & Present*. 1966 (35).

Burke, Thomas. *The Streets of London*. London: B. T. Batsford Ltd., 1940.

Burnett, John, ed. *Useful Toil*. London: Allen Lane, 1974.

Canetti, Elias. *Crowds and Power*. 1962.

Cecil, David. *Melbourne*. London: Constable, 1965.

Cerrah, Ibrahim. *Crowds and Public Order Policing: An Analysis of Crowds and Interpretations of Their Behaviour Based on Observational Studies in Turkey, England, and Wales*. Aldershot: Ashgate, 1998.

Chancellor, E. Beresford. *The West End of Yesterday and Today*. London: The Architectural Press, 1926.

Checkland, S. *The Rise of Industrial Society, 1815–1885*. London: Longmans, 1964.

Chevalier, Louis. *Labouring Classes and Dangerous Classes*. London: Routledge & Kegan Paul, 1973.

Childe-Pemberton, William. *Life of Lord Norton*. London: J. Murray, 1909.

Church, Richard. *The Royal Parks of London*. London: H.M.S.O. Stationery Office, 1956.

Cobb, Belton. *The First Detectives*. London: Faber & Faber, 1957.

Cole, G. D. H. *The British Working Class Politics, 1832–1914.* London: G. Routledge & Sons, 1941.

——. *John Burns.* London: V. Gollancz and the Fabian Society, 1943.

——. *A Short History of the British Working Class Movement.* London: G. Allen & Unwin, 1948.

Cole, G. D. H., and R. Postgate. *The British Common People.* 1937.

Coleman, B. I. *The Idea of the City in Nineteenth-Century Britain.* London: Routledge & Kegan Paul, 1973.

Coleman, Roy. *Reclaiming the Streets: Surveillance, Social Control, and the City.* Cullompton: Willan, 2004.

Collison, Michael. *Public Order and the Rule of Law in England, 1688–1720.* University of Keele, 1987.

Cousens, Michael. *Surveillance Law.* London: LexisNexis UK, 2004.

Cragoe, Matthew, and Antony Taylor. *London Politics, 1760–1914.* New York: Palgrave Macmillan, 2005.

Creighton, M. *Memoir of Sir George Grey.* London: Longmans, Green, 1901.

Critchley, T. A. *A History of Police in England and Wales, 900–1966.* London: Constable, 1967.

Cromwell, Valerie. "Interpretations of Nineteenth-Century Administration: An Analysis." *Victorian Studies* 9.

The Crown Estate, 1960.

Cruse, Amy. *Victorians and Their Reading.* Boston: Houghton Mifflin Co., 1935.

Dahrendoref, Ralf. *Class and Conflict in an Industrial Society.* Stanford, Calif.: Stanford University Press, 1959.

Dark, Sidney. *London.* New York: Macmillan, 1936.

Darvall, Frank. *Popular Disturbances and Public Order in Regency England.* New York: Augustus Kelly, 1934.

Davis, John. *Conflict and Control: Law and Order in Nineteenth-Century Italy.* Atlantic Highlands, N.J.: Humanities Press International, 1988.

——. *Reforming London: The London Government Problem, 1855–1900.* New York: Oxford University Press, 1988.

Debord, G. *The Society of the Spectacle.* New York: Zone Books, 1994.

de Certeau, Michel. *The Practice of Everyday Life.* Berkeley: University of California Press, 1984.

Driver, Christopher. *The Disarmers: A Study in Protest.* London: Hodder & Stoughton, 1964.

Dunbabin, J. P. D. *Rural Discontent in Nineteenth-Century Britain.* New York: Holmes & Meier, 1974.

Dyos, H. J. "Slums of Victorian London." *Victorian Studies.* 1967 (11).

Dyos, H. J., and Derek Aldcroft. *British Transport.* Leicester: Leicester University Press, 1969.

Dyos, H. J., and Michael Wolff. *The Victorian City*. London: Routledge & Kegan Paul, 1973.

Edgar, P. "Festivals of the Oppressed." *Race and Class* 29, no. 4 (1988).

Elton, Godfrey. *England Arise*. London: Jonathan Cape, 1931.

Emsley, Clive. *Crime and Society in England, 1750–1900*. London: Longman, 1987.

——. *The English Police*. London: Longman, 1991.

——. *Gendarmes and the State in Nineteenth-Century Europe*. Oxford: Oxford University Press, 1999.

Emsley, Clive, and Barbara Weinberger. *Policing Western Europe*. New York: Greenwood Press, 1991.

Englander, David. *Britain and America: Studies in Comparative History, 1760–1970*. New Haven, Conn.: Yale University Press, 1997.

Ensor, Sir R. *England, 1870–1914*. Oxford: Clarendon Press, 1936.

Finer, S. E. *The Life and Times of Sir Edwin Chadwick*. London: Methuen, 1952.

Finley, M. I. *Democracy Ancient and Modern*. 1973.

——, ed. *The Legacy of Greece: A New Appraisal*. Oxford: Clarendon Press, 1981.

——. *The World of Odysseus*. 1954.

Fletcher, Anthony, and John Stevenson, eds. *Order and Disorder in Early Modern England*. Cambridge: Cambridge University Press, 1985.

Forshaw, Alec, and Theo Bergstrom. *The Open Spaces of London*. London: Allison & Busby, 1986.

Foster, Steve. *Q & A, Human Rights, and Civil Liberties*. New York: Oxford University Press, 2006.

Gardiner, A. G. *Life of Sir William Harcourt*. London: Constable & Co., 1923.

Gayer, Arthur, W. Rostow, and A. Schwartz. *The Growth and Fluctuation of the British Economy, 1790–1850*. Oxford: Clarendon Press, 1953.

Gibbs-Smith, C. H. *The Great Exhibition of 1851*. London: H.M.S.O., 1950.

Gill, Martin, ed. *CCTV*. Leicester: Perpetuity Press, 2003.

Gilley, Sheridan. "The Garibaldi Riots of 1862." *Historical Journal*. 1973.

Glasier, J. B. *William Morris*. London: Longmans, Green, 1921.

Goodhart, A. L. "Public Meetings and Processions." *Cambridge Law Journal*. 1937.

Goodway, David. *London Chartism, 1838–48*. Cambridge: Cambridge University Press, 1982.

Goold, Benjamin. *CCTV and Policing: Public Area Surveillance and Police Practices in Britain*. Oxford: Oxford University Press, 2004.

Griffiths, Paul, and Mark Jenner, eds. *Londinopolis: Essays in the Cultural and Social History of Early Modern London*. Manchester: Manchester University Press, 2000.

Grubb, A. P. *John Burns*. London, 1908.

Habermas, Jürgen. *The Inclusion of the Other: Studies in Political Theory*. Cambridge, Mass.: The MIT Press, 1998.

——. *The Structural Transformation of the Public Sphere*. Translated by T. Berger. Cambridge, Mass.: The MIT Press, 1989.

Harling, Robert. *The London Miscellany: A Nineteenth-Century Scrapbook*. New York: Oxford University Press, 1938.

Harris, Andrew T. *Policing the City: Crime and Legal Authority in London, 1780–1840*. Columbus: Ohio State University Press, 2004.

Harris, Jose, ed. *Civil Society in British History: Ideas, Identities, Institutions*. Oxford: Oxford University Press, 2003.

——. *Private Lives, Public Spirit: A Social History of Britain, 1870–1914*. Oxford: Oxford University Press, 1993.

——. *Unemployment and Politics*. Oxford: Clarendon University Press, 1972.

Harrison, Brian. *Drink and the Victorians*. Pittsburgh, Penn.: University of Pittsburgh Press, 1971.

——. "The Sunday Trading Riots of 1855." *Historical Journal*. 1965 (8).

Harrison, Mark. *Crowds and History, 1790–1835*. Cambridge: Cambridge University Press, 1988.

Hart, Jennifer. "Nineteenth-Century Social Reform: A Tory Interpretation." *Past & Present* (July 1965).

——. "Reform of the Borough Police, 1935–56." *English Historical Review* (July 1955).

Hay, D., P. Linebaugh, and E. P. Thompson. *Albion's Fatal Tree*. New York: Pantheon, 1975.

Hay, Douglas, and Frances Snyder. *Policing and Prosecution in Britain, 1750–1850*. New York: Oxford University Press, 1989.

Henaff, Marcel, and Tracy Strong, ed. *Public Space and Democracy*. Minneapolis: University of Minnesota Press, 2001.

Hewitt, Patricia. *The Abuse of Power: Civil Liberties in the United Kingdom*. Oxford: M. Robertson, 1982.

Hill, Christopher. *Puritanism and Revolution*. London: Secker & Warburg, 1958.

Hitchcock, Tim, and Heather Shore, ed. *The Streets of London: From the Great Fire to the Great Stink*. London: Ribers Oram Press, 2003.

Himmelfarb, Gertrude. *Victorian Minds*. New York: Knopf, 1968.

Hobsbawm, E. J. *Bandits*. London: Weidenfeld & Nicholson, 1969.

——. "Economic Fluctuations and Some Social Movements Since 1800." *Economic History Review*. 1952 (1).

——. *Industry and Empire*. Middlesex: Penguin, 1969.

——. *Labouring Men*. London: Weidenfeld & Nicholson, 1964.

——. "The Machine Breakers." *Past and Present* (February 1952).

——. "The Nineteenth-Century London Labour Market." In *London: Aspects of Change*, edited by the Centre for Urban Studies. London: MacGibbon & Kee, 1964.

——. *Primitive Rebels*. Manchester: Manchester University Press, 1959.

Hobsbawm, E. J., and George Rude. *Captain Swing*. London: Lawrence & Wishart, 1969.

Hohenerg, Paul, and Lynn Lees. *The Making of Urban Europe, 1000–1994*. Cambridge, Mass.: Harvard University Press, 1995.

Hole, Robert. *Pulpits, Politics, and Public Order in England, 1760–1832*. Cambridge: Cambridge University Press, 1989.

Houghton, Walter. *The Victorian Frame of Mind*. New Haven, Conn.: Yale University Press, 1957.

Hovell, Mark. *The Chartist Movement*. Manchester: Manchester University Press, 1918.

Hulse, James. *Revolutionists in London*. Oxford: Clarendon Press, 1970.

Hutchison, T. W. *A Review of Economic Doctrines, 1870–1929*. Oxford: Clarendon Press, 1953.

Inglis, K. S. *Churches and the Working Classes in Victorian England*. London: Routledge & Kegan Paul, 1963.

Inwood, Stephen. *A History of London*. New York: Carroll & Graf, 1998.

Jones, A. H. M. *Athenian Democracy*. Oxford: Blackwell, 1957.

Jones, David. *Crime, Protest, Community, and Police in Nineteenth-Century Britain*. London: Routledge & Kegan Paul, 1982.

Kasnitz, Philip. *Metropolis: Center and Symbol of Our Times*. New York: New York University Press, 1995.

Keith, M. *Race, Riots, and Policing*. London: UCL Press, 1993.

Kellett, J. R. *The Impact of the Railways on Victorian Cities*. London: Routledge & Kegan Paul, 1969.

Kent, David. "High Church Rituals and Rituals of Protest; the 'Riots' at St. George-in-the-East, 1959–60." *The London Journal* 32, no. 2 (July 2007).

Kent, William. *John Burns: Labour's Lost Leader*. London: Williams & Norgate, 1950.

Kitson Clark, G. *Churchmen and the Condition of England, 1832–1885*. 1973.

——. *The Making of Victorian England*. 1962.

Laski, H. J., et al. *A Century of Municipal Progress*. London: G. Allen & Unwin, 1935.

Lefebvre, Henri. *Critique of Everyday Life*. London: Verso, 1991.

——. *The Survival of Capitalism*. New York: St. Martin's Press, 1976.

LeGates, Robert, and Frederic Stout. *The City Reader*. London: Routledge, 1996.

Lee, H. W., and E. Archbold. *Social Democracy in Britain*. London: Social Democratic Federation, 1935.

Lee, W. L. Melville. *A History of Police in England*. London: Methuen & Co., 1901.

Lees, Andrew. *Cities Perceived*. New York: Columbia University Press, 1985.

Leventhal, F. M. *Respectable Radical: George Howell and Victorian Working-Class Politics*. London: Weidenfeld & Nicolson, 1971.

Liang, Hsi-Huey. *The Rise of Modern Police and the European State System from Metternich to the Second World War*. Cambridge: Cambridge University Press, 1992.

Lillywhite, Bryant. *London Coffee Houses*. London: G. Allen and Unwin, 1963.

Lodhi, Abdul, and Charles Tilly. "Urbanization, Crime, and Collective Violence in Nineteenth Century France." *American Journal of Sociology* (September 1973).

Macdiarmid, H. *Cunninghame Graham*. Glasgow: Caledonian Press, 1952.

MacDonagh, O. "The Nineteenth Century Revolution in Government: A Reappraisal." *Historical Journal*. 1958.

Mace, Rodney. *Trafalgar Square*. London: Lawrence & Wishart, 1976.

Margetson, Stella. *Leisure and Pleasure in the Nineteenth Century*. London: Cassell, 1969.

Mather, F. C. *Public Order in the Age of the Chartists*. Manchester: Manchester University Press, 1959.

McBriar, A. M. *Fabian Socialism and English Politics*. Cambridge: Cambridge University Press, 1962.

McClelland, J. S. *The Crowd and the Mob: From Plato to Canetti*. London: Unwin Hyman, 1989.

Millar, Fergus. *The Crowd in Rome in the Late Republic*. Ann Arbor: University of Michigan Press, 1998.

Mitchell, B. R. *European Historical Statistics, 1750–1970*. London: Macmillan, 1978.

Mitchell, B. R., and P. Deane. *Abstract of British Historical Statistics*. London. 1971.

Mitchell, J. D. B. *Constitutional Law*. Edinburgh: W. Green, 1964.

Mommsen, Wolfgang, and G. Hirschfeld. *Social Protest, Violence, and Terror in Nineteenth- and Twentieth-Century Europe*. New York: St. Martin's Press, 1982.

Mosse, George, ed. *Police Forces in History*. Beverly Hills, Calif.: Sage, 1975.

Mowat, C. L. *The Charity Organization Society*. London: Methuen, 1961.

Nead, Lynda. *Victorian Babylon*. New Haven, Conn.: Yale University Press, 2000.

Newburn, Tim, and Stephanie Hayman. *Policing, Surveillance and Social Control: CCTV and Police Monitoring of Suspects*. Portland: Willan, 2002.

Nippel, Wilfred. *Public Order in Ancient Rome*. Cambridge: Cambridge University Press, 1995.

Norris, Clive, and Gary Armstrong. *The Maximum Surveillance Society: The Rise of CCTV*. Oxford: Berg, 1999.

Oakeshott, Michael. *Hobbes on Civil Association*. Indianapolis: Liberty Fund, 1938.

O'Hagan, Andrew. "Watching Me Watching Them Watching You." *London Review of Books* (October 9, 2003).

Olsen, Donald. *The Growth of Victorian London*. New York: Holmes & Meier, 1976.

Owen, David. *English Philanthropy*. Cambridge, Mass.: Harvard University Press, 1964.

——. *The Government of Victorian London, 1855–1889*. Cambridge, Mass.: Harvard University Press, 1982.

Ozment, Steven. *Magdelena and Balthazar*. New Haven, Conn.: Yale University Press, 1989.

Painter, Kate, and Nicky Tilley, ed. *Surveillance of Public Space: CCTV, Street Legality, and Crime Prevention*. Monsey, N.Y.: Criminal Justice Press, 1999.

Palmer, Stanley. *Police and Protest in England and Ireland, 1780–1850*. Cambridge: Cambridge University Press, 1988.

Pearson, Hesketh. *Bernard Shaw*. London: Collins, 1942.

Pelew, Jill. *The Home Office, 1848–1914*. East Brunswick: Association University Presses, 1982.

Pelling, Henry. "H. H. Champion: Pioneer of Labour Representation." *Cambridge Journal* (January 1953).

——. *A History of British Trade Unionism*. Middlesex: Penguin, 1963.

——. *Origins of the Labour Party, 1880–1900*. London: Macmillan, 1965.

——. *Popular Politics and Society*. London: Macmillan, 1968.

Perkin, Harold. *Origins of Modern English Society, 1780–1880*. London: Routledge & K. Paul, 1969.

Petrow, Stefan. *Policing Morals: The Metropolitan Police and the Home Office, 1870–1914*. Oxford: Clarendon Press, 1994.

Philips, David, and Robert Storch. *Policing Provincial England, 1829–1856*. London: Leicester University Press, 1999.

Pile, Steve. *Real Cities: Modernity, Space, and the Phantasmagorias of City Life*. Thousand Oaks, Calif.: Sage, 2005.

Pile, Steve, Christopher Brook, and Gerry Mooney. *Unruly Cities?* London: Routledge, 1999.

Pile, Steve, and Michael Keith, eds. *Geographies of Resistance*. London: Routledge, 1997.

Pimlott, J. A. R. *The Englishman's Holiday*. London: Faber & Faber, 1948.

——. *Toynbee Hall: Fifty Years of Social Progress*. London: J. M. Dent & Sons, 1935.

Plotz, Jon. *The Crowd: British Literature and Public Politics*. Berkeley: University of California Press, 2000.

Porter, Roy. *London: A Social History*. Cambridge, Mass.: Harvard University Press, 1994.

Postgate, Raymond. *The Life of George Lansbury*. London: Longmans, Green, 1951.

"Protestor = Criminal." *Progressive* (February 2004).

Prothero, I. J. "Chartism in London." *Past & Present* 44 (1969).

——. "London Chartism and the Trades." *The Economic History Review* (May 1971).

Pryce, E. A. "The Notting Hill Carnival." *Caribbean Quarterly* 31, no. 2 (1985).

Raaflaub, Kurt. *The Discovery of Freedom in Ancient Greece*. Chicago: University of Chicago Press, 2004.

Radzinowicz, L. *A History of Criminal Law*. London: Stevens, 1948–1968.

Randall, Adrian, and A. Charlesworth, eds. *Moral Economy and Popular Protest*. Basingstoke: Macmillan, 2000.

Reddaway, T. F. "London in the Nineteenth Century: The Origins of the Metropolitan Police." *Nineteenth Century and After* 147 (1950).

Reith, Charles. *The Blind Eye of History: A Study of the Origins of the Present Police Era*. London: Faber & Faber, 1952.

——. *British Police and the Democratic Ideal*. London: Oxford University Press, 1943.

——. *A New Study of Police History*. Edinburgh: Oliver & Boyd, 1956.

——. *The Police Idea*. London: Oxford University Press, 1938.

Reynolds, Elaine. *Before the Bobbies: The Night Watch and Police Reform in Metropolitan London, 1720–1830*. Stanford, Calif.: Stanford University Press, 1998.

Rhodes, Gerald, ed. *The New Government of London: The First Five Years*. London: London School of Economics and Politics, 1972.

Richardson, John. *The Annals of London*. Berkeley: University of California Press, 2000.

Richter, D. C. *Riotous Victorians*. Athens: Ohio University Press, 1981.

——. "The Role of Mob Riots in Victorian Elections." *Victorian Studies* 15.

Robbins, Michael. *The Railway Age*. London: Routledge & Paul, 1962.

Roberts, David. "Jeremy Bentham and the Victorian Administrative State." *Victorian Studies*. 1950.

——. *Victorian Origins of the Welfare State*. New Haven, Conn.: Yale University Press, 1960.

Robertson, J. M. *Charles Bradlaugh*. London: Watts, 1920.

——. *Public Authorities and Legal Liabilities*. London: University of London Press, 1925.

Rowe, D. J. "The Failure of London Chartism." *Historical Journal*. 1968.

——. "The London Working Men's Association and the People's Charter." *Past and Present*. 1967.

Rude, George. *Captain Swing*. New York: Pantheon Books, 1968.

——. *The Crowd in the French Revolution*. Oxford: Clarendon Press, 1959.

——. *The Crowd in History, 1730–1848*. New York: Wiley, 1964.

——. "English Rural and Urban Disturbances on the Eve of the First Reform Bill, 1830–1831." *Past & Present*. 1967.

——. *Hanoverian London, 1714–1808*. Berkeley: University of California Press, 1971.

——. "The London 'Mob' of the Eighteenth Century." *Historical Journal*. 1959.

——. *Paris and London in the Eighteenth Century*. New York: Collins, 1952.

Rule, James. *Privacy in Peril*. Oxford: Oxford University Press, 2007.

——. *Private Lives and Public Surveillance*. London: Allen Lane, 1973.

Ryan, Alan, ed. *The Idea of Freedom: Essays in Honour of Isaiah Berlin*. Oxford: Oxford University Press, 1979.

Saint, Andrew, ed. *Politics and the People of London: The London County Council, 1889–1965*. London: Reconceverte, 1989.

Sanders, David, Harold Clarke, Marianne Stewart, and Paul Whitely. "The Dynamics of Protest in Britain, 2000–2002." *Parliamentary Affairs* (October 1, 2003).

Savitch, H. V. *Cities in a Time of Terror: Space, Territory, and Local Resilience*. Armonk, N.Y.: M. E. Sharpe, 2008.

Schneer, Jonathan. *London, 1900: The Imperial Metropolis*. New Haven, Conn.: Yale University Press, 1999.

Shoemaker, Robert. *The London Mob: Violence and Disorder in Eighteenth-Century England*. London: Hambledon & London, 2004.

Schumpeter, J. A. *History of Economic Analysis*. New York: Oxford University Press, 1955.

Schwarz, L. D. *London in the Age of Industrialization: Entrepreneurs, Labour Force, and Living Conditions, 1799–1850*. Cambridge: Cambridge University Press, 1992.

Scott, J. W. R. *The Life and Death of a Newspaper*. London: Methuen, 1952.

Shannon, H. A. "Migration and the Growth of London." *Economic History Review*. 1934–1935 (V).

Sheppard, Francis. *London, 1808–1870: The Infernal Wen*. Berkeley: University of California Press, 1971.

Sigmann, Jean. *1848: The Romantic and Democratic Revolutions in Europe*. New York: Harper & Row, 1973.

Slack, Paul, ed. *Rebellion, Popular Protest, and the Social Order in Early Modern England*. Cambridge: Cambridge University Press, 1984.

Smellie, K. "Riot." *Encyclopedia of Social Sciences*. 1934.

Smith, F. B. S. *The Making of the Second Reform Bill*. Cambridge: Cambridge University Press, 1966.

Smith, Paul. *Disraelian Conservatism and Social Reform*. London: Routledge & K. Paul, 1967.

Smith, Phillip. *Policing Victorian London: Political Policing, Public Order, and the London Metropolitan Police*. Westport, Conn.: Greenwood Press, 1985.

Spender, J. A., and Cyril Asquith. *Life of Herbert Henry Asquith*. London: Hutchinson & Co., 1932.

Stansky, Peter. *Gladstone: A Progress in Politics*. Boston: Little, Brown, 1979.

Stedman Jones, Gareth. *Outcast London*. Oxford: Clarendon Press, 1971.

Steedman, Carolyn. *Policing the Victorian Community: The Formation of English Provincial Police Forces, 1856–80*. London: Routledge & K. Paul, 1984.

Stevenson, J., and R. Quinault, eds. *Popular Protest and Public Order*. New York: St. Martin's Press, 1974.

Stevenson, John. *Popular Disturbances in England, 1700–1870*. London: Longman, 1979.

Storch, R. D. "The Plague of Blue Locusts: Police Reform and Popular Resistance in Northern England, 1840–57." *International Review of Social History*. 1975.

———. "The Policeman as Domestic Missionary." *Social History*. 1976.

Taylor, Antony. "Commons Stealers, Land Grabbers, and Jerry Builders: Space, Popular Radicalism, and the Politics of Public Access in London, 1848–80." *IRSH* 40 (1995).

Taylor, David. *Crime, Policing, and Punishment, 1750–1914*. New York: St. Martin's Press, 1998.

———. *The New Police in Nineteenth-Century England: Crime, Conflict, and Control*. Manchester: Manchester University Press, 1997.

Thomas, Dorothy. *Social Aspects of the Business Cycle*. London: G. Routledge & Sons, 1925.

Thompson, E. P. *Customs in Common*. London: Penguin, 1993.

———. *The Making of the English Working Class*. New York: Vintage Books, 1963.

———. "The Moral Economy of the English Crowd in the Eighteenth Century." *Past & Present* 50.

———. *William Morris*. London: Lawrence & Wishart, 1955.

Thompson, F. M. L., ed. *Cambridge Social History of Britain*. Cambridge: Cambridge University Press, 1990.

Thompson, Paul. "Liberals, Radical, and Labour in London, 1880–1900." *Past & Present*. 1964.

———. *Socialists, Liberals, and Labour: The Struggle for London, 1885–1914*. London: Routledge & K. Paul, 1967.

Thurston, Gavin. *The Clerkenwell Riot: The Killing of Constable Culley*. London: Allen & Unwin, 1967.

Tilly, Charles. *Popular Contention in Great Britain*. Cambridge, Mass.: Harvard University Press, 1995.

Tilly, Charles, et al. *The Rebellious Century, 1830–1930*. Cambridge, Mass.: Harvard University Press, 1975.

Tobias, J. J. *Crime and Industrial Society in the Nineteenth Century*. London: Batsford, 1967.

Torr, Dona. *Tom Mann*. London: Lawrence & Wishart, 1936.

Townshend, Charles. *Making the Peace: Public Order and Public Security in Modern Britain*. Oxford: Oxford University Press, 1993.

Trevelyan, G. M. *English Social History*. London: Longmans Green & Co., 1942.

Tschiffely, A. F. *Don Roberto*. London: W. Heinemann, 1937.

Tsuzuki, Chushicki. *H. M. Hyndman and British Socialism*. London: Oxford University Press, 1961.

Uglow, Steve. *Policing Liberal Society*. Oxford: Oxford University Press, 1988.

Vanderbroeck, P. J. J. *Popular Leadership and Collective Behavior in the Late Roman Republic*. Amsterdam: J. C. Gieben, 1987.

Vincent, John. *The Formation of the Liberal Party*. London: Constable, 1966.

Vogler, Richard. *Reading the Riot Act*. Milton Keynes: Open University Press, 1991.

Waddington, P. A. J. *Liberty and Order: Public Order Policing in a Capital City*. London: UCL Press, 1994.

Wade, E. D. S. "Police Powers and Public Meetings." *Cambridge Law Journal*. 1937 (VI).

Wall, Alison. *Power and Protest in England, 1525–1640*. New York: Oxford University Press, 2000.

Ward, J. T. *Sir James Graham*. London: Macmillan, 1967.

Webb, R. K. *The Working Class Reader, 1790–1848*. London, 1958.

Weber, Adna. *The Growth of Cities in the Nineteenth Century*. New York: Macmillan, 1899.

West, Alick. *A Good Man Fallen Among Fabians*. London: Lawrence, 1950.

White, H. P. *A Regional History of the Railways of Great Britain*. 1961.

White, Jerry. *London in the Nineteenth Century*. London: Jonathan Cape, 2007.

Whitfield, Peter. *London: A Life in Maps*. London: British Library, 2006.

Whyte, Frederic. *The Life of W. T. Stead*. London: Jonathan Cape, 1925.

Wilcox, A. F. *The Decision to Prosecute*. London: Butterworths, 1972.

Winsten, Stephen. *Salt and His Circle*. London: Hutchinson, 1951.

Wirth, Lou. *On Cities and Social Life*. Chicago: University Press, 1964.

Wohl, A. S. "The Bitter Cry of Outcast London." *International Review of Social History*. 1968.

——. *Endangered Lives: Public Health in Victorian Britain*. Cambridge, Mass.: Harvard University Press, 1983.

——. *The Eternal Slum: Housing and Social Policy in Victorian London*. London: Edward Arnold, 1977.

Woodward, Sir L. *The Age of Reform*. Oxford: Clarendon Press, 1962.

Wrigley, E. A. *Poverty, Progress, and Population*. Cambridge: Cambridge University Press, 2004.

INDEX

Bennett, Alan, 240

Bergh, Henry, 207

Besant, Annie, 100–101, 122, 143; Law and Liberty League, 124, 127, 131, 133, 134–35

bike ride event, 217–18

Bill for the Regulation of Meetings in Trafalgar Square (1888), 136

birthright tradition, 3–4, 15–16, 139

Black Hole of Calcutta, 90–91

Black Monday (1886, London), 10, 93, 107, 108, 110, 111–16, 133, 270n. 129; press view of, 114, 115, 117, 266–67n. 33; Select Committee on the Origin and Character of the Disturbances, 119–20

Blackstone's principles, 28

Blair, Tony, 3–4, 5, 218

blame, internal, 89–90, 118–19

Bloody Sunday (1887, London), 10, 46, 93–94, 106–8, 126–31, 133. See also Trafalgar Square

Bloomberg, Michael, 4, 5

Booth, Charles, 45, 109–10

Booth, William, 109

Boston, 4

Bowery riots (1857, New York), 157

Bow Street Runners, 69

Bradlaugh, Charles, 107–8, 125, 126, 136, 266n. 13

Bradley, E. R. C., 146

bread-and-circuses policies, 19

bread riots, 114–15, 152

Breyer, Stephen, 7

Brisach, Eugene L., 230

British Union of Fascists, 228

Brooklyn, 203–4

Brooklyn Bridge (New York), xii

Brooklyn Surface Railroad workers strike (1895), 203–4

Bryant Park, 231

Burns, John, 100, 112, 115, 117, 122, 270n. 130; jailed, 129, 135, 138

business interests, 39, 74, 123, 151, 153, 155, 233–34

Byzantine Empire, 19

Caesar's Column (Donnelly), 60–61

Cagan, Leslie, 220

Campbell, Walter, 114

capitalism, 7, 44, 116

"Captain Amy" case, 141

Caroline, Queen, 41

Carpenter, Mary, 85

CCTV (closed-circuit TV), 219, 221–22, 289n. 28

Central Labor Union, 204

Central Park Conservancy (New York), 4, 234–35, 291–92n. 80

Central Park (New York), 4–5, 9, 42, 43, 173, 233–36; Great Lawn, 4, 235, 292n. 80

Chaffee, Zechariah, Jr., 32

Champion, H. H., 122, 124

Charing Cross area (London), 106

Charington, F. N., 145

Charity Organization Society, 110, 116

Chartists, 10, 27–28, 46, 68–78, 103; petition presented, 73–74, 75; three peak periods of activity, 72

Chatham Square (New York), 157

Chicago, Haymarket riot, 31, 126, 224

Child, Lydia Maria, 23

Childers, H. C. E., 108, 118–19, 120–21, 122, 123

Child of the Jago, A (Morrison), 44

children's playgrounds, 43

Church of England, 95

Cicero, 19

City Beautiful movement, 206

City Council (New York), 17, 151–52

city-states (poleis), 18–19

civic discourse, 8–9

civic identity, public spaces and, 43–44

civil liberties, 5, 8, 10, 12–13, 28–33, 122–23, 135, 177

civil service system, 50

Civil War, 29

INDEX

The Columbia History of Urban Life

KENNETH T. JACKSON, GENERAL EDITOR